THE MODERNIST ANTHROPOCENE

Edinburgh Critical Studies in Modernist Culture
Series Editors: Tim Armstrong and Rebecca Beasley

Available

Modernism and Magic: Experiments with Spiritualism, Theosophy and the Occult
Leigh Wilson

Sonic Modernity: Representing Sound in Literature, Culture and the Arts
Sam Halliday

Modernism and the Frankfurt School
Tyrus Miller

Lesbian Modernism: Censorship, Sexuality and Genre Fiction
Elizabeth English

Modern Print Artefacts: Textual Materiality and Literary Value in British Print Culture, 1890–1930s
Patrick Collier

Cheap Modernism: Expanding Markets, Publishers' Series and the Avant-Garde
Lise Jaillant

Portable Modernisms: The Art of Travelling Light
Emily Ridge

Hieroglyphic Modernisms: Writing and New Media in the Twentieth Century
Jesse Schotter

Modernism, Fiction and Mathematics
Nina Engelhardt

Modernist Life Histories: Biological Theory and the Experimental Bildungsroman
Daniel Aureliano Newman

Modernism, Space and the City: Outsiders and Affect in Paris, Vienna, Berlin, and London
Andrew Thacker

Modernism Edited: Marianne Moore and the Dial *Magazine*
Victoria Bazin

Modernism and Time Machines
Charles Tung

Primordial Modernism: Animals, Ideas, transition (1927–1938)
Cathryn Setz

Modernism and Still Life: Artists, Writers, Dancers
Claudia Tobin

The Modernist Exoskeleton: Insects, War, Literary Form
Rachel Murray

Novel Sensations: Modernist Fiction and the Problem of Qualia
Jon Day

Hotel Modernity: Corporate Space in Literature and Film
Robbie Moore

The Modernist Anthropocene: Nonhuman Life and Planetary Change in James Joyce, Virginia Woolf and Djuna Barnes
Peter Adkins

Forthcoming

Modernism and the Idea of Everyday Life
Leena Kore-Schröder

Modernism and Religion: Poetry and the Rise of Mysticism
Jamie Callison

Abstraction in Modernism and Modernity: Human and Inhuman
Jeff Wallace

Visionary Company: Hart Crane and Modernist Periodicals
Francesca Bratton

Asbestos: The Last Modernist Object
Arthur Rose

www.edinburghuniversitypress.com/series/ecsmc

THE MODERNIST ANTHROPOCENE

Nonhuman Life and Planetary Change in
James Joyce, Virginia Woolf
and Djuna Barnes

Peter Adkins

EDINBURGH
University Press

Edinburgh University Press is one of the leading university presses in
the UK. We publish academic books and journals in our selected subject
areas across the humanities and social sciences, combining cutting-edge
scholarship with high editorial and production values to produce academic
works of lasting importance. For more information visit our website:
edinburghuniversitypress.com

© Peter Adkins, 2022, 2024

Edinburgh University Press Ltd
The Tun – Holyrood Road
12(2f) Jackson's Entry
Edinburgh EH8 8PJ

First published in hardback by Edinburgh University Press 2022

Typeset in 10/12.5 Adobe Sabon by
IDSUK (DataConnection) Ltd, and
printed and bound by CPI Group (UK) Ltd, Croydon,
CR0 4YY

A CIP record for this book is available from the British Library

ISBN 978 1 4744 8196 0 (hardback)
ISBN 978 1 4744 8197 7 (paperback)
ISBN 978 1 4744 8198 4 (webready PDF)
ISBN 978 1 4744 8199 1 (epub)

The right of Peter Adkins to be identified as the author of this work has
been asserted in accordance with the Copyright, Designs and Patents
Act 1988, and the Copyright and Related Rights Regulations 2003
(SI No. 2498).

CONTENTS

List of Figures   vi
Acknowledgements   vii
List of Abbreviations   ix

Introduction   1
1   The Matter of Politics in the Novels of James Joyce   31
2   James Joyce and the Revenge of Gaia   62
3   The Beastly Writing of Djuna Barnes   89
4   Sex, Nature and Animal Life in Djuna Barnes's *Ryder*   118
5   The Sympathetic Climate of Virginia Woolf's *Orlando*   145
6   The Disturbing Future of Virginia Woolf's Late Writing   170
Fallout: Modernism in the Nuclear Anthropocene   197

Bibliography   211
Index   232

FIGURES

1.1 Letter from George Russell as editor of the *Irish Homestead* to James Joyce, July 1904. James Joyce Collection. General Collection, Beinecke Rare Book and Manuscript Library, Yale University. 41
3.1 *The Beast*. Djuna Barnes's original line drawn illustration of The Beast Thingumbob and Cheerful for *Ryder*. Djuna Barnes Papers, Special Collections, University of Maryland Libraries. 99
4.1 *The Tree of Ryder* (frontispiece) from *Ryder*. Drawn by Djuna Barnes. Djuna Barnes Papers, Special Collections, University of Maryland Libraries. 122
4.2 Pennyfinder the Bull. Drawn by Djuna Barnes for *Ryder* but removed at the request of her publishers. Djuna Barnes Papers, Special Collections, University of Maryland Libraries. 129
7.1 *Earthrise* (1968) by William Anders. Public Domain. 200
7.2 *Light Coming on the Plains No. II* (1917) (detail) by Georgia O'Keeffe. Amon Carter Museum of American Art, Fort Worth, Texas, 1966.32, © Amon Carter Museum of American Art. 201
7.3 *Blast, I* (1957) by Adolph Gottlieb. Digital image, The Museum of Modern Art, New York/Scala, Florence, © Adolph and Esther Gottlieb Foundation/VAGA at ARS, NY and DACS, London 2021. 202

ACKNOWLEDGEMENTS

This book could not have been written without the support and guidance of many people. My first thanks go to Derek Ryan, who has been an invaluable mentor, colleague and friend over the course of the many years it has taken to write this book. It was his teaching and research that first showed me what might be gained from thinking beyond the human and for this I am extremely grateful. I would also like to thank Wendy Parkins for her role in shaping my research during the formative years of this project and for encouraging me to think more about the Victorians. I am also extremely grateful to Ariane Mildenberg and Vike Martina Plock whose generous insights and incisive questions helped me to see where my argument about the Modernist Anthropocene worked and where I might think harder.

I was encouraged during the writing of this book by friends and colleagues. In particular I would like to thank Miguel Alexiades, Matthew Carbery, Ruth Clemens, Emilia Czatkowska, Jenny Davis, Jeanne Dubino, Angelos Evangelou, Tom Griffiths, Tristan Ireson, Donna Landry, Saskia McCracken, Paul March-Russell, Rachel Murray, Kaori Ngai, Patricia Novillo-Corvalán, Oliver Perrott-Webb, Aaron Pugh, Jo Pettitt, Craig Ritchie, Carrie Rohman, Flicka Small, Harrison Sullivan, Caitlin Stobie, Kiron Ward, Declan Wiffen and Michelle Witen. Special thanks are also due to my colleagues in the Kent Animal Humanities Network whose insights and conversations were always beastly, in the be(a)st sense of the word. This book also owes much to my series editors, Tim Armstrong and Rebecca Beasley, who believed in the project and saw where it could be strengthened.

And special thanks are also due to Jackie Jones, Ersev Ersoy and Susannah Butler at Edinburgh University Press, who have been brilliant editors.

Much of this book was researched and written while at the University of Kent and I am grateful for the institutional support it provided. I am also grateful to the Art and Humanities Research Council for funding the doctoral research on which this monograph is based. The Christine and Ian Bolt Scholarship funded archival research for my chapters on Djuna Barnes and I am hugely grateful to them for the opportunities they afforded me. The University of Maryland's Special Collections library, which holds the Djuna Barnes Papers, are due special thanks for letting me set up camp in their reading room for five weeks and I am especially grateful to lead librarian Amber Kohl for her helpfulness throughout the writing of this book. Thanks are also due to the University of Delaware Special Collections library and the Beinecke Rare Book and Manuscript Library at Yale University.

I am very grateful to the Authors League Fund and St Bride's Church for permission to quote material from Djuna Barnes's published and unpublished writing, and to reproduce her illustrations. They have been supportive of this project from the start, for which I am truly thankful. Thanks are due too to the Estate of Emily Holmes Coleman for permission to quote from her correspondence with Barnes. All quotations by Emily Holmes Coleman are Copyright © by Estate of Emily Holmes Coleman. I was kindly provided permission to use Adolph Gottlieb's *Blast 1* by the Adolph and Esther Gottlieb Foundation and I wish to thank the Design and Artists Copyright Society and the Scala Archives for assisting me with this. I am extremely grateful to have been granted permission to use Georgia O'Keeffe's *Light Coming on the Plains No. II* for my cover image by the Amon Carter Museum of American Art, Fort Worth, Texas.

Deep thanks go to my mum, Jane, and dad, Stephen, Rosie and Nathan Jeffries, and James and Hannah Adkins, as well as Michael, Jane, Ellie and Ami Barnes. Your unwavering love and support got me here and kept me going throughout. Thanks also to my grandad, Ross Adkins, as well as Mary Adkins and Rose and Alfred Morley, who I know would have been proud of me for this book.

Two final special thanks are due. To Wallace, who dragged me out of the house for walks when it all got too much and whose calming presence kept me rooted. And to Maddi, without whose love, encouragement and support, none of this would have been possible. Maddi, thank you.

Earlier versions of material in this book appeared as '"There All The Time Without You": Joyce, Modernism and the Anthropocene', in Jeremy Diaper (ed.), *Eco-Modernism: Ecology, Environment and Nature in Literary Modernism* (Clemson, SC: Clemson University Press, 2021) and as 'The Climate of *Orlando*: Woolf, Braidotti and the Anthropocene' in *Comparative Critical Studies*. I am grateful to the publishers and editors that permission was granted to reprint material from these publications.

ABBREVIATIONS

Djuna Barnes
A	*The Antiphon*
CP	*Collected Poems*
CS	*Collected Stories*
LA	*Ladies Almanack*
N	*Nightwood*
NY	*New York*
R	*Ryder*

James Joyce
FW	*Finnegans Wake*
JJL1–3	*The Letters of James Joyce*
OCPW	*Occasional, Critical and Political Writing*
P	*A Portrait of the Artist as a Young Man*
SH	*Stephen Hero*
U	*Ulysses* (References appear as episode number plus line number)

Virginia Woolf
BTA	*Between the Acts*
E1–6	*The Essays of Virginia Woolf*
MB	*Moments of Being*
MD	*Mrs Dalloway*

O	*Orlando: A Biography*
RO	*A Room of One's Own*
TTL	*To the Lighthouse*
TG	*Three Guineas*
VO	*The Voyage Out*
D1–5	*The Diary of Virginia Woolf*
VWL1–6	*The Letters of Virginia Woolf*

INTRODUCTION: MODERNISM AND THE ANTHROPOCENE

At the conclusion to *A Room of One's Own* (1929), Virginia Woolf imagines the life of a writer in the twenty-first century:

> For my belief is that if we live another century or so – I am talking of the common life which is the real life and not of the little separate lives which we live as individuals – and have five hundred a year each of us and rooms of our own; if we have the habit of freedom and courage to write exactly what we think; if we escape a little from the common sitting-room and see human beings not always in their relation to each other but in relation to reality; and the sky, too, and the trees or whatever it may be in themselves [. . .] then the opportunity will come and the dead poet who was Shakespeare's sister will put on the body which she has so often laid down. (*RO* 86)

It is a vision where changes in the material conditions that determine who can write and what is written might produce not only a wider range of opportunities for women writers but a more ecologically attentive form of writing. Having a room of one's own makes one not more insular, but, rather, provides the opportunity to reflect on the wider more-than-human reality within which we all live. Indeed, from the perspective of our current moment, in which news headlines frequently report of climate change, deforestation and air pollution, Woolf's instruction to see the human in relation to the sky and the trees, to take note of the materiality of our surroundings, takes on a significance that she cannot have foreseen. Even the possibility of extinction articulated in Woolf's 'if we live another century' seems uncannily prescient of current scientific predictions that we are entering the sixth great extinction event, an event whose signs were already marked in the skies and trees of the early twentieth century that Woolf encouraged her readers and future writers to observe.[1]

This book argues that Woolf, along with her modernist contemporaries, James Joyce, and Djuna Barnes intuited the idea of the Anthropocene and that their innovations in writing engage with the aesthetical, ontological and ethical demands of our emergent planetary epoch. Combining the Greek term for the human ('Anthropos') and the unit of time used in geology to differentiate between recent geological epochs ('cene'), the concept of the Anthropocene aims to recognise that we have entered a new phase of planetary history. As its name suggests, this new epoch is defined by the fact that for the first time in the history of the Earth a single species will have marked the planet so profoundly that its influence will be observable for millions of years into the future.[2] For climate scientist Paul Crutzen, the 'rapid expansion of mankind in numbers and per capita exploitation of Earth's resources' is such that humanity must now be considered a telluric force.[3] As such, while, on the one hand, the Anthropocene speaks to the power of the human as the species that can do *so much*, the name simultaneously has a diminutive effect. The human is the species who has been so myopic, so narrowly self-interested, so blind to its impact on the environment and other species, that it has created the conditions for its own demise. The unexpected rise of the term in recent years within popular culture, mainstream media and academic discourse has seen the concept of the Anthropocene become detached from its geological provenance and become imbued with multiple, often contradictory, meanings. This includes its refashioning into a positive term by a small number of commentators who see the techno-utopian possibility of a *good* Anthropocene in which we might fix the world by further accelerating industrialism and large-scale engineering.[4] At the same time, a more critical understanding of the Anthropocene has developed within both the sciences and the humanities under the auspices of what Claire Colebrook has called 'Anthropocene studies'.[5] This emergent, transdisciplinary field of study has come to see the Anthropocene not in terms of humankind's predominance over the planet, but rather as a turning point in how we think about the relationship between the human, the nonhuman and the planetary. It is a field of study characterised by an attention to the way in which human actions are always entangled with nonhuman processes and which relocates human life within a non-hierarchical view of geological history that more broadly distributes who or what is recognised as having agency. As Timothy Clark argues, in this sense the Anthropocene is more than a geochronological measurement of time, rather it stands as 'a cultural threshold' that 'blurs and even scrambles some crucial categories by which people have made sense of the world and their lives. It puts in crisis the lines between culture and nature, fact and value, and between the human and the geological or meteorological.'[6]

Importantly for scholars of modernism, the history of the Anthropocene is also the history of modernity. While, as I explore in more detail below, exactly when the Anthropocene can be said to have begun remains a matter of contention, it nonetheless is bound up with the ascendency of industrialisation, imperialism and capitalism from the late eighteenth century onwards. Fuelled by the industrial capitalism invented by the West and exported to the rest of the planet, a blueprint which inflicted disproportionate levels of ecological harm on poorer populations from the start, the causes and effects of the Anthropocene are closely bound up with the emergence of modernity. As Bruno Latour has argued, the ideology of modernity was premised on an illusionary separation of culture and nature, or the human and the nonhuman, which could not hold. Instead of a safe separation between an autonomous human world and what was perceived to be an inert world of matter, accelerated developments in science worked to hybridise humans and nonhumans through the creation of new technologies that reshaped and further entangled both.[7] While once this entanglement could go largely ignored, the violent 'intrusion' of the Anthropocene, as Isabelle Stengers terms it, into our daily lives through phenomena such as extreme climate events makes clear that the nonhuman can no longer serve as a passive backdrop to human history and society.[8] The humanist ideal of the human as the species set apart from a state of nature is revealed as untenable. Instead, in its implications and consequences, the Anthropocene reiterates Woolf's assertion that we can no longer see the human in isolation. Rather, the human must be seen in in relation to a broader planetary reality.

In the last decade or so, scholars have started to bring to light the ways in which modernist writers were attuned to the material world and alert to the ecological possibilities available in finding new ways of writing about the more-than-human. Initially premised as a 'greening' of modernism, critics such as Elizabeth Black, Jeffrey Mathes McCarthy and Bonnie Kime Scott highlighted how a range of canonical and non-canonical modernist writers were interested in the pastoral and the rural, and drew on literary innovations to find new ways of writing about nature.[9] Moreover, in the same way that ecocriticism's maturation as a field saw it become less narrowly confined to a focus on 'green writing' and 'nature', modernist ecocriticism has undergone a similar transformation.[10] As Kelly Sultzbach has shown, modernism poses 'ecocritical theoretical questions' around coexistence, materiality and nonhuman agency that mean we can look beyond modernist writing that takes 'nature' as its primary subject.[11] In addition to Sultzbach's analysis of how modernist writing presents the ontological liveliness of the material world, critics such as Joshua Schuster and Matthew Griffiths have shown how modernists were exploring topics such as industrial pollution and climate change through their innovations in textual aesthetics.[12] Furthermore, in its ecocritical turn, modernist studies has pointed to the ways in which, as Griffiths frames it, modernism's ability to 'disrupt previously cherished conceptions of the world' remains a generative source for approaching urgent contemporary questions around planetary change.[13]

The three writers who are the focus of this study were deeply preoccupied not so much with a pastoral idea of nature, but with the relationship between the human and the nonhuman more broadly conceived and often on a planetary scale. Woolf's writing bears this imprint from beginning to end, with the visions of the 'vast stretches of dry earth and the plains of the sea that encircled the earth' (*VO* 402) imagined by her characters in her first novel, *The Voyage Out* (1915), echoed in characters preoccupied with thoughts of prehistoric 'swamp[s]' and 'forests' (*BTA* 6–7) in her unfinished final novel *Between the Acts* (1941).[14] As critics such as Derek Ryan have argued, Woolf's writing is marked by a radical understanding of materiality and life that 'extend[s] beyond a purely human concern'.[15] Joyce's interest in thinking about the relation of the human to a broader nonhuman reality can also be traced back to his earliest writing. His 1899 essay 'The Study of Languages', written while at university, criticises the practice of vivisection on ethical grounds, insisting that for '[s]cience, human or divine' to have a morality it must first recognise man 'as an infinitely small actor, playing a most uninteresting part in the drama of worlds' (*OCPW* 14). We find Leopold Bloom making a similar observation in *Ulysses* (1922) when in 'Ithaca', he considers how 'the eons of geological periods recorded in the stratifications of the earth' makes the 'allotted human life [appear] a parenthesis of infinitesimal brevity' (*U* 17.1055–8). In 'Ithaca', however, this diminutiveness does not diminish the human drive to order, manipulate and control that vast cosmos, ironically presented in the catechistic form of the episode, which in its exhaustive questions and answers appears to work towards an impossible completeness of human knowledge and scientific supremacy. As this book will show, a decentring of the human and an ironic depiction of the anthropocentric desire for mastery is present throughout Joyce's writing.[16] Djuna Barnes, too, was preoccupied with finding new ways of writing about the nonhuman world. Writing to her friend and fellow writer Emily Coleman in 1938, two years after her novel *Nightwood* had been published, Barnes cites Shakespeare's image in *Venus and Adonis* (1593) of the snail who 'shrinks backward in his shelly cave with pain', linking it to her own theory of nature:

> That's just what I mean (try and do it Barnes) when I say nature, trees, animals, must for me, somehow, to be of any motion [be] connected with the snail, say, and the lady, with human beings and with the garden, then I get the image, then it means something, then its wedded [. . .] Don't you like it? To be able to write like that is the only permission.[17]

An ecological aesthetic premised on the wedded connections linking human, animal and plant life (and reminiscent in this respect of Woolf's short story 'Kew Gardens' (1919)), Barnes theorises her own literary aesthetic of the nonhuman. Unsurprisingly, it correlates with the beastliness of *Nightwood*, a novel whose animalisation of its human characters unsettles ideas of human exceptionalism and, as Carrie Rohman states, renounces the 'upright humanity' that was being articulated by figures such as Freud in the first half of the twentieth century.[18] We might also detect in Barnes's use of the term 'wedded' in describing the relationship between the human and nonhuman an oblique reference to the suggestion of bestiality with which *Nightwood* concludes, a subject that scandalised Coleman at the time with its 'true implication' of interspecies sexuality.[19] As this book will make clear, for Barnes, Joyce and Woolf, questions of the nonhuman necessarily also opened up questions of gender and sexuality.

By looking at how discourse around the human and the nonhuman was being reimagined within literary modernism, this book aligns itself with a revisionary history that insists that the 'planet's entry into the Anthropocene did not follow a frenetic modernism ignorant of the environment but, on the contrary, decades of reflection and concern as to the human degradation of the Earth'.[20] For the historians of science, Christophe Bonneuil and Jean-Baptiste Fressoz, the emergence of the Anthropocene is sometimes falsely heralded as a moment of twenty-first-century ecological awakening in which humanity finally becomes aware of its precarious relationship to the environments which sustain it. As they counter in their book *The Shock of the Anthropocene* (2016), for as long as humans have been exploiting the Earth on a planetary scale there has been a corresponding 'environmental reflexivity' critiquing such exploitation. Historians, Bonneuil and Fressoz argue, need to 'restore the conceptual grammars' through which this reflexivity was made legible.[21] The innovations associated with the modernist novel, this book argues, are precisely one such set of conceptual grammars through which ideas of the nonhuman were freshly articulated, shedding light on what can be called the Modernist Anthropocene and providing materials with which to think with in the present moment.

Excavating the Modernist Anthropocene

The word 'Anthropocene' is usually credited as having been coined by Paul Crutzen, a Nobel Prize-winning atmospheric chemist, at a conference on Earth Systems Science in Mexico in 1999. In an often-repeated anecdote within discourse on the Anthropocene, during a heated discussion about human impact on the planet Crutzen reportedly exclaimed to his fellow delegates that 'We're not in the Holocene anymore. We're in the . . . the . . . the Anthropocene!'[22] As Crutzen saw it, the planet had entered a new geological epoch in which human activity was now the predominant cause of planetary change. For Crutzen, and other scientists who have subsequently endorsed the concept of the Anthropocene, the industrial extraction of natural resources, particularly fossil fuels, along with mass chemical pollution and changes in land and sea use, has led to such profound shifts in the global environment that the Holocene, the epoch that began 12,000 years ago, has given way to a wholly new geological period. The effects of the Anthropocene are striking both in the short and the long term, with an increase in the frequency of extreme weather events, rising sea levels and ocean acidification being some of the most widely reported phenomena, along with research forecasting a mass extinction event (the sixth in the history of the planet) in which approximately 75 per cent of species stand to be lost.[23] The Holocene, the preceding twelve millennia of unusually stable climatic conditions which made possible agricultural modes of production and thereby provided the conditions for the rise of cities and sophisticated technologies, is in the process of being displaced by the very species that it enabled to flourish.[24]

Exactly *when* the Holocene can be said to have ended and the Anthropocene begun remains a matter of some disagreement. In his early articles on the Anthropocene Crutzen suggested that the epoch could be traced back to the latter part of the eighteenth century since analysis of air trapped in polar ice shows this period as marking 'the beginning of growing global concentration of carbon dioxide and methane'. This time period, as Crutzen outlines, coincides with the beginning of British industrialism and, more specifically, the arrival of James Watt's patented steam engine in 1784.[25] More recently, however, the Anthropocene Working Group (AWG), an international collective of scientists tasked with reporting to the International Commission on Stratigraphy (the body which oversees the formal ratification of new geological periods), have recommended that the 'stratigraphically optimal' starting date for the Anthropocene is 1945, with the radioactive fallout from the detonations of atom bombs and the spike in emissions from the post-war Great Acceleration cited as key geochemical markers.[26] In contrast, other scientists and environmental historians have argued that Crutzen's initial date is not nearly early enough, with the 1492 Columbian expedition to the Americas (and the beginnings of global trade) and, even further back, the advent of agricultural practices and systematised resource extraction in early human civilisations proposed as possible starting dates.[27] The AWG's date of 1945, however, is the one most likely to be ratified and is striking insofar as it suggests that the beginning of the Anthropocene coincides with what is sometimes positioned as an end date for modernism.[28] By 1945, both Joyce and Woolf had died, and Barnes had retreated to a small apartment in New York where she remained an active but reclusive writer until her death in 1982. The Anthropocene, thus dated, might seem to be historically aligned with the emergence of postmodernism, suggesting a clear point of cleavage between a modernist Holocene and a postmodernist Anthropocene. Yet, in the same way that critics have complicated the idea of a clear division between modernism and postmodernism, locating a definitive 1945 boundary between the Holocene and the Anthropocene only serves to conceal the longer history of the Anthropocene.[29]

In particular, the final decades of the nineteenth century and the first few of the twentieth century were crucial to producing the conditions that allowed for a post Second World War acceleration. The period saw the development and use of liquid fuels, the nascence of motor and air travel, the invention of human-made nitrate fertiliser, as well as continued rapid growth in industrialism, urbanisation, fossil fuel extraction, and intensive agriculture, all of which were responding to, and fuelled by, ever-expanding population levels. In the years immediately after 1900, CO^2 levels surpassed three hundred parts per million, a threshold moment in the release of 'lasting anthropogenic traces [. . .] into the atmosphere' as levels of carbon dioxide soared higher than they had been at any point in the previous 10,000 years.[30] Indeed, although the two world wars were responsible for great environmental harm, especially in terms of lead and sulphate emissions, it has been speculated that had it not been for these global conflicts and the economic downturn after the First World War, the Great Acceleration would have occurred earlier, coming into full effect in the early twentieth century.[31] Writers during this period responded to the profound ecological transformations taking place around them, with many of them homing in on the motor car as an aptly overdetermined figure of urban sprawl, chemical pollution and environmental and social decay. E. M. Forster's *Howards End* (1910), for instance, describes how:

> month by month the roads smelt more strongly of petrol, and were more difficult to cross, and human beings heard each other speak with greater difficulty, breathed less of the air, and saw less of the sky. Nature withdrew: the leaves were falling by midsummer; the sun shone through dirt with an admired obscurity.[32]

The 'intensive cultivation' of land both in England and its colonies, encapsulated by the industrious Wilcox family, threatens the pastoralism so highly valued by Margaret and Helen Schlegel, producing what Ted Howell describes as an 'anticarbon and anticar' condition-of-England novel for the Anthropocene.[33] We find a more ambivalent parallel to Forster's anti-car sentiment in D. H. Lawrence's *The Rainbow* (1914), where Ursula is surprised by Skrebensky's arrival at the school where she teaches with 'a motor-car to drive her home'. As in *Howards End* where the car's presence in the countryside becomes symbolic of a transformative influence, Lawrence describes how 'the mud flew in a soft, wild rush from the wheels, the country was blackish green, with the silver of new hay here and there, and masses of trees under a silver-gleaming sky'.[34] Reminiscent in some respects of F. T. Marinetti's paean to automobiles, speed and industrialism in 'The Founding and the Manifesto of Futurism' (1909) which Lawrence read during the writing of his novel, the sky and hay take on the 'gleaming-silver' hues of the machine, while the 'soft' mud of the 'blackish green' fields starts to resemble the colour and liquid form of the oil and petrol propelling the car forward. As in *Howards End* where trees shed their leaves midsummer and dirt from motor cars infiltrates sunbeams, Lawrence presents an image of an unnatural nature, where humans, machines and the nonhuman have become irreversibly entangled, each bleeding into the other. Situated within the broader narrative of *The Rainbow* and its sequel *Women in Love* (1920), it is a scene that contributes to a vision of rural England in the process of becoming mechanised and hollowed-out for its minerals and coal. In *Women in Love*, for instance, the industrialist Gerald Crich gazes out at his Nottinghamshire mine and considers how:

> There was plenty of coal. The old workings could not get at it, that was all. Then break the neck of the old workings. The coal lay there in its seams, even though the seams were thin. There it lay, inert matter, as it had always lain, since the beginning of time, subject to the will of man.[35]

A reflection of early twentieth-century technological developments which were enabling access to deeper and previously harder to extract coal seams, Gerald's perception of coal as inert matter just waiting for the 'will of man' speaks to what Latour describes as modernity's mistake of separating the world into human subjects and nonhuman objects, with the latter characterised as 'inanimate' and 'inert'.[36] Gerald is presented as a figure of extractivist capitalism, whose ambition to 'extend over the earth a great and perfect system in which the will of man ran smooth and unthwarted' encapsulates the rapidly expanding scale of human ambition to exert planetary control and command.[37]

The prominence of the motor car in modernist literature stands as a reminder of the ascendency of oil during the early twentieth century. As Schuster writes, oil was 'everywhere during the modernist era, changing the shape of the landscape with cars, roads, airplanes, military equipment, and spawning suburbs, intensifying land speculation and commodity trading, further mechanizing agriculture, and producing new chemicals and plastics'.[38] And although, as Schuster points out, oil often seems to defy 'direct representation', it by no means went unremarked upon by modernist writers.[39] In a July 1927 diary entry, Woolf recalls a heated discussion during an evening with Vita Sackville-West, Harold Nicolson and Raymond Mortimer, where the subject of the British Empire's benevolence compared to German and French imperialism leads into the specific case of 'the British oil fields' in Persia. While for Nicolson, the oil fields represent the good of British colonialism, since there is a 'hospital there where they take any one [sic], employee or not', Woolf's response is to ask '[b]ut why not grow, change? [. . .] Also, I said, recalling the aeroplanes that had flown over us [. . .] can't you see that nationality is over? All divisions are now rubbed out, or about to be' (*D3* 145). The aeroplane, emblematic of the technological advances made possible through oil, becomes a figure of global connectedness, of divisions made permeable and of a modernity which is liquid and fluid like oil itself. While Woolf's remarks might appear lacking insofar as they elide direct reference to the history of imperial force and subjugation undergirding her vision of a planetary community, she was not naïve to the realities of imperial extractivism and global capitalism. In the 'London Scene' essays that Woolf wrote for *Good Housekeeping* in the early 1930s, she presents the River Thames as flowing with globally extracted materials – '[t]imber, iron, grain, wine, sugar, paper, tallow, fruit' (*E5* 277) – while 'oil' is listed as among the 'new desires [. . .] beginning to grow in us' for foreign commodities, alongside 'rice puddings', 'candles' and 'furs' (*E5* 280). The image of the Thames drawing planetary resources into Britain recalls Eliot's vision of the river sweating 'oil and tar' in *The Waste Land* (1922), a poem Woolf knew well since she handset the type when it was published by the Hogarth Press, and she, too, is similarly aware of the environmental costs.[40] Her essay on the London docklands describes sailing down the Thames:

> The banks of the river are lined with dingy, decrepit-looking warehouses. They huddle on land that has become flat and slimy mud. [. . .] When, suddenly, after acres and acres of this desolation one floats past an old stone house standing in a real field, with real trees growing in clumps, the sight is disconcerting. Can it be possible that there is earth, that there once were fields and crops beneath this desolation and disorder? (*E5* 276)

The outskirts of the city have become a literal wasteland, the river busy with 'rubbish barges, and sewage barges' dumping refuse onto 'long mounds' that have been 'fuming and smoking and [. . .] giving off a gritty, acrid air for fifty years' (*E5* 277). It is an image of a perimeter smouldering with bad air, a border through which ships laden with commodities pass on their way to the city and to which many commodities are destined to eventually return, where they will be added to the heaps of waste. It is a scene that offers a further example of what Colebrook describes as how the apocalyptic tone we find in modernist texts such as Joyce's *Dubliners* (1914) and Eliot's *The Waste Land*, 'anticipate[s] twenty-first-century post-apocalyptic narratives: humans become the walking dead in their own world, not because of any external accident but because the very relation to nature that generated that world tipped over into blind mastery and reification'.[41]

Moreover, Woolf links the accretion of materials, commodities and waste in Britain with corresponding ecological consequences far away, imagining the excavation of 'mammoths that have lain frozen in Siberian ice for fifty-thousand years' destined to be reduced to ivory handles for umbrellas (*E5* 278) and the '[f]locks upon flocks of Australian sheep' whose existence is justified by English 'demand [for] woollen overcoats' (*E5* 280). As Anna Snaith and Michael Whitworth have argued, Woolf 'refused to see imperial space as "out there"'.[42] Her portrait of London compresses scales of time and space, with the planetary and the local becoming superimposed upon each other, as foreign materials are transformed and transported at rapid speed and new commodities are produced, shipped, consumed and eventually discarded. In this respect, Woolf's essay speaks to what James Winter has described as the increasingly complicated relationship between the local and the planetary from the midnineteenth century onwards, when British 'engineers and entrepreneurs' began constructing a 'global environment where the results of building a new railway, digging a new mine or cutting an old forest' in the colonies produced material transformations in Britain thanks to a new abundance of raw materials and commodities.[43] It also speaks to what Bonneuil and Fressoz have described as the way in which in certain respects 'the Anthropocene should rather be called an "Anglocene"', since Britain established the model for industrial modernity, led the way in imperial extractivism and released far more carbon into the atmosphere than other industrial nations, for example, emitting four times as much CO^2 as France during the nineteenth century.[44] The term, in this respect, shares similarities with the notion of the Capitalocene which, for Donna Haraway, provides a corrective to any implied notion that all humans are equally responsible for the causes and consequences of anthropogenic planetary change. Just as for Haraway, for whom the imperative is to recover the more-than-human history of capitalism through 'systemic stories of [. . .] linked metabolisms, articulations, or coproductions [. . .] of economies and ecologies', Woolf attends to the environmental costs of imperialism and global capitalism at both a local and planetary scale.[45]

The Human as Geological Agent

In her book, *Picasso* (1938), Gertrude Stein describes travelling for the first time in an aeroplane and seeing the Earth appear to her as abstract cubist lines. It is evidence for Stein that cubism is *the* visual art form of the twentieth century. The experience, moreover, provides supporting evidence for her theory that 'a creator [. . .] understands what is contemporary when the contemporaries do not yet know it' since cubism had emerged 'when not any painter had ever gone up in an airplane'.[46] The twentieth century, Stein concludes, 'is a century which sees the earth as no one has ever seen it, the earth has a splendor that it never has had, and as everything destroys itself [. . .] and nothing continues, so then the twentieth century has a splendor which is its own'.[47] For Stein, then, modern art brought into focus new modes of perception, insisting that the planet had to be conceptualised afresh. One of the central arguments of this book is that the early twentieth century fostered new structures of subjectivity that modernist writers were also highly attuned to and looking to articulate through innovative new forms, attentive to both, in Stein's terms, the splendour and destruction of the twentieth century. This subjectivity was not only shaped by novel technologies, growing environmental despoilation and emerging global networks of production, but also new ideas about the Earth and its geophysical systems being established in the sciences. Nineteenth-century theories of uniformitarianism, which had argued that the planet was shaped by slow unidirectional geological change, were giving way to a modern understanding of planetary conditions as always in flux and which recognised the human as increasingly shaping geological processes.[48] The Cambridge geographer R. L. Sherlock, for instance, published a book entitled *Man as a Geological Agent* in 1922. Aimed at a broad reading public, the book outlined how 'Man's action on Nature has two aspects: a geological and a biological one.'[49] Sherlock's book offered empirical evidence to argue that earlier science had 'exaggerated the steadiness of Nature' and outlined how the twentieth century had seen humankind taking on an terraforming agency akin to earlier 'natural agents [...] known to have acted with exceptional power at intervals in the earth's history'.[50] Drawing on statistical analysis of mines, quarries, civic infrastructure, roads, railways, waterways, coastal developments, agriculture and forestry, the book charted measurable anthropogenic changes in British geology, ecology and climatology. Sherlock's work was, as Winter states, the first study that recognised the true extent of human 'geomorphological processes'.[51] Moreover, as the British geologist Arthur Smith Woodward recognised in his foreword for Sherlock's book, it also heralded the warning that '[man] may be approaching a stage when he should pause to consider whether his use and alteration of the crust of the earth itself are for future as well as for present advantage'.[52] The book, however, also exposes the gulf between early twentieth-century knowledge and that of the present day. Although he foresaw that 'a considerable increase in the amount of carbon dioxide in the atmosphere [...] is likely to be in some degree inimical to the higher animals', in the final analysis Sherlock believed humankind's influence was 'probably no greater than that of some organic agents of the past'.[53]

Remarkably, in the same year that Sherlock published his book, the word 'Anthropocene' itself was first used, arrived at by Russian geologist Aleksey Pavlov, who suggested that it was a more fitting name than the Holocene since it recognised humanity's long-standing influence on the Earth. The term, however, did not attract the attention of the international scientific community. Hampered by inconsistent translation from Russian (it was sometimes translated as 'Anthropogene') and a Western prejudice towards Soviet science, Pavlov's word would have to wait another eight decades until Crutzen discovered it for the second time to be popularised.[54] More influential was the work of Vladimir Vernadsky, also a Russian scientist, who was establishing the field of geochemistry and arguing that human activities were profoundly altering geochemical systems. Writing in his 1924 book *Geochemistry*, Vernadsky asserted that '[w]e live in a critical epoch of the history of humanity' since 'foundations of our conceptions on the universe, on nature – the unique entity – on everything, of which one heard so much in the eighteenth and first half of the nineteenth centuries, is transforming before our very eyes with extraordinary speed rare in the history of thought'.[55] Like Stein's cubist view of the world from an aeroplane, the key note of Vernadsky's vision is that of accelerated transformation and defamiliarisation. Moreover, and importantly, how humans conceptualise nature was not of secondary concern for Vernadsky. In the same way that for Sherlock, 'the relation between Man's psychology and his geological activities' was '[p]erhaps the most difficult and at the same time the most interesting problem' of the present moment, Vernadsky believed that the cognitive processes of the human species had to be factored within geological history.[56] The term under which Vernadsky would explore the relationship between planetary and cognitive processes was the noosphere (with the prefix 'noo' deriving from the Greek for mind, 'nous'). The noosphere was jointly developed with the theologian and palaeontologist Pierre Teilhard de Chardin and the mathematician turned philosopher Edouard Le Roy in Paris in the 1920s. Intended to map how cognition influences physical systems, it was premised as further developing the nineteenth-century concept of the biosphere, which they saw as unable to account for the way in which thought processes are embedded within, rather than extrinsic to, biological and geological processes. The concept, as Paul Samson and David Pitt outline, aimed to bring together the 'creative world of our imagination and the physical domain of our material existence'.[57] Paralleling the concept of the Anthropocene in several ways, the noosphere not only offered a revised way of understanding the planet but also looked to pinpoint the evolutionary moment in which a single species could consciously transform the biosphere. As le Roy went on to frame it, the noosphere marks the 'hominization' of planetary life, in which 'mankind becomes the key itself of transformational explanations'.[58]

The idea of the noosphere, however, was not widely taken up within either scientific or cultural fields. One of the reasons for this is the degree to which for each of the three figures associated with it, it meant something quite different. For Teilhard, who is credited as being the first to conceive of the concept while working as a non-combatant stretcher-bearer in the trenches of the First World War, the noosphere had a mystical and transcendental dimension, signalling the way in which through collective 'noogenesis [mankind was] ascending irreversibly towards Omega', understood as a final point of unity with the cosmos.[59] For Le Roy, metaphysics was also a central component in understanding the noosphere, seeing it as extending a vitalist understanding of evolution and suggesting that we might even see the Earth itself as a kind of organism, foreshadowing James Lovelock's later Gaia hypothesis (a concept which I return to in Chapter 2). On the other hand, for Vernadsky the noosphere remained largely a geological concept, useful for tracing anthropogenic geochemical changes. There are several striking historical and intellectual parallels between the emergence of the noosphere and modernism. As Samson and Pitt frame it, the noosphere emerged from a 'loose circle' of intellectuals in Paris in the early 1920s, revulsed by the 'horrors of war' but bound by a 'strong faith in human potential and in science'; it was a project that, like modernism, was characterised by both shared aims but also clear vicissitudes.[60] Indeed, it is easy to imagine a Parisian café where, in one corner we find Vernadsky, Le Roy and Teilhard, and in the other, a coterie of modernist writers. Both Barnes and Joyce were living in Paris during the period that the noosphere was being developed and although there is no evidence that their paths crossed during this time, Barnes would later own a copy of Teilhard's *The Phenomenon of Man* (not published until 1955), a work which further developed his argument for noogenesis, and William G. Fallon, Joyce's fellow student at Belvedere and University College, speculated after Joyce's death that he 'would have been attracted to Teilhard's interpretation of Catholicism [. . .] [and his] notion that man is progressing, that science and astronomy all converge on the infinite'.[61]

These suggestive points of connection between modernism and the noosphere are further borne out by a shared influence in Henri Bergson. The three progenitors of the noosphere were all influenced to a varying degree by Bergson, especially Le Roy, whose reputation outside of France remains primarily as having written the first primer on Bergsonian philosophy. More specifically, the concept of the noosphere emerged out of their respective readings of Bergson's *Creative Evolution* (1907; English 1911). An attempt to offer a theory of evolution that could account for how 'the intellectual form of the living being has been gradually modelled on the reciprocal actions and reactions of certain bodies and their material environments', Bergson looked to break away from mechanistic models put forward in the nineteenth century.[62] Arguing that variation and adaptation does not occur through the accumulation of learned traits and behaviours, Bergson instead presented evolution as motored by *élan vital*, a vital impetus that runs through life acting as a differentiating force that creates change. As Elizabeth Grosz has argued, we should not see Bergson's concept of *élan vital* as an extension of nineteenth-century vitalism in which spirit and matter are seen in dichotomous or oppositional terms. Rather, for Bergson life itself was 'an extension and elaboration of matter through attenuating divergence or difference', in which vitality and matter are 'intimately implicated in each other, different degrees of one and the same force'.[63] The tangibility of matter and intangibility of life were not opposites but co-constitutive of one another. Moreover, for Bergson, because of the differentiating force driving evolution, adaptation did not occur through intentional, conscious choices made by autonomous individuals. Rather, life developed through the constant negotiation between vitalism, understood as a chaotic and unceasing propulsion of *élan vital*, and counter-vitalism, understood as a tendency within life towards the stasis inducing structures of memory, identity and sameness. No longer could the human be understood as a rational actor operating on a passive environment; instead, it was an entity wholly entangled within the dynamic ecological and geological processes that it was shaping. Making porous the dividing line between the organic and inorganic, or the biological and the geological, Bergson, like Crutzen in his early articles on the Anthropocene, outlines a geology of mankind.[64]

The widespread popularity of Bergson's philosophy in British society of the 1910s and his specific influence on Anglo-American modernism is well documented. Eliot, for instance, attended Bergson's lectures at the Collège de France in Paris in 1910 and 1911, and T. E. Hulme's readings in Bergson likely had a decisive influence on the emergence of imagism.[65] Like the progenitors of the noosphere, Joyce was influenced by Bergson's *Creative Evolution*. He owned a copy of the book in Trieste when he began work on *Ulysses* and as I have argued elsewhere, we can find traces of a Bergsonian influence in Joyce's interest in our unicellular ancestors, such as algae.[66] There are connections to Woolf and Barnes, too. Although Woolf claimed in the 1930s to have 'never read Bergson' (*VWL5* 91), she was in the audience for a paper on Bergson read by her future sister-in-law, Karin Costelloe, in 1913 and, as critics such as Mary Ann Gillies have shown, Woolf's novels 'manipulat[e] traditional narrative form' in ways that correspond with Bergsonian ideas of flux, intuition and the porousness of the self.[67] As Paul Douglass has suggested, there are plenty of reasons why Woolf might have minimised the influence of Bergson, from simply stating what she felt was true for her at the time of her writing to not wishing to be identified too closely with a philosopher whose reputation had lost some of its lustre by the 1930s.[68] We find a similar downplaying from Barnes, who, writing to Coleman in 1938, admits she has read Bergson but claims to 'really know nothing about [him], like every other book and author I ever read'.[69] Barnes's writing, however, like Woolf's, offers a Bergsonian aesthetic. Robin's body odour in *Nightwood* has 'the quality of that earth-flesh, fungi' (*N* 31) and, throughout the novel, we are presented with processes of dehumanisation and atavism, returning the human to the earth and deconstructing the idea of the human as a rational, autonomous actor. What might be called an 'animal turn' in modernist studies has emphatically demonstrated the degree to which writers such as Woolf, Barnes and Joyce were interested in and responding to new evolutionary theories and emergent knowledge of nonhuman life. As Rohman has shown, modernism is marked by 'a certain crisis in humanism vis-à-vis the animal', enabling not only new insights into animal life but, as Margot Norris writes, encouraging them to write 'not *like* the animal [. . .] but with their animality speaking'.[70] Moreover, it was not only that modernists were inspired by the evolutionary theorists of their day; the opposite was also true. When the biologist Julian Huxley read *Nightwood* in 1936, he felt so 'enthusiastic' about the novel that he asked Ottoline Morrell to invite Barnes to meet him at the Zoological Society in Regent's Park.[71] Huxley, grandson of 'Darwin's Bulldog' T. H. Huxley and one of the most influential evolutionary biologists of his day, would later write the introduction to the 1958 English translation of Teilhard's *The Phenomenon of Man*, the evolutionary theory of noogenesis that Barnes would go on to own in her personal library.

Anthropocene Theorists

As the above section has argued, the early twentieth century was a period during which new ideas about the planet, materiality and species relations were migrating between the sciences, philosophy and literature. Although a wide range of writers responded to the new environmental, technological and scientific contexts that were remaking how we understand life, this book chooses to focus on three modernist writers who were actively theorising the novel as a means of engaging with ontological, ethical and, above all, aesthetical ideas that foreshadow the concept of the Anthropocene. In her study of Joyce, Woolf and Dorothy Richardson, Deborah Parsons highlights what she sees as a shared but divergent commitment to the 'constant exploration and renegotiation of modern fiction's limits and possibilities'.[72] For Parsons, these figures were not only writing novels but theorising what novels could and should do. This study builds on Parson's insight but suggests that the modernist novel, in the hands of Joyce, Woolf and Barnes, more specifically became a space in which human-nonhuman relations could be rethought. In the case of Woolf, we find explicit evidence of a theoretical intent not only in her novels but the voluminous essays that she wrote throughout her life. In 'Poetry, Fiction and the Future' (1927), for instance, Woolf describes how:

> for our generation and the generation that is coming the lyric cry of ecstasy or despair, which is so intense, so personal and so limited, is not enough. The mind is full of monstrous, hybrid, unmanageable emotions. That the age of the earth is 3,000,000,000 years; that the human life lasts but a second; that the capacity of the human mind is nevertheless boundless; that life is infinitely beautiful yet repulsive, that one's fellow creatures are adorable but disgusting; that science and religion have between them destroyed belief; that all bonds of union seem broke, yet some control must exist – it is in this atmosphere of doubt and conflict that writers have now to create. (*E4* 429–30)

It is the task of the writer of both poetry and fiction, Woolf argues, to 'forc[e] the form they use to contain a meaning which is strange to it' (*E4* 429). For Woolf, this means arriving at a mode that is both personal and impersonal; that coexists on both an inhuman and a human plane; and which is alive to the way in which rigid ontological divisions are being erased.[73] For Joyce and Barnes, evidence of a self-reflexive relation to the novel is evident in their finished novels, but also the material archives that surrounds their work. At the same time Woolf was penning the essay quoted above, Joyce, as Cathryn Setz has shown, was compiling notebooks with material about geology, glaciation, hominid ancestors and new theories of evolution for use in *Finnegans Wake* (1939).[74] And as I discuss in Chapter 3, Barnes's correspondence from throughout her life reveals a similar preoccupation with resituating the human in a more-than-human continuum, embedding her characters within the longue durée of evolutionary time that Woolf outlines in her essay. In reimagining the possibilities of what the novel can do, this book argues, these authors were also theorising the Anthropocene.

Certainly, it is true that their theoretical project was not a joint one in the conventional sense of the term. Woolf's initial ambivalence towards and begrudging admiration of *Ulysses* is clear in both her essays and diaries (although, as I show in Chapter 6, this later softened), while, in response, it seems that Joyce had little interest in Woolf's writing. In contrast, Barnes befriended Joyce during her time in Paris and his direct influence on her writing has been both documented and disputed.[75] Surprisingly, given that they moved in similar circles and shared several acquaintances, including Eliot, Morrell and Sackville-West, there is no evidence that Woolf and Barnes ever met, although their respective correspondence shows that they were aware of one another's activities as writers. Barnes, for instance, alludes to *A Room of One's Own* in her correspondence with Coleman while discussing her mother's living conditions, while Woolf, implored to read *Nightwood* in December 1936 by Morrell, explained that she hoped to read it as soon as she had finished working through the pile of manuscripts that had been sent to the Hogarth Press, adding that Eliot had also told her it 'was a remarkable book' (*VWL6* 95–6).[76] In bringing their activities into comparison, this study looks to suggest new correspondences between these writers, arguing that, while their interests and approaches were undoubtedly different, they were united by an interest in refiguring the relationship between the human, the nonhuman and the planetary. It is significant, too, that all three would turn to the novel as their vehicle to do so. As Paul Sheehan has argued, the modern idea of the self and the novel emerged at the same time in the eighteenth century, both deeply influenced by an idea of 'human life' that came to prominence with the rise of humanism. The novel, Sheehan argues, reflected the Enlightenment's foregrounding of 'individualism and innovation', while the 'quintessentially human attribute of logic' was mirrored in the novel's 'narrative logic' of 'seriality [and] causal connection'.[77] In its commitment to mimesis and its formal ability to represent the entire duration of a human life thanks to its extended length, the novel became the literary form that most closely resembled the humanist idea of the human. It also upheld the humanistic values that had been attached to life from Descartes onward. The high humanist credence of teleological progress, Sheehan argues, found its correlative in the *Bildungsroman* novel, where the end is built into the beginning, giving a sense of concordance, harmony and, ultimately, meaning to life.[78] All of this, Sheehan suggests, made the novel an inherently anthropocentric form; it could assimilate the chaotic reality of the world within an aesthetic framework predicated on a human sense of order and meaning. In Sheehan's account, this stability of form and world view was disrupted in the nineteenth century by the emergence of new scientific and philosophical paradigms that challenged the idea of a natural moral order, ushering in the cultural decline of anthropocentric master narratives and 'lay[ing] bare narrative for what it is: a metaphysical scaffolding'.[79] If the humanist ideal of the human, so closely tied to the novel, had proven to no longer be secure, then the novel too needed reinventing. Modernism, Sheehan suggests, arrives on the scene as a response to this crisis, with its experimentations in form and content aimed at reappraising what it means to be human.

Gregory Castle makes a similar argument in the introduction to *A History of the Modernist Novel* (2015), arguing that although the modernist novel is a heterogenous genre covering many different approaches and intentions, it nonetheless can be defined by the fact that it 'was always in an experimental mode and it was always engaged with realism, and in this double-barrelled way it sought narrative access to the Real'.[80] For Castle, part of the 'creative and critical potential of anti-mimetic literature' resides in its ability to 'draw attention to the objects (cows, sky) that are merely background in the realist novel and to the subject's inwardness, his reflections and affections' in such a way that produces not mimetic resemblance but 'register[ing] in language and literary form the lived experience of the present'.[81] Echoing Woolf's command to look at the sky and trees with which I opened this introduction, Castle suggests that modernism is predicated on reassessing the relationship between the inner and the outer. Joyce purportedly outlined similar sentiments in conversation with the art critic Arthur Power, explaining that his object was 'to create a new fusion between the exterior world and our contemporary selves' and stating that 'a writer must maintain a continual struggle against the objective'.[82] Like Woolf in 'Poetry, Fiction and the Future', the form of the novel is seen as needing to be retheorised so as to accommodate an emergent understanding of both human *and* nonhuman life. The modernist novel, thus understood, is predicated on a double movement that returns to the question of what it means to be human, expressed through an interest in consciousness, language and experience, while at the same time paying heightened attention to the nonhuman forces the exist within and without human life.

It is important, therefore, that the three writers in this study retain an ambivalent relationship to notions of nature, a term which as Timothy Morton has argued, is freighted with pastoral ideas of the nonhuman world that often frames it in terms of harmony, order and organic unity, and as a domain separate to human society.[83] As such, while McCarthy's *Green Modernism* singles out Woolf and Joyce as modernists whose interest in human subjectivity signifies a disinterest in the natural world and, therefore, limited as objects of ecocritical analysis, this study suggests that it is precisely their interest in both the human *and* the nonhuman, and the sinewy relationship between the two, that makes them theorists of the Anthropocene.[84] Indeed, in her letters to Coleman on Bergson, Barnes signals her suspicion of 'nature writers' who 'seem to [. . .] clean nature up too much', offering William Wordsworth as one such an example.[85] The notion of cleaning up nature, both in the sense of simplifying and morally improving it, provides the antitheses to Barnes's own aesthetics, where the nonhuman is presented in terms of complexity, excess and degeneracy. Messy points of connection, not clean divisions, become the guiding principle of Barnes's writing and, as I show in my later discussion of her essay 'Against Nature' (1922), her texts register a sustained suspicion towards how the word 'nature' has been used in literary history to sanitise the nonhuman, a suspicion shared by both Joyce and Woolf. As opposed to being nature writers, this study situates Joyce, Woolf and Barnes as posthumanist writers, following Cary Wolfe's definition of posthumanism as a non-anthropocentric opposition to 'fantasies of disembodiment and autonomy, inherited from humanism'.[86] Posthumanism, understood thus, is not 'post' in the sense of looking to transcend or leave behind the embodied biological species of the human.[87] The 'post' of posthumanism instead insists that the humanist idea of the human never existed to begin with; that it was always a transcendent or metaphysical ideal that obscured the material substance of the animal which calls itself human. For Rosi Braidotti, who along with Wolfe has been at the forefront of establishing how posthumanism might challenge the theoretical paradigms through which we conceptualise human-nonhuman relations, posthumanism does not diminish what it means to be human. Instead, it insists that we understand that to be human is to be a 'relational subject constituted in and by multiplicity, [. . .] a subject that works across differences and is also internally differentiated, but still grounded and accountable'.[88]

Posthumanism, it is important to stress, is not a rejection of humanism *tout court*. As Wolfe writes, there are 'many values and aspirations to admire in humanism'. What posthumanism aims to bring to light is how these are 'undercut by the philosophical and ethical frameworks used to conceptualize them'.[89] Braidotti makes a similar point when she argues that sometimes disloyalty is the best form of honour and, in this light, the 'past of European humanism is too rich and important to be monumentalized'. Instead, the imperative is to delink its values from anthropocentric, ethnocentric and patriarchal premises to 'form a different cosmological imaginary'.[90] Joyce, Barnes and Woolf can be seen to share a similar relationship to the humanist institution of the novel, one based on complicated feelings of admiration and dissatisfaction, with their work standing as both a continuation of the form and a radical departure from its anthropocentric conventions. In drawing attention to this aspect of their writing, my study builds on a growing body of criticism alert to, in Ryan's term, the entanglement of 'nonhuman materials, objects, animals and environments' that we find in modernist writing.[91] As Jeff Wallace has argued, modernism's interest in subjectivity and consciousness not only reflected an 'emancipation from the narrow confines of the humanist self' and a 'displacement of anthropocentrism', but in its sustained suspicion towards earlier ideas of the human self was an 'inaugural moment' in the genealogy of posthumanism.[92] Crucially, modernism, in this sense, does not merely foreshadow later posthumanist theory, but lays the ground for it. The poststructuralism of Derrida, Deleuze and Guattari, three thinkers who loom large within posthumanist theory and, indeed, this study, were all deeply influenced by modernism, with their work frequently citing modernist texts by Joyce and Woolf, as well as Lawrence, Kafka and Proust.[93] Such points of continuity persist within posthumanist philosophy itself. For instance, Braidotti's work follows Deleuze not only in further developing many of his insights on materiality and subjectivity but in turning to Woolf as a writer whose texts contain the potential to produce new concepts to think with.[94] Posthumanism, thus understood, presents itself as the latest iteration within a critical trajectory that begins with modernism.

This study, however, situates Joyce, Barnes and Woolf not only as rethinking the novel in ways that would give rise to posthumanism, but more specifically, as anticipating the theoretical challenges posed by the Anthropocene. In a 2009 essay that has subsequently been seen as a watershed moment within Anthropocene studies, Dipesh Chakrabarty argues that as human influence on planetary systems becomes more apparent, one of the greatest challenges is how to reconceptualise agency at multiple scales: individual, collective and planetary. It is a challenge that, in insisting that we need to think on different scales at once, echoes both Bloom's gesture to the disparity between human life and geological eons in *Ulysses* and Woolf's critical reflection on what it means to write fiction against the backdrop of a planetary history that stretches back for billions of years. Similarly, Chakrabarty's observation that the scale of anthropogenic planetary change means we need to reconceptualise 'the category of species' finds a correlative in Barnes's insistence on rethinking the way in which we understand the human as an animal.[95] While for Clark, the Anthropocene, in insisting we think on multiple scales at once, including slow and barely perceptible geological processes, disrupts 'conventions of plotting, characterization and setting' in the novel, since it places 'counter-intuitive demands on representation', this study argues that we find in the modernist novels of Joyce, Barnes and Woolf an attempt to grapple with precisely these problematics of form.[96] No longer hostage to the 'anthropocentric delusion' that Clark identifies as pervading realist fiction, we find in the modernist novel a literary mode that, in Woolf's terms, is 'written standing back from life, [from which] a larger view is to be obtained', able to both 'ris[e] high from the ground [. . .] [while] keeping at the same time in touch with the amusements and idiosyncrasies of human character in daily life' (*E4* 438).[97] Planetary life, not just human life, becomes the purview of the modernist novelist, framed through multiple scales of perspective.

This book does not look to reclaim Joyce, Barnes or Woolf as proto environmentalists, although, like many of their contemporaries, they held what we would now see as environmental concerns. For instance, as I show in this book, Woolf's anxieties around housing developments in the South Downs creep into *Between the Acts* and Joyce's writing registers an awareness of the ecological consequences to British colonialism, while in my coda I present evidence of Barnes's interest in the environmental movements of the 1960s. Rather, the central argument in this book is that in their innovations in form and content, Joyce, Barnes and Woolf engage with ontological and ethical questions that have become increasingly urgent in our current planetary moment. In their willingness to suspend anthropocentric thinking and to figure the human and the nonhuman in new ways, this book reads these three authors as Anthropocene theorists *avant la lettre*. Modernism in this respect, I contend, allows us to not only to historicise the Anthropocene but intervene in contemporary discussions on materiality, species relations and planetary change. At the same time, this study looks to suggest how the Anthropocene offers new ways of theorising and historicising modernism, to understand better how and why Joyce, Barnes and Woolf wrote the novels they did. To do so it draws on archival and historical research to map out points of confluence between literary modernism and the Anthropocene. In resituating the modernist novel as responding to the emergence of the Anthropocene, this book suggests that we can locate a Modernist Anthropocene, understood as both a historical moment within a broader planetary epoch and as an identifiable aesthetic response to that historical moment.

The Modernist Anthropocene begins by setting out modernism's relation to the proto-environmentalist politics that developed in the late nineteenth century. Focusing on how we can trace through Joyce's work an engagement with Revivalist ideas of nature and nationalism, Chapter 1 argues that ambivalence rather than rejection shaped his response to the works of W. B. Yeats, John Eglinton, George Russell and others. Beginning by showing how Revivalist literature was influenced by the Back to Nature movement of late Victorian

England, the chapter goes on to trace how Joyce develops a competing aesthetic theory of nature and nationalism in *Stephen Hero* (posthumously published in 1944) and *A Portrait of the Artist as a Young Man* (1916). I argue that it was Joyce's theory of art and nature that provided one of the motivations to abandon the realism of *Stephen Hero* and develop the experimental prose style of *A Portrait of the Artist as a Young Man*. Moving on to *Ulysses*, the chapter argues that Joyce's continuing formal innovations further insist on an unstable relationship between collective identity and the material world, undermining the natural foundations that the Revival propounded as providing the basis for an organic national identity. By focusing on 'Cyclops', an episode where Joyce demonstrates an acute awareness of the environmental costs to British colonialism, the chapter concludes by suggesting that Joyce could ultimately not wholly disavow nationalist proto-environmentalist concerns. Where *A Portrait of the Artist as a Young Man* represents Stephen's attempt to 'fly by those nets' of nationalism, *Ulysses* shows how ecology is intractable from questions of nation and empire. Drawing on Félix Guattari's concept of tri-ecology, which recognises materiality, subjectivity and social relations as intertwined, I suggest that the environmental politics of Joyce's novels make them important works of Anthropocene fiction.

Taking as its starting point Joyce's assertion that in 'Penelope' Molly speaks as the Earth goddess, Gea-Tellus, Chapter 2 revisits the highly gendered cosmological symbolism through which Joyce schematised his novel and asks if it is possible to reread *Ulysses* in light of recent interest in Gaia theory by Donna Haraway and Bruno Latour. To answer this question, the chapter begins by examining the gendered planetary imaginary of the novel, examining how, although Stephen and Bloom understand the universe in vastly contrasting terms, their respective cosmologies both associate women with a fertile materiality. Showing how Greek and Irish Earth Mother myths are repeatedly referenced and refashioned in the text, I look at whether Molly's monologue – serving to 'countersign' the rest of the novel – might be read as taking a Gaian revenge on what has come before it and examine the vexed question of whether we should see Joyce's novel as complicit with cultural traditions that associate women with an essentialised and feminised idea of the Earth, or subverting them. The chapter concludes by examining how Joyce's interest in Earth Mother myths did not end in 1922 with the publication of *Ulysses*. Looking at how Gaian mythology continued to interest Joyce in *Finnegans Wake*, most strikingly in the figure of ALP as the 'eternal Geo-Mater', I suggest that in Joyce's final novel we find one last attempt to arrive at an aesthetics of material immanence that goes beyond the boundaries of the human, but also a further example of the limited gender politics afforded by the figure of Gaia.

Chapter 3 looks at how Barnes's writing offers a beastly aesthetic that puts the idea of the human – or the Anthropos of the Anthropocene – under pressure. Rather than focusing on a single text, this chapter traces the beastly instances that we find across Barnes's writing, bringing her novel *Nightwood* into a fresh dialogue with her broader body of writing, including her first novel, *Ryder* (1928), her early journalism and the wealth of little-studied materials in her archive. Drawing on Derrida's final seminars, collected and published as *The Beast & the Sovereign* (2009–11), I suggest that we can identify beastliness as a distinct tropological mode in Barnes's oeuvre that differs from either the animal or the creature. While the creaturely turn within animal studies has emphasised relationality and vulnerability, I show how for Barnes the beastly is expressed through terms of queerness, negativity and contagion. Arguing that Barnes's beastly prose enables her to develop a self-reflexive mode of anthropomorphism which gives her texts a lively animality, this chapter makes the case that Barnes insists that it is our beastly differences (rather than similarities) to other animals that might provide the basis for interspecies relations in the Anthropocene.

Continuing to look at how Barnes's literary innovations complicate ideas of the human and the nonhuman, Chapter 4 examines how her writing shows the ecological imagination and the familial imagination to be inextricably entangled. Beginning by looking at Barnes's disavowal of gendered ideas of naturalness in her 1922 essay 'Against Nature', this chapter focuses on her first novel *Ryder*, reading it as a text that is alert to the ways in which discourse around nature all too often work to naturalise heterosexuality and patrilineal genealogies. Set on an unconventional farm in rural America at the turn of the twentieth century, *Ryder* is an experimental and satirical family chronicle that engages with themes of polygamy, genealogy and animal life. It is also a novel, I show, which not only explores modern configurations of sexual identity but writes back to a gendered tradition of American nature writing established by nineteenth-century transcendentalists such as Henry David Thoreau. Barnes's satire of such nature writing, I argue, opens up a space in which patrilineal inheritance is disrupted and more-than-human genealogies are expressed. Showing how Barnes's text offers an ecology that offers new ways of thinking about sexuality, familial structures and species kinship, this chapter brings Barnes into dialogue with Kelly Oliver's theory of multispecies sexual difference and Timothy Morton's queer ecology, situating *Ryder* as a work whose transgressive form insists on a non-heteronormative vision of the nonhuman world.

Chapter 5 turns to Woolf and questions of climate change. Beginning by establishing Woolf's long-standing interest in the relationship between weather and literature, present in her earliest journals and in the reviews and essays she prepared for *The Common Reader* (1925), this chapter argues that the expansive scale of *Orlando: A Biography* (1928) enabled Woolf to experiment with and further develop her interest in climate. In the novel's attentiveness to historical vicissitudes in the British climate, I show how Woolf presents the reader with an image of the past in which human and nonhuman systems are bound together through structures of reciprocity and response. Suggesting that Orlando's status as a nature poet is a satire of the popularity of pastoralism in post-war British poetry (exemplified in the work of A. E. Housman and her lover Vita Sackville-West), I argue that Woolf instead turned to the works of the eminent Victorian scientist of climate, John Tyndall, when it came to writing about the environment. Offering evidence that Woolf was not only familiar with Tyndall's ideas but that she drew on many of them for the atmospheric imagery we find in the novel, the chapter argues that Woolf establishes a climatic ontology that foreshadows contemporary new materialist philosophies. This climatic ontology, I show, is central to questions of identity and transformation at the heart of *Orlando*.

In Woolf's late writings, published in the late 1930s and early 1940s, we find a preoccupation with the end of the world. Chapter 6 examines how during this period Woolf was reconsidering and reconceptualising notions of extinction that are now being theorised within Anthropocene studies. Beginning by looking at how Woolf's diaries, letters, essays and manuscripts written under the threat and eventual arrival of the Second World War are marked by an insistent return to questions of extinction, posterity and futurity, I suggest that throughout this period Woolf was developing a 'tiny philosophy' premised on understanding the relationship between the present and the future. Showing that extinction is the horizon that unites the characters in Woolf's final unfinished novel *Between the Acts*, the chapter brings to light how competing ideas of futurity play out in the novel. Through the concerns of the Oliver family and the villagers attending the pageant, this chapter presents how Woolf understood a dominant narrative of extinction to be structured by anthropocentric and heteronormative ideas of posterity that limited how the future might be imagined. Through analysis of the novel's queer characters and the disruptive agency of the pageant, I suggest that Woolf finds a way of departing from this normative narrative of extinction. In La Trobe's satire of teleological history and in the novel's closing image of the possibility of 'another life', I show how Woolf's novel works towards an ethics of extinction able to ask the radical question of whether we should want our current present to inhere into the future.

The Modernist Anthropocene concludes with a short final chapter that, rather than serving as a coda, presents itself in terms of fallout. Looking at how the detonation of the Trinity nuclear bomb in New Mexico in 1945 inaugurated a new phase in planetary history, I suggest it heralded the beginning of the Nuclear Anthropocene, which, like the Modernist Anthropocene, can be defined both in terms of a historical period and the set of cultural and aesthetic responses it provoked. Suggesting that rather than coming to an end with the Second World War, modernism lived on in the Nuclear Anthropocene, I show how works by Joyce and Woolf seem to uncannily foresee the consequences to life under the threat of nuclear warfare. I also discuss how Georgia O'Keeffe's painting, *Light Coming on the Plains No. II* (1917), which provides the cover art for this book, also points to the ways in which modernist aesthetics would foreshadow and influence responses to the Nuclear Anthropocene. Suggesting that Barnes is comparable to O'Keeffe insofar as both remained active into the 1980s, I show how her late poetry – both published and unpublished – engages directly with the implications of the nuclear age, as well as other emergent environmental crises such as the consequences to chemical pesticides and urban pollution. Presenting evidence that Barnes, far from turning inward in her later years, was engaging with the works of environmentalists such as Rachel Carson, I look at how Barnes's late poetry shows that the fallout from modernism can be traced throughout the twentieth century. Showing how the modernist novel has a half-life that continues to radiate into our present moment, the book concludes by suggesting that the Modernist Anthropocene might guide us in how we respond to our increasingly precarious present.

Notes

1. Atmospheric changes are captured in tree rings and frequently cited as evidence of climate change. Colin N. Waters et al., 'The Anthropocene is Functionally and Stratigraphically Distinct from the Holocene', *Science*, 351.6269 (2016), 137; aad2622-1-aad2622-10.
2. Simon L. Lewis and Mark A. Maslin, 'Defining the Anthropocene', *Nature*, 519.7542 (2015), 171–80 (p. 171).
3. Paul Crutzen, 'Geology of Mankind', *Nature*, 415 (2002), 23.
4. For an overview of the good Anthropocene hypothesis and the critiques that have been made of it see Jamie Lorimer, 'The Anthropo-Scene: A Guide for the Perplexed', *Social Studies of Science*, 47.1 (2017), 125–6.
5. Claire Colebrook, Peter Adkins and Wendy Parkins, 'Victorian Studies in the Anthropocene: An Interview with Claire Colebrook', *19: Interdisciplinary Studies in the Long Nineteenth Century*, 26 (2018) <https://doi.org/10.16995/ntn.819> (last accessed 21 February 2021).
6. Timothy Clark, *Ecocriticism on the Edge: The Anthropocene as a Threshold Concept* (London: Bloomsbury, 2015), p. 9.
7. Bruno Latour, *We Have Never Been Modern*, trans. Catherine Porter (Cambridge, MA: Harvard University Press, 1993), pp.7–10, pp. 43–9. Latour's earlier work on pasteurisation, *The Pasteurization of France* (1984; Eng. 1988), offers an example of one such hybrid.
8. Isabelle Stengers, *In Catastrophic Times: Resisting the Coming Barbarism*, trans. Andrew Goffey (Ann Arbor, MI: Open Humanities Press, 2015), p. 53.
9. See Elizabeth Black, *The Nature of Modernism: Ecocritical Approaches to the Poetry of Edward Thomas, T. S. Eliot, Edith Sitwell and Charlotte Mew* (Abingdon: Routledge, 2018); Jeffrey Mathes McCarthy, *Green Modernism: Nature and the English Novel, 1900 to 1930* (Basingstoke and New York: Palgrave Macmillan,

2015); and Bonnie Kime Scott, *In the Hollow of the Wave: Virginia Woolf and Modernist Uses of Nature* (Charlottesville: University of Virginia Press, 2012). Also see Jeremy Diaper's study of T. S. Eliot's interest in agrarianism and ruralism, *T.S. Eliot and Organicism* (Clemson, SC: Clemson University Press, 2018).
10. Timothy Morton's *Ecology without Nature* was an important moment in this development, with its critique of a range of implicit ideological commitments to romantic ideas of nature in earlier ecocriticism. Morton, *Ecology without Nature: Rethinking Environmental Aesthetics* (Cambridge, MA: Harvard University Press, 2007).
11. Kelly Sultzbach, *Ecocriticism in the Modernist Imagination: Forster, Woolf, and Auden* (Cambridge: Cambridge University Press, 2016), p. 4.
12. Jonathan Schuster, *The Ecology of Modernism: American Environments and Avant-Garde Poetics* (Tuscaloosa: The University of Alabama Press, 2015); Matthew Griffiths, *The New Poetics of Climate Change: Modernist Aesthetics for a Warming World* (London: Bloomsbury, 2017). See also Andrew Kalaidjian's *Exhausted Ecologies: Modernism and Environmental Recovery* (Cambridge: Cambridge University Press, 2020), which traces the rise of national parks as places of rest and rejuvenation alongside modernist works which also link nature and recovery, and Jesse Oak Taylor's *The Sky of Our Manufacture: The London Fog in British Fiction from Dickens to Woolf* (Charlottesville: University of Virginia Press, 2016) which concludes with a section on climate in Woolf and Joseph Conrad.
13. Griffiths, *The New Poetics of Climate Change*, p. 10.
14. Critics have shown how Woolf's interest in the nonhuman was informed by a sustained engagement with the sciences, particularly the emergence of life sciences such as ecology and ethology (Christina Alt, *Virginia Woolf and the Study of Nature* (Cambridge: Cambridge University Press, 2010)), modern astronomy (Holly Henry, *Virginia Woolf and the Discourse of Science* (Cambridge: Cambridge University Press, 2003)) and the new physics (Michael Whitworth, *Einstein's Wake: Relativity, Metaphor, and Modernist Literature* (Oxford: Oxford University Press, 2004)); Rachel Crossland, *Modernist Physics: Waves, Particles, and Relativities in the Writings of Virginia Woolf and D. H. Lawrence* (Oxford: Oxford University Press, 2018)).
15. Derek Ryan, *Virginia Woolf and the Materiality of Theory: Sex, Animal, Life* (Edinburgh: Edinburgh University Press, 2013), p. 2.
16. Robert Brazeau and Derek Gladwin's *Eco-Joyce: The Environmental Imagination of James Joyce* (Cork: Cork University Press, 2014) and Alison Lacivita's *The Ecology of 'Finnegans Wake'* (Gainesville: University Press of Florida, 2015) stand out as trailblazing books in drawing attention to this aspect of Joyce's oeuvre.
17. Djuna Barnes to Emily Coleman, 13 October 1938. Emily Holmes Coleman Papers, Special Collections, University of Delaware Library (hereafter EHCP), Box 4, Folder 39.
18. Carrie Rohman, *Stalking the Subject: Modernism and the Animal* (New York: Columbia University Press, 2009), p. 157.
19. Emily Coleman to Djuna Barnes, 27 August 1935. Djuna Barnes Papers, Special Collections, University of Maryland Libraries (hereafter DBP), Series 2, Box 3, Folder 6.

20. Christophe Bonneuil and Jean-Baptiste Fressoz, *The Shock of the Anthropocene*, trans. David Fernbach (New York: Verso, 2016), p. 76.
21. Ibid. p. 172.
22. Quoted in Jeremy Davies, *The Birth of the Anthropocene* (Oakland: University of California Press, 2016), p. 42. Eugene Stoermer, a University of Michigan ecologist, had been using the word informally since the 1980s. In recognition of this, the first scientific paper on the Anthropocene was co-authored by Stoermer and Crutzen. See Paul Crutzen and Eugene Stoermer, 'The "Anthropocene"', *IGBP Newsletter*, 41 (2000), 17–18.
23. Waters et al., 'The Anthropocene Is Functionally and Stratigraphically Distinct from the Holocene', pp. 2622–8.
24. For analysis of the Holocene as an unusually stable climatic period that produced human culture(s) see Davies, *The Birth of the Anthropocene*, pp. 161–92.
25. Crutzen, 'Geology of Mankind', p. 23.
26. The Great Acceleration names the post-war surge in resource use, population levels and GDP. Jan Zalasiewicz et al., 'When did the Anthropocene Begin? A Mid-Twentieth Century Boundary Level Is Stratigraphically Optimal', *Quaternary International*, 383 (2015), 196–203.
27. See Lorimer's 'The Anthropo-Scene' for an overview of the arguments supporting these earlier dates.
28. See, for instance, Jane Goldman's *Modernism, 1910–1945: Image to Apocalypse* (Basingstoke: Palgrave Macmillan, 2004).
29. On the imbricated relationship between modernism and postmodernism, and beyond, see Susan Stanford Friedman's article on the shifting meaning of modernism and modernity. Susan Stanford Friedman, 'Definitional Excursions: The Meanings of Modern/Modernity/Modernism', *Modernism/modernity*, 8.3 (2001), 493–513.
30. Davies, *The Birth of the Anthropocene*, pp. 98–9.
31. William F. Ruddiman et al., 'Defining the epoch we live in: Is a formally designated "Anthropocene" a good idea?', *Science*, 348.6230 (2015), 38–9 (p. 39); Will Steffen et al., 'The Anthropocene: Conceptual and Historical Perspectives', *Philosophical Transactions of the Royal Society*, A369.1938 (2011), 842–67 (p. 850).
32. E. M. Forster, *Howards End*, ed. Oliver Stallybrass (London: Penguin Books, 1989), p. 115.
33. Forster, *Howards End*, p. 205; Ted Howell, 'An Imperialist Inherits the Earth: *Howards End* in the Anthropocene', *Modern Language Quarterly*, 77.4 (2016), 547–72 (p. 550). The degree to which Forster's novel either endorses or is self-reflexive of the ideological limitations to the Schlegels' pastoral idealism has been much debated. For an ecocritical argument on how 'Forster borrows from the pastoral, but [. . .] also exposes what the pastoral is traditionally meant to evade' see Sultzbach, *Ecocriticism in the Modernist Imagination*, p. 46.
34. D. H. Lawrence, *The Rainbow*, ed. Mark Kinkead-Weekes (London: Penguin Books, 1995), pp. 282–3. On motor car culture more generally in modernist literature see Enda Duffy, *The Speed Handbook: Velocity, Pleasure, Modernism* (Durham, NC: Duke University Press, 2009).

35. D. H. Lawrence, *Women in Love*, ed. David Farmer, Lindeth Vasey and John Worthen (London: Penguin Books, 2000), p. 223.
36. Bruno Latour, *Facing Gaia: Eight Lectures on the New Climatic Regime*, trans. Catherine Porter (Cambridge: Polity, 2017), p. 63. Gerald is, of course, also wrong in thinking that coal has lain in the bedrock since the Earth's beginnings.
37. Ibid. p. 228.
38. Schuster, *The Ecology of Modernism*, p. 162.
39. Ibid. p. 163. Amitav Ghosh has argued that while coal mining became the subject of many nineteenth-century novels, the liquid 'materiality of oil' and the fewer human workers needed to oversee its extraction means that it is 'inscrutable' to the arts in a 'way that coal never was'. See Amitav Ghosh, *The Great Derangement: Climate Change and the Unthinkable* (Chicago: University of Chicago Press, 2017), p. 73.
40. T. S. Eliot, *Collected Poems 1909–1962* (New York: Harcourt, Brace & World, Inc., 1963), p. 63.
41. Claire Colebrook, 'The Future in the Anthropocene: Extinction and the Imagination', in *Climate and Literature*, ed. Adeline Johns-Putra (Cambridge: Cambridge University Press, 2019), pp. 263–80 (p. 273).
42. Anna Snaith and Michael Whitworth, 'Introduction: Approaches to Space and Place in Woolf', in *Locating Woolf: The Politics of Space and Place*, ed. Anna Snaith and Michael Whitworth (Basingstoke: Palgrave Macmillan, 2007), pp.1–30 (p. 25).
43. James H. Winter, *Secure from Rash Assault: Sustaining the Victorian Environment* (Berkeley and Los Angeles: University of California Press, 1999), p. 20.
44. Bonnueil and Fressoz, *The Shock of the Anthropocene*, p. 116.
45. Donna Haraway, *Staying with the Trouble: Making Kin in the Chthulucene* (Durham, NC: Duke University Press, 2016), p. 49. The historian Andreas Malm has also done much to popularise the notion of the Capitalocene, arguing that emergent planetary conditions reveal 'the geology not of mankind, but of capital accumulation'. Malm's theory, however, is more rigid and less useful to this study than Haraway's, not least in its hostility towards the benefits of there being a plurality of optics (or 'cenes) through which to understand the current planetary moment. Andreas Malm, *Fossil Capital: The Rise of Steam Power and the Roots of Global Warming* (London: Verso, 2016), p. 391.
46. Gertrude Stein, *Picasso* (New York: Dover Publications, 1984), p. 50.
47. Ibid. p. 50.
48. Uniformitarian theories had been in decline throughout the second half of the nineteenth century in favour of a more dynamic understanding of geological change. For an account of the developments of geology and ecology in the nineteenth century and its influence on Victorian culture see Wendy Parkins and Peter Adkins, 'Victorian Ecology and the Anthropocene', *19: Interdisciplinary Studies in the Long Nineteenth Century*, 26 (2018) <www.19.bbk.ac.uk/article/id/1717/> (last accessed 22 February 2021).
49. R. L. Sherlock, *Man as Geological Agent: An Account of His Action on Inanimate Nature* (London: H. F & G. Witherby, 1922), p. 13.
50. Ibid. p. 325.

51. Winter, *Secure From Rash Assault*, p. 35.
52. Sherlock, *Man as Geological Agent*, p. 8.
53. Ibid. pp. 343–5. For more on this topic see Christina Alt, '"Restore to Us the Necessary BLIZZARDS": Early Twentieth-Century Visions of Climatic Change', *Modernist Cultures*, 16.1 (2021), 37–61.
54. Lewis and Maslin, 'Defining the Anthropocene', p. 173.
55. Vladimir Vernadsky, 'Geochemistry', in *The Biosphere and Noosphere Reader*, ed. Paul R. Samson and David Pitt, trans. Paul R. Samson (London and New York: Routledge, 1999), pp. 26–8 (p. 26).
56. Sherlock, *Man as Geological Agent*, p. 343.
57. Paul R. Samson and David Pitt, 'Introduction: Sketching the Noosphere', in *The Biosphere and Noosphere Reader*, pp. 1–10 (p. 2). The concept of the biosphere had been established by Austrian geologist Eduard Suess and, as Peter J. Bowler explains, presented a theory of 'global synthesis based on the concept of a gradually cooling earth subject to a steady diminution in the rate of geological change'. Peter J. Bowler, *The Norton History of the Environmental Sciences* (New York: W.W. Norton, 1993), p. 234.
58. Edouard Le Roy, 'The Origins of Humanity and the Evolution of the Mind', trans. Paul R. Samson, in *The Biosphere and Noosphere Reader*, pp. 60–70 (p. 70).
59. Pierre Teilhard de Chardin, 'The Phenomenon of Man', trans. Paul R. Samson, in *The Biosphere and Noosphere Reader*, pp. 71–3 (p. 73).
60. Samson and Pitt, 'Introduction: Sketching the Noosphere', pp. 3–5.
61. Ulick O'Connor (ed.), *The Joyce We Knew: Memoirs of Joyce* (Dingle: Brandon Books, 2004), p. 49. Barnes's personal library is among her papers at the University of Maryland's Special Collections. There are slighter connections with Woolf. A 1940 edition of Teilhard de Chardin's *Sauvons l'humanité* is listed as being present in Virginia and Leonard Woolf's personal library but given the date and Leonard's interest in social science at the time, it is more likely to have belonged to him.
62. Henri Bergson, *Creative Evolution*, trans. Arthur Mitchell (New York: Random House, 1944) p. xi.
63. Elizabeth Grosz, *Becoming Undone: Darwinian Reflections on Life, Politics, and Art* (Durham, NC: Duke University Press, 2011), pp. 30–1.
64. Crutzen, 'Geology of Mankind', p. 23.
65. As Jeff Wallace has argued in the context of D. H. Lawrence's oeuvre, Bergson's 'doubled or distinctly ambivalent stance towards science' and his 'material definition of mind' is part of modernism's intellectual climate, contributing to the revision of the human that became a prevalent site of anxiety for a wide range of modernist writers. Jeff Wallace, *D. H. Lawrence, Science and the Posthuman* (New York: Palgrave Macmillan, 2005), p. 14.
66. See my chapter '"There all the time without you": Joyce, Modernism, and the Anthropocene', in *Eco-Modernism: Ecology, Environment and Nature in Literary Modernism*, ed. Jeremy Diaper (Clemson, SC: Clemson University Press, forthcoming).
67. Paul Douglass, 'Bergson, Vitalism, and Modernist Literature', *Understanding Bergson, Understanding Modernism*, ed. Paul Ardoin, S. E. Gontarski, and Laci

Mattison (London: Bloomsbury, 2013) pp. 107–27 (p. 115); Mary Ann Gillies, *Henri Bergson and British Modernism* (Montreal: McGill Queen's University Press, 1996), p. 110.
68. Douglass, 'Bergson, Vitalism, and Modernist Literature', p. 116.
69. Djuna Barnes to Emily Coleman, 13 October 1938. EHCP, Box 4, Folder 39. Bergson would continue to be discussed in their correspondence throughout the autumn of 1938.
70. Rohman, *Stalking the Subject*, p. 21; Margot Norris, *Beasts of the Modern Imagination: Darwin, Nietzsche, Kafka, Ernst & Lawrence* (Baltimore and London: Johns Hopkins University Press, 1985), p. 1, emphasis in original. See also Caroline Hovanec's *Animal Subjects: Literature, Zoology and British Modernism* (Cambridge: Cambridge University Press, 2018), Rachel Murray's *The Modernist Exoskeleton: Insects, War, Literary Form* (Edinburgh: Edinburgh University Press, 2020), Derek Ryan's *Bloomsbury, Beasts and British Modernist Literature* (forthcoming) and Cathryn Setz's *Primordial Modernism: Animals, Ideas, transition (1927–1938)* (Edinburgh: Edinburgh University Press, 2019).
71. Ottoline Morrell to Djuna Barnes, 19 October 1936. DBP, Series 2, Box 12, Folder 21.
72. Deborah Parsons, *Theorists of the Modernist Novel: James Joyce, Dorothy Richardson, Virginia Woolf* (London: Routledge, 2007), p. 15.
73. Parsons also cites this essay as key to understanding Woolf's theoretical ambitions.
74. Setz, *Primordial Modernism*, pp. 71–4.
75. Phillip Herring locates Barnes's reading of *Ulysses* as 'a turning point' in her writing, while Carolyn Burke has argued that Barnes's 'idiosyncratic modernism' should not be seen as a diluted Joycean aesthetic. Carolyn Burke, '"Accidental Aloofness": Barnes, Loy, and Modernism', in *Silence and Power: A Reevaluation of Djuna Barnes*, ed. Mary Lynn Broe (Carbondale and Edwardsville: Southern Illinois University Press, 1991) pp. 67–79 (p. 73); Phillip Herring, *Djuna: The Life and Works of Djuna Barnes* (New York and London: Penguin Books, 1996), p. 102.
76. Barnes to Coleman, 20 March 1936. EHCP, Box 3, Folder 15.
77. Paul Sheehan, *Modernism, Narrative and Humanism* (Cambridge: Cambridge University Press, 2002), p. 2; p. 10.
78. Ibid. p. 12.
79. Ibid. p. 45.
80. Gregory Castle, 'Introduction: Matter in Motion in the Modernist Novel', in *A History of the Modernist Novel*, ed. Gregory Castle (Cambridge: Cambridge University Press, 2015), pp.1–36 (p. 3).
81. Ibid. p. 7.
82. Arthur Power, *Conversations with James Joyce* (Dublin: Lilliput Press, 1999), p. 86.
83. Timothy Morton, *The Ecological Thought* (Cambridge, MA: Harvard University Press, 2010), p. 3.
84. McCarthy, *Green Modernism*, pp.19–20.
85. Barnes to Coleman, 30 October 1938. DBP, Series 2, Box 3, Folder 12.
86. Cary Wolfe, *What Is Posthumanism?* (Minneapolis: University of Minnesota Press, 2010), p. xv.

87. In this sense, posthumanism is not to be confused with transhumanism, which reimagines the human's relationship to technology in utopian terms, often intensifying Enlightenment ideas of mastery and progress.
88. Rosi Braidotti, *The Posthuman* (Cambridge: Polity, 2013), p. 49.
89. Wolfe, *What Is Posthumanism?*, p. xvi. Wolfe offers the example of animal rights as one such a value.
90. Rosi Braidotti, *Posthuman Knowledge* (Cambridge: Polity, 2019), p. 140; p. 147.
91. Derek Ryan, 'Following Snakes and Moths: Modernist Ethics and Posthumanism', *Twentieth-Century Literature*, 61.3 (2015), 287–304 (p. 300). Ryan's comment comes from the introduction to a special issue of *Twentieth-Century Literature* on 'Modernist Ethics and Posthumanism'. See also the 2016 special issue of *Modernism/modernity* on 'Modernist Inhumanisms' edited by Aaron Jaffe.
92. Jeff Wallace, 'Modern', in *The Cambridge Companion to Literature and the Posthuman*, ed. Bruce Clarke and Manuela Rossini (Cambridge: Cambridge University Press, 2017), pp. 41–53 (pp. 46–8; p. 41). It is worth noting too, in this context, that the *OED* traces the first usage of the word 'posthuman' to 1916 and Joyce used the term in his correspondence while writing *Ulysses*, which I explore in more detail in Chapter 3 of this book.
93. Derrida is most closely associated with Joyce of all the figures named, although both Lawrence and Woolf appear in *The Beast & the Sovereign* (Chicago: University of Chicago Press, 2009–11). As Stephen Ross writes in his introduction to *Modernism and Theory* (2009), many of the 'most important theoretical figures of the last half of the twentieth century were reading and thinking about modernism directly' and their intellectual endeavours can be seen, in a certain sense, as a continuation of the modernist project. Stephen Ross, 'Introduction: The Missing Link', in *Modernism and Theory: A Critical Debate*, ed. Stephen Ross (Abingdon: Routledge, 2009), pp. 1–18 (pp. 13–14).
94. For the relationship between Woolf and Braidotti see the forthcoming special issue of *Comparative Critical Studies* on the subject, edited by Ruth Clemens, Derek Ryan and myself.
95. Dipesh Chakrabarty, 'The Climate of History: Four Theses', *Critical Inquiry*, 35.2 (2009), 197–222 (p. 215).
96. Clark, *Ecocriticism on the Edge*, p. 191.
97. Ibid. p. 191.

1

THE MATTER OF POLITICS IN THE NOVELS OF JAMES JOYCE

The relationship between the brute matter from which the world is composed and the human meaning that we construct from such matter is one of the fundamental concerns played out in James Joyce's *Ulysses* (1922). Leopold Bloom, having just buried his friend Paddy Dignam in Glasnevin Cemetery, reflects on how we are all destined to become 'a tallowy kind of a cheese' in the 'damp earth', in which death is not the end since 'cells or whatever they are go on living' and '[c]hanging about' (*U* 6.778–81). No doubt alert to the fact that the word 'human' likely derives from the same Latin root as 'humus', Joyce has his protagonist intuit the necessity of seeing human life as continuous with earthy nonhuman processes, foreshadowing theorists such as Donna Haraway who argue that '[w]e are humus, not Homo, not anthropos'.[1] Human thought and inhuman matter are caught up within one another, since '[i]n the midst of death we are in life. Both ends meet' (*U* 6.759–60). Stephen Dedalus comes to a similar conclusion at the end of 'Proteus', as he also thinks about processes of decomposition and transformation. Reminded of recent reports of a drowned man and imagining a '[b]ag of corpsegas sopping in foul brine', Stephen is led to consider how 'God becomes man becomes fish becomes barnacle goose becomes featherbed mountain' (*U* 3.476–9). While Stephen's thoughts often veer towards the immaterial and the transcendent, Joyce firmly locates him in the earthy and the bodily: his esoteric musings in 'Proteus', ranging from Aristotle to Shakespeare, conclude with him covertly wiping 'dry snot picked from his nostril on a ledge of rock' (*U* 3.500). Human life and all that it entails does not stand outside of the messy economy of material transformations but is instead, Joyce comically insists again and again, immanent to it.

Joyce's material ontology is not a flat one but constituted by an aggregate of historical, political and symbolic associations that give a depth and textured consistency to the continuum into which he plants his characters. We find a near literal presentation of this earlier in 'Proteus', where Stephen looks out upon an environment constituted by the materiality of history and politics. Mixing free indirect discourse and interior monologue, Joyce presents Stephen amidst:

> damp crackling mast, razorshells, squeaking pebbles, that on the unnumbered pebbles beats, wood sieved by the shipworm, lost Armada. Unwholesome sandflats waited to suck his treading soles, breathing upward sewage breath, a pocket of seaweed smouldered in seafire under a midden of man's ashes. [. . .] Ringsend: wigwams of brown steersmen and master mariners. Human shells. (*U* 3.148–57)

Dublin is presented as a living palimpsest in which the material remainders of historical events are transposed upon matter from the far geological past and still unfolding environmental processes (most notably the seeping of raw sewage from the city). Like Bloom's human as humus, here the image of 'human shells' stands as the intermingling of the human and the inhuman, the personal and the geological. It is a deeply unromantic image of human existence and of Irish existence in particular, and, at first glance, it might seem to stand as evidence of what has been typically seen as Joyce's antithetical stance towards an idealised nature and, more specifically, the pastoralism of the Irish Literary Revival. The Revival, a loose affiliation of writers interested in the rejuvenating potential of Irish folklore and country life, spearheaded by W. B. Yeats, Lady Gregory and J. M. Synge, among others, has long been recognised as an important contemporaneous counterpart to Joyce's modernism. His interest in capturing the realities of Irish life, through ever-changing modes of experimentation with form and genre, and his aesthetic disposition towards irony, fragmentation and difficulty, has historically been read as standing in tension with the romantic works that characterise the Revival.[2] More recently, critics have complicated this narrative, arguing that while Joyce might resist being easily assimilated within the literary history of the Revival, in both the persistent allusions to it that we find across his oeuvre and in his attempts to find new ways of writing about colonial Ireland within the English language, his writing cannot be wholly disentangled from the movement. As Len Platt writes of *Ulysses*, the Revival 'far from being marginal, is actually fundamental' to the novel, arguing that insofar as the 'aesthetics of *Ulysses* are precisely antithetical to the aesthetics of revivalism' we cannot understand one without the other.[3] Gregory Castle makes a similar point in situating an 'immanent critique of Revivalism' within Joyce's writing that appropriates its 'colonial and anthropological' dimensions towards a national literature of *in*authenticity, while more recently John McCourt has suggested that although we should see Joyce as a 'Revival dissenter' this should not overshadow the points of commonalities and connection between his writing and Yeats's, as well as that of other Revivalists.[4]

Yet, where critics have taken pains to nuance Joyce's position in relation to the Revival, his interest in the urban and the cosmopolitan are still largely understood as signifying a complete break with the Revival's interest in nature and rural life. Platt, for instance, contrasts the Revival's 'evocations of a timeless idyllic rurality' with Joyce's 'excessively time-specific urban fictions', while Brendan Kershner argues that Joyce 'explicitly rejects' Revivalist notions of nature.[5] Alison Lacivita, who reads *Finnegans Wake*'s interest in rural Ireland as 'an extension of the revival's project' is so far unique in attending to how Joyce's writing does not constitute an absolute departure from the Literary Revival's ecological interests.[6] One of the central claims this chapter makes is that by looking at Joyce's interest in materiality and the nonhuman world as it develops through his writing, particularly the unfinished *Stephen Hero* (1903–7), *A Portrait of the Artist as a Young Man* (1916) and *Ulysses* (1922), it becomes possible to reassess Joyce's position in relation to the Literary Revival and other forms of Irish cultural nationalism. Certainly, it is the case that Joyce's idea of nature contrasts sharply with the romanticism and pastoralism that coloured much of the Revival's creative output, but, as this chapter will argue, Joyce was interested in the environmental politics that underpinned the Revival's literary aesthetics and this generated a textual ambivalence that should be read as a refashioning or reshaping rather than an outright rejection.

In looking at how Joyce's interest in a more-than-human materiality enables him to engage with sociopolitical cultural discourse around nature, this chapter draws on the ecological theory outlined by Félix Guattari in his late work *The Three Ecologies* (1989). For Guattari there are three ecological categories: 'the environment, social relations and human subjectivity'.[7] Each of these categories is actualised through existential Territories, or what might be described as finite, singular instances or assemblages. Significantly, these Territories are not closed off from each other nor do they exist in opposition to one another, rather they exist in a transversal and dynamic relation of co-production, not unlike Joyce's presentation of the relationship between materiality and meaning with which I opened this chapter. Foregrounding 'process' over 'system or structure', Guattari outlines how the 'principle common to the three ecologies is [that] each of the existential Territories [. . .] is not given as an in-itself, closed in on itself' but instead is a 'for-itself' that intersects with each of the other Territories.[8] The environmental, social and subjective are all deeply imbricated in what Rosi Braidotti, developing Guattari's theory, describes as 'the multiple folds that connect' all 'historical conditions (external) and subject formation (internal)'.⁹ In light of contemporary developments, Guattari's intent to both broaden and politicise what is understood as ecology situates his late work as a key volume of philosophy in Anthropocene studies and its influence is clearly visible in the theoretical work being done on the Anthropocene by figures such as Braidotti and Haraway.[10] Moreover, Guattari cites Joyce, alongside Johann Wolfgang von Goethe, Marcel Proust, Antonin Artaud and Samuel Beckett, as a writer whose work we can turn to to find an 'ecosophical [. . .] conception of subjectivity' in which rather than self-enclosed 'subjects' we find a 'subjectification' which always exceeds the 'terminal' of the 'individual'.[11] Here, we might think of the way in which Joyce shows subjectivity to be produced by bodies (human and nonhuman) that are themselves materially open rather than closed. It is an idea memorably captured in Bloom's thoughts of the human as an open system, 'stuffing food in one hole and out behind: food, chyle, blood, dung, earth, food' (*U* 8.929–30), an example that speaks to what Vike Martina Plock argues is *Ulysses*'s 'sustained scepticism about discourses that emphasise the singularity and wholeness of the human'.[12] Subjectivity in Joyce, as for Guattari, never entirely coincides with the subject.

Guattari's theory is also useful since it examines the close ties between ecology and nationalism, or what he describes as the importance of an ecological 'homeland'. For Guattari the desire for a 'homeland' does not necessitate 'nationalitarian movements (like the Irish or the Basques) [that] have turned in on themselves', rather 'all sorts of deterritorialized "nationalities" are conceivable', even 'music and poetry' might themselves become spaces of collective identity.[13] For Guattari, society is understood in terms of vectors of becoming, containing the potential for new ways of imagining nationality. As this chapter will show, Joyce's own ambivalent understanding of the close ties between nature and nation, and the alternative configuration of both that we find in his writing, similarly looks to reimagine their terms of relation. Building on John Brannigan's observation that Joyce's work explores how 'natural forms might or might not imply correlation with cultural identities', this chapter will examine the degree to which Joyce's writing looked to intervene in and contribute to an emergent national discourse.[14]

Resistance and Revival

The early twentieth century was, as outlined in my introduction, a period of accelerated technological and ecological transformation. Yet, this acceleration, even within Europe, was uneven rather than uniform, and Ireland had not undergone the rapid and widespread industrialisation that England had seen. Although the Dublin of 1904 was more technologically advanced than other cities in some respects (the city's trams that Joyce takes pains to describe at the beginning of 'Aeolus', for instance, had been among the first to be electrified in Europe), it had yet to witness the kind of industrial expansion that had transformed other cities in the Global North. Yet, while Ireland had not seen mass industrialisation, it had nonetheless been subject to profound environmental transformation. One of many countries that suffered the ecological consequences of British imperial policy during the eighteenth and nineteenth centuries, the intensive agricultural regime introduced through the enclosure of agricultural land owned and managed by an often-absent landlord class radically changed the environmental and social fabric of the country. As Marx would observe in 1867 in *Das Kapital,* 'for a century and a half, England has indirectly exported the soil of Ireland'.[15] The results, as is well known, were famines, the erosion of the Irish language, and depopulation, especially in rural communities. The late nineteenth century, however, saw the emergence of new social and political organisations premised on responding to the disastrous effects that these imposed agricultural and environmental changes had inflicted on rural communities. The Irish National Land League, led by Charles Stewart Parnell, organised what became known as the Land War, agitating for the redistribution of land, fairer rents and tenant security. Their success is registered in *Ulysses*, where Bloom notes the quietness of the 'land agent' offices along Sackville Street in the centre of the city (*U* 6.316). The Irish Agricultural Organisation Society (IAOS), founded by Horace Plunkett in 1894 and employing the Revivalist poet George 'A.E.' Russell as a co-operative organiser, worked to similar ends, aiming to 'better the material circumstances of the emerging class of small farmers' through 'forming co-operative societies and credit unions'.[16] Although neither movement can be considered environmental in the modern sense of the term, they nonetheless looked to address the environmental injustices that had alienated people from their own land by means of reasserting an Irish, as opposed to colonial, identity. As Emer Nolan puts it, by the turn of the twentieth century, the 'old ruling class' had largely lost possession of its estates and 'the emerging Catholic bourgeoisie, rural and urban, stood to inherit the Irish earth'.[17]

At the same time in England, where acceleration towards a carbon economy was more visible, similar social movements were also gaining momentum. A recognisably modern strain of anti-industrial, proto-environmentalist literature had emerged in the late nineteenth century in the works of Victorian writers and socialists such as John Ruskin, William Morris, Robert Blatchford and Edward Carpenter. These figures argued for a revival of artisanship, in which small-scale production and locally sourced materials would remedy the effects of industrial capitalism on the English landscape. In both their environmental concerns and celebration of the natural world, the 'Back to Nature' discourse generated by these late-Victorian figures has come to be seen as contributing to the 'most fecund and important period of green politics' prior to the environmental movement of the late twentieth century.[18] For Christophe Bonneuil and Jean-Baptiste Fressoz, who single out these late Romantic Victorian figures as having intuited the emergence of the Anthropocene, their interest in 'protect[ing] the countryside against the aggression of the modern world' contributed to the development of a distinctly modern political mode of literature: the environmental polemic.[19] Victorian writers such as Ruskin and Carpenter, Bonneuil and Fressoz argue, arrived at a 'global critique of industrial capitalism' that mixed 'environmental and health observation, social demands and cultural criticism'.[20] As with the Land League and the IAOS, Joyce was all too aware of such developments in Victorian England, although his feelings towards them were not always favourable. In the 'Scylla and Charybdis' episode of *Ulysses*, which finds Stephen in the National Library in lively conversation with a number of Revivalists including Russell, Buck Mulligan is described as having the '[m]anner of Oxenford' and is associated with the 'Wheelbarrow sun' (*U* 9.1212–3), an allusion to Ruskin's encouragement of Oxford undergraduates to build roads in the countryside whom Joyce elsewhere characterised as 'an effeminate band of Anglo-Saxons [being led] towards the promised land of the society of the future, behind a wheelbarrow' (*OCPW* 148).[21]

Stephen's internal reflection in 'Scylla and Charybdis' is more than incidental. It suggests a point of connection between what might seem to be two otherwise disparate (and, indeed, in some respects antithetical) rural movements in Ireland and England. Namely, it signals the degree to which English and Irish rural movements had a decisive influence on the emergence of the largely Anglo-Irish Revival. Crucially, the late Victorian romanticism that produced 'Back to Nature' socialism was the social and cultural milieu in which the young Yeats immersed himself in the late 1880s, in the years immediately prior to his co-founding of the Irish Literary Society in 1891. Indeed, Yeats, who lived in London and became good friends with Morris, would later describe in *The Cutting of an Agate* (1912) how both Morris and Ruskin had profoundly influenced his early development as a poet and, as Brannigan argues, the 'vision of harmony with nature, and creative labour' that characterises Yeats's early Revivalist poetry is highly suggestive of Morris's mentorship.[22] Yeats's well-known poem 'The Lake Isle of Innisfree' (1890) presents a clear and early example of this, where the poem's speaker aspires to build 'a small cabin' made from 'clay and wattles' in the idealised setting of Innisfree in the west of Ireland.[23] The poem, as Yeats would later reveal in his autobiography, was inspired by an adolescent reading of *Walden*, Henry David Thoreau's narrative of living in a cabin in the woods, a text which had become a key point of reference for 'Back to Nature' socialists in Britain, such as Carpenter and Blatchford.[24] Yet, unlike his British counterparts, the poem finds Yeats coupling a Thoreauvian environmental ethos of simplicity to a Celtic mythology of Ireland's west, in which ecological rejuvenation and national revival are presented as constitutive of one another. For Yeats, as he wrote in 'The Celtic Element in Literature' (1898), rural Ireland was the potential site for the emergence of a new Irish consciousness through the retrieval of 'ancient beliefs about nature'.[25]

Joyce was familiar with this aspect of Yeats's project. In 1902, on the pretext of engaging the 'new generation' of Irish writers, Yeats met Joyce in a café near the National Library where, as Yeats later recounted, he expounded the degradation implicit in urban life to Joyce:

> The folk life, the country life, is nature with her abundance, but the art life, the town life, is the spirit which is sterile when it is not married to nature. The whole ugliness of the modern world has come from the spread of the towns and their ways of thought, and to bring beauty back we must marry the spirit and nature again.[26]

Yeats, writing explicitly against Matthew Arnold's configuration of the Irish as enfeebled and effeminised by their proximity to nature, looked to subvert rather than discard the racialised essentialism in the Victorian imaginary of the Irish 'peasant'. While 'Arnold thought he was criticising the Celts', Yeats explains, 'he was really criticising the [. . .] ancient worship of nature' that has been lost in most of the modern world, but which can still be recovered among the 'beautiful places' of Ireland.[27] 'Surely if one goes far enough into the woods', Yeats asserts, again drawing on a Thoreauvian register, 'there one will find all that one is seeking.'[28] As Seán Hewitt has argued, Yeats's rejection of a post-Enlightenment Victorian idea of nature in favour of a vision of the natural world as enchanted, almost supernatural, was a central component to his intended recovery of an authentic Irish consciousness.[29] Moreover, this was not a simplistic or naïvely nostalgic project to recover a lost Eden, but an attempt, as Castle writes, to bring into being 'a transferential process in which the past yields to the creative force of the present'.[30] Rather than built upon a reactionary anti-modernist foundation, Yeats's poetics were premised on reimagining, rather than disavowing, the present: the final lines of 'Innisfree' return the reader to the grey pavements of the metropolis, insisting on a continuity between the city and the culturally redemptive possibilities of the natural world, both literal and imagined. While in Britain, 'Back to Nature' socialists were proclaiming that a turn to the natural world might overthrow the alienation of modern capitalist life, Yeats was drawing on similar proto-environmentalist rhetoric to articulate the conviction that a renewed national consciousness might emerge from the retrieval of an earlier and now forgotten relationship with nature.

The Literary Revival's yoking of nature and nation might be seen as intuitive of the emergent demands of the Anthropocene, in which the terms through which the world is conceptualised are not only highly politicised but understood to be bound up with imperial and counter-imperial histories. Yet its politics were nonetheless limited, as Lacivita frames it, by an 'idealisation of the environment and of the peasant's intrinsic connection to the land' that fostered 'a false conception of the Irish landscape' and helped to perpetuate 'patronising stereotypes [of] rural Irish culture'.³¹ Joyce's letters from the time register exactly this sentiment. Writing to his brother, Stanislaus, in the aftermath of the Abbey Theatre riots in 1907, Joyce describes Yeats as 'a tiresome idiot' 'quite out of touch with the Irish people' (*JJL2* 211). Yet, Yeats was not alone in seeing the potential for the Irish landscape to provide the basis for an organic nationalism. The Gaelic League and Athletic Association encouraged traditional sports and activities such as hurling, football and camogie that were premised not only on building strength and community, but a connection to the land. In addition, other Anglo-Irish Revivalists also saw the potential for nature to not only provide a mode of retrieving a national consciousness but overcoming sectarian differences. The writer and librarian William Kirkpatrick Magee, who wrote under the name John Eglinton and appears in the 'Scylla and Charybdis' episode of *Ulysses* alongside Russell, argued in *Anglo-Irish Essays* (1917) that 'Mother Nature' might unify Ireland since nature worship predates all racial and religious differences on the island and, for this reason, the 'future of Irish literature is mainly an affair between the poet and this kindly mother'.³² Here, Eglinton took a political ideal implicit in Yeats's romanticism and made it explicit: nature might serve as an organic foundation uniting religious, class and political differences. An example of Bruno Latour's theory that environmental discourse often presents 'nature [as] already composed, already totalized [and thereby] already instituted to neutralize politics', in Eglinton's essay we find an intrinsically Irish nature, bound up with discourse around racial essentialism and placed in contrast with an urbanised modernity, and wholly premised on constructing a national identity without recourse to conventional (and divisive) nationalist politics.³³ Irish nature is at once political and depoliticising, serving as the natural foundation for an Irish nation.

While John Rignall and H. Gustav Klaus have argued that the colour green, associated throughout the nineteenth century with a romantic ecology, is eclipsed at the turn of the twentieth century by its association with Irish nationalism, we can actually see these two shades of green merge and work to strengthen one another in the construction of an organic national identity.³⁴ Indeed, in *A Portrait of the Artist as a Young Man* the young Stephen makes precisely this connection. Having 'coloured the earth green and the clouds maroon' in his geography schoolbook, Stephen recalls Dante's press, where the 'brush with the green velvet back [stands] for Parnell and the brush with the marron velvet back for Michael Davitt' (*P* 12). As Vincent Cheng suggests, this is an early indication that for Stephen politics and aesthetics will be coupled.³⁵ The green of the earth and the green of Irish nationalism occupy an unarticulated association in the young Stephen's mind. Just as important, however, is the moment that immediately follows, as Stephen turns to the flyleaf of his book and reads what he has previously written there:

Stephen Dedalus
Class of Elements
Clongowes Wood College
Sallins
County Kildare
Ireland
Europe
The World
The Universe (*P* 12)

A hierarchical list that reflects both a cosmological imaginary and an anti-colonial sentiment (the British Empire is noticeably absent) as well as the anthropocentrism of his education, the stability and order that this assertion of location seems to promise is not forthcoming. Instead, it is the inability of the list to do what it should – epistemologically or politically – that is emphasised, as Stephen 'wearily' returns to the image of 'the green round earth' and feels 'pained [. . .] that he did not know well what politics meant and that he did not know where the universe ended' (*P* 13). The young Stephen, who has imbibed the cultural nationalism of the late nineteenth century and dreams of 'sleep[ing] for one night in [a] cottage before the fire of smoking turf, in the dark lit by the fire, in the warm dark, breathing the smell of the peasants, air and rain and turf and corduroy' (*P* 14), is able to perceive an affinity between the green vision of a romantic nature and that of Irish nationalism. Yet, it will be his inability to reconcile the two or accept the terms on which they are presented to him that will come to shape his growth as an artist.

The Nature of *Stephen Hero* and *A Portrait of the Artist as a Young Man*

Joyce, famously, did not follow Yeats's advice to privilege the Irish countryside in his writing. Nonetheless, as *Ulysses* acknowledges, the Literary Revival provided the material context of his early publications. When Russell appears in the 'Scylla and Charybdis' episode, presented as a 'tall figure in bearded homespun' wearing a 'cooperative watch' (*U* 9.269–70), Stephen puns on his pseudonym, 'A. E. I. O. U.' (*U* 9.213). It is a moment that recognises not only a monetary debt owed to Russell within the narrative but Joyce's own ambivalent indebtedness to Russell for having published his earliest works of fiction in the *Irish Homestead*, the paper of the IAOS. Edited by Russell and referred to in *Ulysses* as the 'farmer's gazette' (*U* 14.525), the paper promoted both agricultural reform and Revivalist literary aesthetics. It was a publication where, as P. J. Mathews states, readers were likely to encounter a new poem by Yeats 'side-by-side with an article on fertilizers'.[36] Indeed, Joyce's first short story, published in the 13 August 1904 edition of the *Homestead*, was placed above a large advertisement for 'dairy machines and appliances'.[37] Moreover, the material archive that survives from

Joyce's early work demonstrates the degree to which he would have been aware that his writing was being put to the use of an agricultural reformist agenda. While the July 1904 letter from Russell to Joyce, asking him to write something 'simple, rural' for the paper is often quoted, the physical letter presents the larger context of their correspondence. The letter's headed stationery, proclaiming in block capitals the paper's stature as 'The Organ of Agricultural and Industrial Developments in Ireland', makes explicit the socio-aesthetic context within which his work would be published (figure 1.1).[38]

While Joyce was writing stories for the *Irish Homestead*, he was also working on an autobiographical novel that self-reflexively engaged with the politics, aesthetics and ecology of revivalism. Begun in 1903, *Stephen Hero* was intended to consist of sixty-three chapters which would cover the life of Stephen Daedalus from childhood onward. Joyce abandoned the novel in 1907, when he began reworking the material into what would become *A Portrait of the Artist as a Young Man*.[39] Only fragments of the manuscript remain, largely covering Stephen's time at university, and they present a less stylised prose than that which would come to characterise his later texts, with Joyce later disavowing the aborted book.[40] At the time, however, Joyce sent chapters of the novel to Russell as he wrote them, who admired the writing and encouraged him to continue to work on the project.[41] As critics have noted, *Stephen Hero* differs from *A Portrait of the Artist as a Young Man* in a number of important ways, both at a narrative and stylistic level, but there are also clear points of continuity. Stephen, for instance, is situated in terms of his ambivalence towards Irish nationalism and is reluctant to assimilate himself within Revivalist trends. Stephen and the nationalist Madden (who would become Davin in *A Portrait of the Artist as a Young Man*) are opposed in terms of 'metropolitanism' and 'rustic[ism]' in the text – neither term appears in the later novel – yet are connected through an 'affectionate familiarity' (*SH* 51–2). While Madden tries 'in vain to infect Stephen with nationalistic fever', Stephen's reluctance to acquiesce to the 'so-desired community' is shown to be primarily aesthetic rather than overtly political (*SH* 52). Accused of 'despis[ing] the peasant since you live in the city', Stephen responds that it is not contempt he feels but rather the sense that 'the Irish peasant [does not] represent a very admirable type of culture' (*SH* 53) and, crucially, that he cannot use the 'phrases of the platform' since he is an 'artist' and therefore when confronted with political questions of Irish self-determination needs to 'think them out' (*SH* 54).

Here, as becomes amplified in *A Portrait of the Artist as a Young Man*, art is premised as that which cannot be subordinated to politics (although, as I discuss below, Joyce later qualifies the ability of the artist to be autonomous). The romanticised Irish peasant becomes a symbol not of Irish nationalism in the text, but a failure of the political imagination. While Stephen initially agrees to attend Irish classes, it is not the political content but its literary aesthetics that

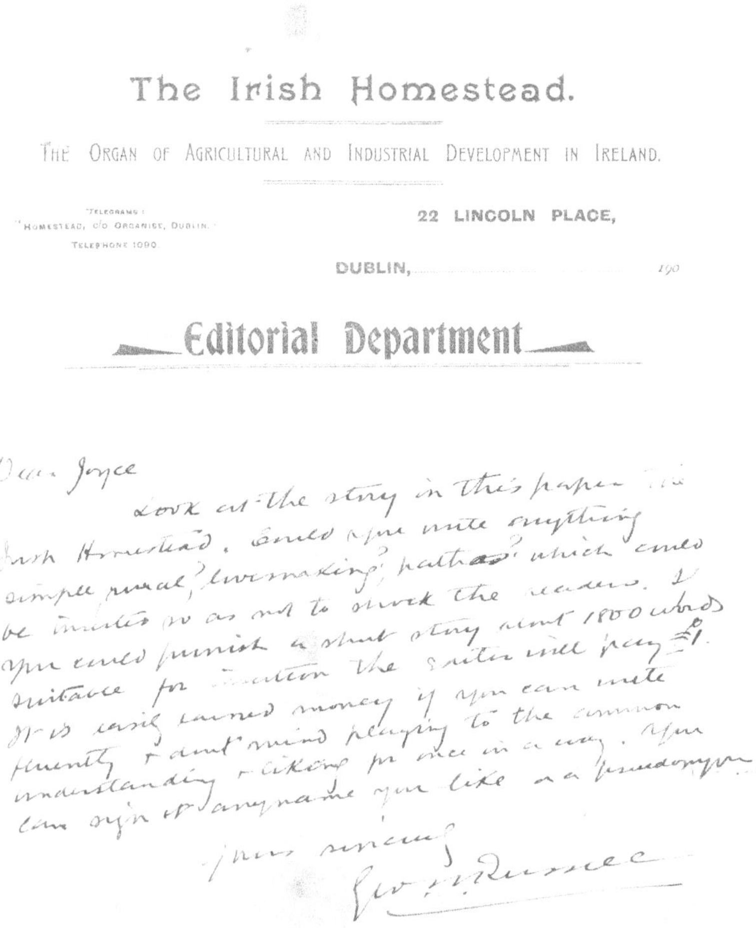

The Irish Homestead.

THE ORGAN OF AGRICULTURAL AND INDUSTRIAL DEVELOPMENT IN IRELAND.

TELEGRAMS:
"HOMESTEAD, c/o ORGANISE, DUBLIN."
TELEPHONE 1090.

22 LINCOLN PLACE,

DUBLIN, 190

Editorial Department

Dear Joyce
Look at the story in this paper The Irish Homestead. Could you write anything simple, rural?, livemaking?, pathos?, which could be inserted so as not to shock the readers. If you could furnish a short story about 1800 words suitable for insertion the editor will pay £1. It is easily earned money if you can write fluently and don't mind playing to the common understanding and liking for once in a way. You can sign it any name you like as a pseudonym.
Yours sincerely
Geo. W. Russell

Figure 1.1 Letter from George Russell as editor of the *Irish Homestead* to James Joyce, July 1904. James Joyce Collection. General Collection, Beinecke Rare Book and Manuscript Library, Yale University.

leads him to angrily resign, prompted by the reading of a 'piece of verse entitled *Mo Náire Tù* – (My shame art thou)', comprised of the kind of 'mournful idealism' and 'tawdry lines' that epitomises what he sees as the unsophisticated and untruthful thrust of politicised art (*SH* 77). The reader is implicitly positioned to sympathise with Stephen here, who is associated in the text with the naturalism of Zola and Ibsen (whom Stephen frequently praises), since the narrative's realism itself explicitly eschews an idealised Ireland and avoids romanticisation. The last image of the surviving manuscript, for instance, is of a female corpse fished out of a canal in the country town of Mullingar, the 'body [. . .] curved upwards with legs abroad' and 'nightdress' drawn down (*SH* 220).

Yet, if for Joyce romantic idealism did not square with the realities of modern Ireland, *Stephen Hero* nonetheless engages with the mythology and anthropology that were at the centre of the Revivalist project.[42] In the trip to Mullingar (omitted entirely from *A Portrait of the Artist as a Young Man*), the narrator retells a tale told to Stephen and his companions by an officer stationed in the town:

> The story was this. The officer and a friend found themselves one evening surprised by a heavy shower far out on the Killucan road and forced to take refuge in a peasant's cabin. An old man was seated at the side of the fire smoking a dirty cutty-pipe which he held upside down in the corner of his mouth. The old peasant invited his visitors to come near the fire as the evening was chilly and said he could not stand up to welcome them decently as he had the rheumatics. (*SH* 212)

Framed in a manner reminiscent of Revivalist texts by Yeats and Synge, the story within the story goes on to describe how the peasant's fireplace is decorated with primitive drawings of circus elephants 'scrawled in chalk', the work of the peasant's grandson, concluding with his assertion that 'Aw, there must be terrible quare craythurs at the latther ind of the world' (*SH* 212–13). Joyce was evidently unsure of how to include the tale within the narrative, with his revisions to the manuscript showing that he initially considered only alluding to the fact that a story had been told and jumping straight to the reaction from the listening audience, with the story present only as a lacuna within the narrative. It is clear to see why Joyce would have been tempted by this: its inclusion in the draft stands uneasily with the disavowal of an authentic national identity that we find elsewhere in the novel and what is described later as the 'aristocratic' and 'zealous patronage' undergirding the 'championing of the Irish peasant' (*SH* 217). Notably, however, Joyce did not abandon this story when it came to *A Portrait of the Artist as a Young Man*, instead opting to rework it within the stylised fabric of the later novel. Coming in the final section of the last chapter, where the prose is presented as diary entries, Stephen recounts a friend's trip to 'the west of Ireland' and his encounter with an old man in a mountain cabin who tells him in Irish, 'Ah, there must be terrible queer creatures at the latter end of the world' (*P* 212). While in *Stephen Hero* 'Stephen thought that the officer told this story very well and he joined in the laughter' (*SH* 213), in *A Portrait of the Artist as a Young Man*, the story is followed by the remarks 'I fear him [. . .] It is with him I must struggle all through this night till day come[s]' (*P* 212). Where earlier Joyce hesitated between either including or excluding the story, here its presentation comes in the highly mediated form of a diary entry recounting a story that has already been told and retold. Anxiety is substituted for mirth, although it remains unclear whether it is the primitive figure of the peasant that strikes fear in Stephen or the towering figure of the peasant within Irish culture that he fears he cannot escape despite his desire for artistic autonomy. As Castle argues, while in *Stephen Hero* Stephen is shown to be complicit with the Revival's ethnographic gaze, in *A Portrait of the Artist as a Young Man*, the shift to the diary form 'reflects an ironic detachment not only from the Revival but also from Stephen's own investments in it', with the recasting of the peasant's dialogue into a standardised English further suggesting 'a reluctance to "redeem" the old man's language and thus replicate the ethnographic gesture' found in Revivalist literature.[43]

What might be described as Joyce's focus on the material rather than the ideal is explained in *Stephen Hero* through Stephen's own theory of the relationship between art and nature. In conversation with one of the priests at the university, Stephen is described as unable to 'conceive a divorce between art and nature', since for him 'art was neither a copy nor an imitation of nature: the artistic process was a natural process' (*SH* 154). Here, as will become more apparent in his later works, nature is understood not in terms of a romantic pastoralism but rather the material processes underpinning life itself. Moreover, art is situated as immanent to these natural processes. As Katherine Ebury has argued in relation to the epiphanies that Joyce was writing during this time, Joyce locates 'the animal inspiration of life' as continuous with the 'human control of art'; fiction emerges from the materiality of life itself rather than standing outside of it, offering merely a reflection.[44] For Ebury, the epiphanies are, on one level, an attempt to get closer to the immediacy and intensity of life, diminishing the divide between art and nature that Stephen outlines as false in *Stephen Hero*.

Building on this insight, we can read Joyce's reworking of *Stephen Hero* into the more experimental style of *A Portrait of the Artist as a Young Man* as a further attempt to make form as well as content reflect his rejection of a divide between art and nature. Akin to Guattari's understanding of ecology as a complex weave of environmental, social and subjective territories, *A Portrait of the Artist as a Young Man*'s highly stylised realism derives from its movement between interior monologue, free indirect discourse and a more distant third-person narration. Moreover, these different narrative perspectives are presented on the page without explicit delineation, seamlessly transitioning from one to the other yet remaining distinct in themselves, analogous to Guattari's tri-ecology. We see this, for instance, at the end of the fourth chapter, where, as Stephen walks along the coastline at Dollymount, the narrative slips in and out of his subjectivity:

> He drew forth a phrase from his treasure and spoke it softly to himself:
> – A day of dappled seaborne clouds.
> The phrase and the day and the scene harmonised in a chord. Words. Was it their colours? He allowed them to glow and fade, hue after hue: sunrise gold, the russet and green of apple orchards, azure of waves, the greyfringed fleece of clouds. No, it was not their colours: it was the poise and balance of the period itself. Did he then love the rhythmic rise and fall of words better than their associations of legend and colour? (P 140)

As a result of the shifting semantics and the ambiguous drift between different narrative perspectives, neither the objective materiality of the landscape nor the subjective meaning Stephen associates with the scene can be considered to hold a primary position in relation to the other. Instead, we see the landscape shape Stephen's perception and Stephen, in the questions and equivocations at the front of his mind, reimagine the landscape around him. Thought and matter both work on each other, offering a textual representation of the relation between art and nature that Joyce could only explain in *Stephen Hero*. By presenting a porous rather than rigid boundary between interior and exterior, further amplified by the absence of conventional speech marks, continuity between materiality and language becomes the stylistic keynote. Stephen is himself drawn to this conclusion, when a short while later he thinks about his Greek namesake as a 'symbol of the artist forging anew in his workshop out of the sluggish matter of the earth a new soaring impalpable imperishable being' (P 142). What will be further explored in *Ulysses* through the leitmotifs of transubstantiation and metempsychosis – both premised on there being a dynamic, even unstable, continuity between matter and life – is here already present. The quotation that Stephen is drawn to is also revealing in this respect, with the 'dappled seaborne clouds' being lifted from Hugh Miller's *The Testimony of the Rocks; or Geology in Its Bearings on the Two Theologies, Nature and Revealed* (1857).[45] Miller, who was both a geologist and evangelical Christian, hoped his book would contribute to a reconciliation of theology with the geological discoveries that seemed to increasingly challenge and destabilise Christian teaching. The passage from which Stephen quotes describes man as 'vitality . . . united to matter, but in whom also, as in no inferior animal, responsibility was to be united to vitality!'[46] It is a scene pregnant with a kind of geological creativity, in which materiality and meaning shape each other, neither able to claim precedence. Stephen, with 'a new wild life [. . .] singing in his veins' experiences a moment of 'profane joy', desiring to 'recreate life out of life' and, shutting his eyes, feels his 'eyelids tremb[le] as if they felt the vast cyclic movement of the earth and her watchers' (*P* 144–5).

GEOLOGY AND AUTONOMY IN *A PORTRAIT OF THE ARTIST AS A YOUNG MAN* AND *ULYSSES*

What might be described as Stephen's geological vision is returned to and further developed in *Ulysses*. As I have already suggested, Joyce's entangling of free indirect discourse and interior monologue is further amplified in the early episodes of *Ulysses* and in 'Proteus' we again find Stephen walking along Dublin's coastline. Yet, if in *A Portrait of the Artist as a Young Man*, Stephen's allusion to the myth of Daedalus offers traces of anthropocentrism, insofar as an implicit human exceptionalism is staked on the ability to submit the earth to human mastery, from the start 'Proteus' engenders ambivalence and ambiguity about the status of the human as the measure of all things. Indeed, the episode's opening lines establish the degree to which this will be a primary concern:

> Ineluctable modality of the visible: at least that if no more, thought through my eyes. Signatures of all things I am here to read, seaspawn and seawrack, the nearing tide, that rusty boot. Snotgreen, bluesilver, rust: coloured signs. Limits of the diaphane. (*U* 3.1–4)

Stephen's thoughts here are indebted to Aristotle, whose argument in *On the Soul* is that each sense has a 'proper' object, with 'the visible' being the proper object of sight. As Aristotle explains, what is visible is primarily colour but also 'a certain kind of object which can be described in words but which has no single name'.[47] While, as Castle points out there is a danger in too neatly mapping this episode back onto the philosophies that are being invoked since Stephen's 'promiscuous (if not flawed) use of philosophical theories' makes it hard to know if he is using them in 'bad faith' or 'intentionally misusing them', his indebtedness to Aristotle is important here.[48] As I discuss in the following chapter, it informs Stephen's gendered perception of the earth in which, following Aristotle, materiality is associated with the feminine. Moreover, Aristotle's empiricism enables Stephen to take an oppositional position to the explicitly Neo-Platonic Revivalists. When Stephen later encounters Russell and Eglinton in the National Library in 'Scylla and Charybdis', Eglinton declares how it makes his 'blood boil to hear anyone compare Aristotle with Plato', while Russell's invocation of 'the dreams and visions in a peasant's heart' for whom 'the earth is not an exploitable ground but the living mother' marries a Neoplatonic occultism with the ecological sensibilities of the Revival (*U* 9.80–1; 9.105–8).

Stephen's preoccupation in 'Proteus', however, is primarily with the 'modality' through which the material world makes itself known to him, a process which takes place via 'thought through my eyes' (a sentence which insinuates the shared etymology of 'sight' and 'form' in the Greek word *eidos*, from which the English word 'idea' can be traced). As Stephen reflects, what is 'ineluctable' is not the visibility of the world itself, a fact he proves to himself by walking a short distance with his eyes closed, but rather the 'modality' through which the visible gives itself to sight and thereby thought. The question as to whether that modality resides in the perceiving subject or the perceived object appears to be at stake in Stephen's thoughts, as the entities in his line of vision, 'seaspawn and seawrack; the nearing tide, that rusty boot', present themselves as '[s]ignatures' to be 'read' (*U* 3.3–4). Further developing his younger self's thoughts on the relationship between language and materiality while stood on the same stretch of coastline in *A Portrait of the Artist as a Young Man*, Stephen's thoughts return to an ambivalence around the location of signification and meaning. The uncertainty as to whether humans create meaning or whether the nonhuman world has the agency to produce meaning itself is further developed later in the episode: 'These heavy sands are language tide and wind have silted here. And these, the stoneheaps of dead builders, a warren of weasel rats' (*U* 3.288–9). Here, there is a sense of nonhuman agents actively producing signification. While Hunter Dukes points out that Stephen observes 'lithic striation as a form of language', it is noticeable that while the geological strata is the linguistic medium, it is water and air that Stephen credits with the act of inscription.[49] Moreover, the 'stoneheaps of deadbuilders' (breakwaters constructed in the deep past) and the maze of 'warren[s]' constructed by uncertain animals, adds to the scene's material presentation of indeterminate signs, writers and readers. These are signs whose meanings do not wholly coincide with the human. When Bloom is later also on Sandymount Strand, seeing 'rocks with lines and scars and letters' and thinking about the pertinence to Martha Clifford's mistakenly writing 'world' instead of 'word', Joyce again appears to be insisting on the alterity of language; not only its materiality but also its status as something profoundly other than human (*U* 13.1261–313). The 'signatures' that Stephen and later Bloom observe present themselves as both human and nonhuman, living and dead, organic and inorganic, with the distinction as to whether meaning is found in their other-than-human production or their human reception remaining in suspension.

Yet, Stephen's ability to see beyond a romanticised nationalism does not allow him to straightforwardly 'discover the mode of life or of art whereby [his] spirit could express itself in unfettered freedom' (*P* 207). As Cheng reminds readers, we should not mistake Stephen's views on nationalism for Joyce's, and in both *A Portrait of the Artist as a Young Man* and *Ulysses* Joyce takes pains to locate Stephen not only within the material ecology of the Irish landscape, but the cultural ecology of the Revival also, often at the same time.[50] Stephen's epiphany watching the swallows on the steps of the National Library towards the end of *A Portrait of the Artist as a Young Man* offers a clear example of where the transversal movement between free indirect discourse and interior monologue opens up an ironic distance between protagonist and author around questions of nature and nation:

> What birds were they? He stood on the steps of the library to look at them, leaning wearily on his ashplant. [. . .] The air of the late March evening made clear their flight, their dark darting quivering bodies flying clearly against the sky as against a limphung cloth of smoky tenuous blue. [. . .]
>
> The inhuman clamour soothed his ears [. . .] an airy temple of the tenuous sky soothed his eyes [. . .]
>
> What birds were they? He thought that they must be swallows who had come back from the south. Then he was to go away for they were birds ever going and coming, building an unlasting home, under the eaves of men's houses and ever leaving the homes they had built to wander. (*P* 188–90)

While it is, as Jeff Wallace describes, an instance of modernism's 'heroic mode of the posthuman' articulated through 'the pursuit of aesthetic autonomy', it is also an epiphany that fails on its own terms.[51] Stephen's experience moves from a recognition of nonhuman alterity ('dark darting quivering bodies', 'inhuman') to an implicitly anthropomorphic romanticism ('ever going and coming' 'building an unlasting home') that seems closer to the idealised nature that can be found in the literature of the Revival. Indeed, any suggestion that such a connection is incidental is quashed by the sentence which follows the above extract, in which Stephen recollects four lines from Cathleen's farewell speech in Yeats's *The Countess Cathleen* (1892), where the self-sacrificing heroine likens herself to the 'swallow' who must 'wander the loud waters' in exile (*P* 190). While a short while earlier he has declared how he will 'fly by [the] nets' of 'nationality, language, religion' (*P* 171), at this crucial moment of self-determination Joyce presents Stephen as ensnared within them. Stephen's desire that, like the swallows, he might enjoy autonomy and free expression, is undermined by their symbolic assimilation within a Revivalist codification of the natural world, as the lines from Yeats's play suggest the degree to which Stephen is already inescapably steeped within its literary culture. Moreover, the lines from Yeats's play not only show the degree to which Stephen cannot disavow the influence of the Revival, but, contributing to the dense intertextual weave of *A Portrait of the Artist as a Young Man*, they also stand as Joyce's own acknowledgement of his ambivalent yet unavoidable indebtedness to Revivalist literature.

It is perhaps unsurprising then that Stephen's encounter with the swallows comes back to haunt him in *Ulysses*. At the end of 'Scylla and Charybdis', standing on the same spot outside the library, Stephen reflects how '[h]ere I watched the birds for augury' but that now there are '[n]o birds' (*U* 9.1206–18).[52] The absoluteness of Stephen's observation suggests not just the literal absence of birds from the scene, but rather a new-found awareness of the absence of properly natural subjects free from cultural associations which might offer themselves up to himself in the pursuit of autonomy. In the same way that Stephen rejects the romantic ecology of the Revival and its veneration of the Irish peasantry, Joyce shows that Stephen cannot claim unmediated access to the natural world either. That his insight arrives at the end of an episode of *Ulysses* which has long been recognised as representing one of Joyce's clearest and most direct engagements with the Revival and, more specifically, its material culture adds to its significance.[53] Indeed, as Frank Budgen suggested in his 1934 book *James Joyce and the Making of 'Ulysses'* (written with Joyce's involvement), central to the narrative of 'Scylla and Charybdis' is Stephen's aim to get 'a commission for an article in *Dana*', the literary journal edited by Eglinton and fellow Revivalist Frederick Ryan and named after the Celtic Earth goddess.[54] Many of the episode's allusions speak to the Literary Revival's interest in pre-modern rural life and mythology. A remark by Eglinton, for instance, reminds Stephen of 'Gap-toothed Kathleen [and] her four beautiful green fields' (*U* 9.36–7), a reference to the heroine of Yeats's *Cathleen Ni Houlihan* (1902), while the 'enthusiastic' Englishman Haines, it is revealed, has snubbed Stephen in favour of going to buy Douglas Hyde's *Love Songs of Connacht* (1895). Eglinton's comment that '[t]he peatsmoke is going to [Haines's] head' offers an echo of the pastoral romanticism that had seduced Stephen as a child in *A Portrait of the Artist as a Young Man* but which he now holds in derision (*U* 9.100).

Stephen's assessment of the limitations to the Revival parallel Guattari's critique of 'ecosophical' narratives that rely on mythic or archetypal ideals and, thereby, limit how individuals and collectives come to fashion themselves. Associating archetype and myth with psychoanalytic paradigms that regulate subjectivity through 'subjectification', Guattari warns against ecosophical revivals that express a desire 'to return to the past in order to reconstruct former ways of living'.[55] In the light of Guattari's philosophy, Yeats's figure of the ancient Celt farmer, along with the variations of Celtic mythology that we find expressed by nationalists of various stripes in *Stephen Hero*, *A Portrait of the Artist as a Young Man* and *Ulysses*, represent not possible ecological futures, but the narrow limits imposed by 'archaic fixations' with an idealised 'collective past'.[56] Moreover, as Stephen appears aware, in the context of Irish nationalism such limitations present themselves as aesthetically complicit with an imperialist imaginary in which, as Declan Kiberd frames it, Ireland can only exist as a pristine 'elsewhere' that necessarily needs a colonial master to serve as its counter-image.⁵⁷ Notably, however, Guattari, like Joyce, reimagines rather than outrightly rejects revivalism. For Guattari, a successful 'ecosophical revival (or whatever we wish to call it)' involves not retrieving a forgotten authentic relationship with the land, but rather, 'rearticulat[ing] the three fundamental types of ecology' and recognising the way in which subjectivity is always entangled within social and environmental processes.⁵⁸ This understanding of revival as destratification, in which instead of returning to supposedly natural foundations the relation between the individual, the collective and the nonhuman is returned to afresh and reimagined, offers a new way of understanding Joyce's dissatisfaction with the Revival. In Stephen's desire to revivify language and in Joyce's presentation of this as a process in which environmental and social forces are as much in play as the subjective self, we find a portrait not of artistic autonomy but of literature as the product of more-than-human material processes that resist assimilation to pre-established forms or political ideals.

'Scylla and Charybdis' not only marks the half-way point of *Ulysses*, standing as the ninth episode out of eighteen, but it is also, as Karen Lawrence states, the point at which 'we witness the breakdown of the initial style and a departure from the novelistic form of the book's first half'.⁵⁹ The episodes that follow take on distinctive rhetorical masks, each written in a self-contained literary mode and departing from what I have been described as Joyce's highly stylised realism.⁶⁰ The last episode focalised through Stephen, 'Scylla and Charybdis' is not only a moment of transition within the internal style of the novel but brings to a close a narrative trajectory which began with *Stephen Hero*, in which Joyce has self-reflexively examined what it means to be a writer caught up in and struggling against the cultural politics and aesthetic ideals of the Irish Literary Revival. While the episodes that follow 'Scylla and Charybdis' do not turn away from nationalist constructions of an Irish nature, they employ different strategies to examine the relationship between the environment, history and literature.

The Problem of the Environment in *Ulysses*

'Cyclops' presents one of the novel's most sustained engagements not only with nationalism and the mythic constructions of an Irish nature that underpin it, but also the environmental catastrophes inflicted by British imperialism. Taking place in Barney Kiernan's pub, questions of land and nature are a repeated point of concern among the drinkers gathered around the citizen, as well as in the thirty-three nonsequential parodies that intersect the pub narrative and which are generally seen as interpolations or interruptions.⁶¹ As Platt notes, a large proportion of these interpolations present themselves as parodies of the Revival in some form and, moreover, these Revivalist parodies often operate through an ironic veneration of Irish nature.⁶² The description of the 'land of holy Michan', for example, where in 'the mild breezes of the west and of the east the lofty trees wave in different directions their firstclass foliage' (*U* 12.68–76), presents itself as an exaggerated version of the rustic mysticism avowed by Russell in 'Scylla and Charybdis'. The militant patriotism of the citizen is to outward appearances a stark contrast to the cultural nationalism of the Revival, however. Introduced by the episode's narrator as a 'rapparee' (U 12.134), the name for the Catholic landowners forced to turn to plundering after British clearances dispossessed them of their land, the citizen is presented in terms of a more militant nationalism than has been encountered previously in the novel. His confrontational assertion to Bloom that '*Sinn fein amhain!* The friends we love are by our sides and the foes we hate before us' (U 12.523–4) aligns him with nationalist movements that emphasised the importance of the Irish language, such as the Gaelic League, and which, as Roy Foster has argued, were responsible for the 'radicalization of Irish politics' at the turn of the twentieth century.[63]

Although Irish history looms large in 'Cyclops', the episode itself is surprisingly anachronistic in places. Joyce, for instance, has the drinkers refer to the 'report of lord Castletown's' (U 12.1260–1), a government report published in 1908 which detailed the exhaustion of forests owing to recent changes in land legislation and made recommendations for afforestation schemes. The report is mentioned in a section of the episode that explicitly foregrounds the ecological consequences of colonisation, in which the citizen and the other drinkers in the pub discuss British exploitation of Ireland's forests and rivers, and the financial recompense 'the yellowjohns of Anglia owe us for our ruined trade and our ruined hearths' (U 12.1254–5). The collective lament for the damaged riverbeds of the 'Barrow and Shannon', the 'acres of marsh and bog' that threaten populations with 'consumption', and the 'trees of the conifer family [that] are going fast' are for the nationalists all connected with the material and the symbolic decline of Ireland (U 12. 1240–65). Both Yi-Peng Lai and James Fairhall have argued that the conversation reflects political sensitivities around land usage and deforestation in nationalist circles at the turn of the century, a fact which Joyce makes clear in the citizen's epithet 'Save the trees of Ireland for the future men of Ireland' (U 12.1263–4).[64] Moreover, as Fairhall explains, the reference to Castletown's report gestures to the consequences of the Land Purchase Acts which had led to an increase in Protestant landowners selling woodland that could be felled and transformed into agricultural land.[65] Joyce's notes for the episode substantiate Fairhall's analysis, with Joyce's description of 'timber' as 'a crop that must be cut' suggesting that he understood and was interested in the political currency of Irish trees.[66] British attempts to dampen Irish nationalism in the late nineteenth century had also involved trees, with Prime Minister William Gladstone having planned to plant three million acres of new trees in Ireland as a means of restoring 'peace and quietness'.[67] Neither Lai nor Fairhall, however, address why Joyce includes a reference to a 1908 report produced by a government committee that in 1904 was not yet formed. One possible answer is that Joyce, like the citizen, is making a political rather than historical point. Joyce's early writing exhibits, in places, an understanding of what would now be termed environmental justice, and this is particularly true of the political writing he produced in 1907 while living in Trieste. In these works of journalism, intended for an Italian audience unfamiliar with Irish history, Joyce rehearses the arguments that he will later have the men in the pub make, arguing that imperial control had been established through a 'system of agriculture' that 'reduced the power of the native leaders and granted huge estates to her soldiers' (*OCPW* 119). Elsewhere Joyce, like the citizen, misidentifies Ireland's 'vast central bog' with a wasteland, asserting that the English government owes both a moral and financial debt to the Irish for 'not having seen to the reforestation of this disease-ridden swamp' (*OCPW* 144).[68] Deforestation would have also represented a broader political point in 1918 when Joyce returned to the subject when writing *Ulysses*. The demand for wood during the First World War saw Britain fell nearly half of all its commercial woodlands to satisfy military demands and Joyce describes the practice of 'deforesting for military reasons' in his notes for 'Cyclops', again insisting on a close proximity between ecological and political change within a colonial context.[69]

On one level, the conversation in the pub presents a history of the Anthropocene through colonial conquest and environmental destruction, or what Haraway calls the Plantationocene, in which the story of planetary change is one of 'diverse kinds of human-tended farms, pastures and forests [transformed] into extractive and enclosed plantations'.[70] Yet, to see the figures in the pub as straightforwardly ventriloquising Joyce's earlier stated views on the politics of afforestation is to overlook the way in which the episode's formal operations reveal the limitations to the arguments being made by the citizen and his fellow drinkers. The discussion around deforestation is immediately followed by a parodic vignette often referred to as the Tree Wedding. Taking the form of a lengthy marriage announcement for 'Jean Wyse de Neaulan, grand high chief ranger of the Irish National Foresters [and] Miss Fir Conifer of Pine Valley', all the guests reported as having attended the ceremony have names such as 'Miss Grace Poplar' or 'Miss Blanch Maple' (*U* 12.1268–73). Parodying a romantic veneration for Ireland's forests, the Tree Wedding is an example of the way in which a number of the interpolations operate in terms of what Castle has described as 'stylistic travesties of the Literary Revival's ethnographic imagination'.[71] On one level, the parody brings into relief the comparatively historically and politically incisive analysis of the nationalists in the pub compared to their Revivalist counterparts. Yet, the parodies also present points of similarity between the Gaelic nationalists and the largely Anglo-Irish Revivalists around the question of Ireland's natural environment. For instance, the citizen's declaration that they must 'save' the 'giant ash of Galway and the chieftain elm of Kildare' presents itself as a foray into gigantism that operates in not dissimilar terms to the tree wedding (*U* 12.1262–3). Moreover, in the use of racialised language to describe how the 'future' is bound up with the 'trees of Ireland' (*U* 12.1263–4), Joyce has the citizen make a point that, in both tone and content, is similar to Eglinton's 1912 essay 'Reafforestation'. Eglinton's essay argues that one of the central responsibilities of any new Irish state will be 'to restore the balance of nature where it has been upset by the reckless behaviour of man in the past: to determine, for example, what portions of the earth's surface it can now afford to set apart for the ancient races of the trees'.[72] Moreover, Eglinton's essay is a very plausible source of inspiration for the conversation that takes place in the pub: Joyce had access to the essay while writing *Ulysses* via the copy of Eglinton's *Anglo-Irish Essays* (1917) in his Trieste library and Eglinton's name appears in his notes for the Cyclops episode.[73] If Eglinton's organic nationalism was indeed Joyce's source for the citizen's sense of environmental outrage, the implications are surely intended to be deeply ironic. Despite their clear differences, both the firebrand nationalist and the mannered librarian Revivalist share common ground insofar as they rely on an idealised Irish nature for the basis of an essentialised Irish identity. Eglinton's proto-environmental rhetoric might differ from the citizen's in its mystical underpinnings, but both look to the retrieval of a lost Irish environment which might rekindle and sustain a racial identity capable of self-determination.

If the citizen and Eglinton unwittingly share certain rhetorical strategies through appeals to an Irish nature, the style of 'Cyclops' can also be read as insisting on a close proximity between the citizen's Gaelic nationalism and the Revivalist parodies. Rather than operating as interruptions in the pub narrative, in the sense of drawing the reader away from the action taking place, the parodies instead tend to operate in a supplementary mode, largely falling into three broad categories: they either redramatise what has just occurred in the pub, stand in for a section of the narrative in the pub that is not otherwise presented to the reader or expand on a theme that has either been discussed or will be discussed in the pub. As such, the pub discussion cannot be straightforwardly understood as the primary narrative to which the parodies are secondary, since in certain instances the parodies give meaning to the pub narrative, while at other points this relationship is reversed. For instance, the parodic description of Ireland as a 'pleasant land' with 'murmuring waters' in which 'heroes voyage from afar to woo' '[l]ovely maidens' (*U* 12.70–83) appears immediately prior to the introduction of the citizen, serving to presage the mock-heroic description of him as an agrarian freedom fighter. Instead of an oppositional relationship between the two parts of the episode, we can instead detect an internal logic of supplementation akin to Jacques Derrida's description of the way in which the desire for a primary source or origin will always be frustrated by the discovery that the foundation itself is already a kind of supplement.[74] Such a relationship is clearly discernible in the episode's presentation on the page where, rather than presenting breaks between the two narrative strands clearly demarcating and differentiating them, we find continuity. Indeed, this was even more clear when the episode was serialised in four instalments in *The*

Little Review, a number of which opened with the parodies, implying not an interpolative relation to the pub narrative, but an equal standing. In intertwining the Gaelic nationalism of the citizen and Revivalist cultural nationalism, the 'Cyclops' episode establishes points of continuity between their respective constructions of nationhood. In both we find a rhetoric of race reliant upon and constructed through an aesthetics of nature. The parodic descriptions of the 'gentle declivities of the place of the race of Kiar' whose dairy herd produce a 'superabundance of milk' (U 12.113–14), the heroic 'brawnyhanded hairylegged ruddyfaced' figure 'seated on a larger boulder' wearing a 'long unsleeved garment of recently flayed oxhide' (U 12.151–68) and the importance of the 'Revival of ancient Gaelic sports' for the 'development of the race' (U 12.898–911) supplement and are supplemented by the citizen's racialised constructions of agriculture, traditional clothing and masculine athleticism. Indeed, in this context, a further possible rationale behind the anachronous inclusion of Lord Castletown's report is suggested. Castletown was not only the author of an influential report on the deleterious effects of Ireland's deforestation, but as Kaori Nagai has shown, an Irish landlord whose endorsement of pan-Celtic Revivalism was bolstered by the perception that his aristocratic lineage represented 'the quintessence of not only Irish-Ireland but also the ancient Celtic race'.[75] Castletown's appearance in the 'Cyclops' episode carries not only political authority, but an implicit endorsement of a racialised Irish nature that would have likely been attractive to Gaelic nationalists and Revivalists alike.

Signs of Nature

The organic nationalism of 'Cyclops' foregrounds the way in which, as Guattari argues, 'an ecosophical revival' can 'suddenly flip into reactionary closure'.[76] In a parallel to Joyce, Guattari draws on Cyclopean imagery in his writing about the dangers of ecofascism, warning of a 'fascinating and repulsive [. . .] one-eyed man' who 'force[s] his implicitly racist and Nazi discourse onto the French media and into the political arena'.[77] On one level, this is an overt reference to the eyepatch-wearing Jean-Marie Le Pen, whose National Front party was enjoying political ascendency while Guattari was writing in the 1980s. Guattari's writing is prescient in this respect: Le Pen's daughter, Marine, who currently leads the party, has recently signalled that she will be exploiting environmental anxieties to win the support of French citizens.[78] Guattari's cyclopean imagery is also, however, a reference to the concept of 'one-eyed' 'Binder-Gods or magic emperors' that he developed with Gilles Deleuze in *A Thousand Plateaus* (1980). For Deleuze and Guattari, the 'one-eyed men' concept represents a pole of political sovereignty in which power is accrued through 'capture, bonds, knots and nets' and which stands in contrast to the 'jurist-priest-king' which proceeds by 'treaties, pacts, contracts'. These one-eyed men amass their sovereignty through acts of monolithic encoding, in which they '[emit] from their single eye signs that capture [and] tie knots at a distance', establishing their dominance through a 'regime of signs'.[79]

Deleuze and Guattari's 'one-eyed' tyrant invites identification with the violently singular-minded citizen in 'Cyclops', whose vision of a naturalised Ireland actively excludes those who he sees as unnatural or foreign. When the citizen pointedly remarks to Bloom that '[w]e want no more strangers in our house', he invokes Ireland's peasants as figures of a naturalised racial identity at risk from exploitation and contamination from outsiders (*U* 12.1150–1). Although Joyce might be sympathetic to the environmental injustices inflicted under British imperialism, over the course of the episode the rhetoric around the 'revival of [. . .] ancient Ireland, for the development of the race' (*U* 12.899–901) is shown to project an ultimately limiting symbolic order. Within such an order the vital materiality of life, a force that Joyce has shown to be dynamic and transformative, risks being forcibly subsumed and mastered. Indeed, despite the citizen's protestations around deforestation, his description of the 'giant ash of Galway and the chieftain elm of Kildare with a fortyfoot bole' subordinate real trees to extravagantly anthropomorphic figures of masculine identity (*U* 12.1262–3), as the trees of Ireland are situated as standing timber for symbolic constructions of national identity. The natural environment is thus reduced to a reserve, exploited in the service of an aesthetic construction of national and racial identity, as the pastoralism we find in both the parodies and the pub conversation cultivate and regulate nature, subjecting it to a form of extractivism from which modern Ireland can be fashioned. If as I argued at the start of this chapter, *Ulysses* begins by foregrounding the overdetermined relationship between materiality and meaning, in the 'Cyclops' episode we see the political stakes to insisting on a homeostatic and essentialised Irish nature that, once purged of the contaminating influences of either modernity or imperialism, can provide the foundations for a self-determining, decolonised future. In this respect, 'Cyclops' offered a warning of the environmental dangers that would accompany Irish independence. As Dipesh Chakrabarty has argued, any history of the Anthropocene is complicated by the fact that industrial 'acceleration' and 'decolonisation' often went hand in hand as postcolonial countries looked to industrialise and increase the standard of living for their citizens.[80] Ireland was no exception. In her ecocritical study of *Finnegans Wake*, Alison Lacivita details the extent to which the policies of the newly formed Irish Free State were ecologically 'exploitative' and 'land-hungry', spurring Joyce to respond through the experimentation of his final major work.[81]

In reading the citizen as a one-eyed tyrant submitting nature to his symbolic regime, Bloom might be read as his opposite: the novel's countervailing jurist-priest-king, to use Deleuze and Guattari's term. Bloom's fantasy in 'Ithaca' of accruing a smallholding through a 'feefarm grant, lease 999 years', becoming 'a justice of the peace' and 'upholding the letter of the law' (*U* 17.1519; 1610–27) invokes the 'treaties, pacts, contracts' of Deleuze and Guattari's description.[82]

The extensive description of Flowerville in 'Ithaca', Bloom's imaginary '5 or 6 acres' of smallholding (*U* 17.1511), both parallels and departs from the pastoral fantasies of 'Cyclops' in its detailing of its prospective livestock and plants, along with the inventory of the tools and instruments with which he would tend it. As William Kupinse has argued, in Flowerville's solar energy and self-sufficiency, this section of the novel appears 'invested to a surprising extent in what we today would understand as discourses of sustainability'.[83] Yet, while Bloom responds to the citizen's nationalism in 'Cyclops' by arguing against 'force, hatred, history' (*U* 12.1481), occupying an apparent position of measured diplomacy, his figuring in 'Ithaca' as the jurist-priest-king of Flowerville reveals that, like the citizen, Bloom is similarly invested in structures of sovereignty and punishment. In his exhaustive attention to the organisation and cultivation of a 'country residence' (*U* 17.1657) and his hope that this will provide the impetus for him to be invested with a judicial power over 'all menial molesters of domestic conviviality' (*U* 17.1632), Bloom's Flowerville presents itself as a fantasy that proceeds via contracts and laws to '[lay] out a field [. . .] imposes a discipline upon it, subordinates it to political ends'.[84] As Bloom's fantasy enlarges, turning to the 'vast wealth' that can be generated through 'the exploitation of white coal (hydraulic power)' obtained by developing a 'hydroelectric plant' on the North Bull, the undeveloped coastal area rich in wildlife that Stephen had observed in Chapter 4 of *A Portrait of the Artist as a Young Man*, to be accompanied by 'golf links and rifle ranges' as well as 'casinos, booths, shooting galleries, hotels, boarding houses [and] readingrooms', it becomes clear that there is an entrepreneurial and managerialist logic, as opposed to an ecological ideal, behind Flowerville (*U* 17.1699–1718). Joyce's prescience is again notable here, with the North Bull becoming the centre of political disputes in the 1930s between those who wanted to preserve it as a bird sanctuary and those who argued that development on the land was vital to Dublin's urban expansion.[85] As such, if the citizen's vow to save the trees of Ireland relies on a political rhetoric that, in fact, reduces them to a kind of symbolic timber ready to be literally felled after independence, Bloom's vision is explicitly destructive in the name of peace and diplomacy. Although according to Joyce's design, Bloom's humanitarianism might be preferable to the citizen's xenophobia, his dispassionate and moderate politics is shown to be just as complicit with the force and systemic violence that is all too readily observed in the citizen's cyclopean demeanour.

In 'Cyclops' both the mythical Irish forests and the idealised racial purity of the Celts are called into question, while in 'Ithaca' Bloom's more capacious civic nationalism is shown to rely on a perspective that also views nature as standing reserve. For the citizen and Bloom alike, nature is a source of symbolic and material plenitude that can be exploited in the service of an idealised identity. As Joyce shows, aesthetic invocations of nature all too often serve to assert an apparently self-evident foundation that can naturalise and legitimise collective and individual identities, as well as police their boundaries. Nature, in this sense, is at its most political at the point at which it is claimed to be its most self-evidently natural and, therefore, apolitical. In contrast, Joyce's body of writing presents an open and ever-changing relationship between the materiality of the nonhuman world and the meaning that human societies impose on it. If in *Stephen Hero* we find Joyce first rejecting a division between nature and art, and in *A Portrait of the Artist as a Young Man* we see an attempt to stage at both a formal and narrative level the way in which nature shapes art, the later episodes of *Ulysses* show Joyce directly engaging with nationalist rhetoric that would, post-independence, have dire environmental consequences. For Joyce, writing in 1907, the nation state was best understood not through organic metaphors, but as 'an immense woven fabric in which very different elements are mixed' and in which it is 'pointless searching for a thread that has remained pure, virgin and uninfluenced by the threads nearby' (*OCPW* 118). It is a metaphor that insists on an heterogenous materiality, in which no authenticating origin can be appealed to, and in which admixture and entanglement are its condition of being. It is a metaphor for unification but not cohesion nor sameness; a fabric where individual threads remain discernible but which also influence those around them. This chapter has shown how Joyce's relation to the Revival and other forms of nationalism in *Ulysses* is not one of straightforward rejection but rather ambivalence. Like them, he was highly cognisant of the lasting environmental damage that colonialism had inflicted on Ireland. Joyce shared, in this respect, the Revival's attention to the natural world, but rather than seeing it as a lost organic foundation that might be recovered and thereby authenticate a national consciousness, for Joyce, the brute materiality of the Irish landscape was the material from which wholly new forms of identity might be shaped. Joyce's ambivalence towards the various strands of Irish nationalism at the turn of the century and his ability to see their respective shortcomings capture what Guattari describes as the way in which when 'individual [. . .] subjectivities' remove themselves from the collective they are able to discover alternative forms of 'creative expression' that contain new 'ecosophical' modes.[86] Joyce, whose self-imposed exile surely places him in such a category, demonstrates that acts of deterritorialisation are not limited to the Thoreauvian retreats, but can be formed from the quotidian materials encountered in daily life.

Notes

1. Donna Haraway, *Staying with the Trouble: Making Kin in the Chthulucene* (Durham, NC: Duke University Press, 2016), p. 55.
2. Early and influential accounts of Joyce and his writing that made these arguments include Harry Levin's 1944 book *James Joyce: A Critical Introduction* (London: Faber and Faber, 1971) and Richard Ellmann's 1959 biography of Joyce.

3. Len Platt, *Joyce and the Anglo-Irish: A Study of Joyce and the Literary Revival* (Amsterdam: Rodopi, 1998), p. 8; p. 178.
4. Gregory Castle, *Modernism and the Celtic Revival* (Cambridge: Cambridge University Press, 2001), p. 175; John McCourt, 'Introduction: Joyce, Yeats, and the Revival', *Joyce Studies in Italy*, 17 (2015), 7–30 (p. 9; pp. 17–18). See also Emer Nolan, *James Joyce and Nationalism* (New York: Routledge, 1995), pp. 23–54.
5. Platt, *Joyce and the Anglo-Irish*, p. 8; Brendan Kershner, 'Joyce Beyond the Pale', in *Eco-Joyce: The Environmental Imagination of James Joyce*, ed. Robert Brazeau and Derek Gladwin (Cork: Cork University Press, 2014), pp. 123–35 (p. 126).
6. Alison Lacivita, *The Ecology of 'Finnegans Wake'* (Gainesville: University Press of Florida, 2015), p. 43.
7. Félix Guattari, *The Three Ecologies*, trans. Ian Pindar and Paul Sutton (New Brunswick, NJ: The Athlone Press, 2000), p. 28.
8. Ibid. p. 44; p. 53.
9. Rosi Braidotti, *Posthuman Knowledge* (Cambridge: Polity, 2019), p. 69.
10. Braidotti sees the 'Anthropocene condition' as expressing Guattari's three ecologies. See Braidotti, 'Critical Posthuman Knowledges', *The South Atlantic Quarterly*, 116.1 (2017), 83–96 (p. 84).
11. Guattari, *The Three Ecologies*, pp. 35–7. Far less attention has been afforded to the points of confluence between Joyce and Guattari than with other poststructuralists, and even less work has considered Joyce in relation to Guattari's solo writing as opposed to that which he co-authored with Deleuze. The 'Deleuze-Guattari Cluster' of essays in the Winter 1993 issue of the *James Joyce Quarterly* and Beatrice Monaco's *Machinic Modernism: The Deleuzian Literary Machines of Woolf, Lawrence and Joyce* (Basingstoke, Palgrave Macmillan, 2008) currently represent the most sustained analysis, but also reflect the attention paid to Deleuze over Guattari.
12. Vike Martina Plock, 'Bodies', in *The Cambridge Companion to 'Ulysses'*, ed. Sean Latham (Cambridge: Cambridge University Press, 2014), pp. 184–99 (p. 184).
13. Guattari, *The Three Ecologies*, p. 65.
14. John Brannigan, *Archipelagic Modernism: Literature in the Irish and British Isles, 1890–1970* (Edinburgh: Edinburgh University Press, 2015), p. 68.
15. Quoted in Christophe Bonneuil and Jean-Baptiste Fressoz, *The Shock of the Anthropocene*, trans. David Fernbach (New York: Verso, 2016), p. 225.
16. P. J. Mathews, *Revival: The Abbey Theatre, Sinn Féin, The Gaelic League and the Co-Operative Movement* (Notre Dame, IN: University of Notre Dame Press, 2003). Also see Patrick Doyle's study of the cooperative movement, *Civilising Rural Ireland: The Co-Operative Movement, Development and the Nation-State, 1889–1939* (Manchester: Manchester University Press, 2019).
17. Emer Nolan, 'Modernism and the Irish Revival', in *The Cambridge Companion to Modern Irish Culture*, ed. Joe Cleary and Claire Connolly (Cambridge: Cambridge University Press, 2005), pp. 157–72 (p. 158). Nolan's emphasis on the declining favour of the Anglo-Irish is somewhat qualified by the activities of the IAOS, however.
18. Peter C. Gould, *Early Green Politics: Back to Nature, Back to the Land, and Socialism in Britain, 1880–1900* (Brighton: The Harvester Press, 1988), p. viii.
19. Bonneuil and Fressoz, *The Shock of the Anthropocene*, p. 271.

20. Ibid. p. 271.
21. This quotation comes from Joyce's essay on Oscar Wilde, where he gives an account of Wilde studying with Ruskin.
22. W. B. Yeats, *The Cutting of an Agate* (New York: Macmillan, 1912), p. 120; Brannigan, *Archipelagic Modernism*, p. 26.
23. W. B. Yeats, *Collected Poems* (London: Macmillan, 1982), p. 44.
24. W. B. Yeats, *Autobiographies* (London: Macmillan, 1955), pp. 71–4. I have elsewhere given a detailed account of the influence of *Walden* on Carpenter's aesthetics and its broader influence on British socialism. See Peter Adkins, 'Transatlantic Dialogues in Sustainability: Edward Carpenter, Henry David Thoreau and the Literature of Simplification', in *Victorian Sustainability in Literature and Culture*, ed. Wendy Parkins (London and New York: Routledge, 2018), pp. 51–68.
25. W. B. Yeats, *Writings on Irish Folklore, Legend and Myth*, ed. Robert Welch (London: Penguin Books, 1993), p. 190.
26. Quoted in Richard Ellmann, *James Joyce* (Oxford: Oxford University Press, 1983), p. 100; p. 103. For a critical account of this much mythologised meeting, see Ronan Crowley, 'Things Actually Said: On Some Versions of Joyce's and Yeats' First Meeting', *Joyce Studies in Italy*, 17 (2015), 31–54.
27. Yeats, *Irish Folklore*, p. 191.
28. Ibid. p. 194.
29. Seán Hewitt, 'Yeats's Re-Enchanted Nature', *International Yeats Studies*, 2.2 (2018), 1–19 (pp. 10–11).
30. Gregory Castle, 'Irish Revivalism: Critical Trends and New Directions', *Literature Compass*, 8.5 (2011), 291–303 (p. 297).
31. Alison Lacivita, 'Wild Dublin: Nature Versus Culture in Irish Literature', *Green Letters*, 17.1 (2013), 27–41 (p. 28). Edward Hirsch also makes clear that Irish rural communities did not see themselves in terms of a peasantry and the term, even in its use by nationalists, was a literary construct rather than a social reality. Hirsh, 'The Imaginary Irish Peasant', *PMLA*, 106.5 (1991), 1116–33 (p. 1123).
32. John Eglinton, *Anglo-Irish Essays* (Dublin: The Talbot Press, 1917), p. 9.
33. Bruno Latour, *Politics of Nature: How to Bring the Sciences into Democracy*, trans. Catherine Porter (Cambridge, MA: Harvard University Press, 2004), p. 3.
34. H. Gustav Klaus and John Rignall, 'Introduction: The Red and The Green', in *Ecology and the Literature of the British Left: The Red and The Green*, ed. Valentine Cunningham, H. Gustav Klaus and John Rignall (Farnham: Ashgate, 2012), pp. 1–17 (pp. 1–2).
35. Vincent J. Cheng, *Joyce, race, and empire* (Cambridge: Cambridge University Press, 1995), p. 72.
36. Mathews, *Revival*, p. 32.
37. James Joyce, 'The Sisters', *The Irish Homestead*, 13 August 1904, pp. 676–7. Dathalinn O'Dea's recent analysis of Joyce's contributions to *The Irish Homestead* situates his writing as 'in dialogue' with the agricultural material context of the paper. Dathalinn O'Dea, 'Joyce the Regionalist: *The Irish Homestead*, *Dubliners* and Modernism's Regional Affect', *Modern Fiction Studies*, 63.3 (2017), 475–501 (p. 485).

38. George Russell to James Joyce, July 1904. James Joyce Collection, General Collection, Beinecke Rare Book and Manuscript Library Box 2, Folder 42.
39. For the compositional history of both *Stephen Hero* and *A Portrait of the Artist as a Young Man* see Hans Walter Gabler's introduction to the 1993 Garland edition of the latter.
40. Ellmann, *James Joyce*, p. 683.
41. Ibid. p. 163.
42. For the Revival as an anthropological project see Castle, *Modernism and the Celtic Revival*.
43. Castle, *Modernism and the Celtic Revival*, pp. 204–6.
44. Katherine Ebury, 'Becoming-Animal in the Epiphanies: Joyce Between Fiction and Non-Fiction', in *Joyce's Non-Fiction Writings: Outside His Jurisfiction*, ed. Katherine Ebury and James Alexander Fraser (Cham: Palgrave Macmillan, 2018), pp. 175–94 (p. 188).
45. See Don Gifford and Robert J. Seidman, *'Ulysses' Annotated: Notes for James Joyce's 'Ulysses'* (Berkeley and Los Angeles: University of California Press, 1986), p. 219.
46. Quoted in Gifford and Seidman, *'Ulysses' Annotated*, p. 219.
47. Aristotle, *The Complete Works of Aristotle*, ed. Jonathan Barnes, rev. edn (Oxford: Oxford University Press, 1995), p. 1457. As Gifford and Seidman highlight, Stephen amalgamates ideas from both *On the Soul* and *Sense and Sensibilia*. See Gifford and Seidman, *'Ulysses' Annotated*, pp. 44–5. For an extended account of Aristotle's philosophy in 'Proteus' see David Ayers, 'De Anima: or, *Ulysses* and the Theological Turn in Modernist Studies', *Humanities*, 6.3 (2017) <www.mdpi.com/2076-0787/6/3/57> (last accessed 25 February 2021).
48. Gregory Castle, '"I Am Almosting It": History, Nature, and the Will to Power in "Proteus"', *James Joyce Quarterly*, 29.2 (1992), 281–96 (p. 285).
49. Hunter Dukes, '*Ulysses* and the Signature of Things', *Humanities*, 6.3 (2017) <www.mdpi.com/2076-0787/6/3/52> (last accessed 23 February 2021).
50. Cheng, *Joyce, race, and empire*, p. 67.
51. Jeff Wallace, 'Modern', in *The Cambridge Companion to Literature and the Posthuman*, ed. Bruce Clarke and Manuela Rossini (Cambridge: Cambridge University Press, 2017), pp. 41–53 (p. 44).
52. Stephen's observation of 'no birds' is also possibly a reference to Keats's 'no birds sing' in 'La Belle Dame sans Merci' (1819). I am grateful to Tim Conley for suggesting this connection. Keats's poem also inspired the title of Rachel Carson's groundbreaking work of environmental science *Silent Spring* (London and New York: Penguin Books, 1962), which was an influence on Djuna Barnes's late poetry, as I discuss in the final chapter to this book.
53. For accounts of the Revival's importance in the episode see Clare Hutton, 'Joyce and the Institutions of Revivalism', *Irish University Review*, 33.1 (2003), 117–32.
54. Frank Budgen, *James Joyce and the Making of 'Ulysses' and Other Writings* (Oxford: Oxford University Press, 1972), p. 117. Joyce had unsuccessfully submitted the experimental autobiographical essay 'A Portrait of the Artist' to the journal in 1904, while also working on *Stephen Hero*.

55. Guattari, *The Three Ecologies*, pp. 37–8; p. 42.
56. Ibid. p. 38.
57. Declan Kiberd, *Inventing Ireland: The Literature of a Modern Nation* (London: Jonathan Cape, 1995), p. 337. Castle makes a similar argument but reaches a different conclusion, arguing that the Revivalist interest in myth is part of a dialectical logic in which misrecognition serves to correct historical misrepresentation. Castle, 'Irish Revivalism', pp. 301–2.
58. Guattari, *The Three Ecologies*, p. 35.
59. Karen Lawrence, *The Odyssey of Style in 'Ulysses'* (Princeton: Princeton University Press, 1981), p. 80.
60. 'Rhetorical masks' is Lawrence's term.
61. The notion of the parodies as interpolations is present both in the foundational works of modernist criticism on *Ulysses* and later criticism that has taken a more political or historical approach. For the former see Hugh Kenner, *Ulysses* (London: George Allen & Unwin, 1980), p. 100; and Richard Ellmann, *Ulysses on the Liffey* (Oxford: Oxford University Press, 1982), p. 111. For more recent approaches see Nolan, *James Joyce and Nationalism*, p. 91; and Brigitte L. Sandquist, 'The Tree Wedding in "Cyclops" and the Ramifications of Cata-Logic', *James Joyce Quarterly*, 33.2 (1996), 195–209 (p. 207).
62. Platt, *Joyce and the Anglo-Irish*, pp. 144–5.
63. R. F. Foster, *Modern Ireland 1600–1972* (London: Penguin Books, 1988), pp. 456–7.
64. James Fairhall, 'Ecocriticism, Joyce, and the Politics of Trees in the "Cyclops" Episode of *Ulysses*', *Irish Studies Review*, 20.4 (2012), 367–87 (pp. 373–4); Yi-Peng Lai, 'The Tree Wedding and the (Eco)Politics of Irish Forestry in "Cyclops": History, Language and the Viconian Politics of the Forest', in *Eco-Joyce: The Environmental Imagination of James Joyce*, ed. Robert Brazeau and Derek Gladwin (Cork: Cork University Press, 2014), pp. 91–110 (pp. 94–5).
65. Fairhall, 'Ecocriticism', p. 373.
66. James Joyce, *Joyce's 'Ulysses' Notesheets in the British Museum*, ed. Phillip Herring (Charlottesville: University Press of Virginia, 1972), p. 458.
67. Lacivita, *Ecology of 'Finnegans Wake'*, p. 190.
68. As Fairhall has pointed out, Joyce was wrong to suggest deforestation created Ireland's bogs, many of which had developed after the last Ice Age. See Fairhall, 'The Bog of Allen, the Tiber River, and the Pontine Marshes: An Ecocritical Reading of "The Dead"', *James Joyce Quarterly*, 51.4 (2014), 567–600 (p. 574).
69. Joyce, *Joyce's 'Ulysses' Notesheets*, p. 460.
70. Haraway, *Staying with the Trouble*, p. 206.
71. Castle, *Modernism and the Celtic Revival*, p. 241.
72. Eglinton, *Anglo-Irish Essays*, p. 112.
73. Joyce, *Joyce's 'Ulysses' Notesheets*, p. 119.
74. For Derrida, the 'supplement is always the supplement of a supplement. One wishes to go back from the supplement to the source: one must recognize that there is a supplement at the source.' Derrida, *Of Grammatology*, trans. Gayatri Chakravorty Spivak (Baltimore: Johns Hopkins University Press, 1997), p. 304.

75. Kaori Nagai, '"'Tis Optophone Which Ontophanes": Race, the Modern and Irish Revivalism', in *Modernism and Race*, ed. Len Platt (Cambridge: Cambridge University Press, 2011), pp. 58–76 (p. 61).
76. Guattari, *The Three Ecologies*, p. 35.
77. Ibid. p. 58.
78. Norimitsu Onishi, 'France's Far Right Wants to Be an Environmental Party, Too', *The New York Times*, 17 October 2019 <www.nytimes.com/2019/10/17/world/europe/france-far-right-environment> (last accessed 25 February 2021).
79. Gilles Deleuze and Félix Guattari, *A Thousand Plateaus: Capitalism and Schizophrenia*, trans. Brian Massumi (London: Bloomsbury, 2014), p. 494.
80. Dipesh Chakrabarty, 'The Anthropocene and the Convergence of Histories', in *The Anthropocene and the Global Environmental Crisis: Rethinking Modernity in a New Epoch*, ed. Clive Hamilton (Abingdon: Routledge, 2015), pp. 44–56 (p. 52).
81. Lacivita, *Ecology of 'Finnegans Wake'*, pp. 8–9.
82. Deleuze and Guattari, *A Thousand Plateaus*, p. 494.
83. Kupinse also finds parallels between Bloom and William Morris's arts and crafts aesthetics, suggesting further English Romantic influences on constructions of Irish nature. See William J. Kupinse, 'Private Property, Public Interest: Bloom's Ecological Fantasy in "Ithaca"', *James Joyce Quarterly*, 52.3–4 (2015), 593–621 (p. 597; p. 609).
84. Deleuze and Guattari, *A Thousand Plateaus*, p. 494.
85. As Lacivita shows, Joyce incorporated these disagreements around the island's use within *Finnegans Wake*. Lacivita, *Ecology of 'Finnegans Wake'*, pp. 157–8.
86. Guattari, *The Three Ecologies*, p. 52.

2

JAMES JOYCE AND THE REVENGE OF GAIA

In August 1921 Joyce wrote to Frank Budgen informing him of the progress of the final episode of *Ulysses*. '*Penelope* is the clou of the book', Joyce explained, before continuing:

> The first sentence contains 2500 words. There are eight sentences in the episode. It begins and ends with the female word *Yes*. It turns like the huge earthball slowly and surely and evenly round and round spinning. Its four cardinal points being the female breasts, arse, womb and cunt expressed by the words *because*, *bottom* (in all senses, bottom button, bottom of the glass, bottom of the sea, bottom of his heart), *woman*, *yes*. Though probably more obscene than any preceding episode it seems to me to be perfectly sane full amoral fertilisable untrustworthy engaging shrewd limited prudent indifferent *Weib*. (*JJL*1 170, emphasis in original)

Joyce's characterisation of Molly as 'the huge earthball' spinning in a slow orbit would not have surprised Budgen, who was already alert to the planetary scale Joyce envisioned for the novel's conclusion. Earlier in 1921, Joyce had explained that the penultimate episode, 'Ithaca', took the 'form of a mathematical catechism' in which '[a]ll events are resolved into their cosmic, physical, psychical etc. equivalents [. . .] Bloom and Stephen thereby become heavenly bodies, wanderers like the stars at which they gaze', while '[t]he last word (human all-too-human) is left to Penelope' as the 'indispensable countersign to Bloom's passport to eternity' (*JJL*1 159–60). By the time he had finished 'Penelope' and sent it to Harriet Shaw Weaver he was describing Molly's monologue as an attempt to 'depict the earth which is prehuman and presumably posthuman' (*JJL*1 180). No longer constrained to a 'human apparition' (*JJL*1 180), Molly's expansive monologue instead took the form of the Earth itself speaking. Indeed, this is exactly how Bloom, climbing into bed at the end of 'Ithaca', perceives her: 'reclined semilaterally, left, left hand under head, right leg extended in a straight line and resting on left leg, flexed, in the attitude of Gea-Tellus, fulfilled, recumbent, big with seed' (*U* 17.2312–14). An amalgamation of the Greek Earth Goddess, Gea, or Gaia, and her counterpart in Roman mythology, Tellus, Bloom's odyssey concludes with him returning to the 'amoral fertilisable untrustworthy' Earth Mother herself.

Despite this brief description of Molly as Gea-Tellus being the only explicit reference to Gaian mythology in the novel, the connection between Molly and classical Mother Earth myths were foregrounded in accounts of *Ulysses* by Joyce's contemporaries. Valéry Larbaud, in an influential article that appeared in the *Nouvelle Revue Française* in April 1922 and in English in the October 1922 issue of the *Criterion*, explained to readers that 'Bloom's wife' is 'the symbol of Gaea, the Earth'.[1] Ezra Pound, in a favourable review of *Ulysses* in the June 1922 issue of *The Dial*, further developed this highly gendered connection, describing how Bloom's 'spouse Gea-Tellus, the earth symbol, is the soil from which the intelligence strives to leap, and to which it subsides *in saeculurn saeculorum*. As Molly she is a coarse-grained bitch, not a whore, an adulteress, *il y en a*.'[2] In this context, T. S. Eliot's '*Ulysses*, Order and Myth', published in *The Dial* a year after Pound's essay and which noticeably avoids any direct mention of the novel's content, might be read as offering a similar, if more oblique, description of the gendered relationship between matter and meaning. Eliot's argument that Joyce submits 'living material' to myth as a way 'of ordering, of giving a shape and a significance' to the 'futility and anarchy which is contemporary history', sets up a binary between a passive materiality that has historically been gendered feminine and a heroic understanding of history that finds its symbol in the figure of Homer's Odysseus.[3] These early critical alignments of Molly with Gea, including Eliot's more allusive insinuation, reached their culmination in Stuart Gilbert's *James Joyce's Ulysses: A Study* (1930), a work shaped by Joyce's guidance, and which argues in detail that Molly represents 'the Great Mother [. . .] Gaea, the Earth, [who] according to the Greeks, [was] the first being that sprang from Chaos'. She is assigned the symbol of 'Earth' in the schema Joyce produced for the book and Gilbert goes on to describe in detail the chapter's 'geotropic' structure.[4] As Suzette Henke and Elaine Unkeless have argued, these early accounts ensured that the dominant critical approach to Molly in the decades to come would see her 'not only as an "earth-goddess" but as a sensuous embodiment of material inertia'.[5] If Bloom's glimpse of Molly as Gea-Tellus in the closing moments of 'Ithaca' is relatively brief, Joyce and his circle of friendly critics went some way to make sure that his early readers nonetheless saw her in this highly gendered planetary light.

While Gaia was of interest to Joyce and his modernist contemporaries as a mythic figure of feminised materiality and as a maternal embodiment of the Earth, the Greek goddess's significance in the second half of the twentieth century was as a metaphor for a systems-based understanding of the planet and radical ecological philosophies. The Gaia hypothesis, established by scientist and inventor James Lovelock in the late 1960s and subsequently co-developed with the biologist Lynn Margulis from the early 1970s onwards, argued that the Earth itself should be considered a living entity. Lovelock had developed the theory while working for NASA in the 1960s on the possible presence of life forms on other planets, when he had been struck by the unlikely combination of gases that were needed for life on Earth. In studying the relationship between atmospheric gases, surface rocks, water and organisms, he discovered that the Earth's unlikely composition resembled a 'physiological system [that] appears to have the unconscious goal of regulating the climate and the chemistry [of the planet] at a comfortable state for life'.[6] The Earth's various systems, Lovelock and Margulis showed, were not only co-dependent on one another but seemed to regulate themselves in such a way so as to be amenable to the over-all life of the planet. In a reversal to Joyce's intent to remove any 'human apparition' from Molly as Gea-Tellus, Lovelock decided to anthropomorphise his scientific model, giving it the name Gaia, with the goddess's fitting stature as the primordial deity and ancestral mother of all life being suggested to him by the novelist William Golding. Indeed, Lovelock was seduced by exactly the kind of romanticism which, as I argued in my previous chapter, Joyce was highly suspicious of. In a preface that Lovelock wrote in 2000 for the republication of his first book on Gaia, he describes how he started writing it 'in 1974 in the unspoilt landscape of Western Ireland, [where] it was like living in a house run by Gaia', going on to suggest that '[w]ritten in Ireland, perhaps it is Irish in spirit'.[7] Lovelock's theory, which he has wryly suggested in retrospect is 'a fairy story about a Greek goddess [. . .] with science as [. . .] an incidental part', was both the product of a new way of thinking about the planet and one more re-animation of an ancient maternal figure who had interested Joyce just as much.[8]

In recent years there has been a resurgence of interest in Lovelock's Gaia, as philosophers and scientists return to his hypothesis in the Anthropocene. For Bruno Latour, one of the most vocal proponents of Gaia, the concept's usefulness resides in its ability to offer an understanding of the planet without reverting to holism. As he explains, the Gaia theory of planetary systems does not imply unity or coherence, rather it is premised on 'captu[ring] the distributed intentionality of all [. . .] agents, each of which modifies its surroundings for its own purposes'. In this respect, Gaia speaks to one of the Anthropocene's most urgent epistemological provocations: 'how to speak about the Earth without taking it to be an already composed whole'.[9] As Latour, and other advocates of Gaia have argued, although it is easy to dismiss the concept as implying a homeostatic or idealised idea of planetary life to reach such a conclusion would be a profound misreading of what Gaia means.[10] In her 1998 book, *The Symbiotic Planet*, Margulis makes clear that self-regulation should not be confused with the teleological idea of a 'living planetary system [that] behaves together to optimize conditions for all its members'. Gaia is not normative in the sense of proscribing how the planet *should* be composed but is a useful scientific theory for mapping the 'interweaving network of all life'.[11] Gaia, then, should not be misconstrued as a model for planetary conditions conducive for human habitation. Rather, it is an analytic for thinking about the systems and processes which all life emerges from and relies upon. For Isabelle Stengers, this is precisely why the figure of Gaia has critical purchase in the Anthropocene: it becomes the name for an 'intrusion' within global capitalism, a 'being' with 'its own regime of activity and sensitivity' that we have been ignoring for too long and whose 'brutality [. . .] corresponds to the brutality of what has provoked her'.[12] Lovelock has also returned to his theory in the face of global challenges. In a 2006 book entitled *The Revenge of Gaia: Why the Earth is Fighting Back – and How We Can Still Save Humanity*, Lovelock argues that the 'metaphor' of Gaia is more important than ever, since 'to deal with, understand, and even ameliorate the fix we are in now over global change requires us to know the true nature of the Earth and imagine it as the largest living thing in the solar system, not something inanimate'.[13] Lovelock concludes his book with a description of Gaia that, in many respects, strikes a not dissimilar note to the modernists fascinated with Joyce's mythic gendering of Molly: 'Gaia [. . .] acts as a mother who is nurturing but ruthlessly cruel towards her transgressors, even when they are her progeny.'[14]

This chapter reassesses Joyce's interest in Gaia and the gendered cosmology of his writing in the light of recent critical and theoretical interest in Gaia. Building on the insights and concerns of the previous chapter by continuing to look at Joyce's interest in the dynamics between materiality and meaning, this chapter shifts in scale from the nation to the Earth itself. Recent criticism has begun to elucidate how Joyce's writing might be read alongside theories of the planet from early twentieth-century science and philosophy, with Katherine Ebury examining how Joyce moves towards a concept of relativity akin to that being explored in the new physics and Ruben Borg suggesting we can employ Husserl's genetic phenomenology as a way of reading how Joyce figures the 'phenomenality of the earth'.[15] This chapter suggests that by focusing on Joyce's interest in materiality and his refiguring of Gea-Tellus, his writing can also be brought into dialogue with contemporary attempts to rethink planetary life in the Anthropocene. It will foreground the way in which, as Joyce was all too aware in the letters he wrote to Budgen, the story of Gea-Tellus is also a story of how sex and gender influence how we perceive and figure the Earth. Not just in the final episode, but throughout *Ulysses* we see this fact presented through the perspectives of Bloom and Stephen. While their ideas on planetary life might vary, Joyce presents them as sharing a gendered perception of matter that is complicit with a long but overdetermined cultural tradition that associates women with the Earth. It is in this respect that we might see Molly as taking revenge on the gendered cosmology that precedes her monologue. Here, too, we can find parallels with contemporary interest in Gaia. Margulis wrote that she 'regret[ted]' the personification of Gaia as 'a living goddess' who 'will supposedly punish or reward us for our environmental insults or blessings to her body' and offered an alternative figure of Gaia as a 'tough bitch'.[16] More recently, Donna Haraway has argued that the sexual politics of Gaia have become further heightened in the Anthropocene, with a pressing need to dismiss the idea of a single Earth Mother in favour of recognising multiple 'Gaians' who exist as a 'queer planetwide litter of chthonic ones'.[17] With these recuperative readings that seem to reclaim the figure of Gaia for a feminist understanding of the Anthropocene in mind, this chapter looks at how Joyce's own highly gendered design of Molly as the speaking Earth reveals the possibilities and limitations to the metaphors through which we conceptualise planetary life.

Sexualised Figures of the Earth

Stephen's Aristotelian musings in 'Proteus', outlined in the previous chapter, not only signal an interest in the relation between the senses and the material world, but also produce a planetary imaginary at whose centre is a 'manshape ineluctable' (*U* 3.413). This phrase comes from a moment in the episode where Stephen is considering the finitude of his own shadow:

> His shadow lay over the rocks as he bent, ending. Why not endless till the farthest star? Darkly they are there behind this light, darkness shining in the brightness, delta of Cassiopeia, worlds. Me sits there with his augur's rod of ash, in borrowed sandals, by day beside a livid sea, unbeheld, in violet night walking beneath a reign of uncouth stars. I throw this ended shadow from me, manshape ineluctable, call it back. Endless, would it be mine, form of my form? (*U* 3.408–14)

Stephen's shadow, which he identifies with an Aristotelian inflection as the 'form of my form', is held in contrast to the inhuman and seemingly infinite scale of the universe. As with Stephen's other reflections on the human and the more-than-human materiality that subtends it, the tension between the two is left unresolved. While the gendered language that Stephen employs is representative of linguistic conventions in the early twentieth century, it nonetheless gestures to a broader question of sex and gender at work in the question of the mind and matter, a lineage which we can trace back through Stephen's Aristotelian readings. In *Generation of Animals*, Aristotle makes the distinction between male rationality and female matter, setting out a model of reproduction in which 'it is the soul that is from the male' while the 'body is from the female' and can be aligned with the organic materiality of 'the soil'.[18] This gendered dualism between body and mind, thought and matter, active and passive that we find in Aristotle is also present in Stephen's planetary imaginary. Watching two midwives approach the beach, Stephen thinks:

> Like me, like Algy, coming down to our mighty mother. [. . .] One of her sisterhood lugged me squealing into life. Creation from nothing. What has she in her bag? A misbirth with a trailing navelcord, hushed in ruddy wool. The cords of all link back, strandentwining cable of all flesh. (*U* 3.31–7)

Echoing Buck Mulligan's remarks in the opening of the novel that the sea is 'a great sweet mother' (*U* 1.77–8), Stephen aligns childbirth with a mythic idea of female fertility associated with the ocean. His unease with this fertile matter becomes clearer as he considers the possibility of '[c]reation from nothing', a fantasy of divine, as opposed to biological, creation that is played out in his mind several times over the course of the novel, emphasising a desire for mastery over, rather than continuity with, materiality. For Borg, Stephen's revulsion at matter is why the umbilical cord, figured as the 'strandentwining cable of all flesh', comes to symbolise a horrifying physical tie to a 'sexualized earth-mother engendering the sensory world'.[19] As such when Stephen subsequently reflects on Eve's lack of a 'navel', he figures her as a kind of Christian Earth Mother, her '[b]elly without blemish, bulging big, a buckler of taut vellum' with a '[w]omb of sin' (*U* 3.41–4). A short while later, when Stephen looks out to a woman collecting cockles he sees her as a 'handmaid of the moon', his thoughts on the 'tide westering, moondrawn, in her wake' conflating her menstrual cycle with the movements of the tide (*U* 3.93–5) and foreshadowing Molly who, as the daughter of 'Lunita Laredo', figures as another kind of maiden of the moon (*U* 18.848).[20] As Borg argues in his phenomenological analysis of sex and materiality in Joyce, 'Proteus' stages the way in which matter becomes sexualised as it passes through the 'genesis of sense perception'. For Borg, who reads the earth as a 'generative matrix' that gives itself to human perception, as soon as materiality is perceived it undergoes an 'anthropomorphic rendering' in which the 'sensible world' is assimilated within sexualised figurations.[21] As Joyce shows in Stephen, materiality is not given cultural associations after the fact of its having been integrated within linguistic frameworks. Rather, these material processes are themselves always bound up with questions of sex, gender and sexuality in advance of the cultural and linguistic associations we assign them, in what Haraway describes as 'material-semiotic fields of meaning'.[22]

'Proteus' is important to the planetary imaginary that follows in the rest of the novel, not least in assessing the degree to which Molly, as Gea-Tellus, can be seen as speaking back to Stephen's gendered figuring of the Earth. While Maud Ellmann is right to point out that Joyce's writing is part of a tradition that goes back to 'Greek philosophical thought [in which] femaleness has been conflated with everything that Reason has transcended, dominated or simply left behind', it is nonetheless also the case that *Ulysses* emphasises the degree to which the feminisation of materiality is overdetermined.[23] We see this overdetermination perhaps most clearly in the competing Mother Earth myths present in the novel. The Celtic Earth goddess Dana, for instance, was an important figure in Revivalist culture, becoming a popular poetic subject and the title for the short-lived Dublin literary magazine edited by John Eglinton and Frederick Ryan. As mentioned in the previous chapter, one of Stephen's motivations for appearing at the National Library in 'Scylla and Charybdis' is to win a commission for *Dana* and we find Stephen drop a rather unsubtle hint to this when he declares that '[a]s we, or mother Dana, weave and unweave our bodies [. . .] from day to day, their molecules shuttled to and fro, so does the artist weave and unweave his image' (*U* 9.376–8). Writing in 1984 in one of the first feminist analyses of Joyce's mythic frameworks, Bonnie Kime Scott lists the worship of Dana among 'Ireland's basic Celtic groups, the Milesians' as an example of a 'strong female prehistory and myth' in Ireland that Joyce would have been aware of.[24] Scott points, too, to Robert Graves's suggestion that such Celtic myths can be traced back to ancient Aegean cultures, suggesting a point of continuity between Gaia and Dana. Joyce's interest in the specifically maternal dimension to this Irish myth finds clear evidence in his decision to add 'mother' to Stephen's invocation of 'mother Dana' while revising 'Scylla and Charybdis', emphasising the gendered dimension to Stephen's view of materiality and foreshadowing the appearance of Molly as the Earth Mother herself at the novel's end.[25] Scott also highlights the figure of Medb from the Ulster Cycle of myths, a 'strong-willed' queen who is equated with both 'Ireland' and 'the earth itself' and whom, in having greater power than the king, Scott suggests is comparable to the demanding Molly in 'Calypso'.[26] This is, perhaps, the Irish Earth Mother George Russell invokes earlier in 'Scylla and Charybdis', when he describes those hillside peasants for whom 'the earth is not the exploitable ground but the living mother' (*U* 9.106–7).

It is not only prehistoric and classical myths that are shown to perpetuate the association of women, especially mothers, with the land. As touched upon in my previous chapter, the Revival relied on archetypal mothers within Irish folklore, such as Kathleen Ni Houlihan who symbolises the 'four beautiful fields' of Ireland in Yeats's play of that title (*U* 9.37). The milkwoman who visits Stephen and the others at the Martello Tower in 'Telemachus' presents a corrective to this myth: Stephen watches her 'pour into the measure and thence into the jug rich white milk, not hers' since, as he observes, she has '[o]ld shrunken paps' (*U* 1.397–8). He then goes on to sardonically entertain the idea of her '[c]rouching by a patient cow at daybreak in the lush field' with the 'silk of the kine'; she is to Stephen not a goddess but a 'wandering crone' and 'common cuckquean' dispossessed by the English (*U* 1.400–5). Inverting rather than rejecting the sexual politics of Revivalist mythology, Stephen merely substitutes female infertility for fertility, paralleling Bloom's near simultaneous reflection on how the 'barren' Levant, once the home of the 'first race', is now 'the grey sunken cunt of the world' (*U* 4.219–28). In both instances, the novel foregrounds the degree to which not only prehistorical and classical myths, but contemporary discourse around nationalism and empire continues to conceptualise land and earth through figures of femininity which are themselves equated with fertility and (re)birth.[27]

Moreover, Bloom's own predisposition towards science over myth does not inure him from the gendering of matter. Bloom is more willing than Stephen to recognise the autonomy of matter, with his thoughts often ascribing agency to objects that would be considered inert or inanimate. The phosphorescence of codfish in his pantry, for instance, fascinating him with its 'bluey silver' and 'all the smells in it waiting to rush out' (*U* 8.22–3), offers one such example of Bloom considering the life of the lifeless, an idea that has already been explored at length in 'Hades', where the 'damp earth' is situated as a generative medium underpinning all biological life, in which 'cells or whatever they are go on living' and 'changing about' (*U* 6.778–81). For Bloom, mind and matter resolutely do not exist in a binary, not least since, as he explains to Stephen in 'Eumaeus', 'brainpower' is itself an effect of 'grey matter' (*U* 16.749–52). Bloom's disposition is to accept the liveliness of matter and the dynamic, often messy, systems of interrelation that underpin all life. Yet, while Bloom's materialism is more open, and arguably more radical, than Stephen's, it does not translate into a straightforward rejection of human exceptionalism. While he does not believe in the Catholic dualism of 'body and soul', he nonetheless *does* believe that science shows us how human 'intelligence' is 'distinct from any outside object, the table, let us say, that cup' (*U* 16.748–50). Moreover, while he departs from the Aristotelian binary that separates soul (male) from matter (female), his materialism still works towards an androcentric cosmology. In 'Nausicaa', for instance, Bloom notices that his wristwatch appears to have stopped at the exact time of Molly and Boylan's planned rendezvous:

> Back of everything magnetism. Earth for instance pulling this and being pulled. That causes movement. And time, well that's the time the movement takes. Then if one thing stopped the whole ghesabo would stop bit by bit. Because it's all arranged. (*U* 13.987–90)

Bloom's thoughts on the relationship between his wristwatch and planetary movement are understood not in terms of contingency but arrangement, in which the apparent inevitability of Molly's sexual liaison is likened to the subterranean movements of the Earth. As Borg suggests, Joyce is here drawing a connection between 'the motions of the earth and the theme of female sexuality', serving as a further example of matter as feminine and fertile.[28] In one of the earlier drafts, this point was made even more strongly, with a longer final sentence reading: 'Because it is arranged that way down to the smallest: no mistakes.'[29] The geological and the historical, the impersonal and the personal, are fundamentally intertwined in such a way that the Earth itself takes on the shape of the adulterous wife.

Bloom's aforementioned likening of the Levant to a 'grey sunken cunt' offers further evidence of a predisposition towards a cosmology that, while recognising the vitality of matter, remains deeply attached to the association of matter with fertility and, by extension, femininity. And it is in 'Ithaca', where his scientism is on fullest display, that the sexual politics of his materialism are most clear. Turning his mind to the question of 'human life', Bloom explains to Stephen his views on 'the generic conditions imposed by natural, as distinct from human law, [that are] integral parts of the human whole', in which 'the fact of vital growth, through convulsions of metamorphosis' means progress is also always a form of 'decay' (U 17.993–1006). It is a vitalism, which like his speculations in 'Hades', situates the human as continuous with the nonhuman materiality that subtends it, in which life is epiphenomenal and death is akin to Rosi Braidotti's description of it as 'not the horizon against which the human drama is played out' but part of 'ever-recurring flows of vitality'.[30] Unlike Braidotti's vital materialism, however, Bloom's thoughts on vital flows leads him to associate it with 'the monotonous menstruation of simian and (particularly) human females extending from the age of puberty to the menopause' as well as 'innate lunacy and congenital criminality' (U 17.995–1002). Indeed, in this respect, Bloom falls into precisely the trap that Braidotti warns against, namely perceiving the planet in terms of 'an undifferentiated vitalist system [formed of] flat equivalences across all species, all technologies and all organisms under one common Law'.[31] Stephen's Aristotelian response that man can be set apart as the 'conscious rational animal' (U 17.1012) offers both a departure from Bloom's professed views but also an implicit gender bias linking their two cosmologies. While Bloom's attentiveness to the chaotic vitalism underpinning life destabilises his elsewhere professed belief in human exceptionalism and seems to imply a broadly distributive model of agency, it is a vitalism that simultaneously works to naturalise sexual difference. It is perhaps little surprise that 'Ithaca' culminates with Bloom returning to the earth through his mythic association of Molly with 'Gea-Tellus', an image that presents itself as continuous, rather than at odds, with the scientific outlook on life that has gone before.

A Goddess Called Gaea

Certainly, Bloom's cosmology is not a straightforward articulation of Joyce's views. Yet, Bloom's thoughts on it all being 'arranged' in 'Nausicaa' are surely also a meta-textual joke about Joyce's careful arrangement and construction of the novel and raise questions of how easily one can distinguish the various characters' sexual politics from Joyce's own. The letters which Joyce wrote to Budgen, for instance, suggest a creative reinheritance rather than rejection of a tradition that associates women with a fertile materiality that stands in opposition to masculine reason. And it is not only Joyce's letters to Budgen that suggest he was drawn to Earth Mother myths. In 1912, when visiting Percy Bysshe Shelley's grave in Rome, Joyce made notes for his play *Exiles* (1918), writing of a feminised 'earth', figured as a 'dark, formless, mother, made beautiful by the moonlit night' and 'darkly conscious of her instincts'.[32] In the finished play, Robert Hand, in anticipation of his liaison with Bertha Rowan, exclaims that '[t]onight the earth is loved – loved and possessed',[33] a turn of phrase that parallels Bloom's poem for Molly, whose concluding line of 'You are mine. The world is mine.' (*U* 17.416) takes on suggestive connotations in the context of his elsewhere association of her with the Earth. Perhaps most revealing in this respect are Joyce's notes for 'Penelope', where near the top of the notebook for the episode is written 'her cunt, darkest Africa',[34] likely an allusion to Joseph Conrad's *Heart of Darkness* (1899) and adding a further essentialised, not to mention racist, connotation to his later equating of Molly's 'yes' with 'cunt' in his correspondence with Budgen (*JJL*1 170).

Joyce was not alone in being fascinated by fertility myths and their relationship to a modern understanding of sexuality. T. S. Eliot's insistence on the centrality of Jessie Weston's *From Ritual to Romance* (1920) to the 'plan and [. . .] symbolism' of *The Waste Land* foregrounds a continuity between human and nonhuman (in)fertility and D. H. Lawrence's *The Rainbow* (1915) presents the pregnant Anna Brangwen as being in 'the fecund storm of life [. . .] feeling] like the earth, the mother of everything'.[35] What sets Joyce apart in this context, however, is his use of Gaia mythology. Joyce would have likely known the Gaia myth from the account Hesiod gives in the *Theogony*, or at the very least the sanitised version that appears in the Victorian book *Myths of Hellas or Greek Tales* (1883) which Joyce had in his library while writing *Ulysses*.[36] In Hesiod's *Theogony*, the 'broad-breasted' Gaia is 'the eternal ground of all | The deathless ones'.[37] The primordial goddess, she emerges out of the dark formless mass of Chaos and gives birth to successive litters of children, including the Titans, many of them incestuously sired by another one of her children, Uranus. In the *Theogony*, she is presented as a figure who is both loving and cunning. When Uranus banishes her children, she encourages one of her sons, Cronus, to kill him with a sickle that she has made. Later she poisons Cronus, creating the conditions for one of his own children, Zeus, to overthrow him. As the *Oxford Classical Dictionary* characterises her, Gaia is 'generally ambivalent: she can be deceitful and threatening, dangerous, and gives birth to creatures that pester gods and men'.[38]

Molly's physical characteristics, temperament and Mediterranean background all suggest that Joyce had Gaia in mind while writing *Ulysses*. Her appearance and personality parallel what Latour describes (in a manner that ostensibly replicates the problematic gender dynamics of the myth) as the 'chthonic power, dark skinned, dark-haired and somber [nature]' of Gaia.[39] Although Molly's skin might be, according to Bloom, 'white like wax' (*U* 5.492), she is associated with a Mediterranean darkness throughout the novel. Bloom broods on the 'darkness of her eyes' which he associates with her being 'Spanish' (*U* 5.494–5), an idea amplified in the description of her in 'Cyclops' as the '[p]ride of Calpe's rocky mount, the ravenhaired daughter of Tweedy' (*U* 12.1003).[40] Molly's uncertain origins add a further shadow of darkness, an aspect which Bloom, whose Jewishness is also aligned with darkness in the novel by various characters, can identify with. Making good on Joyce's notes for the episode, Molly's darkness is both racialised and associated with the primordial Earth.[41] Again, it is difficult to delineate as to whether we should see this association as Joyce's own characterisation of Molly or whether, since her association with a dark and fertile materiality is largely presented through the thoughts of male characters, Joyce intends the reader to be critical of this figuration of her. It is notable, for instance, that by the time we reach 'Penelope', Molly challenges the Spanish exoticism through which she has been figured, identifying with the occupying British military force rather than what she calls 'the Spanish girls' (*U* 18.776–7) and displacing any anxieties she might have about her racial identity on to Bloom, by way of his appearance as a 'dark man' in her reading of her cards earlier that morning (*U* 18.1428–9). Where Molly perhaps most clearly fits the Gaia myth is in her characterisation as simultaneously caring and callous. Such changeability is integral to the vicissitudes of her monologue, where a sympathetic view of Bloom as someone who 'understood or felt what a woman is' gives ways to musings on his disposability (*U* 18.1579–1604). Thoughts on Boylan and Milly are also subject to sudden shifts from affection to disdain. Molly's inconsistency of temperament is not coincidental to her monologue. Like both the classical Gaia and Lovelock's modern characterisation of an ecological Gaia as vengeful and liable to be provoked, she stands outside of reason and disrupts human order: her ability to switch between the poles of virtue and vindictiveness is constitutive of a consciousness that has none of the supposed self-reflexivity or coherency that comes with male rationality. Joyce's formal innovations in 'Penelope' also figure her as Gaia. The episode's division into eight sections brings to the fore a number which when turned (and resting on its side like Molly) resembles the infinity symbol, which Joyce gave as the time for the episode in his Linati schema. Here, Molly as Gea-Tellus stands outside of the historical time of the novel, emphasised through the unpunctuated flow of her monologue, which like the life-giving Gaia is a fertile source of generative energy, bringing matter into being. In all these senses, Joyce's figuration of Molly as Gaia appears to succumb to the misogyny and essentialism that continues to colour the popular image of the Earth as a universal mother who gives life but lashes out at the slightest provocation.

It is the interrelation between the episode's formal qualities and its shifts in tone that Stuart Gilbert homes in on in his 'geotropic' reading of Molly as 'a trinity of personages: Penelope, Calypso, and the Earth herself, Gaea-Tellus' in his 1930 guide to *Ulysses*.[42] Gilbert's account of 'Penelope' is worthy of careful engagement for a number of reasons. Firstly, despite its publication date, it continues to stand as the most sustained analysis of Molly and Gea-Tellus. Secondly, Joyce was involved in its publication: Gilbert read the book to him chapter by chapter and benefitted from suggested corrections and additions, meaning we might cautiously read it as an extension of Joyce's dialogue with Budgen on Molly as Gea-Tellus. Finally, to a large extent it set the tone for the way in which Molly would be understood by Joyceans in the post-war period, as well as more recent responses that have disparaged approaches that read Molly as an Earth Mother figure. For Gilbert, Molly actively speaks as 'Gaea-Tellus', a 'divinity of the earth', since her monologue is 'unmistakably earthy' in the literal sense that it 'sing[s] down towards the earth', as 'except for occasional moments when she bethinks herself of her Catholic upbringing, she applies to her conduct but one test, simplicity itself – Is it natural?'[43] This association with naturalness both justifies and elevates Molly's adultery for Gilbert, since the Earth Mother's 'function is fertility' and her 'pleasure is creation', a description which chimes with Bloom's own view of Molly as 'big with seed' as he climbs into bed (*U* 17.2314), even if over the course of the episode it becomes clear that Molly has not been impregnated.[44] Even Molly's uncertain age is marshalled as evidence, paralleling the failure of geologists to reach a 'positive conclusion' regarding the age of the Earth.[45] Having established that Molly has 'the voice of Genetrix, the Earth', Gilbert then turns to the episode's form. Focusing on what he describes as the 'movements' of Molly's monologue, Gilbert explains that although the episode appears 'subject to no law', under 'close examination' the repetition of certain words ('woman', 'bottom', 'he' and 'man') form a pattern that resembles a planetary force. Each moment in the monologue where we find a repetition of words represents what he terms 'wobbling-points', in which Molly's thoughts, 'which, as a general rule revolve about herself', are temporarily directed towards someone else. These 'wobbling-points', in Gilbert's reading, resemble 'the movements of the earth' in which the 'continuous [. . .] rotation about her axis' stands in tension with the gravitational attraction of other planets. Paralleling Bloom in the suggestion of the uniformity of a single natural law guiding both women and planetary cosmology, Gilbert situates Molly as 'egocentric' yet aware of a succession of 'outside force[s]' towards whom 'her thoughts, half reluctantly, turn'.[46]

Gilbert's reading of Molly as the Earth does not suffer from the overt misogyny that we find in Pound's early assessment of her as a 'bitch', but it is clearly informed by an essentialised understanding of the Earth, continuously conflated with a 'Nature' characterised by femininity and fertility. Gilbert's reading of Molly as Gaia might follow Joyce's intention that she should not be read as a 'human apparition' (*JJL*1 180), but he achieves this by projecting an essentialised figuration of 'Woman' back onto the planet.[47] Indeed, in this respect, Gilbert anticipates the literary strategies of Lovelock while developing his Gaia hypothesis. As Lovelock explains, although the scientific community were uneasy with the metaphor, he had hoped that the figure of Gaia would 'enliven and entertain' an audience of general readers, conveying how Gaia was 'an entity that kept herself and all who lived with her comfortable throughout time and season'.[48] Like Gilbert's reading, which concludes by emphasising Gaea-Tellus as 'timeless' and 'artless', Lovelock presents Gaia as the bedrock of all human civilisation and, paradoxically, a feminised matter that stands outside of history, culture and science.[49] Lovelock's Gaia, as in Gilbert's reading, implicitly inscribes the nature-culture binary that it appears to ostensibly overturn.

Molly, Gaia and Ecofeminism

In their 1982 feminist account of the reception of 'Penelope', Henke and Unkeless suggest that Gilbert's study was decisive in establishing a critical approach which saw post-war Joyceans such as Hugh Kenner, William York Tindall and S. L. Goldberg read Molly in symbolic or archetypal terms as representing 'Woman', 'Earth', 'Nature' and, ultimately functioning less as a character than a 'sexual abstraction'.[50] Indeed, as late as 1972, Richard Ellmann was describing Molly as 'earth to Bloom's sun'.[51] Kathleen McCormick has convincingly argued that one of the ulterior motives to these prominent critics reading Molly as an Earth Mother was to aestheticise and thereby sanitise the perceived immorality of the episode, aiding the novel's safe passage into the literary canon.[52] Yet, it is important to note that it was not only male critics who drew upon essentialised ideas of femininity when reading Molly in the 1960s and 1970s. Hélène Cixous's concept of *écriture féminine* turns to Molly's monologue as evidence of the possibility of feminine writing and her description of female writing as having a force comparable to the natural power of the 'sea, earth [and] sky' invokes a surprisingly similar planetary rhetoric to Gilbert.[53] Certainly, *écriture feminine* is far from the reductive kind of sexual essentialism we find in Gilbert's reading. Cixous's argument is that female writing is at once essential *and* marked by difference: it is the expression of 'a universal woman subject' of which there is 'no general woman, no one typical woman'.[54] Where Gilbert situates Molly as a planet slowly and passively turning on her axis, Cixous situates female writing in terms of 'an earthquake' that 'sweeps order away', a force analogous to the tremulous intensity in the final moments of Molly's monologue.[55]

The points of overlap between Gilbert's influential Gaian reading of Molly and Cixous's theory of female difference are useful to bring to light, since they also point to a confluence with the emergence of ecofeminism during the 1970s. First developed by the French feminist Françoise d'Eaubonne, who coined the term *écoféminisme* in 1974, ecofeminism looked to reclaim Mother Earth myths as a means of 'revaluing' the 'woman/nature' connection, aiming to retrieve a maternal connection with the Earth that had been 'degraded and distorted through centuries of patriarchal cultural and economic domination'.[56] Rising to prominence in France and the US, ecofeminism highlighted the structural inequalities linking environmental violence and violence against women, arguing that one could not be addressed without also addressing the other. Certain branches of ecofeminism were also invested in resurrecting the myth of Gaia. Inspired by Lovelock's theory, these ecofeminists looked to refashion 'age-old images of Mother Earth', with Gaia becoming a 'shorthand for holistic approaches' that saw the planet as an organism to be cared for and who, in turn, would care for her children.[57] Although Cixous is not usually seen as an ecofeminist, and her grounding in a poststructuralist understanding of gender, subjectivity and textuality all point to important differences to early ecofeminists, her attention to natural symbols, her insistence on femininity as a force of nature, and her deconstruction of a gendered humanism all run parallel to those who were looking to reclaim Mother Earth as a way of redefining both women and the planet. That Cixous finds an example of *écriture feminine* in Joyce's refiguring of Gea-Tellus in the same cultural moment in which ecofeminists were rediscovering the power of the Gaia myth suggests that we might approach her reading as a radical reinterpretation rather than rejection of the mythic Earth Goddess approach which had dominated masculinist analyses of 'Penelope' up to that point.

A further parallel between *écriture feminine* and ecofeminism can be seen in the way both were subsequently criticised by later feminists for relying on a limiting and essentialised idea of gender. Maud Ellmann's critique that *écriture feminine*'s 'oceanic' readings of 'Penelope' mistake the episode's carefully controlled structure for a bountiful feminine voice, for instance, parallels what Danielle Sands describes as the way in which the woman/nature connection, celebrated by ecofeminists, has been seen by other feminists as a discursive construction deeply rooted in patriarchal conventions.[58] Indeed, as Sands suggests, it was ecofeminism's gravitation towards the figure of Gaia, revivified and brought to notoriety by Lovelock, that many feminists most strongly rejected.[59] Such division explains why ecofeminism has occupied an uncertain and at times maligned relation to wider feminist discourse, particularly third-wave feminism that looked to epistemological, psychological and historical structures rather than natural foundations to understand sex and gender.[60] A similar trend is visible in Joyce studies, where feminist readings of 'Penelope' from the 1990s onwards have largely drawn on third-wave feminist criticism as a means to understand Molly's monologue in singular, historically situated terms rather than as a symbolic or archetypal representation of her sex.[61] Although varying greatly in methodology and argument, what these approaches tend to have in common is a downplaying of Joyce's original Mother Earth symbolism and a turn towards Molly's experience of her own body and bodily processes as situated in a specific place and within historical time.

While offering a necessary critique of explicit and implicit gender essentialisms present in masculinist *and* feminist readings of Molly as Mother Earth, the critical severing of Molly from Gea-Tellus in Joyce studies has meant that critics have not fully engaged with the possibility of reading Molly alongside more recent theoretically sophisticated and ecologically alert configurations of Gaia. As Sands outlines in her survey of ecofeminist approaches to Gaia, more recent ecofeminists have forged a third way between either accepting or rejecting the woman/nature connection by refusing to recognise the nature-culture binary inherent within such a choice and have instead looked to create 'ironic, critical or strategic recuperations of the alliance'.[62] Haraway, for instance, argues against understanding Gaia as either a 'resource to be exploited or ward to be protected', arguing instead that 'Gaia is not a person but complex systemic phenomena that compose a living planet'. For Haraway, Gaia needs to be understood as pluralistic, composed of 'nonlinear couplings between processes that compose and sustain [. . .] a partially cohering systemic whole'.[63] Gaia, in this sense, speaks to the way in which the Earth is comprised not of individual or autonomous subjects, but of organisms that emerge through complex interactions with one another (hence Haraway's preference for the term sympoiesis over autopoiesis). Where Stephen's misogynistic fantasies home in on divine creation out of nothing, Haraway insists on the messy and material processes of 'becoming with' that provide the basis for all life.[64] Far exceeding the normative categories through which biology is commonly understood, Haraway paints a picture of life as brimming with queer potentiality, exceeding any and all binaries of sexuality, gender or sex, with Gaia naming a material-semiotic complexity from which radically new figurations of planetary existence come into view. Much like Guattari's transversal ecology discussed in the previous chapter, Haraway's Gaia undoes constructions of autonomy and sovereignty at individual, collective and planetary levels. And it is for all these reasons that, for Haraway, an 'unfurling Gaia' can be untethered from its roots in the myth of a primordial Greek maternal goddess and the accompanying heroic tradition of storytelling inherited from classical times. Her Gaia 'resists figuration and dating, and demands myriad names', arising from material and cultural histories found in multiple locations, and in which, no longer constrained to anthropo-, euro- or andro-centric myths that pin down our origins and futures, we can instead tell 'geostories' that open out onto untold possibilities.[65]

For Haraway, Gaia signals the need to 'change the story, to learn somehow to narrate – to think – outside the prick tale of Humans in History', and for Joyce, Molly's monologue also necessitated a wholly different mode of writing that could countersign the rest of the novel not as its coda but as its 'clou' or central idea (*JJL*1 170).[66] Indeed, we can read this final episode as challenging what has gone before, or an act of taking Gaian revenge on the cosmology that has been established by way of Bloom and Stephen up until this point. This act of speaking back is not only present in what Margot Norris has argued is the episode's riposte to the 'almost exclusively male construction' of Molly that the reader has encountered until this point, but also in the episode's position directly following 'Ithaca', the apotheosis of Bloom's sense of the universe as arranged and rational, in which the 'necessity of order' is reflected in there being 'a place for everything and everything in its place' (*U* 17.1410).[67] This trust in an underlying order means that even when Bloom seemingly acknowledges non-anthropocentric propositions, calculating the possible 'annihilation of the planet' via collision with other planets or stars (*U* 17.2181) and the 'inevitable' extinction 'of the human species' (*U* 17.464–5), he is able to reduce the materiality of the cosmology to human knowledge. The oversized full stop that in certain editions of *Ulysses* draws the scientific reductionism of 'Ithaca' to a close, operates, as Eliot's Prufrock phrases it, to 'have squeezed the universe into a ball'.[68] Providing the answer to the episode's final question of 'Where?' (*U* 17.2331–2), it is one last example of the hyperbolic scientific rationalism and reductionism that has characterised the episode, not only operating as a final act of containment and certainty but offering a visual representation of all planetary space squeezed into a singular, neat, circular mark.[69] On one level, it is this scientific and ordered view of the planet that Molly takes her revenge on, not least since, although Joyce wrote in his notes that she should have 'no science words', she has an interest in the same planetary questions discussed in 'Ithaca'.[70] While Bloom looks out into the stars and tries to explain to Stephen the 'parallactic drift of socalled fixed stars' before turning to the subject of 'the eons of geological periods recorded in the stratifications of the earth' (*U* 17.1052–8), Molly questions what she calls the 'bad conscience' of 'atheists' who despite insisting on an objective basis for their claims, cannot say:

> who was the first person in the universe before there was anybody that made it all who ah that they dont know neither do I so there you are they might as well try to stop the sun from rising the sun shines for you he said (*U* 18.1569–72)

Here, the designation 'no science words' presents itself not as a lack (although it is true that Molly has been denied a formal education) so much as a suspicion towards the authority imbued in a word that has been deemed objective or beyond contestation. Molly's description of the universe, like Bloom's, asserts its prior existence to and diminishing effect on the figure of the human, but unlike Bloom she affirms its ability to endlessly escape any empirical definition that might assimilate it within an epistemological structure once and for all. In this, we might read a foreshadowing of Latour's argument that facts are indeed only 'the final results of very complex assemblages that allow reliable witnesses to validate the testimony of laboratory tests' and which must remain open to dispute.[71] Certainly, it is true that Molly affirms a deistic view of the universe. Yet, she also imagines the human as being wholly without the possibility of recourse to absolute knowledge of it, the desire for which taints Bloom's supposed scientific objectivity with a wish for Godlike omniscience. Even her misunderstanding that the sun orbits the Earth can be read as contributing to a reluctance towards the ordering and arranging that is the basis of a residual anthropocentrism in 'Ithaca'. And we should not forget that Bloom's scientism does not preclude his getting planetary facts wrong, for instance, describing the 'perpetual motion of the earth' as being in 'westward' rather than eastward motion (*U* 17.2307–10).

In form, too, 'Penelope' rejects a conventionally ordered cosmos. The episode's long, unpunctuated and ever-expanding sentences project a kaleidoscopic imaginary in which images and propositions incessantly emerge and dissipate. Moreover, in contrast to the episodes that precede it, which in various ways all present human characters against the narrative background of a material world, the most arresting and immediately differentiating quality of 'Penelope' is that Molly's voice is presented on the page without the stabilising frame of an external environment. The reader is confronted with having to make sense of the episode purely from Molly's voice. Unlike the presentation of human subjects placed in nonhuman environments that we find in earlier episodes, Molly's voice further collapses the distinction between subject and object, as the reader is presented with a monism in which nothing is external, since her words provide the context of the episode as well as its content. This framelessness coincides with Latour's insistence that there is 'nothing external in Gaia', since '[i]f climate and life have evolved together, space is not a frame, not even a context: *space is the offspring of time*'.[72] Although Latour might appear to privilege time over space here, his broader argument insists on an understanding of contingency in which the two co-produce each other and where neither time nor space develop along a determined, linear trajectory. A similar disruption to chronological time is produced through the spatiality of 'Penelope'. Joyce described 'Ithaca' as 'in reality the end as *Penelope* has no beginning, middle or end' (*JJL*1 172), an idea which finds its formal expression in the aforementioned design of the episode's syntactic invocation of infinity, as well as the circularity established through the repeated return to certain words and topics of concern. For Robert Spoo, who resists the idea of Molly as a 'monocausal deity, a Gea-Tellus' and instead reads Molly's monologue 'as perpetually imminent, *about* to coalesce into style and discourse but remaining forever on the edge of formulation', the episode stands not as the novel's 'telos' but as 'a ground from which forms emerge as meaning is discovered and isolated'.[73] Spoo's description of the monologue as the 'ground' from which meaning emerges highlights not only imminence but also the sense of immanence that arises from the episode's departure from chronological time. The clap of 'thunder' that earlier awoke Molly brings to mind the 'awful thunderbolts in Gibraltar' (*U* 18.134–5), drawing together the present, near past and Molly's youth in a single instance, as well as folding the geographies of Dublin and Gibraltar onto one another. This effect is repeated and amplified over the course of the episode, not least through the lack of punctuation that usually works to delineate and separate clauses that occupy different spatial or temporal locations. This culminates in the final section in which the use of repetition transposes different moments in time and space, imbricating one within another rather than safely spacing them apart, both on the page and in the narrative:

> and O that awful deepdown torrent O and the sea the sea crimson sometimes like fire and the glorious sunsets and the figtrees in the Alameda gardens yes [. . .] and then he asked me would I yes to say yes my mountain flower and first I put my arms around him yes and drew him down to me so he could feel my breasts all perfume yes and his heart was going like mad and yes I said yes I will Yes. (*U* 18.1598–9)

Even the repeated 'I' that grows and swells in these final moments of the episode serves not to mark out a position of transcendent space from which to observe the world but constitutes itself within an incessantly accretive bricolage of places and events remembered and imagined, far and near. Joyce's geo-story fundamentally challenges what it means to narrate in the same way that for Haraway, 'Gaia stories' bring to light how there 'are no guarantees, no arrow of time, no Law of History or Science or Nature' which can offer permanent or transcendent structures of meaning.[74] Where for Haraway, there is an urgent need to engage in creative and critical 'compositionist practices' that attend to ever co-evolving material relations between organisms and the planet they live on, in Joyce's design of Molly as the prehuman and posthuman voice of the earth we can detect a similar foregrounding of process, change and transformation, actualised in the unpunctuated forward movement of Molly's excessive, associative and affirmatory thrust.[75]

In contrast to the philosophical allusions of 'Proteus' that invoke a long history of feminising matter or the over-straining scientific diction of 'Ithaca' which looks to erase its own linguistic condition but ends up proliferating it, 'Penelope' portrays material subjectivity as inseparable from the language through which we articulate the idea of the human and its environment. Where both Stephen and Bloom offer a cosmological vision of the universe in which the human, always implicitly male, retains its status as a transcendent category, Molly as Gea-Tellus offers a planetary vision in which structures of meaning are passed over in favour of a view of life as emergent (both *pre-* and *post-*human), in which definitions are suspended in favour of attention to transformations and, perhaps most importantly in relation to the context of the narrative itself, in which a female voice can take revenge on those who have spoken for her. Richard Ellmann describes how Joyce almost concluded Molly's monologue with the words 'I will' but decided them to be 'too Luciferian', while the word 'yes' invoked a 'submission to a world beyond himself' as an 'acknowledgement of the universe'.[76] This affirmation of contingency, but also the limits of representation, is mirrored most clearly in the novel by Molly herself, for whom 'life' is 'always something to think about every moment and see it all around you like a new world' (*U* 18.738–9). As *Ulysses* repeatedly insinuates, the gap between new words and new worlds is slight.

An Earth which is Posthuman: Gaia in the *Wake*

The *OED* cites the first instance of the term 'posthuman' in a 1916 textbook entitled *Poverty and Social Progress* by the sociologist Maurice Farr Parmelee, but it is likely that for Joyce the term was a neologism that presented itself at the time of writing to Weaver about 'Penelope'.[77] Joyce's use, however, arguably stands as the more important inaugurating moment. As I have argued above, in the episode's attempt to reimagine how we might conceptualise the human and the planetary, Joyce's intention 'to depict the earth which is prehuman and presumably posthuman' (*JJL*1 180) foreshadows the rise of a posthumanist critical discourse premised on 'the dencentering of the human in relation to either evolutionary, ecological, or technological coordinates'.[78] Importantly, however, Joyce's posthumanist project did not end with Molly's concluding 'Yes' but continued into his final work, *Finnegans Wake*. As Jean-Michel Rabaté has argued, the idea of the 'posthuman' became central for Joyce in the years immediately following the publication of *Ulysses*. Having enabled Joyce to push Molly's 'character beyond [. . .] human psychology' so as to resemble the 'inhuman and posthuman figure of the revolving Earth', the notion of a 'posthuman earth' presented a range of aesthetic possibilities through which he might depart from the traditional constraints of plot and character.[79] Recent years have seen critics establish the degree to which *Finnegans Wake* should be considered a deeply ecological text. Alison Lacivita's *The Ecology of Finnegans Wake* (2015) has shown how studying the genetic development of the text brings to light Joyce's interest in the environmental questions facing Ireland in the 1920s and 30s, and, as Katherine Ebury argues, it is a book in which we see characters 'frequently and easily move between human and nonhuman identities', with 'Joyce definitively locat[ing] the *Wake* above and below the human scale'.[80] What is more, the ecological aesthetics of the *Wake* influenced Joyce's fellow modernist writers. As I discuss in the following chapter, the book's surfeit of animal figures was a key influence on Djuna Barnes's beastly literary experiments. In the final section of this chapter, however, I will focus on one specific aspect of Joyce's posthuman and ecological aesthetics in the *Wake*, examining how Joyce did not abandon the figure of Gaia in his final work, but developed it further in one final attempt to arrive at an aesthetics of materiality and immanence, and the implications for sex and gender that accompanied his decision to go beyond the limits of the human.

Insofar as the *Wake* can be considered to have characters, its five principal figures are Humphrey Chimpden Earwicker (HCE), his wife, Anna Livia Plurabelle (ALP), and their three children, twins Shem and Shaun, and daughter Issy. Rather than being self-contained individuals, however, these characters instead constantly transform into other entities and assemblages, each affiliated with a set of associations and characteristics. HCE is associated, at various points, with Ireland's mountains, burial mounds and cities, whereas ALP is primarily associated with Ireland's rivers (particularly the Liffey), flora and rural landscapes. Over the course of the book, HCE, as Adam Barrows suggests, tends to be aligned with a masculinist drive to order a feminised nature, with the natural world repeatedly 'suppressed and violated in order to make room for [HCE]' with nature 'symbolized most often, although not exclusively in the text, by ALP and by different forms of water'.[81] More explicitly than in *Ulysses*, this carries an environmental message, with Barrows arguing that the effect is a growing sense of an imminent catastrophe in 'humanity's compact with nature' so severe that 'there will be no future at all'.[82] Joyce's presentation of gender roles in *Finnegans Wake* has long been commented on, especially the way in which womanhood is associated with fertility and maternity, with recent attention being paid to the way in which the novel's sexual politics cannot be easily disentangled from its ecological aesthetic. While for Finn Fordham ALP is 'a force that makes civilization possible [. . .] by making fertile flood plains', for Bonnie Kime Scott, Joyce invites us to see in ALP 'the land of Ireland [. . .] subjected to bodily invasion'.[83] Like Molly, ALP is a posthuman Earth Mother, there to 'elp the ealth of the ole' (*FW* 76), the 'turf-brown mummy' (*FW* 194) not only of Shaun, Shem and Issy, but of everyone who relies on her fertile sustenance. Fluid and flowing, she is associated with nature's life-giving vitality, arriving on the scene 'ducking under bridges, bellhopping the weirs, dodging by a bit of bog [and] rapidshooting round the bends' as the 'giddy-gaddy, grannyma, gossipaceous Anna Livia' (*FW* 194–5).

Irreducible to any one cultural association or myth, Gaia nonetheless looms large within ALP's constellation of forms. At the end of I.4, a chapter largely focused on HCE, ALP arrives to the cry of 'Do tell us all about. As we want to hear allabout. So tellus tellas allabouter' (*FW* 101). Here, ALP as Tellus (the Roman name for Gaia) is invited to tell us all, yoking together the ancient Earth Mother and a chatty Dublin housewife, foreshadowing the opening moments of one of the book's most well-known passages, which centres on two gossiping washerwomen in the Liffey and begins with the sentence 'O tell me all about Anna Livia' (*FW* 196). Akin to Latour's insistence that 'Gaia has a thousand names' and that the only certainty that surrounds her is that 'she is not a figure of harmony', Joyce presents ALP as Tellus flowing into the narrative to *tell us* of HCE, his indiscretions and crimes, while also defending his innocence.[84] As with Molly, however, the question of whether ALP ultimately emerges as a figure who upends deep-rooted gender essentialisms or confirms them remains in tension. In II.2, the 'Nightlessons' chapter, ALP manifests as the 'eternal geomater' as Shaun and Shem complete their geometry homework (*FW* 296–7). As Joyce would have known, the prefix 'geo' in words such as geometry, geography and geology all derive from the same ancient Greek word which also gave Gaia her name.[85] Here ALP in the guise of the original geo-mother returns the abstraction of knowledge to the primordial substrate of the feminised and fertile Earth. As the twins work through their geometry problems, Shem suggests that they might find the solution by looking under their mother's skirt to 'see figuratleavely the whome of your eternal geomater' (*FW* 296–7). Gazing into the 'dark' cavernlike space the twins light a match to make out the 'flument, fluvey and fluteous [. . .] muddy old triagonal delta' of ALP (*FW* 297). As Borg helpfully glosses, in presenting 'a geometry problem the solution of which doubles as an anatomy of their mother's vulva' the passage combines the pure 'minimalist formalism [of geometry] with a natural, messy fecundity'.[86] Again, any opposition between meaning and materiality is deconstructed in the process, as abstract forms and living matter are each revealed to be composed of the other. In the same way that Molly as Gaia-Tellus stands as a figure of excessive materiality in opposition to Bloom's desire for a scientific meta-language that can order the universe, ALP returns the concepts and epistemological structures through which space and time are quantified to their material origins and insists on the impossibility of a purely abstract form of knowledge. That this knowledge is gained through the twins' desire to glimpse their mother's 'sluice' (*FW* 297) echoes both the blurred role of mother and mate in the Gaia myth in the *Theogony* and the suggestions of incest found throughout the *Wake*.[87] If, as Norris suggests, at the centre of the Nightlesson is 'the secret of procreation, a knowledge that will eventually enable [the child] to replace the father as creator', then in the figure of the 'Eternal Geomater', we find not an Oedipal myth so much as the fertile maternal soil whose 'constant of fluxion' is the guarantee of birth, reproduction and eventually death (*FW* 297).[88]

There is, however, a further Gaian dimension to the aesthetic of the *Wake*, one which relies less on entrenched figurations of gender (irrespective of how mutable they might be). In what Fordham suggests is its textual status as 'a wild natural object rather than as a constructed text to be understood', *Finnegans Wake*'s formal aesthetic parallels what Margulis describes as the consciousness of Gaia; a consciousness which relies not on cognition but is '[a]nalogous to proprioception', understood as the unconscious perception of the body itself.[89] A decentralised system that is self-generating through inexhaustible linguistic associations, multiple narratological layers and endless shifting figurations, *Finnegans Wake* resembles the unbounded and undirected proprioceptive liveliness of Gaia. As Latour states, in a description that could pass as advice for novice readers of *Finnegans Wake*, Gaia encourages us to 'follow the connections without being holistic'.[90] In this sense, we find that *Finnegans Wake*'s formal operations produce a kind of Gaian planetary system in which there is no centre or foundation, but only parts whose meaning emerge in relation to other parts.[91] We find this idea metonymically represented in the *Wake* itself, in ALP's letter exonerating her husband that is dug up from an 'organgeflavoured mudmound', or dung heap, by a hen (*FW* 111). Standing in for the text itself, this heap of composting waste offers both the hope of meaning in the form of a promised letter and a hot mess of decomposing material. Resembling what Haraway describes as 'a material-semiotic composting' or 'theory in the mud', it stands for the self-conscious experience of transforming meaning from matter that accompanies any encounter with *Finnegans Wake* itself.[92] Posthuman in the sense of going beyond a humanist division between meaning and materiality, in addition to all the other binaries it undoes in what Fordham calls its 'unravelling' of universals, the text offers a model of the decentred, dynamic and ever shifting processes of relation that characterise a Gaian understanding of the planet in which meaning emerges from the materiality to which it is destined to return.[93]

As in *Ulysses*, we do not find anywhere in *Finnegans Wake* a straightforward binary between masculine and feminine or culture and nature. Yet, while it is true that categories or identities are never stable for long in the novel, it is nonetheless also the case that certain figurations or principles reform over and over, almost as if there are natural laws within the cosmology of the book itself. In Joyce's presentation of ALP we find an echo of Stephen in 'Proteus', in her 'reminding uus ineluctably of nature at her naturalest' (*FW* 120), destined to forever slosh through time and space since 'Woman will water the wild world over' (*FW* 526). Danielle Sands, in a critique of Latour, has argued that the insistence on disunity that we find in Gaia theory in many respects re-enacts the 'historical perception of the female's lack of bodily integrity' while never making clear how this 'non-sovereignty could be translated into a form of agency that would evade recuperation by masculine sovereignty'.[94] A sympathetic feminist reading of *Finnegans Wake* might suggest there is an implicit environmental message in the moments where HCE appears in pursuit to tame and master ALP, at which points the text's broader aesthetic of disunity and multiplicity position the reader to side with vitalism and flow over reason and order. Yet, as ALP flows out in the unfinished sentence at the end of the book to join the unfinished sentence at its beginning, the novel concludes, as with Molly's final word, by insisting on a gendered association of woman with earth and life. Margulis, who as I stated above, co-developed Gaia theory with Lovelock from the 1970s onward, was never a great fan of the metaphor he had picked, writing in 1998 that in her mind it was just 'a convenient name for an Earthwide phenomenon'.[95] Like Haraway's attempt to transform Gaia from a singular goddess into a queer planet-wide litter of chthonic ones, Margulis's description is a reminder that it should always be asked whose interests are being served in the metaphors and figures through which we imagine the planet, as well as the possibility of always imagining it differently. In Joyce's decision to radically rewrite the historic woman/nature association in Molly and, later, ALP, through the figure of Gaia, we find a modernist mode of writing that could scrutinise, lampoon but also, in some respects, entrench a gendered planetary imaginary. Whether in Molly taking revenge as Gaia-Tellus or in the vitalism of *Finnegans Wake*'s formal disunity, Joyce's writing presents the reader with both the possibilities and the limitations that accompany the re-emergence of Gaia within the Anthropocene.

Notes

1. Valery Larbaud, 'The *Ulysses* of James Joyce', *The Criterion*, 1.1 (1922), 94–103 (p. 103).
2. Ezra Pound, *Pound/Joyce: The Letters of Ezra Pound to James Joyce, with Pound's Essays on Joyce*, ed. Forrest Read (New York: New Directions Books, 1967), p. 198.
3. T. S. Eliot, *Selected Prose*, ed. Frank Kermode (New York: Harcourt Brace Jovanovich Farrar, Straus and Giroux, 1975), p. 177.
4. Stuart Gilbert, *James Joyce's 'Ulysses': A Study* (London: Penguin Books, 1963), pp. 339–40. 'Penelope' is not assigned a symbol in Joyce's earlier Linati schema.
5. Suzette A. Henke and Elaine Unkeless, 'Introduction', in *Women in Joyce*, ed. Suzette A. Henke and Elaine Unkeless (Brighton: The Harvester Press, 1982), pp. xi–xxii (p. xii).
6. James Lovelock, *The Revenge of Gaia: Why the Earth Is Fighting Back – and How We Can Still Save Humanity* (London: Penguin Books, 2007), p. 19.
7. James Lovelock, *Gaia: A New Look at Life on Earth*, rev. edn (Oxford: Oxford University Press, 2000), p. ix; p. xiv.
8. Ibid. p. xiv.
9. Bruno Latour, *Facing Gaia: Eight Lectures on the New Climatic Regime*, trans. Catherine Porter (Cambridge: Polity, 2017), p. 98; p. 86.

10. Confusion on this topic has been partially fuelled by the fact that Lovelock has himself appeared to propound this view in several of his books.
11. Lynn Margulis, *The Symbiotic Planet: A New Look at Evolution* (London: Phoenix, 1999), pp. 155–8.
12. Isabelle Stengers, *In Catastrophic Times: Resisting the Coming Barbarism*, trans. Andrew Goffey (Ann Arbor, MI: Open Humanities Press, 2015), p. 45; p. 53.
13. Lovelock, *Revenge of Gaia*, p. 21.
14. Ibid. p. 188.
15. Katherine Ebury, *Modernism and Cosmology: Absurd Lights* (Basingstoke: Palgrave Macmillan, 2014), pp. 66–99; Ruben Borg, 'Figures of the Earth: Non-Human Phenomenology in Joyce', *Humanities*, 6.3 (2017) <www.mdpi.com/2076-0787/6/3/71> (last accessed 22 February 2021).
16. Margulis, *The Symbiotic Planet*, pp. 148–9.
17. Donna Haraway, *Staying with the Trouble: Making Kin in the Chthulucene* (Durham, NC: Duke University Press, 2016), p. 175.
18. Aristotle, *The Complete Works of Aristotle*, ed. Jonathan Barnes, rev. edn (Oxford: Oxford University Press, 1995), p. 2500. Laura Lovejoy has highlighted the degree to which this Aristotelian binary remains at play in *Finnegans Wake*. See Laura Lovejoy, 'The Bestial Feminine in *Finnegans Wake*', *Humanities*, 6.3 (2017) <https://www.mdpi.com/2076-0787/6/3/58> (last accessed 25 February 2021).
19. Borg, 'Figures of the Earth', n.p.
20. Molly also reiterates Stephen's metaphor when she describes her menstrual blood as 'pouring out of me like the sea' (*U* 18.1123).
21. Borg, 'Figures of the Earth', n.p.
22. Donna Haraway, 'Situated Knowledges: The Science Question in Feminism and the Privilege of Partial Perspective', *Feminist Studies*, 14.3 (1988), 575–99 (p. 588).
23. Maud Ellmann, '*Ulysses*: The Epic of the Human Body', in *A Companion to James Joyce*, ed. Richard Brown (Oxford: Wiley-Blackwell, 2011), pp. 54–70 (p. 67).
24. Bonnie Kime Scott, *Joyce and Feminism* (Bloomington: Indiana University Press, 1984), p. 10.
25. James Joyce, *Ulysses: A Critical and Synoptic Edition*, ed. Hans Walter Gabler, Wolfhard Steppe and Claus Melchior (New York: Garland Publishing, 1984), p. 414.
26. Scott, *Joyce and Feminism*, p. 10; p. 280.
27. Emer Nolan argues that *Ulysses* is consciously writing back to a historical tendency to deploy symbols of femininity and maternity onto 'national territory'. See Emer Nolan, *James Joyce and Nationalism* (New York: Routledge, 1995), p. 167.
28. Borg, 'Figures of the Earth', n.p.
29. Joyce, *Ulysses: A Critical and Synoptic Edition*, p. 804.
30. Rosi Braidotti, *Transpositions: On Nomadic Ethics* (Cambridge: Polity, 2006), p. 247.
31. Rosi Braidotti, *Posthuman Knowledge* (Cambridge: Polity, 2019), p. 51.
32. Richard Ellmann, *James Joyce* (Oxford: Oxford University Press, 1983), p. 324.
33. James Joyce, *Poems and Exiles*, ed. J. C. C Mays (London: Penguin Books, 1992), p. 228.

34. James Joyce, *Joyce's 'Ulysses' Notesheets in the British Museum*, ed. Phillip Herring (Charlottesville: University Press of Virginia, 1972), p. 494.
35. T. S. Eliot, *Collected Poems 1909 – 1962* (New York: Harcourt, Brace & World, Inc., 1963), p. 80; D. H. Lawrence, *The Rainbow*, ed. Mark Kinkead-Weekes (London: Penguin Books, 1995), pp. 192–3.
36. *Myths of Hellas* was a popular re-telling of the Greek myths, originally in German by the philologist Carl Witt of the Alstadt Gymansium at Königsberg and translated into English by Frances Younghusband.
37. Hesiod, *Theogony and Works and Days*, trans. Catherine M. Schlegel and Henry Weinfeld (Ann Arbor: University of Michigan Press, 2010), pp. 26–7.
38. Christiane Sourvinou-Inwood, 'Gaia, Gē', *The Oxford Classical Dictionary*, Oxford University Press < https://oxfordre.com/classics> (last accessed 22 September 2020).
39. Latour, *Facing Gaia*, p. 83.
40. The Rock of Gibraltar was called Mons Calpe by the Romans.
41. There is, of course, a long history of equating dark skin with primordial origins in the West. Vincent Cheng's *Joyce, race, and empire* examines race in Joyce at length, including a chapter that addresses Bloom's characterisation in *Ulysses* as a 'dark horse' (*U* 12.1557).
42. Gilbert, *James Joyce's 'Ulysses'*, p. 336.
43. Ibid. pp. 339–40.
44. Ibid. p. 340. Gilbert noticeably occludes all references to Molly's menstruation. As Van Boheemen-Saaf has argued, Molly's blood arguably stages not a celebration of fertility but a modern anxiety around its disappearance. Christine Van Boheemen-Saaf, 'Joyce's Answer to Philosophy: Writing the Dematerializing Object', in *Joyce, 'Penelope' and the Body*, ed. Richard Brown (Amsterdam: Rodopi, 2006), pp. 31–46 (p. 46).
45. Gilbert, *James Joyce's* 'Ulysses', p. 341.
46. Ibid. pp. 339–42.
47. Ibid. p. 339.
48. Lovelock, *Gaia*, p. xiv.
49. Gilbert, *James Joyce's* 'Ulysses', p. 342.
50. Henke and Unkeless, 'Introduction', p. xii.
51. Richard Ellmann, *Ulysses on the Liffey* (Oxford: Oxford University Press, 1982), p. 166.
52. Kathleen McCormick, 'Reproducing Molly Bloom: A Revisionist History of "Penelope", 1922-1970', in *Molly Blooms: A Polylogue on 'Penelope' and Cultural Studies*, ed. Richard Pearce (Madison: University of Wisconsin Press, 1994), pp. 17–39 (p. 20).
53. Hélène Cixous, 'The Laugh of the Medusa', trans. Keith Cohen and Paula Cohen, *Signs*, 1.4 (1976), 875–93 (p. 889).
54. Ibid. pp. 875–6.
55. Ibid. p. 879.
56. Catriona Sandilands, *The Good Natured Feminist: Ecofeminism and the Quest for Democracy* (Minneapolis: University of Minnesota Press, 1999), pp. 6–7.

57. Ursula K. Heise, *Sense of Place and Sense of Planet: The Environmental Imagination of the Global* (Oxford: Oxford University Press, 2008), p. 24.
58. Maud Ellmann, '"Penelope" Without the Body', in *Joyce, 'Penelope' and the Body*, pp. 97–108 (p. 103).
59. Danielle Sands, 'Gaia, Gender, and Sovereignty in the Anthropocene', *philoSOPHIA*, 5.2 (2015), 287–307 (pp. 288–93).
60. See Sandilands for a survey of some critical responses to ecofeminism. Sandilands, *The Good Natured Feminist*, pp. xvi-ii.
61. For an overview of the heterogeneity of approaches this encompasses see Richard Brown (ed.), *Joyce, 'Penelope' and the Body* (2006) and Richard Pearce (ed.), *Molly Blooms: A Polylogue on "Penelope" and Cultural Studies* (1994).
62. Sands, 'Gaia, Gender, and Sovereignty in the Anthropocene', pp.290–1.
63. Haraway, *Staying with the Trouble*, p. 43.
64. 'Becoming with' is Haraway's preferred ontological term to 'becoming'. She develops this concept at length in *When Species Meet* (Minneapolis: University of Minnesota Press, 2007).
65. Haraway, *Staying with the Trouble*, pp. 51–2; p. 41.
66. Ibid. p. 40.
67. Margot Norris, *Virgin and Veteran Readings of 'Ulysses'* (New York: Palgrave Macmillan, 2011), p. 229.
68. T. S. Eliot, *Collected Poems*, p. 6.
69. As critics such as Vike Martina Plock have pointed out, the form and content of 'Ithaca' is also defined by expansion, meaning that Bloom's reductionism is always ironically undermined by its momentum. Plock, *Joyce, Medicine and Modernity* (Gainesville: University Press of Florida, 2010), pp. 127–9.
70. Joyce, *'Ulysses' Notesheets*, p. 491.
71. Latour, *Facing Gaia*, p. 164.
72. Ibid. p. 106, emphasis in original.
73. Robert Spoo, *James Joyce and the Language of History: Dedalus's Nightmare* (Oxford: Oxford University Press, 1994), p. 78, emphasis in original.
74. Haraway, *Staying with the Trouble*, pp. 40–1.
75. Ibid. pp. 40–1.
76. Richard Ellmann, *James Joyce*, p. 522.
77. 'Posthuman', in *OED Online* <www.oed.com/view/Entry/263433> (last accessed 23 October 2020).
78. Cary Wolfe, *What Is Posthumanism?* (Minneapolis: University of Minnesota Press, 2010), p. xvi.
79. Jean-Michel Rabaté, *Think, Pig!: Beckett at the Limit of the Human* (New York: Fordham University Press, 2016), pp. 38–9.
80. Ebury, 'Joyce's Non-Human Ecologies' forthcoming in *New Joyce Studies*, ed. Catherine Flynn. My thanks to the author for sharing this work with me in advance of its publication.
81. Adam Barrows, 'Joyce's Panarchy: Time, Ecological Resilience, and *Finnegans Wake*', *James Joyce Quarterly*, 51.2–3 (2014), 333–52 (pp. 337–8).
82. Ibid. p. 339.

83. Finn Fordham, '*Finnegans Wake*: Novel and Anti-Novel', in *A Companion to James Joyce*, pp. 71–89 (p. 80); Bonnie Kime Scott, 'Joyce, Ecofeminism and the River as Woman', in *Eco-Joyce: The Environmental Imagination of James Joyce*, ed. Robert Brazeau and Derek Gladwin (Cork: Cork University Press, 2014), pp. 56–69 (p. 66).
84. Latour, *Facing Gaia*, p. 82.
85. Margulis, *The Symbiotic Planet*, p. 147.
86. Borg, 'Figures of the Earth', n.p.
87. We find this connection elsewhere in the *Wake* too. HCE is describe as 'heaven-gendered, chaosfoedted, earthborn' (*FW* 137), occupying the roles of Uranus and Chaos and, therefore, offspring and mate.
88. Margot Norris, *The Decentered Universe of 'Finnegans Wake': A Structuralist Analysis* (Baltimore: Johns Hopkins University Press, 1977), p. 46.
89. Fordham, '*Finnegans Wake*', p. 75; Margulis, *The Symbiotic Planet*, p. 158.
90. Latour, *Facing Gaia*, p. 97. Norris's *The Decentered Universe of 'Finnegans Wake'* was one of the first studies to suggest that the *Wake* should be not read in terms of an organic unity or totality.
91. Erin Walsh has similarly proposed that the puns of the *Wake* suggest 'a model for an ecological discourse'. Walsh, 'Word and World: The Ecology of the Pun in *Finnegans Wake*', in *Eco-Joyce: The Environmental Imagination of James Joyce*, pp. 70–90 (p. 70).
92. Haraway, *Staying with the Trouble*, p. 31. Haraway prefers the term 'composthumanism' to 'posthumanism', which also finds an affinity with the *Wake*.
93. Finn Fordham, *Lots of Fun at 'Finnegans Wake': Unravelling Universals* (Oxford: Oxford University Press, 2007), p. 33.
94. Sands, 'Gaia, Gender, and Sovereignty in the Anthropocene', p. 293; p. 302.
95. Margulis, *The Symbiotic Planet*, p. 150.

3

THE BEASTLY WRITING OF DJUNA BARNES

What does it mean to be, as Robin Vote is described in Djuna Barnes's *Nightwood* (1936), a 'beast turning human' (*N* 33)? As Rachel Potter notes, it is a description that draws attention to both continuity and difference between humans and beasts, operating as a linguistic construction that foregrounds an uncertain relation between the two.[1] An example of the idiomatic language that produces *Nightwood*'s unsettling and often obscure presentation of animals and humans, it is an image of transgression and contamination that resists being understood in any singular sense. Yet, whether we understand this image of a 'beast turning human' in terms of an evolutionary temporality, a physical transformation, or a change in temperament or personality, what remains at stake is the question of what it means to be recognised as human. As I outlined in my introduction, the Anthropocene in its very name similarly brings into crisis ideas of the human. It is a concept that both centres and decentres the human, foregrounding both humanity's exceptionalism as a species that can shape planetary systems, but also its precariousness in that, like all other animals, it is wholly dependent on those systems for survival. Adapting Barnes's phrase, we might say that the Anthropocene represents the planet turning human, a turning that, as with Robin, suggests we need to revise how we understand both terms. Indeed, for Sverre Raffnsøe the 'shift in the situation of the human, and in the very quality of being human' accelerated by the Anthropocene precisely constitutes a 'human turn'. That is, at the same time that 'world seems to have turned towards the human, insofar as the human being is perceived as having a decisive impact on even very fundamental conditions in the world [. . .] the human being [. . .] turns towards itself, as it investigates, articulates and redefines its own role'.² The Anthropocene brings into crisis the idea of humanity as a stable or transcendent category, or what Rosi Braidotti calls an understanding of '"Man" as the universal humanistic measure of all things' and, as suggested in Barnes's image of Robin, requires us to think of ourselves in relation to all the other-than-human subjects that often serve as oppositional categories through which we define ourselves.³

The question of what it means to be human in the Anthropocene requires us to rethink not only about what it means to have evolved into the species we have become, but also the implications for those other species with whom we have co-evolved and who remain, to use Donna Haraway's term, entangled in 'ongoing multispecies stories' with us.⁴ At stake in the Anthropocene is a question of our collective identity as and alongside other animals. Indeed, our relationship with other animals is one of the beastly markers of the Anthropocene, whether in the form of the fossil record left behind by the 65 billion broiler chickens consumed each year or the methane produced by cattle livestock populations that contributes to climate change.⁵ For Barnes, the question of what it means to be a beast, whether human or otherwise, was not limited to the animal imagery and metaphors that populate the pages of *Nightwood*. An interest in questions of animality and species, nearly always bound up with questions of sex, gender and sexuality, were a mainstay of her activities as a writer. From the journalism, poetry, drama and short fiction that she produced in the 1910s and early 1920s, through her major fiction of the 1920s and 1930s, and into the late drama and poetry that she produced from the 1940s until her death in 1982, beastly figures, animal bodies, and more-than-human encounters occur over and over again. Indeed, as readers of Barnes have observed, an interest in animal life and species discourse is integral to her modernist aesthetic. Jane Marcus's memorable description of *Nightwood*'s 'modernism of marginality', for instance, associates what she sees as the text's transgressive sexual politics with its carnivalesque presentation of animality, primitiveness and abjection.⁶ Barnes's writing in this respect contributes to a body of modernist works which Carrie Rohman has argued were jolted by a 'post-Darwinian crisis in humanist identity' into a 'dramatic reckoning with the animal' and which, for Margot Norris, inaugurated what she terms a 'biocentric tradition'.⁷ For Rohman, the figure of Robin in *Nightwood* challenges a brand of humanism that would safely separate the human from the animal, with her silence in the novel indicative of a 'non-identity' that challenges the logocentrism that upholds human exceptionalism.⁸ Moreover, while Barnes's work has benefitted from the turn to animals in literary studies more broadly, in its ability to, as Bonnie Kime Scott frames it, 'blu[r] the distinctions between the human and the animal', it would be more correct to see her writing as prefiguring the concerns and debates that have emerged under the heading of animal studies.⁹ In the image of the beast turning human, we find an invitation to reconsider the proximity between humans and animals, as well as the epistemological, ontological, and aesthetical distinctions that have been constructed over time in order to hold them apart.

Yet, while animal-orientated approaches might now be considered a fairly well-established way of reading *Nightwood*, less attention has been given to how species discourse figures in Barnes's broader oeuvre,[10] and even less attention has been paid to the way in which the material collected in her archive complicates, substantiates or sheds new light on her animal figures.[11] In this chapter, I look at a range of Barnes's published and unpublished writing to explore how she fashions a language of beasts and beastliness in order to interrogate the figure of the human. The research in this chapter draws on the manuscripts, notebooks, letters, textual annotations and clippings that Barnes amassed over the course of her life, showing how reading her back through her archive not only confirms a lifelong interest in animals and animality, but reveals that questions around the nonhuman were central to her literary practices. If Barnes's image of Robin as a 'beast turning human' has been singled out as a moment that threatens a humanist fantasy of autonomy and exceptionalism, this chapter will show how throughout her writerly life Barnes developed a beastly aesthetic that called into question human identity. Moreover, to call Barnes's oeuvre beastly, this chapter contends, is to draw attention to a specific set of figurations and literary strategies. As Derrida insisted in his final seminar, posthumously published as *The Beast & the Sovereign*, 'the beast is not exactly the animal'; it has cultural connotations, linguistic implications and aesthetic traditions that are related to, but distinct from the broader category of 'the animal'.[12] If 'the animal' is too often a 'hypostatic fiction', the figure of the beast and the adjectival quality of beastliness are less determined, more open to contestations and transgressions that worry the notion of categorisation itself.[13] Showing how we might read Barnes's beastly tropes across and through her texts, and charting how these tropes change and take on new dimensions depending on the (con)textual space in which they are presented provides, this chapter argues, a way of better understanding the themes of interspecies contamination, transformation and queerness that recur through her work. Turning to Barnes's beasts might, in this sense, offer a new way of thinking about the Anthropocene's human turn.

Following Beastly Trails

Beasts are of clear centrality to Barnes's oeuvre. They appear again and again in her writing, often with contrasting connotations and meanings. In her 1913 article on Coney Island for the *Brooklyn Daily Eagle*, for example, resort attendants are likened to zoo animals as they pace 'back and forth' like 'dim beasts' in front of a restless crowd of pleasure seekers waiting to enter, who are in turn described in terms of an animalised physicality (*NY* 33).[14] Barnes's presentation of beastly resemblances among New York's lower classes, reflective of a broader discourse that equated the masses with an unthinking animality, also finds expression in the short fiction she was writing at the time. In 'The Coward' (1917), Monk, a professional criminal and member of the New York underworld, is described as 'an ugly beast', his grotesque presence causing those around him to feel 'physical pain . . . [and] repulsion' (*CS* 167; 159). Foreshadowing the way in which Robin's beastly animality in *Nightwood* will make those who meet her feel 'the structure of [their] head and jaws ache' (*N* 34), Monk's beastliness is presented in terms of an atavistic regression that threatens to contaminate those who encounter him. Beastliness, however, takes on a different set of meanings in 'Oscar', Barnes's 1920 story for the *Little Review*, where the arrival of the eponymous child murderer is prefigured in the story's opening description of frequent 'speeches in the town hall on the mark of the beast, sin, and democracy' (*CS* 279). Here, 'the' beast, given the definite article, is associated with a set of biblical allusions, restaging St John's vision of the arrival of the beast in the Book of Revelation. Like Yeats's contemporaneous image of the 'rough beast' that '[s]louches towards Bethlehem' in 'The Second Coming' (1920), it traces an apocalyptic imaginary over modern history.[15] Such images reveal the influence of a biblical literary tradition on Barnes's beasts, shaped by her keen reading in Dante, Milton and Blake, among others. As Daniela Caselli has pointed out, in the image of Robin as 'beast turning human' we might read an intentional reversal of John Donne's humans who 'turne beasts' in *Satyre IV* and, reversing the biblical teleology, an obscene avowal of the beastly origins of human life.[16]

While beasts and beastliness carry charges of atavism and apocalypse in Barnes's work, they also take on associations with the desiring body. The posthumously published 1923 lyric 'Love and the Beast', dedicated to Natalie Clifford Barney, figures a spurned lover as a beast 'Pacing down mortality | With a lost, immortal cry' (*CP* 101). Decades later, in an untitled fragment from her Patchin Place period, where poems were constantly being redrafted, we find a similar expression of desire figured in the imperative, 'Say I am a beast | lowing in the isle of my dimension'.[17] In both instances, beastliness is aligned with isolation and suffering, expressed through a non-linguistic cry, an animal sound that not only exceeds language but suggests the paucity of language's ability to contain or fully represent emotion and feeling. It is an idea which circles back to the beastly silence associated with Robin in *Nightwood*, which, as Rohman has argued, is representative of a break with the logocentric economies that underpin an ontology which is not only anthropocentric, but heteronormative and patriarchal.[18] Indeed, beastliness as a figure of queer sexuality is present throughout Barnes's 1920s writings. In 'Dusie' (1927), a story that looks ahead to *Nightwood* in many respects, the young and anonymous

Dusie, who finds herself at the centre of a lesbian coterie, is treated like a 'pet or beast' according to the feelings of the people around her (*CS* 406). Barnes's *Ladies Almanack*, privately published a year later in 1928, noticeably does not use the word beast, but nonetheless insinuates an uncertain contiguity between female sexuality and beastliness, with Dame Musset (loosely based on Barney) described as having 'mooed with the Herd, her Heels with their Hoofs, and in the wet Dingle hooted' (*LA* 15). Here, the hoofed Dame Musset hooting in the dingle takes on the form of a beast in the word's colloquial meaning to refer to cattle. An association between women and cattle takes on starkly different sexual politics in Barnes's novel *Ryder* published in the same year. As I discuss in more detail in the following chapter, *Ryder*'s critique of patriarchal conventions that associate female sexuality and livestock constitutes a key element of the novel's feminist aesthetic. Similarly, in the late lyric-drama *The Antiphon* (1958), Barnes returns to the same subject and autobiographical material, drawn from her own unconventional childhood on a farmstead. Here, the lead character Miranda describes her dead father's 'monstrous act of polygamy' as a means by which he could 'beast' those around him while, in contrast, 'woman is most beast familiar' (*A* 110; 176). In these examples beastliness articulates both potential forms of female sexual agency and the painful limits to such formations, sharing a language with a misogynistic fantasy that associates women with an idea of animal bodies that can be taken at will.

If there is an aesthetic principle that loosely binds all of the beastly tropes in Barnes's modernist bestiary, it is the proximity of the beastly to the grotesque.[19] Barnes's human beasts are invariably figured through what Mikhail Bakhtin described as the 'combination of human and animal traits' that define the grotesque, in which the human is not a stable entity, but a 'phenomenon in transformation, an as yet unfinished metamorphosis of death and birth, growth and becoming'.[20] Indeed, this grotesque quality of *Nightwood* was observed at the time of its publication. In a largely admiring review of the novel for *The Tablet* that Barnes retained a cutting from, Graham Greene compared the book to *Ulysses*, drawing on the novel's own language to describe its 'sometimes obscene, though never pornographic "gaudy, cheap cuts from the beast life"'.[21] Barnes's characterisation, Greene rightly observes, is premised on obscene transgression. Robin is figured as 'outside the "human type" [. . .] a wild thing caught in a woman's skin' (*N* 131), a woman who has 'the long unqualified range in the iris of wild beasts who have not tamed the focus down to meet the human eye' and who 'carrie[s] the quality of "way back" as animals do' (*N* 33–4). Robin's seductiveness to those around her is presented in terms of an atavistic allure that not only associates the sexual and bodily with the animal but threatens to reveal that the idea of civilised human identity premised on separation from the animal is but a thin veneer. As Scott argues, *Nightwood* presents the 'beast as the other of the human [. . .] and provides it with a sense of origin', undermining the binaries that separate the human from the animal.[22]

Yet, while Scott sees the beast in terms of a disruption to a humanist binary, Barnes's work resists readings that emphasise a schematic or allegorical understanding of her beastly figures. In the two pages of corrections she sent to the prospective Italian translator of *Nightwood*, Bruno Maffi, in 1948, Barnes explicitly dispels the notion of 'the beast' as a self-identical or coherent figure. Responding to Maffi's query regarding a metaphor offered by the unlicensed doctor Matthew O'Connor, in which he likens the loss of innocence to a 'child going small in the claws of a beast' (*N* 75), Barnes corrects Maffi's use of the definite article: it is 'a (not *the*) beast' she instructs him.[23] Here, the definite article is replaced by the indefinite, both in the implication that this is one of perhaps many beasts, but also in the sense of semantic indefinability. 'I can't give an exact account of the phrase', Barnes goes on to explain, '[it] has to be understood as it stands'.[24] The difference between *the* beast and *a* beast is considerable. While the former is open to the criticism that Derrida makes of the term 'the animal' as a false (and even asinine) philosophical category through which humans negatively construct themselves, the latter implies a multiplicity and heterogeneity that escapes binary oppositions.[25] Indeed, the heterogeneity of the term is precisely what Barnes's instructions to Maffi insist upon: since the phrase is in an important sense untranslatable, in that it can only be understood 'as it stands', the translation must necessarily bestialise the original English and become something beastly itself.

As captured in Barnes's ironic statement in a letter to Natalie Clifford Barney that, for the modernist writers who lived to see the 1960s, it was a 'beastly time for beasts', Barnes's beasts are never wholly identical with themselves or inherently unequivocal constructions.[26] They are themselves beastly, roaming about and transgressing semantic boundaries. Indeed, Barnes was conscious of the mutability of beastly figures during the composition of *Nightwood* itself. Writing to Emily Coleman in 1935, Barnes suggested that *Night Beast* (noticeably without either the definite or indefinite article) would be a fitting title for the novel if it was not for 'the debased meaning now put on that nice word beast'.[27] Bearing in mind the circumstances around the publication of her first novel, *Ryder*, in which passages had been expurgated by the publisher due to anxieties around censorship, the degree to which Barnes's comments on debasement in this letter should be understood as ironic has previously been overlooked by critics.[28] Debasement, which shares an etymological commonality with 'beast' in that both historically describe a sense of lowness, finds direct expression in *Nightwood*, not only explicitly invoked in chapter titles such as 'Bow Down' (another early title for the novel) and 'Go Down, Matthew' and in Robin's act of going down alongside the dog in the novel's final moments, but also in what Kenneth Burke identified to be the novel's structural 'transcendence downwards'.²⁹ Here, to be beastly is to be low not only in the sense of being close to the earth like all other animals but in the euphemistic associations of transgression and debasement suggested within such beastly acts of going down.

This lowness and debasement also gives Barnes's beastly aesthetic a discernible interspecies charge. Robin's beastly descent sees her repeatedly likened to animals by other characters; she is, as O'Connor puts it, like 'an animal, born at the opening of the eye, going only forward, and at the end of the day, shutting out memory with the dropping of the lid' (N 122). Yet, as with her husband Felix, O'Connor's description of Robin largely works towards a sentimental and romanticised notion of her perceived animality. Robin is simultaneously a figure of human animality, a reminder of the human *as* animal, but also an exoticised figure of sexual otherness. In this latter role, Robin serves as the negative image of those around her, allowing them to feel more fully human because of their difference to her. It is in this sense that *Nightwood* foregrounds the historical tensions between 'beastly' as a word that denotes the human as animal and as a pejorative term that works to displace animality. The OED's two foremost definitions of 'beastly' go some way toward capturing the contradictions at play here. The first definition gives beastly as 'the nature of living creatures (including man); animal, natural, "carnal"'. This is what might be summarised as animal life in general. The second definition, in direct contradiction, situates beastly as 'pertaining to the lower animals (as opposed to man); merely animal, bestial'.³⁰ Here, beastliness is the animal kingdom which the human stands outside of. With both definitions having been in use since at least the fourteenth century, and as Barnes's characterisation of Robin affirms, beastliness is a concept without essence or foundations, its linguistic and aesthetic agency operating as a site of contested meaning that simultaneously acknowledges and displaces human animality.

Barnes's ability to exploit beastliness as a mode that foregrounds an undecidability around the status of the human also structures her earlier novel, *Ryder*. As Alex Goody notes, the novel insists on the close 'proximities of grotesque bodies' in its presentation of life on a rural farmstead, where humans and animals are repeatedly juxtaposed and brought into close contact, unsettling 'the boundaries of the subject and the proper body'.³¹ We see this not only in the novel's imagery of humans and animals living alongside each other, but in the linguistic attention to the contradictions inherent to constructions of beastliness. The polygamy of Wendell Ryder, the farm's eccentric patriarch, is excused by his mother, Sophia, on the basis that he 'lust[s] openly and sweetly like [. . .] the beast of the field', implicitly insisting upon the human's place within a natural, animal state (R 238). A little later, however, having advised him that he should leave one of his two wives since he risks being prosecuted for bigamy, Sophia warns him that if he ignores her advice he will 'fall alone' and 'be as the beast', a description that positions beastliness in terms of a moral fallenness (*R* 239). Here, being 'like [...] the beast' and 'as the beast' take on oppositional meanings in the space of a few paragraphs. The former is a description of beastliness whose proper applicability is to nonhuman animals and in which to act beastly is to be animalised. The latter essentially reverses this, in which beastly behaviour, since it implies a moral transgression, is that which is only proper to the human. We see this contradiction elsewhere in the novel. The livestock are figured as 'beasts' luxuriating in a brute innocence that affords them a 'holy look' in their eyes, insisting on beastliness as a space of animality outside of the human, yet a short while later when Wendell is accused of being a 'beast' by his legal wife, Amelia, it is precisely because of the lack of morals that, as a human, he should have (*R* 187; 224). Beastliness, as such, is not simply a description of animal characteristics in either a general or specific sense. Instead, it functions to signify a mode of properness or improperness as it relates to perceived ideas around the body and moral behaviour that include but extend beyond human life.

What might be described as Barnes's beastly deployment of beasts in her writing foregrounds what Derrida would later describe as the inherent undecidability of *la bête* and the way in which its overdetermination always complicates the question of 'what is proper to the beast'. Identifying how *la bête* can be used to describe stupidity, Derrida identifies the irony that the attribute of being *bête*, being beastly stupid, is 'appropriate only to a person' not an animal since to be *bête* is to lack the sense or intellect, which, according to dominant humanist and theological paradigms, are the exclusive domains of the human.[32] In both Derrida's and Barnes's foregrounding of such contradictions inherent to a beastly language, what emerges is that the beast, unlike the animal, does not work towards a categorising function. Rather than simply subverting binary oppositions, the beast points to slippages between categorical definitions and their inability to contain what they purport to define. In the same speech wherein Sophia likens Wendell to the beast of the fields, she asserts that a 'woman can be civilized beyond civilization and she can be beast beyond beast' (*R* 238), a description that emphasises the potentially infinitely circular logic and ungroundedness of the appellation. As in *Nightwood*, where the bestial figures as an excessive site of anxiety around the human body, but particularly the female body, and its relation to and difference from other animals, beastliness correlates not to a certain subject position but the processes of affiliation and displacement through which subjects are formed.

Creaturely Life and Beastly Violence

If Barnes's beasts do have an oppositional aesthetic, it is not so much towards the human, since, as I have already shown, the human is bound up with all sorts of beastly operations and negations, but rather the creature. The figure of the creature has seen its critical stock rise in recent years, with discourse around the creaturely emerging as one of the central paradigms through which categories of life have been theorised within literary studies, animal studies and biopolitical theory. Tobias Menely, offering an overview of the way in which the creaturely has gained purchase within the humanities, suggests that the figure's origin is in Walter Benjamin's notion of creaturely life in *The Origin of German Tragic Drama* (1928). The Benjaminian creature, Menely explains, approaches human animal life through terms of relationality and vulnerability, characterised 'above all by the supplanting of eschatological with natural-historical time'. In place of grand historical human narratives, creaturely time asserts a 'natural world bereft of transcendental signature or promise'.[33] In recent work within animal studies, this Benjaminian creatureliness has provided the basis for a trans-species ethics.[34] As David Herman writes, slightly modifying the term, the 'creatural' foregrounds our 'status of being a creature, subject to the requirements of the surrounding environment, the vicissitudes of time, and the vulnerabilities of the body' and 'emphasizes the fundamental continuity between humans and other animals'.[35] For Anat Pick, who takes her figure of the creaturely from Simone Weil as well as Benjamin, the creaturely names the condition of being a 'living body – material, temporal, and vulnerable', and like Herman, it is ultimately this vulnerability that, in operating as a 'universal mode of exposure', might help us rethink the human and its animal others.[36]

Arguably, the most prominent and widely influential example of the creaturely within animal studies is to be found in the work of a theorist who does not use the term at all. Donna Haraway's concept of 'critters', the American vernacular she borrows to name the planet's 'motley crowd of lively beings', similarly emphasises relationality between humans and other living beings.[37] While Haraway, always alert to the material-semiotic entanglements which mean that words matter, 'pray[s] that all residual tones of *creation* have been silenced in the demotic *critter*', the figure of the critter affirms attachment, companionship and, even, love, all terms that find similar expression in the affective economy of the creaturely as theorised by Herman, Pick and others.[38] Moreover, for Haraway, the imperative of a critterly perspective has become even more pronounced in the Anthropocene, as the 'destruction of places and times of refuge for people and other critters' becomes an increasingly pressing issue.[39] In contrast to those mourning the potential extinction of the humanist idea of the human, Haraway argues that the Anthropocene calls for a critterly human to emerge through affiliative acts of 'making kin' with more-than-human forms of life, a realigning of species relations that will provide the foundation for a future planetary ethics.[40] In a manner that might seem to parallel Benjamin's argument, Haraway looks to supplant the apocalyptic temporality of the Anthropocene with a critterly philosophy of life.

For Barnes, however, in the same way that the word beast constitutes a distinct although varied aesthetic mode, the creaturely also contains a set of aesthetic associations that overlap with but depart from the critical idiom that has emerged in recent times. Primarily, the creaturely takes on a satirical register in her writing. In *Nightwood*, for instance, O'Connor employs the term in affectionate condescension. Destitute aristocrats keeping up appearances are 'poor creatures', while O'Connor is himself 'the funniest looking creature on the face of the earth' (*N* 89; 87). Creatureliness here might name a shared form of exposure and vulnerability, but, within the self-mythologising monologues of O'Connor, suggests a superficial form of relationality that is unlikely to provide the grounds for genuine empathy. In *Ryder*, a similar condescension inherent to the creaturely is drawn out. In the epistolary chapters written by Wendell's religious moralist sister-in-law, Ann, creaturely figures again point to failed moments of relation or empathy, such as her complaint that she may have to work as a live-in maid for 'some creature who cannot hold his, or her, wind' (*R* 181). Here the creaturely rather than affirming the material continuity across bodies, becomes a term of abject repulsion. This makes sense considering Ann's foregrounding of the term's deep etymological roots in a biblical discourse of divine creation and destruction. Ann's lament that the 'creatures' who currently live 'do so disgrace [the world], root and branch, that the Lord will have none of it in another generation' (*R* 152) situates the creaturely as a mode that, in contrast to contemporary theorists, is grounded in an eschatological rather than natural history. Indeed, it is when life is no longer creaturely, in the sense of reflecting the divine order of creation, signified by the news that a 'fisherman in Sicily has netted a fish with a human eye [and] that a child in Wales was born with the foot of a kid and the foot of a lamb', that Ann feels sure that she is among 'the last generation' (*R* 112–3). While for Haraway the 'taint of [. . .] "creation"' is a 'semiotic barnacle' to be 'scrape[d] off' from her critters, Barnes's novel suggests that creaturely imaginaries and apocalyptic narratives are constitutive of one another. If Barnes's insistence that 'a beast' be not translated as 'the beast' is a rejection of an eschatological understanding of the beastly, here we find that the creaturely is just as associated with shrill cries of moral apocalypse.[41]

In contrast to the condescension and moralism of the creaturely, premised on superficial bonds of attachment and divine resemblance, Barnes's beasts are often characterised by negativity and non-recognition. In early 1955, T. S. Eliot sent Barnes a copy of T. H. White's recently published translation of a Latin Bestiary, *The Book of Beasts* (1954), which opens with the assertion that the word 'beast' should 'properly be used about lions, leopards, tigers, wolves, foxes, dogs, monkeys and others which rage about with tooth and claw [. . .] They are called Beasts because of the violence with which they rage.'[42] The association between beasts and violence can be seen in *The Antiphon*, which Barnes was writing at the time, where 'half of a gryphon' watches over the play's events, until, at the drama's conclusion, the murdered Miranda and her mother who has murdered her 'fall across the gryphon, pulling down the curtains, gilt crown and all' (*A* 7; 201).⁴³ Yet, it is not only in her later work where beasts are associated with violence and destruction. In *Ryder*, a dichotomy between beastly violence and creaturely harmony is presented in explicitly gendered terms in a chapter entitled 'The Beast Thingumbob', accompanied by one of Barnes's hand-drawn illustrations (figure 3.1). Here, Wendell tells his children the story of 'a great beast' with horns, wings and 'eyes like flakes of fire' named Thingumbob, who is 'stricken for the love of a strange creature' named Cheerful (*R* 119). Cheerful, who has coiled hair, ten breasts and a face which 'was not yet', is described as 'fettered to the earth' and characterised in terms of virginal equanimity: she 'was a virgin, but not as other women, for [. . .] she had a greater share than any mortal woman could bear [. . .] but to her the putting up was no great business' (*R* 119–20). Inculcated with a sense of responsibility to male desire and dutiful reproduction, she agrees to 'die beneath' Thingumbob in the process of giving him 'ten sons' who will 'burst [her] asunder' (*R* 121). Presenting, as Sheryl Stevenson notes, a suffocating

Figure 3.1 *The Beast.* Djuna Barnes's original line drawn illustration of The Beast Thingumbob and Cheerful for *Ryder*. Djuna Barnes Papers, Special Collections, University of Maryland Libraries.

image of the female body as homogenous, inert matter, the story concludes with Thingumbob 'pluck[ing] his sons from her belly' and carrying them back 'to his nest' where he sits amidst the 'smoke of his sorrow' (R 121).[44] Relying on an oppositional understanding of sexual difference, it is a narrative where creaturely passivity is constitutive of a masculinist ideal of femininity and beastly violence undergirds patriarchal authority.

In *Nightwood*, Barnes offers a more complex portrayal of beastly violence as it relates to sex, gender and sexuality. Here beastliness is understood to be a wilful and violent transgression of creaturely aesthetics, crossing demarcations of sex and gender, as well as species, and resisting being neatly mapped onto oppositional relations. Where creatureliness is framed in terms of relationality (and satirised through O'Connor's monologues), beastliness is figured as a contagion that produces difference, discontinuity and nonidentification. This is particularly clear in scenes of interspecies encounters. When Robin and Nora meet for the first time in the circus, it is a shared experience with a lioness that galvanises their desires:

> Then as one powerful lioness came to the turn of the bars, exactly opposite the girl, she turned her furious great head with its yellow eyes afire and went down, her paws thrusting through the bars and, as she regarded the girl, as if a river were falling behind impassable heat, her eyes flowed in tears that never reached the surface. At that the girl rose straight up. Nora took her hand. 'Let's get out of here!' the girl said, and still holding her hand Nora took her out. (N 49)

The passage initially appears to invite itself to be read as a moment that erodes beastly differences for a moment of creaturely transcendence. The long sentences and the shifting subject of the third person pronoun engender an ambiguity that implies interchangeability; it is not immediately clear, for instance, whether the weeping subject 'regard[ing] the girl' is the lioness or Nora, through whom the chapter is largely focalised. Moreover, both sorrow and desire appear to traverse species boundaries in a manner not dissimilar to the affective terms of kinship often foregrounded in accounts of the creaturely. In such a reading, the lioness, as desiring and subjugated subject, becomes representative of female subjectivity trapped within what Derrida describes as a hierarchal configuration in which 'the right of man over the beasts' places the 'master, king, husband, father' above 'the beast, the woman, the child'.[45]

Yet, to read the circus scene in this way involves overlooking how, although a certain trans-species empathy is established, the novel's language emphasises distance and asymmetry rather than intimacy and unity. Literalised in the 'bars' of the cage, the passage insists rather more on separation than straightforward affiliation. The awkward, paradoxical syntax of eyes flowing with tears which never reach 'the surface' intimates an image before undoing it; the tears of the lioness/Nora, at first apparently perceptible, retreat from the surface. Having teased at a moment of recognisable interspecies empathy, Barnes instead insists on an unrecognisability that takes form at the level of the sentence itself. In the syntactical contradiction, the reader experiences the same movement from recognition to unrecognition. Rather than producing a stable representation, the passage's meaning and affect emerges not from nouns but adjectives ('furious', 'afire', 'impassable', 'powerful') and verbs ('thrusting', 'falling', 'flowed'), abstractions which insist on vicissitude, difference and violence. While James B. Scott is certainly correct in suggesting that the scene establishes symbolic parallels between Robin and the lioness, illustrated in her mane-like hair and the later description of her Paris apartment as a 'lair', what emerges is not a creaturely similarity, but rather a beastliness premised on undoing identity.[46] The lion, foremost in White's definition of the beast as that which rages and roams, becomes emblematic of Robin's own bestial nature. It presents an understanding of human-animal relations premised not on identification and recognition. Rather, the scene suggests the kind of beastly contagion which Derrida identifies as traversing species boundaries and which we see passing between the human and nonhuman characters in the circus scene, not establishing forms of identity but undoing them.[47]

Beastliness, in this sense, present itself in similar terms to a certain understanding of queerness. As Lee Edelman argues, queerness should not be understood as naming a category, but as a desiring force that negates and unsettles identity. Queerness in this sense 'can never define an identity; it can only ever disturb one'.[48] In *Nightwood*, beastliness operates as a contagion that seems to travel between bodies and species, threatening to undo the bonds that keep a culturally proscribed heterosexuality in place. Indeed, this beastly sexuality embodies an offensiveness, both in the sense of upsetting moral sensibilities and in the sense of launching an offence, that can be linked to White's insistence that violence is the defining characteristic of beastliness. The female circus performers whom Felix befriends in the first chapter are 'stronger than their beasts' and driven by 'desires utterly divergent' from the genteel Felix, their queerness all the more powerful for being 'inappropriate' (N 10). Robin, as an 'infected carrier of the past' (N 34), presents a dangerous and ultimately deathly threat of sexual contagion to those around her, with the contact she has with others framed in terms of non-identity. The description of Nora and Robin 'looking into each other's face, their two heads in their four hands, so strained together that the space that divided them seemed to be thrusting them apart' replicates the syntax of attraction and repulsion that characterised the earlier circus scene, leading Nora to realise that the only way 'Robin would belong to her' is in 'death' (N 52). Here, akin to Edelman's 'queer negativity' which opposes 'every substantiation of identity', Robin's beastliness threatens to not only violently transpose heterosexual constructions of identity, but to expose the hollowness of the humanist ideal of man as the master of himself and the beasts around him.[49]

This beastly negativity finds its clearest expression in the much-disputed ending to *Nightwood*, where Robin retreats to a 'decaying chapel' somewhere in America and in a final moment of textual ambiguity goes down on all fours with the dog she finds there (N 151–3). Although critics have read the final scene in widely contrasting terms, nearly all see the novel's final moment as central to Barnes's understanding of animal life, with early critics reading Robin's going down as a withdrawal from civilised humanity and more recent critics reading the scene as an ambivalent affirmation of animality.[50] Much like the scene in the circus, however, Barnes's language resists straightforward exegesis:

> The dog, quivering in every muscle, sprang back, his lips drawn, his tongue a stiff curving terror in his mouth; moved backward, back, as she came on, whimpering too, coming forward, her head turned completely sideways, grinning and whimpering. Back now into the farthest corner, the dog reared as if to avoid something that troubled him to such agony that he seemed to be rising from the floor; then he stopped, clawing sideways at the wall, his forepaws lifted and sliding. Then, head down, dragging her forelocks in the dust, she struck against his side. He let loose one howl of misery and bit at her, dashing about her, barking, and as he sprang on either side of her he always kept his head towards her, dashing his rump now this side, now that, of the wall. (N 152–3)

As with Robin's encounter with the lioness, the passage engenders uncertainty through its accumulation of clauses, as new, mostly intransitive verbs incessantly transform and disorient the syntax, making it initially difficult to be certain if it is the dog or Robin who is the grammatical subject of any given verb, as the structure of the sentence reflects the morphological transformations taking place in the scene itself. An insinuation of beastly sexual impropriety, even masochism, is suggested through the unstable imagery of 'quivering', 'stiff curving', 'whimpering' and 'grinning' bodies, as dog and human coalesce into unfamiliar and strange assemblages. Indeed, in one of the earlier typescript drafts of *Nightwood* from 1936 the insinuation of sexual transgression is even stronger. The dog looks to Robin as 'a mistress', with the final sentence ending in a description of 'his eyes bloodshot and waiting'.[51]

In September 1935, having read a draft of the novel with the earlier version of the ending, Coleman wrote to Barnes to say that both she and Peggy Guggenheim had recoiled at what they assumed to be the unintended insinuation of a sexual act with a dog. 'The end, the part about the dog', Coleman wrote, 'is definitely sexual. I told Peggy you had no such thought in mind. She then told me about Fitzi's [Eleanor Fitzgerald's] dog, the original of this, and the things it made her feel. You did not know this when writing, but you understood unconsciously the true implication of that dog.'[52] Barnes's response was cautious and defensive: 'if it sounds sexual, then sexual it sounds I can't change it, wouldn't know what to do about it, unless the word Mistress was crossed out, would that help?'[53] Barnes's tautological emphasis on the passage's phonic attributes, the way in which the ambiguous images of human and dog sound like (rather than describe) sex, suggest a broader understanding than allowed for in narrow definitions of sexuality. As Barnes insinuates, the queerness of the scene resides not in ascertaining whether what is taking place constitutes sexual intercourse, or what Barnes later described in a 1979 letter to her unwelcome biographer Andrew Field as an exasperation with readers who understand the scene as Robin 'trying to make love to the dog', but rather a more broadly dehumanised, or, more aptly, beastly, understanding of sex itself that emerges from the scene's negativity and undecidability.[54] If the scene sounds sexual, this is because sex itself is bound up with precisely these beastly qualities and associations. Robin's beastliness in this final passage emerges not as a mode of identity or even a form of becoming that emphasises affirmation, rather it resides in the queer vicissitudes of sexual figuration through which identity is incessantly constructed, deconstructed and ultimately negated. In contrast to both the idea of the human as a transcendent category and a weak creaturely universalism, Barnes's beastly aesthetic serves to undermine forms of relation, undoing the coherency not only of identity but recognisability itself.

Anthropomorphism and Surface Reading

Nightwood's ending stands as a prime example of the recalcitrant quality of Barnes's writing, where stable semantic meaning often seems to be at risk of withdrawing back into highly stylised language and problems of recognisability and readability are repeatedly foregrounded, as the reader is made aware of the beastly otherness of the text itself. Indeed, the final pages of the novel, rather than offering a direct representation of human and animal relations, instead draw attention to the formal structures, literary phonetics and figurative devices through which structures of meaning are produced. Barnes's use of conditional language and metaphor, describing the dog rearing 'as if to avoid something that troubled him' consciously imbues the scene with an anthropomorphic quality.[55] It is a moment that, as with the earlier circus encounter with the lion, brings to the surface the fact of anthropomorphism and invites questions around how human and animal relations are encoded within literature. Anthropomorphism, however, need not be inherently or reductively anthropocentric; indeed, Barnes's interest in the textual operations through which animals are mediated and presented within literature can be seen to foreshadow an increasing concern with questions of how anthropomorphism might be strategically employed to non-anthropocentric ends. Ron Broglio, for instance, emphasises the way in which anthropomorphism has long influenced how we understand and behave towards animals since, as the ontological interiority of other species is closed off from us, it is 'the surface' that has historically provided the zone of 'interaction between humans and animals'.[56] As Broglio explains, the fact that we cannot easily ascertain the ontology of other species, what it is like to 'be' a dog or a lion, has led to animals being seen as only 'living on the surface', without the interiority, self-reflexivity or depth so highly prized in humans.[57] Yet, rather than arguing for the importance of recognising the rich inner life of other animals, as biologists and ethologists increasingly demonstrate to be the case, Broglio looks to deconstruct the value placed on depth at the expense of surface. Staying on the surface, at the level at which human and animal encounters take place, 'affords us an invaluable modality for thought, and for pursuing the unthought of thought'.[58] Surfaces, rather than being understood as superficial or shallow, might be sites of generative insight and imagination.

Broglio's emphasis on the way in which surface encounters mediate how we perceive and understand other animals also resonates with what Rosi Braidotti describes as the fundamental role of anthropomorphism within human ontology. Rather than being a mode which we can choose to switch on or off in any given instance, Braidotti situates anthropomorphism as being the fundamental condition of human life, since we encounter the world through an 'anthropologically bound structure'. That is, since our sensory and cognitive experiences, and, therefore, our epistemological and aesthetic figurations, are, in Braidotti's terms, 'embedded and embodied, enfleshed, affective, and relational' they will always already be anthropomorphic.[59] Anthropomorphism for Braidotti is not limited to interactions with other animals but influences all experience of life in the Anthropocene. Yet, as with Broglio, for Braidotti this fact is not inherently limiting, but opens the possibility for a 'self-aware anthropomorphism' which, by creatively and critically embracing the limits and possibilities of our boundedness, has the potential to 'overcome anthropocentrism'.[60] Paul De Man, in a study of anthropomorphism within literary language in the decades before the concept of the Anthropocene had been coined, can be seen to reach a similar conclusion. As an 'identification on the level of substance', the standard understanding of anthropomorphism 'takes one entity for another and thus implies the constitution of specific entities prior to their confusion'.[61] In other words, such an understanding of anthropomorphism relies on essential distinctions between the human and the nonhuman made ahead of time; a process through which the human comes to define itself by falsely recognising a reflection of its own self in the world around it. Anthropomorphism, then, for De Man, Braidotti and Broglio, contains the potential to defamiliarise the human, by drawing attention to the processes and figurations through which the human encounters and understands its nonhuman others, and thereby comes to understand itself. Rather than a blithe or inherently anthropocentric mode of seeing, it contains possibilities for understanding life both human and other.

Barnes's writing, already seemingly aware of what is at stake in such questions, is filled with instances where anthropomorphism is deployed to bestialise an anthropocentric or originary notion of the human. Moreover, it is possible to chart a developing set of literary strategies within her work that reveal a shifting approach to human and animal relations. Her journalism from the 1910s, for instance, ironically deploys an exaggerated anthropomorphic optic, that foregrounds its own insufficiencies and gaps. One of the clearest examples of this is 'The Girl and the Gorilla', Barnes's 1914 *New York World Magazine* 'interview' with Dinah, a three-year-old gorilla captured in the French Congo and brought back to the Bronx Zoo. The short and witty article sees Barnes 'freely interpret' Dinah's answers to her questions through the 'rules' of communication established by the man who had caught her, the primatologist, Richard L. Garner. Treading a fine line between biting, deadpan humour and an attempt to creatively document a modern interspecies encounter, Barnes puts human words into Dinah's mouth, offering a comic account of the gorilla's 'high intelligence' and 'queer [. . .] drawing-room caution' as she gives forth on New York's modern electric lighting, its taxis and chewing gum.[62] Barnes's anthropomorphism is knowingly reductive:

> 'Let me see' – she cupped her hand about her ear and dusted a piece of lint from her shoulders. [. . .] 'The first thing that really attracted my attention was the meter upon the taxi that the professor hired to bring me here to the zoo. That thing climbed exactly three-and-a-half times faster than a chimpanzee, four times faster than an ordinary monkey, and six times faster than a gorilla.'[63]

As Nancy Levine notes, Barnes's decision to put her own words in the mouth of Dinah is not unique to this article but was a strategy she repeatedly employed in her interviews, contributing to her destabilising of the boundaries between journalism and fiction.[64] Yet, while ventriloquism might be a common feature of Barnes's interviews, her article on Dinah draws specific attention to the intersections between language and species representation. The insufficiency of the ethological 'rules' that Garner has devised to delineate and regulate Dinah's modes of communication are satirised through what might be described as an exaggerated anthropomorphic realism. Barnes's satirical representation of Dinah intentionally blurs the line between verisimilitude and artifice: it both claims to be authentic or truthful in the sense of being a work of journalism and is, at the same time, clearly a fiction. What is natural or truthful about the situation can only be determined by negotiating questions of style and representation.

The problem of representation is further gestured towards in the article's conclusion. The interview's final line is given not to Dinah, but the zookeeper who, having had to restrain the now agitated gorilla, asserts that 'Kipling's remark about the female of the species holds true'.[65] A reference to Kipling's poem 'The Female of the Species', published three years previously in 1911, the newspaper article invites readers to recall that Kipling's survey of various animal species and racial groups culminates in the conclusion that throughout the human and animal world 'the Female of Her Species is more deadly than the Male'.[66] Barnes's interview with Dinah, then, concludes with a citation of an anthropomorphic truism that, if not already a cliché by this point in time, is reductively essentialist in its portrayal of race, gender and species. The ironic ambiguity as to whether Barnes is ventriloquising the zookeeper in the same way that she earlier ventriloquised Dinah is surely intended. The reader, alert to the interview's status as a fiction purporting to be truth, is already primed to read this intertextual reference against the grain and to be suspicious of its veracity and sentiment. Creating a complex tissue of uncertainty around the origins and authenticity of the text, Barnes problematises the straightforward ability of language to directly represent its subject (whether human or nonhuman) through an unequivocal language or within stable categories.

Bonnie Kime Scott has argued that Barnes's portrayal of Dinah's gender and sexuality allows a certain alliance between herself and the gorilla to emerge.[67] Such an interpretation is further borne out by the fact that Barnes had also been uprooted and moved with her mother and brothers to the Bronx, only a few blocks south of the zoo, when in 1912 her parents separated because of her father's polygamy. In a letter from her father, Wald, shortly after the move, he wrote the he was glad that she was 'next to the zoo' since she 'no doubt appreciates George Bernard Shaw's remark [. . .] "They put all their good citizens in jail!"'.[68] While Wald, who like Wendell in *Ryder* feared criminal prosecution for bigamy, is drawing parallels between the incarceration of zoo animals and men such as himself, it also speaks to Barnes's own sense of kinship with Dinah. Her description of the 'faraway' look in Dinah's eyes as she gazes 'upon a life called civilised' and ironises about the banality of her new metropolitan environment allows a beastly resemblance to emerge despite Barnes's satirical anthropomorphic realism.[69] If in *Nightwood* and *Ryder* beastliness is a force of negativity and difference, here beastliness speaks to a limited sense of trans-species kinship. Indeed, the fragility of such a kinship is emphasised in giving the last word to Kipling, self-reflexively acknowledging not only the inadequacy of language but its active distortions. Barnes might want the reader to feel mistrustful of anthropomorphism, but the interview also suggests that there is not a different, more authentic position from which she can describe this more-than-human encounter.

The sense of both intimacy and distance that is evoked by Barnes's self-reflexive anthropomorphism presents an example of a certain modernist trope:

the figure of the primate who speaks to us and whose very speaking signifies both the human's intimate proximity to nonhuman animals and an unassailable ontological difference. It is this anthropomorphic sense of intimacy and distance that is also apparent in the figure of Red Peter, the ape who delivers a paper to a room of scientists in Franz Kafka's 'A Report to an Academy' (1917) and which is inverted in David Garnett's narrative of a human voluntarily moving into a Large Ape-House in *A Man in The Zoo* (1924).[70] Subjected not only to taxonomical categorisation and ethological observation but also the demands of a modern entertainment culture, the modernist primate exposes the mutually constitutive identities of scientific subject and public spectacle, as well as the fragility of claims to human exceptionalism based on intelligence, language or psychology. In her interview with Dinah, Barnes foregrounds the 'rules' through which early twentieth-century ethnologists and zoologists sought to represent and thereby authoritatively map animal interiority. As Derrida argues, drawing on the example of King Louis XIV's ceremonial observation of an elephant autopsy at the Menageries of Versailles in 1681, representation, epistemology and sovereign power are constitutive of one another. The 'wanting-to-see' that drives a 'question of knowledge' produces a 'knowing-power' in which epistemology enables 'possession and mastery of its object'.[71] This is an optics, Derrida continues, which cannot be dissociated 'from spectacle, theater, ceremony as representation, and representation as representation of the king [as sovereign]'. This optical relationship between sovereign subject and beastly object is not interrupted with the ascendency of democracy. Instead, the 'sovereignty of the people or of the nation merely inaugurates a new form of the same fundamental structure', a fact reflected both in the claim to scientific objectivity in Garner's 'rules' for reading Dinah's gestures and 'the crowd roar[ing] in delight' as they look in through the bars.[72] As Barnes's satirical portrayal of Dinah shows, this sovereign gaze is inseparable from epistemological modes of knowing and, thereby, mastering animals.

If in Barnes's 1914 interview with Dinah we see her ironising a mode of discourse that claims to be able to penetrate and bring to light the inner life of beastly subjects, her fiction of the 1920s is even more explicit in its disruption of the representational strategies through which knowledge is produced and categories of species identity are constructed. In its collage of contrasting literary styles and registers, *Ryder* foregrounds the way in which textuality is itself always the site of meaning rather than a mediating sign of something external to it. Instead of realism's conceit of a direct relation between a signifier and a signified, the first chapter of *Ryder*, written in the idiom of the *King James Bible*, instructs the reader to '[r]each not beyond the image' (R 3). The archly authoritative voice goes on to outline a kingdom of 'Beasts' with 'the eyes back and the eyes front' and 'fishes [that] have a hard smile within their mouths, and go forward always' (R 4). Here, in contrast to the mode of sovereign possession that Derrida outlines as the dominant mode of knowing, anthropomorphic surface images are privileged over depth, and in the chapters that follow, Barnes's highly stylised language repeatedly presents animals in overtly figurative terms, eschewing verisimilitude and mimesis for artifice and metaphor. The messianic ox who tells Amelia in a dream that 'I am also' (R 99), the peewit who calls 'alone from across the lands' waiting for someone to answer to his question of 'Watchman, what of the night?' (R 158) and the obscene drawing of Pennyfinder the Bull that illustrates Wendell's bawdy and fantastical tale of animal sex all offer examples of *Ryder*'s anti-mimetic animal figures (see Chapter 4 for an image of Pennyfinder). These are animal figures that, in contrast to Dinah, have no depth at all; they are paper thin. If in her journalism, Barnes appears troubled by claims of representation, in *Ryder*, Barnes suspends all claims to literary or epistemological realism and instead forcibly orients attention to the surface of language itself.

Barnes's interest in surface over depth in *Ryder* has been identified by Julie Taylor as central to the novel's affective charge: in resisting a 'direct and singular relationship' between sign and referent the novel forestalls a mode of reading that would look to plumb its depths for its true autobiographical meaning. Instead, 'Barnes's text points us in the direction of [. . .] feelings and sensations that are not hidden but sit beside – and often in tension to – each other on the surface of the text.'[73] The novel's earliest readers were also alert to its captivating surfaces. Eugene Jolas, who published parts of *Ryder* in *transition*, noted how the novel, in attending to surface over depth, succeeded in having 'caught life prismatically'.[74] Life, here, invites itself to be understood in terms of more-than-human figurations, the surface of *Ryder*'s pages teeming with stylised images of both humans and animals. Much like Joyce's similarly prismatic *Work in Progress* (later to become *Finnegans Wake*), also partially serialised in *transition*, Barnes's figurative, metaphoric and fabular animals foreground their own anthropomorphic artificiality as textual compositions.[75] Indeed, there is evidence that the animals of Joyce's *Work in Progress* may have influenced the prismatic beasts of *Ryder*. Barnes, who as discussed in the introduction to this book, befriended Joyce when she lived in Paris in the 1920s, cut out and kept the first published part of *Work in Progress*, which was printed in the same April 1924 issue of the *transatlantic review* that also included her short story 'Aller et Retour'. The extract from Joyce opens with the following:

> And there they were too listening in as hard as they could to the solans and the sycamores and the wild geese and gannets and the migratories and mistlethrushes and the auspices and all the birds of the sea, all four of them, all sighing and sobbing, and listening. They were the big four, the four master waves of Erin.[76]

As Bonnie Kime Scott recounts, when Barnes first met Joyce in Paris, he allegedly 'regaled [her] with a story that mixed animal and procreative themes, Ovid's *Fasti*',[77] and here, in what would become a chapter of *Finnegans Wake* that resounds with the 'shrillgleescreaming' of '[a]ll the birds of the sea' (*FW* 383), we find a similar attention to surface, transformation and excess over depth, stability and restraint, as well as a similar dissolving of the boundary between the human and animal. Drawing the reader's attention to the textual surface, Joyce's prose emphasises its own figurative, anthropomorphic operations and diminishes stable, mimetic processes of representation, paralleling Barnes's own later figurations, including the grammatical blurring of human and animal subjects that I have shown to be constitutive of *Nightwood*'s beastly aesthetic.

In their anti-representational disruptions to established modes of writing animals, both Barnes and Joyce draw attention to the processes that do not so much mediate as produce the reader's relation with the animals on the page. Barnes arguably goes further than Joyce in this respect insofar as her accompanying illustrations challenge the semantic predominance or transcendence of the word itself, the simple yet highly stylised designs influenced by a French book collecting medieval animal drawings entitled *L'Imagerie Populaire* (1926). If, as the narrator instructs in the first chapter, the reader should not reach beyond the image, then text and image can be seen to work beside one another (although not always harmoniously) to produce a novel of surfaces in more ways than one. Indeed, there is something animalistic in producing a work that is all surface. As Broglio writes of contemporary visual art that depicts animal subjects, 'allusive and illusive surfaces' have the potential to form an 'expressive language [. . .] for thinking the problem of contact between the "surface" animal world and our own'.[78] Broglio's argument that by staying on the surface one can resist an aesthetic mode that, in continuing to valorise interiority over exteriority, tends towards mastery and assimilation, is reflected not only in *Ryder* but *Nightwood* also. In the character of Frau Mann, *Nightwood*'s circus acrobat, we find a figure who as she flies through the air 'seemed to have a skin that was the pattern of her costume: a bodice of lozenges, red and yellow' (*N* 12). Mann, whose tights are 'no longer a covering' but are 'herself' (*N* 12) and whose name worries distinctions of male and female, as well as man and beast, embodies an aesthetic of surface, speed and metamorphosis. In its dazzling fluidity, the prismatic body of Mann presents itself as a metaphor for the novel's own form; the emphasis on surface over depth, the ambiguities and morphic instability, the beastly speed and trajectory all mirror the novel's stylistic operations. If, *pace* Derrida, the 'wanting to see' of the sovereign finds expression in the courtly autopsies of exotic animals in early modern France, an optics that equates to a literal cutting open, then Barnes's refusal of depth and celebration of surface reorients the animal away from a being to be tamed and vivisected, into a force of beastly negativity that resists being pinned down. Robin as 'beast turning human' comes to stand as a metonym for this process. Her initial emergence in front of Felix (and the reader) from the Rousseau-like 'jungle trapped in a drawing room' (N 31–3) and her return to the bestial in the final moments of the novel present an anthropomorphism that stands in opposition to essence and categorisation. As Barnes's writing repeatedly insists, anthropomorphism is not only the mode through which we tropologically assimilate the nonhuman otherness of the world into recognisable forms, but the ontological mode through which the human constructs and regulates its own image. Unsettling the transcendence of meta-categories such as 'the human' and 'the animal', she instead foregrounds the beastly resemblances that travel across surfaces.

The Impossibility of a Beastocene

In her copy of Marcel Proust's *The Past Recaptured* (1927) Barnes marked the following passage:

> Thanks to art, instead of seeing only one world, our own, we see it under multiple forms, and as many as there are original artists, just so many worlds have we at our disposal, differing more widely from one another than those that roll through infinite space [. . .] This work of the artist, to seek to discern something different underneath material, experience, words, is exactly the reverse of the process which, during every minute that we live with our attention diverted from ourselves, is being carried on within us by pride, passion, intelligence and also by our habits, when they hide our true impressions from us by burying them under the mass of nomenclatures and practical aims which we erroneously call life.[79]

In Proust's avowal of the heterogeneity of existence and the centrality of art in unveiling the varied experientialities and materialities of life, Barnes likely found an aesthetic vision in sympathy with her own. The encounter with literature produces an experience of otherness which, temporarily, appears to transport us beyond our usual experience of a bounded, stable self. As Proust asserts, aesthetic modes reveal the world 'under multiple forms' in a way that is unavailable to pragmatic or practical modes of discourse. Yet, while we might see Proust's description of art as humanising a cold and indifferent universe, in Barnes's writing it remains a resolutely inhuman world. In contrast to Proust's harmonious image of human life and the universe, in *Nightwood* Barnes writes:

> Life, the pastures in which the night feeds and prunes the cud that nourishes us to despair. Life, the permission to know death. We were created that the earth might be made sensible of her inhuman taste; and love that the body might be so dear that even the earth should roar with it. (N 75)

The anthropomorphised earth, '[in]sensible' of its inhuman taste, roars like the beasts who feed upon her. While such a description might appear to lend itself to the neologism of a 'beastocene', an understanding of our planetary moment as defined by the beastly aesthetics outlined across Barnes's work, such a term would introduce the kind of anthropomorphism that, as De Man writes, 'freezes the infinite chain of tropological transformations into one single assertion or essence which, as such, excludes all others'.[80] Instead, the difference and negativity inherent to Barnes's beastly anthropomorphism exposes the tropological processes through which such figures calcify, and, eventually, crack. As Barnes wrote to Coleman, 'there is always more surface to a shattered object than a whole object' and in the fragmented, yet prismatic aesthetic of Barnes's beastly writing, she exposes the processes through which the human names its others and, thereby, casts its own identity.[81]

In this respect, Barnes's writing can be seen to embody what Claire Colebrook argues is the way in which the Anthropocene requires us 'to consider that the question of [. . .] the human is not something that might be added to the problem of planetary change' but that 'what may need to be rethought is the very concept of the human' itself. Colebrook suggests that the starting point for such a reimagining is the acknowledgement that there is 'no longer [. . .] man (historically and socially determined and determining) but a species tied to rhythms [. . .] beyond the historical and familial imagination'.[82] In Barnes's writing, the emphasis on surface speaks to a similar displacement of species discourse in favour of an anthropomorphic ontology in which identity and relation are always in a state of transformation and subject to beastly contagions. Indeed, if, as quoted in my introductory chapter, Barnes insisted to Coleman that for her nature must be understood in terms of 'motion' and 'wedded[ness]', it is unsurprising that in *Nightwood* there is a similar emphasis on movement and equivocation. As O'Connor states, when describing sheltering in a cellar during a bombardment in the First World War with a Breton woman and her cow, 'there are directions and speeds that no one has yet calculated, for believe it or not that cow had gone somewhere very fast that we didn't know of, and yet was still standing there' (*N* 21). This is interspecies relations understood in terms of rhythm or intensity, rather than category or essence. Moreover, Barnes's beastly aesthetic allows a negative relationality to emerge from such prismatic surfaces of species coexistence. O'Connor's tragicomic description of the cow, recalling how in the momentary illumination of a 'flash of lightning' he 'saw the cow turning her head straight back so her horns made two moons against her shoulders, the tears soused all over her great black eyes' (*N* 20), anthropomorphically aestheticises animal fear and sadness that, like Barnes's portrayal of Dinah, gestures towards both an intimate interspecies proximity and a profoundly insurmountable alterity. O'Connor's own fear and distress as he shelters with 'the poor beast trembling on her four legs' (*N* 20) presents itself as akin to what Derrida describes as the risk of madness that comes from 'cry[ing] in conjunction with an animal'.[83] An example of the way in which trans-species contagion transforms bodies and material relations, the scene plays out as a metonymy for beastly dehumanisation in the Anthropocene. While violent, negative affects circulate in Barnes's beastly writing, it is a negativity that traverses species boundaries. Beastliness here speaks to an embodied mode of being which, although inherently anthropomorphic, is produced through processes of negation and negativity that, paradoxically, produce new (but not always positive) modes of relation. Beastliness, then, operates not as an aesthetic mode that might save us from our fate and enable a recognisably human figure to sustain itself indefinitely. Rather, it insists that the human was never fully human to begin with. Instead, as captured in the fragmentary image of a 'beast lowing | in the isle of [its] dimension', beastliness orients us towards the morphic processes through which we imagine ourselves and the scenes upon which we speak.

Notes

1. Rachel Potter, '*Nightwood*'s Humans', in *Shattered Objects: Djuna Barnes's Modernism,* ed. Elizabeth Pender and Cathryn Setz (University Park: Penn State University Press, 2019), pp. 61–74 (p. 61).
2. Sverre Raffnsøe, *Philosophy of the Anthropocene: The Human Turn* (Basingstoke: Palgrave Macmillan, 2016), p. xiii.
3. Rosi Braidotti, 'Four Theses on Posthuman Feminism', in *Anthropocene Feminism*, ed. Richard Grusin (Minneapolis: University of Minnesota Press, 2017), pp. 21–48 (p. 26).
4. Donna Haraway, *Staying with the Trouble: Making Kin in the Chthulucene* (Durham, NC: Duke University Press, 2016), p. 55.
5. In his first article on the Anthropocene for *Nature* in 2002, Paul Crutzen singled out industrial agriculture as one of the defining features of the new epoch. See 'Geology of Mankind', *Nature*, 415 (2002), 23. For more see *Animals in the Anthropocene: Critical perspectives on non-human futures*, ed. the Human Animal Research Network (Sydney: Sydney University Press, 2015), and *Thinking About Animals in the Age of the Anthropocene*, ed. Morten Tønnessen, Kristin Armstrong Oma and Silver Rattasepp (Lanham, MD: Lexington Books, 2016).
6. Jane Marcus, 'Laughing at Leviticus: *Nightwood* as Woman's Circus Epic', in *Silence and Power: A Reevaulation of Djuna Barnes,* ed. Mary Lynn Broe (Carbondale and Edwardsville: Southern Illinois University Press, 1991), pp. 221–50 (p. 223). Also see Karen Kaivola's discussion of *Nightwood*'s 'representation of [. . .] primitive otherness'. Kaivola, 'The "Beast Turning Human": Constructions of the "Primitive" in *Nightwood*', *Review of Contemporary Fiction*, 13.3 (1993), 172–85 (p. 173). More recent accounts of Barnes's texts have drawn out how her work foregrounds a posthumanist aesthetic of material continuity with the nonhuman world, such as Robert Azzarello's *Queer Environmentality: Ecology, Evolution and Sexuality in American*

Literature (Farnham: Ashgate, 2012), Erin Edward's *The Modernist Corpse: Posthumanism and the Posthumous* (Minneapolis: University of Minnesota Press, 2018) and Andrew Kalaidjian's 'The Black Sheep: Djuna Barnes's Dark Pastoral', in *Creatural Fictions: Human-Animal Relationships in Twentieth- and Twenty-First-Century Literature*, ed. David Herman (Basingstoke: Palgrave Macmillan, 2016), pp. 65–87.

7. Norris does not include Barnes in her survey of biocentric writers, but her description of them as 'creat[ing] *as* – not like the animal [. . .] with their animality speaking' fits what I will argue is Barnes's beastly aesthetic. Carrie Rohman, *Stalking the Subject: Modernism and the Animal* (New York: Columbia University Press, 2009), p. 28; Margot Norris, *Beasts of The Modern Imagination: Darwin, Nietzsche, Kafka, Ernst & Lawrence* (Baltimore and London: Johns Hopkins University Press, 1985), pp. 1–3.
8. Rohman, *Stalking the Subject*, p. 133.
9. Bonnie Kime Scott, *Refiguring Modernism Volume 2: Postmodern Feminist Readings of Woolf, West and Barnes* (Bloomington: Indiana University Press, 1995), p. 73.
10. Bonnie Kime Scott's groundbreaking chapter on Barnes in the second volume of *Refiguring Modernism* (1995) is an important exception here, drawing connections between animal figures across the breadth of her oeuvre and remaining alert to the 'variable construction of "beast" in language'. Scott, *Refiguring Modernism Volume 2*, p. 102.
11. Daniela Caselli's *Improper Modernism* (2009) remains the most sustained analysis of Barnes's published writing in relation to the materials in her archive, arguing that Barnes's body of work constitutes an 'inopportune modernism' in which 'what has been read as her obscurity is the result of her still unacknowledged poetics of impropriety'. Caselli, *Improper Modernism: Djuna Barnes's Bewildering Corpus* (London and New York: Routledge, 2016), p. 2. See also Julie Taylor's *Djuna Barnes and Affective Modernism* (Edinburgh: Edinburgh University Press, 2012) which draws on archival materials in its examination of affect and subjectivity in Barnes's oeuvre.
12. Jacques Derrida, *The Beast & the Sovereign, Volume 1*, trans. Geoffrey Bennington (Chicago: University of Chicago Press, 2009), p. 1.
13. Ibid. p. 106. For Derrida on the paucity of 'the animal' as both a term and a category see Derrida, *The Animal That Therefore I Am*, trans. David Wills, ed. Marie-Louise Mallet (New York: Fordham University Press, 2008), pp. 47–51.
14. As Alex Goody has convincingly argued, while Barnes's article is typical of the reformist agenda of the time it resists the moral superiority of 'the woman journalist-observer'. Goody, 'Djuna Barnes on the Page', in *Shattered Objects: Djuna Barnes's Modernism*, pp. 26–45 (p. 31).
15. W. B. Yeats, *Collected Poems* (London: Macmillan, 1982) p. 210. Barnes would later single out Yeats's image of the slouching beast, annotating it with a large red line in the copy of Edwin Muir's *The Present Age* (1939) that she obtained after moving back to the US.
16. Caselli, *Improper Modernism*, p. 179.
17. Djuna Barnes, untitled poem headed 'Say I am a Beast', Typescript, Undated. Djuna Barnes Papers, Special Collections, University of Maryland Libraries (hereafter DBP), Series 3, Box 7, Folder 6.

18. Rohman, *Stalking the Subject*, p. 134.
19. Joanne Winning has argued that the grotesque is central to both Barnes's literary and visual works, constituting a 'lesbian modernist grotesque'. Winning, 'Djuna Barnes, Thelma Wood and the Making of the Lesbian Modernist Grotesque', in *Shattered Objects: Djuna Barnes's Modernism*, pp. 95–112 (p. 95).
20. Mikhail Bakhtin, *Rabelais and His World*, trans. Hélène Iswolsky (Bloomington: Indiana University Press, 1984), p. 316; p. 24.
21. Graham Greene, 'Fiction Chronicle', *Tablet*, 14 November 1936, pp. 678–9 (p. 678).
22. Bonnie Kime Scott, *Refiguring Modernism Volume 2*, p. 102.
23. Barnes, 'Attention Signor Maffi', c. 1948. DBP, Series 2, Box 1, Folder 5, emphasis in original.
24. Ibid.
25. Derrida, *The Animal That Therefore I Am*, p. 31.
26. Djuna Barnes to Natalie Clifford Barney, 12 April 1968, DBP, Series 2, Box 1, Folder 46.
27. Djuna Barnes to Emily Coleman, 5 May 1935, Emily Holmes Coleman Papers, Special Collections, University of Delaware Library (hereafter EHCP), Box 2, Folder 10.
28. See Cheryl J. Plumb's introduction to the restored version of *Nightwood* and Dana Seitler's reading of Barnes's letter as a 'disavowal' of the 'cultural valences' attached to beasts. Plumb, 'Introduction', in *Nightwood: The Original Version and Related Drafts*, ed. Cheryl J. Plumb (Normal, IL: Dalkey Archive Press, 1995), pp. vii–xxvi; Seitler, *Atavistic Tendencies: The Culture of Science in American Modernity* (Minneapolis: University of Minnesota Press, 2008), p. 114.
29. Kenneth Burke, *Language as Symbolic Action: Essays on Life, Literature and Method* (Berkeley: University of California Press, 1966), p. 244. These chapter titles also have religious connotations that, in later years, Barnes wished to emphasise at the expense of their clearly euphemistic associations. Writing to James Scott, who was researching a monograph on her, Barnes insisted that he should 'stop this tiresome phallic symbolism, and sex business in everything. Very tiresome and usually incorrect, such as the comment on "go down" it means exactly what it says, from "Go down Moses, let my people go."' Djuna Barnes to James Scott, c. October 1971. DBP, Series 2, Box 14, Folder 57.
30. 'Beastly', in *OED Online* <www.oed.com/view/Entry/16601> (last accessed 20 February 2020).
31. Goody, *Modernist Articulations: A Cultural Study of Djuna Barnes, Mina Loy and Gertrude Stein* (Basingstoke: Palgrave Macmillan, 2007), p. 169.
32. Derrida, *Beast & Sovereign*, p. 138. An equivalent can be found within English, where the *OED* gives the third definition of 'beastly' to mean 'resembling a beast in unintelligence; brutish, irrational, without thought'.
33. Tobias Menely, *The Animal Claim: Sensibility and the Creaturely Voice* (Chicago and London: University of Chicago Press, 2015), p. 14.
34. For the creaturely as it has been articulated within biopolitical theory see Giorgio Agamben's reading of Benjamin in *The Open: Man and Animal* trans. Kevin Attell (Stanford: Stanford University Press, 2004), pp. 81–4, and Eric L. Santner's *On*

Creaturely Life (2006). In contrast to animal studies, these accounts tend to approach the creaturely as 'a specifically human way of finding oneself in the midst of antagonism in and of the political field'. Santner, *On Creaturely Life: Rilke, Benjamin, Sebald* (Chicago: University of Chicago Press, 2006), p. xix.

35. David Herman, 'Introduction: Literature Beyond the Human', in *Creatural Fictions*, pp. 1–18 (p. 3).
36. Anat Pick, *Creaturely Poetics: Animality and Vulnerability in Literature and Film* (New York: Columbia University Press, 2011), p. 5.
37. Importantly for Haraway, her critters include not only animals but other organisms including microbes, fungi, plants, cyborgs and aliens. Haraway, *When Species Meet* (Minneapolis: University of Minnesota Press, 2007), p. 330 n33.
38. Ibid. p. 330, emphasis in original. On critterly love see Haraway's *The Companion Species Manifesto: Dogs, People, and Significant Otherness* (Chicago: Prickly Paradigm Press, 2003).
39. Haraway, *Staying with the Trouble*, p. 100.
40. Ibid. p. 40; p. 89. Haraway's argument that such a world will necessarily entail a reduction in the global human population to two or three billion and her injunction to 'Make Kin, Not Babies!' has come under fierce criticism from feminist critics. See Sophie Lewis, 'Cthulhu Plays No Role For Me', *View Point Mag*, 2017 <https://viewpointmag.com/2017/05/08/cthulhu-plays-no-role-for-me/> (last accessed 12 May 2020); and *Making Kin Not Population: Reconceiving Generations*, ed. Adele Clark and Donna Haraway (Chicago: Prickly Paradigm Press, 2018).
41. Barnes's *Creatures in an Alphabet* (1982), which she was preparing for publication shortly before her death, represents a different approach to writing the creaturely. See Caselli on how this late work disrupts the notion of a divine cosmos of creation and uses simplistic creaturely idioms to estrange language. Caselli, *Improper Modernism*, pp. 109–20.
42. T. H. White, *The Book of Beasts: Being a Translation from a Latin Bestiary of the Twelfth Century* (London: Jonathan Cape, 1956), p. 7.
43. Caselli has argued that the gryphon functions as the central allegory of the play as a figure of both birth and death. Caselli, '"If Some Strong Woman": Djuna Barnes's Great Capacity for All Things Uncertain', in *Shattered Objects: Djuna Barnes's Modernism*, pp.147–62.
44. Sheryl Stevenson, 'Writing the Grotesque Body: Djuna Barnes's Carnival Parody', in *Silence and Power: A Reevaulation of Djuna Barnes*, pp. 81–93 (p. 90).
45. Derrida, *Beast & Sovereign*, pp. 29–30. Several critics have read this scene as an enacting a moment of trans-species affiliation; see Erin Edwards, *The Modernist Corpse*, p. 170; Monica Faltejskova, *Djuna Barnes, T. S. Eliot and the Gender Dynamics of Modernism: Tracing 'Nightwood'* (New York and Abingdon: Routledge, 2010), pp. 156–7; and Rohman, *Stalking the Subject*, p. 145.
46. James B. Scott, *Djuna Barnes* (Boston: Twayne Publishers, 1976), p. 111.
47. Derrida, *Beast & Sovereign*, p. 158.
48. Lee Edelman, *No Future: Queer Theory and the Death Drive* (Durham, NC: Duke University Press, 2004), p. 17. As Ery Shin notes, Edelman's notion of queerness as a negative agency that undoes structures of identity offers a queer theory that is

more sympathetic to Barnes's texts than those which are premised on more straightforwardly emancipatory models of queer identity or performance. See Shin, 'The Apocalypse for Barnes', *Texas Studies in Literature and Language*, 57.2 (2015), 182–209 (pp. 183–5). For queer readings of *Nightwood* that emphasise contagion and negativity see Caselli, *Improper Modernism*, pp.151–90; and Julie Taylor, 'Making Contact: Affect, Queer Historiography, and "Our Djuna"', in *Shattered Objects: Djuna Barnes's Modernism*, pp. 193–206.

49. Edelman, *No Future*, pp. 4–6.
50. For earlier humanist readings of the scene see Burke, *Language as Symbolic Action*, pp. 246–7 and Joseph Frank, *The Widening Gyre: Crisis and Mastery in Modern Literature* (Bloomington: Indiana University Press, 1963), p. 49. For more recent critical readings see Goody, *Modernist Articulations*, pp. 169–73 and Rohman, *Stalking the Subject*, pp. 156–8.
51. Barnes, *Nightwood* Typescript, TSC1, 1935. DBP, Series 3, Box 6, Folder 8.
52. Coleman to Barnes, 27 August 1935, DBP, Series 2, Box 3, Folder 6. Hank O'Neal recalls that in 1978 Barnes told him that the ending of the novel was 'taken from a real life situation she observed. A friend of hers, Fitzie [sic], was "drunk as a hoot and crawling around on all fours and her dog, Buff, was running around her, growling and barking". She then gave her opinions on how animals feel when they see their masters in an "unusual" state.' Phillip Herring, in his biography of Barnes, suggests that Fitzgerald was known to have 'curiously sexual feelings for her dog'. Hank O'Neal, *'Life is Painful, Nasty and Short . . . in my Case it has only been Painful and Nasty': An Informal Memoir* (New York: Paragon House, 1990), pp. 36–7; Phillip Herring, *Djuna: The Life and Works of Djuna Barnes* (New York: Penguin Books, 1996), p. 225.
53. Djuna Barnes to Emily Coleman, 20 September 1935. EHCP, Box 2, Folder 11. Eliot, in a letter to Coleman at the time of the novel's preparation for publication by Faber & Faber in early 1936 and which Coleman forwarded to Barnes, also voiced concerns: 'I should certainly advise *strongly* the omission of the last chapter, which is not only superfluous, but really an anti-climax.' Having acquiesced to the inclusion of the final chapter, Eliot then wanted her to substitute 'unclean' for 'obscene' in the final paragraph, an editorial suggestion which Barnes successfully resisted. See Coleman to Barnes, 26 January 1936. DBP, Series 2, Box 3, Folder 8.
54. Barnes to Andrew Field, 15 May 1979. DBP, Series 2, Box 7, Folder 4.
55. Elizabeth Blake has argued that the use of anthropomorphic figures in this scene makes it, paradoxically, the novel's most human moment. Blake, however, overlooks the way in which anthropomorphism can open onto non-anthropocentric modes of thinking and feeling. Blake, 'Obscene Hungers: Eating and Enjoying *Nightwood* and *Ulysses*', *The Comparatist*, 39 (2015), 153–70.
56. Ron Broglio *Surface Encounters: Thinking with Animals and Art* (Minneapolis: University of Minnesota Press, 2011), p. xix.
57. Ibid. p. xvi.
58. Ibid. p. xx.
59. Braidotti, 'Four Theses', p. 32; p. 35.
60. Ibid. p. 35.

61. Paul De Man, *The Rhetoric of Romanticism* (New York: Columbia University Press, 1984), p. 241.
62. Djuna Barnes, 'The Girl and the Gorilla', *New York World Magazine*, 18 October 1914, p. 9.
63. Ibid. p. 9.
64. Nancy J. Levine, '"Bringing Milkshake to Bulldogs": The Early Journalism of Djuna Barnes', in *Silence and Power: A Reevaulation of Djuna Barnes*, pp. 27–37 (p. 30).
65. Barnes, 'Girl and the Gorilla', p. 9.
66. Rudyard Kipling, *Selected Poems* (London: Penguin Books, 2001), p. 142.
67. Bonnie Kime Scott, *Refiguring Modernism Volume 2*, pp. 102–3.
68. The word 'cages' is written above 'jail' on the letter. It is not clear which of Shaw's remarks Wald Barnes is paraphrasing here. Wald Barnes to Djuna Barnes, c. 1912. DBP, Series 1, Box 6, Folder 1.
69. Barnes, 'Girl and the Gorilla', p. 9.
70. For analysis of the parallels between Kafka's and Garnett's modernist animals see Derek Ryan, 'Literature' in *The Edinburgh Companion to Animal Studies*, ed. Lynn Turner, Undine Sellbach and Ron Broglio (Edinburgh: Edinburgh University Press, 2018), pp. 321–36.
71. Derrida, *Beast & Sovereign*, pp. 280–2.
72. Derrida, *Beast & Sovereign*, p. 287; p. 282; Barnes, 'Girl and the Gorilla', p. 9.
73. Julie Taylor, *Djuna Barnes and Affective Modernism*, p. 83.
74. Eugene Jolas, 'Glossary', *transition*, 16–17 (1929), 326–8 (p. 326).
75. For analysis of Joyce's animal figurations in *Finnegans Wake* see Cliff Mak, 'Joyce's Indifferent Animals: Boredom and the Subversion of Fables in *Finnegans Wake*', *Modernist Cultures*, 11.2 (2016), 179–205; Margot Norris, 'The Animals of James Joyce's *Finnegans Wake*', *Modern Fiction Studies*, 60.3 (2014), 527–43 and Cathryn Setz's *Primordial Modernism: Animals, Ideas*, transition *(1927–1938)* (Edinburgh: Edinburgh University Press, 2019).
76. Barnes's clipping of Joyce's work in the *transatlantic review* is in her archive. James Joyce, 'From Work in Progress', the *transatlantic review*, 1.4 (April 1924), 215–23 (p. 215).
77. Bonnie Kime Scott, *Refiguring Modernism Volume 2*, p. 160.
78. Broglio, *Surface Encounters*, p. xvii.
79. Marcel Proust, *The Past Recaptured*, trans. Frederick A. Blossom (New York: Albert & Charles Boni, 1932), p. 225.
80. De Man, *The Rhetoric of Romanticism*, p. 241.
81. Barnes to Coleman, 8 November 1935. EHCP, Box 2, Folder 12.
82. Claire Colebrook, *Death of the Posthuman: Essays on Extinction, Vol.1* (Ann Arbor, MI: Open Humanities Press, 2014), p. 56.
83. Derrida is here invoking the story of Friedrich Nietzsche's breakdown after witnessing the flogging of a horse in Turin in 1889. Barnes's lifelong love of horses offers an implicit parallel. Writing to Coleman on the death of her horse, Buck, in 1941, Barnes wrote 'you know what I feel about death for animals in general, so what I must feel for you and Jake [Coleman's partner] and Buck'. Derrida, *Animal That Therefore I Am*, p. 35; Barnes to Coleman, 6 April 1941. DBP, Series 2, Box 3, Folder 17.

4

SEX, NATURE AND ANIMAL LIFE IN DJUNA BARNES'S *RYDER*

In the autumn of 1935, in a long letter to Djuna Barnes that touches on the horror of attending bullfights in Spain and her anxieties about getting the manuscript of *Nightwood* into the hands of T. S. Eliot, Emily Coleman recounts how she 'always remember[s] what you said, when I asked you if you considered yourself really Lesbian: "I might be anything. If a horse loved me, I might be that."'[1] Coleman's description of Barnes's rejection of lesbianism, with its bold capital letter, for a less categorical or identifiable form of identity hinges not only on an unsettling of sureties around sexuality, but species also. Desire might produce 'anything', even a more-than-human transformation. While Barnes's reported sentiment that if one felt strongly enough for a horse one might, in some way, become a horse is clearly ironic, it also speaks to a playfulness around species boundaries and a comic interest in holding all distinctions in suspension that we find elsewhere in her writing, perhaps most notably in the 'fit of laughter' ((N 153) that accompanies Robin's descent at the end of *Nightwood* that I discussed in Chapter 3. It speaks, too, to the slipperiness of what we mean when we invoke nature. Within a heteronormative framework, Barnes's reported formulation on the nature of both desire and biology would be considered distinctly unnatural. In this respect, we might read in Coleman's letter a queer supplement to what Raymond Williams described as nature's stature as 'perhaps the most complex' word in the English language since its meanings are 'variable and at times even opposed'. As Williams explains, 'nature' can mean, at any given point, the 'essential character and quality' of something, the 'inherent force' within life, or the entirety of the 'material world itself, taken as including or not including human beings'.[2] Barnes's supposition, which nimbly glosses the essential nature of lesbianism, the sexual force inherent to life itself, and the material world of species relations, arguably invokes all three meanings without using the word at all.

In Coleman and Barnes's correspondence, playfully alert to the intersections between sex and nature, they foreshadow recent interest in the relationship between animal life and sexual difference. The feminist philosopher Kelly Oliver argues in *Animal Lessons* (2009) that dismantling the human-animal binary has important implications for how we think about sex. Following Derrida's disavowal of 'the animal' as only serving to centre the idea of 'the human', Oliver argues that if we attend to the 'nearly infinite variety of living beings' that come under the category of the animal we might start attending to the 'various sexes, sexualities and reproductive practices of animals', or the way in which sexual difference differs *within* animal life. In turn, Oliver argues, by situating the human within this context of animalised sexual difference, we can 'reconsider the sexes, sexualities, and reproductive practices of humans beyond the tight-fitting binary of man/woman or homosexual/heterosexual'.[3] As in Coleman's letter, sexual difference is no longer beholden to a binary construction along the lines of identity and desire, since by 'opening animal differences to the vast varieties of animals, we might also open sexual differences to varieties of sexes, sexualities, and genders'.[4] Oliver's animalising of sexual difference and sexualisation of animal life is representative of a broader turn to examining the longstanding overlaps between discourses around nature and cultural configurations of gender and sexuality. As Catriona Mortimer-Sandilands and Bruce Erickson outline in *Queer Ecologies* (2010), the co-emergence of sexology and evolutionary biology in the nineteenth century led to the modern understanding of sex and nature being 'linked [. . .] through a strongly evolutionary narrative that pits the perverse, the polluted and the degenerate against the fit, the healthy, and the natural'.[5] Nature and naturalness increasingly became terms that offered not only a descriptive function, but a proscriptive agency, measuring an individual's behaviour against what was seen to be the 'natural' moral and social standards of the species.

With the ascendancy of the concept of the Anthropocene, the critical stakes around ideas of naturalness have become further heightened. While in popular discourse, the Anthropocene is frequently invoked to mourn the threatened loss of a perceived state of nature – often figured through the demise of seemingly harmonious biosystems and charismatic species that operate as synecdoches for a natural order – ecocritics and queer theorists alike have suggested the necessity of interrogating how prevalent concepts of nature have served to distort the relationship between the human and the nonhuman. For Timothy Morton, in his influential argument for an ecology 'without' nature, nature is 'a transcendental term in a material mask' that often conceals the inherent contingency, mutability and vicissitudes of life behind pastoral ideals of holistic unity.[6] Developing this line of argument, Morton has elsewhere made the case that a proper understanding of Darwinian evolution would recognise that ecology is inherently queer since it insists on an anti-foundationalist understanding of life, in which there can be no stable categories of sexual difference and that sexuality is premised on 'relationality' rather than identity or essence.[7] In this, Morton shares common ground with queer theorists turning to points of connection that link human sexuality and nonhuman life. As Mortimer-Sandilands and Erickson argue, giving the example of the homoeroticism associated with cowboys in the American West and its representation in *Brokeback Mountain* (2005), 'ideas and practices of nature, including both bodies and landscapes, are located in particular productions of sexuality and sex' and vice versa.[8] Sex, sexuality and nature are terms that not only need to be contested, but contested in relation to one another. While Barnes's idea that one might become a horse if one felt the right kind of desire works as a joke, it is a joke that nonetheless speaks to the queer intersections between sex and nature.

Similarly comic in tone, Barnes's first novel *Ryder* (1928) explores precisely these interstices between sex, nature and animal life. Relatively little studied within Barnes's corpus and even less so within broader discussions of modernism, *Ryder* is an unconventional family saga set largely in rural New York that centres on the picaresque exploits of the eponymous patriarch Wendell Ryder. A comic figure of self-absorption, Wendell is presented as a philosopher farmer and polygamist, who justifies his two wives and many lovers on the basis of a natural autonomy that makes him an 'outlaw' from society and social niceties (R 131). While Eugene Jolas in his review of the novel for *transition* described Wendell Ryder as a 'swashbuckling super-male', Ryder's identity is, in reality, rather less straightforward.[9] A figure of 'changing countenance' who wishes to be 'all things to all men, and all women's woman', explaining that at one moment he can be a 'young and tender girl', the next 'a whore in a ruffled petticoat' and at other times a 'man-with-a-trowel, digging [. . .] for the tangible substance of re-creation' (R 164), Wendell, like O'Connor in *Nightwood*, is able to vacillate between positions and identities. He nonetheless holds onto a position of familial authority, complicating the idea that patriarchal power is synonymous with a stable masculine identity. A 'sensitive man [. . .] racked with women, and with beasts' (R 220), the novel narrates the course of his life from birth to moment of sexual crisis where, under threat of law, he is forced to submit to monogamy. Yet, the most immediately striking quality of *Ryder* is not its transgressive narrative content, but its bold modernist form. Eschewing the typical structure of the family saga, the novel's fifty episodic chapters adhere only obliquely to a linear chronology, each chapter drawing on a different stylistic mode, often recycling and ventriloquising earlier literary forms, such as Chaucerian, Gothic, sentimental, fabular, biblical and catechistic modes, and are accompanied by eleven illustrations that Barnes drew. Censored by her publisher, Boni & Liveright, who feared that the novel would be seized and destroyed by the New York Postal Service under obscenity laws, two of these illustrations were removed and a number of the novel's passages deemed most likely to offend replaced with asterisks, producing a text that, as Barnes ironically states in her foreword, has had its 'beauty [. . .] damaged' thanks to the 'havoc of [. . .] nicety' (R vii).[10]

While the revival of interest in Barnes's life and writing in the 1990s saw some attention paid to the novel, early criticism on *Ryder* looked to decode its autobiographical aspects to fill blanks in Barnes's biography, reading Wendell as a stand-in for Barnes's father, Wald, and the figure of Julie in the novel as representing Barnes's young self.[11] Barnes, however, disparaged autobiographical readings of the novel. When James B. Scott wrote to Barnes in 1971, asking if the character of Julie represented her, Barnes responded by complaining of the 'superficial drive to find out [. . .] at what point the author is the person named in any portion of the story, play or verse' and 'the frivolous attempt to drag the author back through his or her works to confront him or her at the porch of the mother', explaining that if it was biographical details he wanted, he should instead 'come for tea and I will give them to you, as well as I remember them'.[12] Insisting on the formal unity of the work as speaking for itself rather than serving as a psycho-biographical puzzle to be resolved into its latent meanings, Barnes's remarks anticipate the recent turn to reading *Ryder* as presenting a 'non-dichotomous relationship' between 'auto/biography and fiction'.[13] Looking at how Barnes's formal innovations refashion, rather than represent, familial relations, the novel's departure from the linear structure of the family saga has been read as disrupting the patrilineality that typifies the generic conventions of biographies and novels alike.[14] Less attention, however, has been paid to the way in which Barnes's denaturalising of familial structures, and the sexual categories that undergird them, intersect with conventions around nature and species. Yet, such a connection is suggested even before the narrative has begun. The original frontispiece illustration, depicting the Ryder family arranged on various branches of a tree, presents a literalised family tree (figure 4.1). While Louis Kannenstine has argued that it gives the impression of 'pastoral serenity in an orderly universe with everything in its place', it is also an image that questions natural order.[15] Family members are poised precariously, as if about to slip on to a different branch or tumble to the ground at any moment. Similarly, humans and animals crowd the base of the trunk, bringing into question the species barrier that is usually a defining feature of a family tree, and suggesting an analogous resemblance to the diagrams of evolutionary trees that had caused so much controversy during the nineteenth century. In all these respects, it both represents the family and

THE MODERNIST ANTHROPOCENE

Figure 4.1 *The Tree of Ryder* (frontispiece) from *Ryder*. Drawn by Djuna Barnes. Djuna Barnes Papers, Special Collections, University of Maryland Libraries.

questions that frame of representation, setting up a movement that will prevail throughout the novel.

This chapter examines Barnes's interest in showing how the familial imagination that regulates sexual difference and the ecological imagination that regulates the human's relation to the natural world are inextricably tangled, suggesting that, as the Anthropocene is increasingly bringing to light, questions of relationality must consider both intra- and interspecies dynamics. Beginning by examining Barnes's polemical engagement with a masculinist aesthetics of nature within her journalism and letters, it suggests that Barnes perceived discourse around nature as often naturalising heterosexual ideas of sexual difference. Moving to consider how in *Ryder* Barnes shows that a progressive or transgressive ecological outlook might not always be inherently at odds with patriarchal sovereignty, but can, in fact, entrench it, I suggest that rather than reading Wendell as a swashbuckling superman, we should attend to how the novel's formal and stylistic operations critique the genealogical structures that uphold both anthropo- and androcentrism. *Ryder*, this chapter will argue, instead draws on disparate matter to construct an alternative, queer genealogical mode and invites new ways of thinking about sexual difference, familial structures and species kinship.

Barnes Against Nature

'Against Nature', Barnes's August 1922 article for *Vanity Fair* written under the pseudonym Lydia Steptoe, opens with a bold, arch assertion: 'I hate Nature. Nature and simplicity. I always have.'[16] Echoing the title of the English translation of Joris-Karl Huysmans's *Á rebours* (1884), the article, like much of Barnes's early writing, displays a debt to the decadence movement's celebration of artificiality and intricacy over naturalness and simplicity, taking on the mannered and ironical voice of the world-weary 'cultivated woman'. As the article proceeds, however, it becomes clear that the disavowal of nature is not just rooted in an aesthetic revulsion from the simple and plain, but a rejection of the gendered societal values that surround them. Challenging the tendency for anything 'inadequate, young or tiresome [to be] called natural', the article outlines the sexual politics of discourse around nature, in which women interested in 'advanced ideas' are considered to contravene natural qualities of feminine 'simplicity'.[17] Here we find Barnes foreshadowing what Woolf in 1931, in an address to the National Society for Women's Service (which would go on to become the starting point for both *The Years* (1937) and *Three Guineas* (1938)), described as the male belief that 'nature had meant women to be wives, mothers, housemaids, parlourmaids and cooks'.[18] For Barnes, however, it is the reduction of women to motherhood, or the idea that 'babies are [. . .] justifiers of a woman's existence', that becomes the focus of the article's ire. 'To justify yourself more than five or six times in a life is rather insisting on the point', Barnes writes, 'a point that even Nature would drop – and Nature almost never drops a point.'[19] Ironically drawing on the impersonal language of biological reductionism in order to satirise it, Barnes's rejection of Nature, its capitalisation speaking to its standing as a signifier of metaphysical authority, insists that the category of the natural is, in fact, a tissue of cultural proscriptions around sexual difference.

As Mortimer-Sandilands and Erickson argue, drawing on Foucault's history of sexuality, the early twentieth century saw sexuality become increasingly naturalised, with sexual behaviours codified in terms of biological norms (and pathological deviations from those norms).[20] Barnes's article, seemingly alert to this process, concludes with what must have been shocking advice for the readers of the 1920s, asserting the dual need for 'women [to] solve their destiny without children' and for both men and women to embrace 'intricacy' and 'falsity' rather than 'eternal simplicity'.[21] Necessary to the rejection of a falsely naturalised notion of female reproduction is, Barnes shows, a turn from an idealised nature to the aesthetic, the artificial and the corrupt. Yet while critics have sometimes seen Barnes's interest in aesthetic artifice as premised on a wholesale rejection of nature, it might instead be understood to be a certain 'natural' aesthetic of nature that is being rejected, as the article clears the ground for the highly stylised presentation of humans, animals and the rural in her subsequent fiction.[22] A further indication of Barnes's article foreshadowing *Ryder*, is its mockery of the rise of an American veneration for the rustic, or what Barnes describes as the increase in 'Nature lovers'.[23] Framing the uptake as a largely masculine hobby, the article outlines 'how dangerous it is to love Nature', describing men who are:

> always pulling your spirits down by lurid descriptions of home with roses clinging to the front porch and smoke issuing from the chimney and hens laying eggs in the backyard. [. . .] Through love of plants men have lost their ability to stand alone, and have become permanently hooked. Through preoccupation with crawling, bivalvular creatures, they have neglected to shave for such a lengthy period that they become too heavily bearded to be of any further use in the home.[24]

Presenting echoes of Bloom's pastoral Flowerville fantasy in the 'Ithaca' episode of *Ulysses* that I discussed in Chapter 1, and which Barnes may have had freshly in mind as she wrote this article in August 1922, the passage satirises the gendered expectations and domestic labour that enable the pursuits of nature lovers. Again, there are parallels here with Mortimer-Sandilands and Erickson's genealogy of sex and nature here, who note that in early twentieth-century America, 'white men came to assert their increasingly heterosexual identities' through outdoor hobbies and sports that cultivated values of self-reliance and an ability to navigate and master the natural world.[25]

For Barnes, a masculine veneration for the natural world was constitutive to an American literary tradition that she felt she was outside of and, at times, actively writing against. In a letter to Coleman in the late 1930s, Barnes described what she called the 'open shirt prophets' who had influenced her father, Wald. Offering as examples Henry David Thoreau and Walt Whitman, Barnes describes such prophets as being 'full of theories and whiskers, but underneath, [having] a really passionate feeling for truth and right and "how to live"'.[26] These nineteenth-century writers are presented as faintly ridiculous bearded figures of sincerity, but, as she explained in a further letter, they had established a masculinist aesthetic of nature that stretched into the modernist present. Declining Coleman's invitation to visit her ranch in Arizona, Barnes exclaimed that she disliked the idea of 'the West' on the basis that it 'personifies everything in my father that I hated – Mark Twain – Bret Harte – Walt Whitman sort of thing – Ezra Pound and his hick-prune-chewing prose'.[27] As in 'Against Nature', Barnes highlights the prevalent cultural and literary constructions of nature in America and, implicitly, the sexual politics attached to them.

In both Barnes's correspondence and article, we find a suggested lens through which to read the traces of American romanticism that run through *Ryder* and, more specifically, Wendell's role as, in an example of Barnes's recycling a term from her journalism, a 'nature lover' (*R* 7). While Wendell has previously been read as a grotesque refashioning of transcendentalism – with Daniela Caselli wittily describing him as a 'Whitmanian hero who has misread Emerson' – I want to suggest that his presentation in the novel should be seen as premised on a more explicit refusal of an American nature writing tradition than has previously been acknowledged.[28] Indeed, perhaps unsurprisingly given the way in which she would later equate her father with Thoreau in her letters to Coleman, *Walden; or Life in the Woods* (1854) emerges as an intertext that clearly shapes the way in which Wendell is figured in the novel. Thoreau's book, which was among Wald Barnes's favourite texts and possibly inspired his name (which he gave himself as an adolescent), would likely have been familiar to Barnes. We find distorted iterations of *Walden*'s ideals in Wendell Ryder's reported maxims, such as that one should 'ris[e] in the dawn and goest among the green things' (*R* 4) and his belief that 'the great man lives and dies alone' (*R* 223).[29] Similarly, the construction of the 'Ryder cabin' in the rural Hudson valley, 'fifteen feet high and twenty-nine feet wide [. . .] and [with] steps three to its stoop', made of 'hewn cedar, by Wendell cut [. . .] when he had gone with his axe into the forest' (*R* 86) parallels the precision and asceticism of *Walden*, whose opening chapter, 'Economy', details the dimensions, materials and location of his cabin in the woods. Yet, unlike Thoreau's *Walden*, which obscures the female labour that supported his project, *Ryder* takes pains to foreground the physical and emotional toll of Wendell's idealism on his family.[30] In the same short chapter that Wendell is described 'furnishing' the 'little log cabin', Amelia, his wife, must 'cha[r] the day out below in Wendell's brother's mansion', taking up the 'task of providing for the family' (*R* 86). Moreover, on her return to the family home, Amelia discovers Wendell has furnished the cabin according to his philosophy in more than one sense, when she is greeted by the 'smiling' arrival of his new, second wife Kate. At first a complicit partner in Wendell's scheme, observing that they 'have it very comfortable here' (*R* 87), Kate is yet unaware of the physical labour that will be required of her and which is, at least partially, the motivation for her presence.

Certainly, it is true that, as Andrew Kalaidjian has argued, Barnes is in a sense indebted to the 'dark pastoral' mode that Thoreau developed through his presentation of the nonhuman world's strangeness and opacity.[31] Yet, *Ryder* is equally preoccupied with scrutinising the implicitly gendered dimension to the ideals of self-reliance that Thoreau's aesthetic gravitates towards. Like Woolf, whose ambivalent feelings towards Thoreau were derived from the way that she saw him as 'never speaking directly to us [but always] speaking partly to himself and partly to something mystic beyond our sight' (*E2* 137), Barnes presents transcendentalist modes of writing about nature as enacting an androcentric obfuscation of social relations and responsibilities. It is not so much, as Susan Edmunds argues, that Wendell is a 'grotesque parody of transcendentalism' that both 'degrades and revives its loftier sentiments', so much that Barnes reveals those supposedly lofty sentiments to have their foundations in a philosophy of self-reliance that not only naturalises a certain aesthetic ideal of nature, but of sex and gender too.[32] Where Wendell differs from both Thoreau and the account of heterosexual masculinity that Barnes outlines in 'Against Nature', however, is in his challenge to monogamy. For Wendell, the fallacy that 'animal and man be set apart' can be overcome by observing animal procreation and following suit, behaving like a 'cock-hen' indiscriminately mating with 'speckled wyandotts' and letting 'like a fountain [. . .] the eggës pour' (R 61–2). A return to nature for Wendell not only involves retreating to the country, but what Alex Goody describes as an 'earthly spirituality of phallic fecundity'.[33] Nonetheless, Wendell's polygamy cannot be traced back solely to transcendentalism. The novel also insists on its germ in his childhood in *fin de siècle* London, where his mother, Sophia, having 'the stuff of a great reformer' and 'mov[ing] among the Pre-Raphaelites', is the matriarch of a fashionable salon (R 9; 34). It is within this progressive, liberal environment that an adolescent Wendell first articulates his 'rosy picture [. . .] of polygamy' as 'a perfect prostrate tapestry of fecundity' (R 39–41). Yet, as the novel repeatedly makes clear, at the root of Wendell's ideals around sex, sexuality and reproduction is a radical understanding of nature in which self-reliance, providence and fertility are all foregrounded. As this next section will discuss, the coherency of Wendell's philosophy of polygamy relies upon a view of the nonhuman world that appears to question human exceptionalism while simultaneously strengthening the grounds upon which patriarchal sovereignty is naturalised.

Man, Woman and Animal

Mimicking the language of the *King James Bible*, the opening chapter of *Ryder* establishes Wendell's ecological credentials, introducing him as Jesus Mundane: a messiah not of the heavens, but the earth and the earthy.[34] In contrast to the Bible, however, the divine law of Wendell insists on a humility in which man recognises he is 'part and parcel of thy pastures' (R 5). Where in Genesis, God gives dominion over the beasts, Jesus Mundane teaches that 'the beasts [are not] for thee' and further sets out that:

> When thou goest into the field and markest thy goat's eye, think not that thou knowest why it lies like meek fluid in the head, or why thy kine have an unknown regard from under their eyelids, nor why the hawk flies among its feathers [. . .] These also are within the way, but all things are not equal about His feet. (R 4)

The inscrutable gaze of the animal disrupts the promise of mastery, yet as the clause regarding 'equal[ity]' makes clear, this act of recognising nonhuman life does not itself necessitate the dismantling of species hierarchy. Rather, it engenders a position that, in emphasising his ability to observe and recognise the interdependence of the parts within the whole, maintains Wendell's centrality as the subject who has oversight over all relations. From the start Wendell's ability to think beyond human life is marked by a doubleness that entrenches the anthropocentrism which it professes to disavow. In the chapters that follow, Wendell's messianic mundanity is further developed, with his apparently self-effacing view of humankind's position within nature enabling him to occupy a role that can vacillate at will between animality and sovereignty. In the mock-Chaucerian chapter, 'The Occupations of Wendell', for instance, Wendell outwardly professes a wish to topple the ontological division between humans and other animals, asking 'what [. . .] have we that all y-beasts have not?' (*R* 62). Challenging the notion that language separates man from beast, Wendell instead situates animals as subjects who, given the chance, might speak for themselves. In a fable told to his children, Wendell weaves a tale in which his wizardry enables the farm horse, Hisodalgus, to speak in rhyming couplets. Suggestive not only of Jonathan Swift's Houyhnhnms but also the anthropomorphic tales about the family horse, Dick, that Wald would recount to Barnes while she was a child, the story pivots on Hisodalgus's attempt to warn the animals on the farm of their imminent slaughter.[35] Recognising that it is their perceived lack of language that permits their death, the mannered Hisodalgus instructs his fellow animals to follow his example:

> Now I would have each one of you to mull,
> This cud of thought, that right into each skull
> A flowing brook of speech by haply hung
> To rill in wordës all adown your tongue,
> So that you take not only to the bit
> But both to wisdom and alike to wit,
> That nevermore your throat y-corve is none
> For man be fright to pick the rack of bone
> That to him spoken has [. . .] (*R* 67)

Wendell's speaking horse, absurdly anthropomorphised, encourages his fellow animals to not only disrupt the human prejudice that 'animals go silent before all' (*R* 65), but to literally intervene in human discourse, reasoning through 'wisdom' and 'wit' to argue for their recognition as subjects worthy of ontological, and by extension ethical, recognition.

While, on one level, Wendell's anxiety around the silence of animals parallels what Derrida describes as the 'brutally false' assertion of animal silence inherent to Western philosophy, Wendell's desire that 'every beaste in kindë mightë speak'(*R* 65) is itself rooted in a narrowly logocentric understanding of language.³⁶ Conflated with reason and rationality, language is situated as a medium through which animals might make a claim for their moral worth through their resemblance to the humanist idea of the human as the rational animal, in which 'wisdom' and 'wit' are defining properties. Reiterated in his later description of a potential future language between humans and animals where the calls of a 'thousand several throats' will be '*common* to the human' (R 210 emphasis added), Wendell strains to collapse the distinction between the human and animal by configuring the latter within the dominant humanist measure of the speaking subject. Wendell might acknowledge the animality of his own being, and in doing so, recognise the being of animals, but he does so through an uncritical anthropomorphism that implicitly entrenches the basis for his own sovereignty.

Moreover, if, as Rosi Braidotti has argued, the humanist configuration of the human operates through a 'systematized standard of recognizability' that subsumes difference in favour of sameness in such a way that is not only anthropocentric but androcentric, enshrining man as the measure of all things, it is unsurprising that Wendell's sovereignty extends beyond his livestock.³⁷ Described as performing 'the samë office for his cow[s]' as he does his wives and setting out how 'child and cattle' will eat from the same 'bin' since 'kine [. . .] were kith and infants kin' (R 55–6), Wendell's farm is an attempt to construct a trans-species commune structured on the principles of shared fecundity and procreation. Yet, where Wendell's sovereignty relies on anthropomorphising his livestock, it simultaneously requires that he animalises his family, situating both within a general ecology at his command. The description, for instance, of Amelia and Kate, simultaneously going into labour (and discovering that they were both impregnated by Wendell 'nine months back to a day') while in his pastures all the cows lie with 'a little cow within' (R 95) presents an image of the farm operating according to Wendell's strict management of reproduction. The bawdy story of Pennyfinder the Bull that Wendell recounts to his daughter Julie further explicates the resemblance between women and livestock, as Wendell describes Pennyfinder, 'a Bull as great as any tree', whose 'roar' brings '[m]any a dame [. . .] running to her door' (R 62–3). Inviting further comparison between Barnes and Joyce, the tale of Pennyfinder parallels the moment in the 'Oxen of the Sun' episode of *Ulysses* set in Holles Street Maternity Hospital, where the medical student Dixon retells the bawdy fertility fable of an 'Irish bull' seducing a 'maid, wife, abbess and widow' in the 'dark of a cowhouse' (U 14.581; 14.595–7). While the passage in *Ryder* that describes what happens once the dames meet Pennyfinder was expurgated, the reader can nonetheless infer the censored narrative from the surviving illustration (restored in the 1990 Dalkey Archive edition) which shows two women bathing in a pool of bodily fluids beneath the giant bull (figure 4.2).

Figure 4.2 Pennyfinder the Bull. Drawn by Djuna Barnes for *Ryder* but removed at the request of her publishers. Djuna Barnes Papers, Special Collections, University of Maryland Libraries.

As in the aforementioned section of *Ulysses*, where Dixon's parable of bestiality serves as a misogynistic portrayal of female sexuality and male virility, Wendell's Pennyfinder bestialises female sexuality in order to position his wives within the same sexual economy as his livestock where, it is implied, prize sperm will sate both.

For Wendell, who conceives of himself not as a father but a 'ranchman' to his children (*R* 170), nature is understood in terms where survival of the fittest is applied not so much to species as spermatozoa. Disavowing the artifice of civilisation, while still upholding the tenets of wisdom and wit that undergird his authority as man, Wendell believes that a return to nature means 'bedding in all beds, and in bedding, sow[ing] no seed of doubt' (*R* 211). Structured by a distorted Darwinian logic of survival, Wendell rejects monogamy but wholly embraces genealogy, seeing polygamy as nature's way of securing his line. As he explains to one of his lovers, in a long speech immediately prior to copulation, polygamy multiplies the channels through which he can be 'Father of All Things' and, akin to a logic of species survival, enables him to extend his fatherly presence beyond his own mortality through 'the Race that shall be Ryder' (*R* 210):

> Now this is the Race that shall be Ryder – those who can sing like the lark, coo like the dove, moo like the cow, buzz like the bee, cheep like the cricket, bark like the dog, mew like the cat, neigh like the stallion, roar like the bull, crow like the cock [. . .] My children shall come forth, grow, rise, decline and fall in a manner hithertofore unknown to man [. . .] They shall follow the hounds, and herd with the beasts and know the way of birds and fish. They shall be fleshed with all fleshes now alien to man and unknown, and shall be by that flesh made so tender with wisdom that they shall know how the hoof strikes, the fin cleaves, the wing soars, the paw runs, the claw clings, and the web swims. (*R* 210–11)

A description of species kinship premised upon his own procreative agency, Wendell embeds himself and his kin within the animal kingdom, while marking out his own exceptionalism. Metonymically defining animals through conventional linguistic representation ('moo', 'crow', 'mew', 'bark' and so forth) the accumulation of anthropomorphic designations has a nominative effect. In this respect, Wendell's speech operates according to what Derrida emphasises as the authority the human bestows upon itself through the act of naming which, he argues, runs all the way back to the story of Adam being given dominion over the beasts.[38] In operating as a kind of performative creation myth itself, Wendell's speech embodies what Oliver describes as the way in which the 'sovereign operation of naming' not only creates the illusion of human dominion, but the conditions for 'animal and sexual difference [to] arrive at the same time'.[39] His assertion that in a 'thousand several shapes shall they be created and named all things' (*R* 211) is a recognition of animal life that entrenches his own identity as a male speaking subject and sovereign over his livestock, sexual partners and offspring.

For Wendell, then, recognising the human as an animal is a means of arriving at newly essentialised ideas of sex and gender. His description of his daughter Julie as destined to 'eat, function and die, looking neither backward nor forward' (*R* 202), for instance, not only situates her in terms that resemble his livestock, but closely echoes O'Connor's patronising description of Robin in *Nightwood* as an 'animal, born at the opening of the eye, going only forward, and, at the end of the day, shutting out memory with the dropping of the lid' (*N* 122), discussed in my previous chapter. The relationship between sex and nature, for Wendell, means returning to a question that has been asked a 'thousand times [and] in as many tongues':

> What is woman? Wherein comes that of her which we are not? What destroys our reason in her, when we see it enter her as we would, and

come forth as she will? What in her, like a shadow jackal, preys upon the mound of our accomplishment, dragging off that of it we thought most rotten with defeat, to make of it an halter and a noose? For man rides the monster civilization, but to woman goes the shoe cast of it, in which is the exact record of that journey. (*R* 206)

An example of Wendell's ability to vacillate between positions, the description of 'woman' as a jackal shadowing man and feeding on the fringes of his accomplishments, defines both women and animals through what they lack in comparison with the reasoning figure of man. Women here are 'cast' in the same shoe as a nature that must necessarily be tamed in order to be transformed. Oliver observes that Western philosophy has historically associated women with 'instincts to procreate, which place them in the vicinity of the animal realm' while man, figured as a rational subject, is placed outside of it.[40] Although Wendell appears on the one hand to transgress this division, by rejecting sexual relations based on monogamy and resituating the human within a natural economy of sexuality, these sexual transgressions entrench his mundane messianism in which the 'lives that [he] begettest, and the lives that shall spring from them' produce a 'world without end' in which he remains at the centre (*R* 3).

In his ability to vacillate between a position of animality and patriarchal power, Wendell presents the reader with what Derrida describes as the troubling resemblance between the beast and the sovereign.[41] For Derrida, both beast and sovereign stand outside of the law; the law is applied neither to animals nor the sovereign upon whose authority the law relies. Indeed, Wendell explicitly identifies himself in such terms. When a concerned social worker arrives on the farm and instructs him to send his unschooled children to school, he warns her that 'Ryder as an outlaw is less trouble than citizen Ryder' (*R* 131). As Edmunds notes, Wendell not only occupies a position of both criminality and authority, but worries the 'stable opposition' between the two.[42] Able to vacillate between being above and before the law, in much the same way as he can vacillate between being human and animal, Wendell enjoys a sovereign subjectivity that can, as Derrida writes, 'posit itself as [the] "I, me"' of the autonomous subject.[43] In this respect Wendell occupies almost exactly the kingly position that Barnes will have O'Connor later set out in *Nightwood*:

A king is the peasant's actor, who becomes so scandalous that he has to be bowed down to [. . .] And why must he be bowed down to? Because he has been set apart as the one dog who need not regard the rules of the house, they are so high that they can defame God and foul their rafters! (*N* 35)

O'Connor's mixed metaphor situates the king 'as' the dog who in being outside the law enjoys a sovereignty unbeholden to any authority, to the extent that he, the kingly dog, has the right to defile his own environment.[44]

As *Ryder* repeatedly shows, it is not for lack of a transgressive ecological imaginary that Wendell is able to claim sovereignty over the animals and women around him. Rather, his authority derives precisely from his ability to reconfigure the relation between the human and the animal. Indeed, the manner in which Wendell's philosophy legitimates his patriarchy serves to highlight how, as Derrida has argued, ecology is bound up with familial structures ahead of time. Drawing attention to the well-known etymological root of the prefix eco- in 'oikos', the Greek word for both family and home, Derrida argues that epistemologies such as ecology and economics remain indebted to the notion of 'furnishing a house'; that is to say, establishing and regulating laws of domesticity and relationality. Just as in ancient Greece 'oikos' functioned to situate women, slaves and animals within 'a habitat for beasts', in which processes of 'domestication, [. . .] taming, training, stock raising, so many modalities of master and sovereign power' were enacted, Derrida suggests that later, modern epistemological or discursive modes of 'oikos' operate through similar operations of sovereign knowledge and power. In establishing a proper set of relations between species and their environments, ecology always has the potential to extend 'the laws of the family home [. . .] the house of the master' beyond the boundaries of what is usually considered the domestic sphere.[45] Wendell's challenging of the rigid boundary between the human and the animal does not transgress patriarchy. Rather, his ability to reconceptualise human-animal relations provide the grounds for patriarchal authority itself.

Bringing Laughter to Slaughter

As I have shown above, Wendell's philosophy of nature establishes a sexual economy in which both women and animals are cast as material resources to be exploited in the service of a genealogical line. Throughout *Ryder* this exploitation is thematised through images of violence that foreground a correlation between sexual sacrifice and structures of male sovereignty. In the early chapter, 'Rape and Repining', which does not directly feature any of the Ryder family, procreation is disturbingly and satirically presented through seasonal cycles of sexual violence. Spoken by a female chorus, an unidentified 'Council of Women' (R 26) who have internalised the misogyny enacted against them, the chapter opens with the sentiment, 'What ho! Spring again! Rape again, and the Cock not yet at his Crowing!' (R 21), before detailing how 'the Waters melt, and the Earth divides, and the Leaves put forth, and the Heart sings dilly, dilly, dilly! It is Girls' Weather and Boys' Luck' (R 29). Presenting rural environments as spaces of danger for young women, the chapter laments the

'Deflowering' of an adolescent in Tittencote, the English village where Wendell's wife Amelia grew up:

> A Girl is gone! A Girl is lost! A simple Rustic Maiden but Yesterday swung upon the Pasture Gate, with Knowledge nowhere, yet is now, to-day, no better than her Mother, and her Mother's Mother before her! Soiled! Despoiled! Handled! Mauled! Rumpled! Rummaged! Ransacked! No purer than Fish in Sea, no sweeter than Bird on Wing, no better than Beasts of Earth! (*R* 21)

An example of what Bonnie Kime Scott describes as a 'repeated Barnes plot' of women hunted like animals and forcibly brought down to the earth, the chapter refashions springtime fertility myths into narratives of violent sexual conquest.[46] Here women, 'no better than Beasts', are literally positioned as coterminous with an undifferentiated nature that exists only as it is organised by the sovereign agency of man, whose questions of 'Whose child do you harvest? Whose First-Born springs from your Lap?' (*R* 27), mirrors Wendell's own rhetoric of a naturalised genealogy. Indeed, in both the chapter's misogynistic content – its assertion that it is the girls' own 'ambushed Flesh' (*R* 21) that generates the ritual of springtime predation – and its verbose pronouncements on sexual conduct, Barnes encourages the reader to hear a clear echo of the opening apostrophe delivered by Wendell as Jesus Mundane. That the chapter following 'Rape and Repining' details Wendell's seduction of Amelia, is another suggestion that we should read this pastoral scene as a mytho-poetic justification of Wendell's adoption of a naturalised genealogy.

The positioning of women alongside the bodies of livestock and fields of wheat as grist for the mill in Wendell's grand vision of nature makes literal what in contemporary feminist theory has been suggested is the structural relation between misogyny and the consumption of animal bodies. Most notably, Carol Adams in *The Sexual Politics of Meat* (1990) has argued that the slaughtering and consuming of animals is an entrenched 'symbol and celebration of male dominance'. This dominance, Adams argues, can be traced through overt and covert 'association[s] between meat eating and virile maleness' in cookbooks, novels, advertisements and other cultural representations.[47] To a certain extent, Barnes's oeuvre offers examples that support Adams's argument. The maidens of 'Rape and Repining', for instance, are described as 'Quarry' promising 'White meat or Dark' to their captors, who see them as 'Sweet Chops' (*R* 24). The theme is returned to in an early draft of Barnes's 1958 play *The Antiphon*. As Andrew Field summarises, an unpublished draft includes a speech by the play's protagonist Miranda describing how at the age of sixteen she was bound 'up like a side of beef and [hoisted] to hang from a rafter in the barn' while her father, a figure who resembles both Wendell Ryder and Wald Barnes, 'goes off to barter her virginity for a goat among the local men'. Like the adolescent Julie in *Ryder*, whose virginity it is implied is 'flung down into the market place' (*R* 109), Miranda is, as Field puts it, 'the first virginal sacrifice of [her father's] new religion'.[48]

Yet, while such moments in Barnes's oeuvre speak clearly to Adams's description of 'images of women [as] butchered, fragmented, or consumable', her writing resists straightforwardly mapping animal slaughter onto a model of binary gender relations.[49] The 1917 short story 'The Rabbit', which she revised substantially in 1962 for republication in the collection *Spillway*, offers a good example of the way in which Barnes complicates the connection between sex, animality and slaughter. The story's main protagonist, Amietiev, a timid, newly arrived Armenian immigrant in New York, is early on in the narrative shocked by a Manhattan butcher's grotesque window display of 'bright quarters of beef, calves' heads and [. . .] remnants of animals, pink and yellow layers of fat' (*CS* 199). This 'harvest of death' stands in explicit contrast to his bucolic memories of his home farm in Armenia where he had 'ploughed and tended his crops', 'groomed the feathers and beaks of his ducks' and 'watched his cows grazing' (*CS* 197–9). Subsequently falling in love with a confident and sardonic New Yorker named Addie, who not only refuses to return his affection but tells him that he is too feminine to ever 'be anything', Amietiev avows to become 'less like a woman' to win the affection of his love (*CS* 202–3). Associating masculinity with a heroism defined by violence, since 'all heroes were men who killed or got killed', Amietiev returns to the butcher's shop with its 'calves' heads in ranks on their slabs, looking like peeled women' (*CS* 204; 206). Covertly entering the shop while it is briefly unattended and overcoming the nausea he experiences from the smell of the 'choked scrap barrel, spilling out its lungs and guts', he discovers in the backroom a live rabbit in a box (*CS* 206). Strangling the rabbit despite his repulsion at the act, he returns with the carcass to Addie as proof of his masculinity. The story, however, concludes with her 'harsh, back-bending laughter' at his deed, while Amietiev, now 'shaking', runs out on to the streets of New York in terror at what he has done (*CS* 208). In its presentation of the mutability of Amietiev's masculinity, 'The Rabbit' is a story that draws upon a lurid aesthetic of meat and slaughter to explore the construction of gender roles. Yet while the story explicitly associates women with slaughtered animals in its likening of calves' heads to skinned women, it also foregrounds the degree to which cultural practices surrounding the production and consumption of meat resist being neatly correlated with stable male and female identities. The protagonist's masculinity is not at any point synonymous with an aesthetic of meat eating, although the romanticism with which he remembers his previous life in Armenia suggest that it is an aesthetic revulsion at impersonal, mass-produced meat production that horrifies him rather than meat itself. Most striking, however, is the way in which it is Addie who has more clearly internalised an ideal of masculinity associated with the killing and consumption of animals. Meat eating in 'The Rabbit' provides the basis for a construction of female, rather than male, agency, although, as the story's ending suggests, where Amietiev's terror makes Addie suddenly 'afraid of him' (*CS* 208), it is a form of agency that does not translate into progressive gender relations. Instead, like the meat on display, things are left sticky, raw and in a state of decay.[50]

Ryder also complicates this relation between sexual violence and carnivorousness, showing it not only to cut across demarcations of sex and gender, but to be constitutive to a certain figuration of subjecthood. In 'Rape and Repining', for instance, the female chorus not only liken maidens to 'Quarry', but encourage married women to be like hounds in their pursuit of women who have fallen short of moral standards:

> This way, good Wives! Muzzles to Windward! [. . .] The Hare is running, and you are well behind! She whisks over the Common and you cannot get scent of her! [. . ..] Who is the most Infallible Pointer among you? [. . .] Now, now! She falls at yonder Ditch, and, like a Deer, turns face on, weeping for clemency. Now, have at her!' (*R* 24)

While elsewhere in the novel 'a man's member' is likened to a 'mighty bloodhound' sniffing out its prey (*R* 230), here the canine figure of the 'Infallible Pointer' stands as an internalised phallus that impels women themselves to 'make a catch of [maidens] and an example' (*R* 24). Moreover, as in 'The Rabbit', the novel shows the mutability of meat tropes across gender distinctions that are themselves mutable. Wendell might fashion himself as a sovereign ranchman securing his genealogical line, but elsewhere sees himself as 'a well-done fowl' whose 'aroma' teases the 'authorities of the state' like a 'pack of hounds, all slavering at the jaws' (*R* 169). Wendell's mother, Sophia, also offers a clear example of the way in which it is possible to occupy a position of both hunter and hunted. Described as '[b]eggar at the gates [and] [. . .] queen at home', she is, like Wendell, able to vacillate between positions, as she is both subject to and requires 'obeisance'. As the novel simply states, 'She was the law' and in being the law 'gave herself to be devoured' (*R* 16).

Here, then, we find a dynamic that, rather than paralleling the vegetarian feminist critique of Adams, speaks rather more to Derrida's concept of carnophallogocentrism. For Derrida, carnophallogocentrism is a concept that outlines the degree to which the dominant notion of sovereign or autonomous subjecthood relies upon a carnivorous 'ingestion, incorporation, or introjection' of otherness which has often been both symbolised and actualised through meat eating.[51] Like Adams, Derrida highlights how this structure of subjecthood has historically operated through phallogocentric constructions of subjectivity (hence the neologism) in which '[a]uthority and autonomy' are attributed to 'the man . . . rather than to the woman, and to the woman rather than to the animal'. Yet, in a manner foreshadowed in Barnes's images of meat, slaughter and gender, Derrida's 'carnivorous virility' does not describe a certain identity but a set of social relations. For Derrida, as Amietiev in 'The Rabbit' also realises, meat eating is a practice that undergirds a 'heroic schema'.[52] Derrida, however, emphasises that this 'carnivorous virility' is not a symptom of a certain kind of masculinity, rather, this 'sacrificial schema' underpins the (patriarchal) Western idea of sovereign subjecthood itself. Indeed, for Derrida this carnivorous incorporation of otherness cannot be simply disavowed since, to a certain extent, it constitutes a fundamental set of relations between 'the self' and 'the other'. As such, the 'moral question is thus not [. . .] should one eat or not eat' but, rather, what does it mean to 'eat well'.[53] What constitutes eating well is a question that is also constantly at stake in *Ryder*. While Sophia 'offer[s] her heart for food' to her family, Julie, her granddaughter, 'spew[s] it out' since she 'taste[s] a lie' (*R* 16), a metaphor that self-reflexively points to the carnivorous processes of consumption, digestion and sublimation that Sophia appears to have capitalised upon in order to construct a position of power within the family's social relations.

In contrast to Carol Adams's argument for a vegetarian ethics as a response to the structural relation between patriarchy and meat eating, *Ryder* suggests that the notion of eating well cannot be straightforwardly associated with vegetarian practices. Wendell's experimentation with a 'meatless diet of vegetables' while a young man, proving to Sophia that her son is 'an artist' (*R* 34), is a moment that provides a further link with the transcendentalist philosophy of Thoreau, for whom the 'uncleanness' inherent to slaughter is an intolerable reminder of the 'slimy beastly life' and best replaced by a vegetable diet that will cultivate the 'higher or poetic faculties'.[54] While it is implied that the adult Wendell is no longer vegetarian, his queasiness around animal slaughter and general aesthetic distaste for the visceral means his wives are responsible for cleaning up the 'dirty mess' of animal waste that accrues on the farm (*R* 114). The lapsed vegetarianism of Wendell lives on in the abjection that he continues to associate with meat and animal bodies, but which extends to the bodies of his wives, shoring up his patriarchal sovereignty through a disavowal of the abject and the deathly associated with the feminine.[55] An example of what Derrida describes as the way in which vegetarians are not situated outside of the carnophallogocentric schema but simply 'practice a different mode of denegation', *Ryder* demonstrates how carnivorous identities are capable of occupying positions that outwardly appear to renounce meat eating and slaughter.[56]

While Derrida suggests that an ethics attentive to carnophallogocentrism should be premised on eating well, Barnes, more provocatively, presents a mode of feminist agency grounded in eating badly. The chapter 'Ryder – His Race', situated towards the end of the novel, is prefaced with an epigraph that situates it as 'a treatise on carnivora' (R 205). A nineteenth-century taxonomic term that again points to Wendell's distortion of Darwinian science, the carnivora are an order of animal within the mammalian class with carnassial molars effective for shredding flesh. Although humans are not technically part of this taxonomical order, the chapter opens with the assertion that, 'Of all carnivora man holds woman most dear' (R 205). Presented as a tract written by Wendell, the chapter continues the abject association of women with meat, praising females who practise the 'art of gourmandising' and detailing how the sight of 'some sweet creature [. . .] putting away sides of ox' fills him with 'pure ravishment' (R 205). In 'consuming whole lamb[s], trawls of fish, an hundred guinea fowl, woodcock and grouse per annum', the chapter explains, 'slaughter may be transfigured' into female beauty (R 205). Where Wendell associates himself with the quasi-vegetarian realms of the artistic and the philosophical, women are associated with the carnal and excessive. The chapter subsequently shifts in its form to a narrative account of Wendell's seduction of the wealthy widow Lady Terrance Bridesleep, a former attendee of Sophia's salons. Attractive to Wendell since she is the apotheosis of an 'epicure and gustator', Bridesleep is a woman who knows 'scarcely a bird or beast that [holds] adequate intricacies' for her tastes (R 208). Importantly, however, Bridesleep has not only internalised the carnivorous animality ascribed to her by Wendell but subverted its abject carnality into a form of agency and resistance. 'Men had come to her as men', the novel explains, 'and had left as little girls' (R 208). Although Bridesleep explains that she can no longer conceive children, for Wendell her lust for meat is proof of her 'fecundity' (R 207). Their subsequent act of intercourse is premised on Wendell's intention that she will contribute to 'the Race that shall be Ryder' (R 210). Her 'smiling' post-coital revelation, however, that the child she will bear for him will take the name 'Nothing and Never' and that through this 'No Child' she will have accomplished what 'all the others leave undone', namely enjoyed sexual pleasure without the consequence of impregnation, sees Bridesleep turn her carnivorousness on Wendell's projected genealogy (R 211). Subsequently calling to her maid to 'bring [. . .] the calf's head that you'll find on the ice', a doubly horrified Wendell 'open[s] his mouth, but no sound came' (R 211). It is, as Tyrus Miller suggests, an 'image of carnivorous woman' defeating Wendell's 'narcissistic vision' by forcing him to confront oblivion, as Wendell is reduced to the status of a silent, brute animal.[57] Death, however, is not incidental to Bridesleep (whose very name suggests a putting to sleep of a bridal idea of womanhood). Instead of displacing the carnophallogocentric schema within which she has been interpolated, her affirmation of negativity and violence, symbolised in the decapitated 'calf's head' that stands in for the 'No Child', refuses the feminine passivity that Wendell's treatise of carnivora ascribes. Instead, she fashions her own form of aesthetic pleasure from within the carnality to which she has been consigned. Bridesleep's lavish and grotesque taste for the very meat she is associated with becomes an act of cannibalism which disrupts patriarchal claims on female bodies by consuming the offspring she is expected to produce.

Genealogies of Difference

Bridesleep's cannibalistic mode of resisting the Ryder name by consuming the offspring which the structure of patrilineal genealogy relies upon is implicitly endorsed by the novel's own cannibalistic form. The grotesque refashioning of recognisable literary genres does not just wryly affiliate *Ryder* with a recognisable literary history, but gorges on this literary history as means of subverting established tropes and modes. Yet unlike Bridesleep, whose cannibalism is premised on eating her own offspring, the generative excess of Barnes's refiguring of literary history produces what Caselli describes as 'the text as illegitimate offspring'.[58] Central to this illegitimacy is a questioning of conventions around species kinship in relation to genealogy. Embodying a challenge to both species difference and patrilineality is the character of Molly Dancer, a 'dog fancier' who breeds 'fine bitches', producing 'pedigree[s] that would put a king to shame' (*R* 191). Like Wendell, Molly takes great interest in animal sex. She 'chaperon[s] her kennel assiduously' to protect against cross-breeding and has become so knowledgeable about canine copulation that her 'ears could tell, to a howl, that which heralded, in the future, a brindle with a hound's ear' (*R* 191). Yet, where for Wendell animal procreation is the undifferentiated material from which a human genealogy can be shaped, Molly, to Wendell's horror, reverses this order. Molly, described as 'no better than her dogs and seldom as good', believes that 'the human breed was of no importance' and, indeed, does not know who has 'sire[d]' any of her ten children (*R* 191). Her pedigree dogs and unfathered children stand in ironic counterpoint to one another: her 'outhouse stunk and sounded with this breed and that; the kitchen stunk and sounded with her own' (*R* 193).[59]

As Molly makes clear to Wendell when he visits 'to buy a bitch, and stayed to talk' (*R* 194), her approach to animal sex is informed by a reimagining of nature, history and literature. Mirroring the novel's formal irreverence towards an authoritative literary history, Molly asserts that she believes 'Henry James was a horse-thief and Caesar the betrayer of Jesus', prompting Wendell to accuse Molly of not knowing 'the fundamentals of anything' (*R* 194). This accusation of a lack of fundamentals, understood both in the sense of beginnings and underlying principles, is met with a response by Molly in the form of an origins story that undoes the authority of all fundamentals. A chaotic, fragmented and exuberant description of creation that stands in contrast to Wendell's harmonious origin myth in 'Ryder – His Race', Molly's tale begins with Jonah as 'the First

Man', emerging 'out of a whale's mouth [. . .] all decked out in olive branches and briars, and a crown of thorns, and his underneath all scaled' and stepping out into a world 'struck full of grass and flowers of all sorts and kinds' (R 195). This is followed by a sped-up version of Darwinian evolution, as 'Jonah's scales dried in the sun, [. . .] turned to feathers, and a bit later [. . .] into furs of all sorts and kinds, and after the fur [. . .] skin' and a chronological reordering of historical events and biblical narratives with the fall of Rome followed by Cain's slaughtering of Abel, which itself becomes the catalyst for 'the animals' to come down to land from where they 'had always herded in the sky' (R 195–6). A narrative composed of 'peelings and pits left scattered about' (R 195) that eschews sequential temporality and logic for an absurd collage of detritus, it is a creation myth intended to defy Wendell's framing of nature through linear heterosexual reproduction. Indeed, when challenged that she has forgotten about women's involvement in 'original sin', an assertion that looks to impose a teleological narrative of sexual morality on the tale, Molly responds by relaying the visionary message of a winged 'calf's-foot', outlining that 'original sin was not a woman's' and although there was an apple involved it was man who 'snapped it up, scattering the seeds [which] he uses to this day to get his sons by' (R 197–8). Exposing what Caselli describes as the 'lexical and syntactical choices' through which historical explanations derive 'causality, value and power', the exuberance of Molly's narrative self-reflexively points to its own artifice and self-fashioning.[60] In contrast to Wendell's naturalised polygamy, Molly's creation myth suggests that if there is an original sin, it comes, paradoxically, in believing too readily in an authentic idea of Eden.

Rejecting, like Barnes's newspaper article 'Against Nature', the possibility of a natural history which can be narrated without artifice and falsity, Molly's creation myth lambasts the notion of a pure or linear genealogy that Wendell sees as naturalising patriarchy. Instead, in her exuberant splicing of biblical myth, Darwinian evolution and modern history, in which the 'First Man' has only a 'hint [of] the human' to him (R 195) rather than a definitive essence or clear outline, Molly's narrative of origins displaces man (in both the universalising and gendered sense of the word) and queers nature. Reflecting what Morton describes as the way in which a queer approach to ecology recognises that life is not 'organic [or] coherent' but 'catastrophic, monstrous, nonholistic, and dislocated', Molly's origin tale fuses new forms of relation between humans, other species and their environment.[61] A self-fashioned ecology that finds expression in her activities as both a mother and a dog breeder, Molly's approach to animal sex opens up new genealogies and kinships that depart from heteronormative accounts of nature. Where Wendell's transgressive view of nature is indicative of what Morton calls an 'organicism' that polices sex and gender by 'naturalizing sexual difference', the queer agency of Molly's vision of nature finds emphasis in the chapter's closing moments.[62] Wendell, still disgusted at Molly's lack of fundamentals, is driven by a desire to force one upon her, namely that she will 'for once [know] the father' of her child (*R* 198). Although Molly initially agrees, with bold asterisks marking out where Barnes's description of the sexual act has been removed, her admission afterwards that 'Dan, the corner policeman' had the same idea 'two nights ago' (*R* 199) is, like Lady Bridesleep's post-coital remarks, a revelation that retrospectively reframes the sexual act outside of the genealogy Wendell has looked to establish. For Molly, who has always 'done her best with a very bad tangle' (*R* 192), sex, genealogy and species are always already entangled. Indeed, it is the tangle's badness, its improperness, that becomes the basis for a sexual agency that subverts any participation in Wendell's 'setting things in order' (*R* 198).

As Molly sees it, 'one man's thoughts are not worth much more than another's' (*R* 199) since they can only think of sex and reproduction in singular terms. Her own pleasure in heterogeneity, creativity and artifice, instead, speaks to what Oliver describes as the potential for animal sex to open the 'imagination to the possibility of alternative sexes and sexualities' in which we are able 'to see and to imagine alternatives to the limited and claustrophobic binary that reduces sex to a war between two'.[63] A genealogy that affirms difference rather than opposition, the 'bad tangle' through which Molly approaches her 'fine bitches' pre-emptively affirms Oliver's assertion of sex as an 'open rather than closed system [. . .] [comprised] of multiple sexes, sexualities, and even multiple reproductive practices'.[64] Like Barnes's ironic remark to Coleman imagining the forms of desire and subjectivity that might emerge between a human and a horse given the right circumstances, Molly playfully challenges the ideals of binary sexual difference that structure patrilineality. Where Wendell's interest in animal sex is premised on a heteronormative logic of passive feminine fecundity and fertility, Molly, like Bridesleep, uncouples sex and reproduction from patriarchal genealogy. Mirrored in the novel's various bad tangles, knotting together contrasting styles from literary history, as well as biography with fiction and illustration with text, *Ryder* explodes traditions of writing about nature that look to profess their naturalness of form and content. Foreshadowing arguments that the Anthropocene necessitates a deconstruction of how we use and understand the word 'nature' and that we remain critical of its proscriptive agency in policing not only landscapes but bodies and sexualities, Barnes insists on reimagining the nature of literature, in all senses of the phrase.

Notes

1. Emily Coleman to Djuna Barnes, 27 October 1935. Djuna Barnes Papers, Special Collections, University of Maryland Libraries (hereafter DBP), Series 2, Box 3, Folder 7.
2. Raymond Williams, *Keywords: A Vocabulary of Culture and Society* (Abingdon: Routledge, 2011), p. 184.

3. Kelly Oliver, *Animal Lessons: How They Teach Us to Be Human* (New York: Columbia University Press, 2009), pp. 131–2.
4. Ibid. p. 145.
5. Catriona Mortimer-Sandilands and Bruce Erickson. 'Introduction: A Genealogy of Queer Ecologies', in *Queer Ecologies: Sex, Nature, Politics, Desire*, ed. Catriona Mortimer-Sandilands and Bruce Erickson (Bloomington and Indianapolis: Indiana University Press, 2010), pp. 1–51 (p. 3; pp. 7–10).
6. Timothy Morton, *Ecology without Nature: Rethinking Environmental Aesthetics* (Cambridge, MA: Harvard University Press, 2007), p. 14.
7. Timothy Morton, 'Queer Ecology', *PMLA*, 125.2 (2010), 273–82 (p. 277).
8. Mortimer-Sandilands and Erickson, 'Introduction: A Genealogy of Queer Ecologies', p. 4. See also *Queering the Non/Human*, ed. Noreen Giffney and Myra Hird (Aldershot: Ashgate, 2008); and Nicole Seymour, *Strange Natures: Futurity, Empathy, and the Queer Ecological Imagination* (Urbana: University of Illinois Press, 2013).
9. As noted in the previous chapter, *transition* published chapters from the novel prior to its publication. Eugene Jolas, 'Glossary', *transition*, 16–17 (1929), 326–8 (p. 326).
10. Since manuscripts for the novel are not known to exist and Barnes declined to reinstate the offending passages in the 1979 republication of the novel the asterisks remain in all current editions of the novel. For analysis see C. F. S. Creasy, 'Of Matter and Manner: Djuna Barnes's *Ryder* and Censorship as Style', *Modern Philology*, 117.3 (2020), 370–92.
11. See for instance, Anne B. Dalton, 'Escaping from Eden: Djuna Barnes' Revision of Psychoanalytic Theory and Her Treatment of Father-Daughter Incest in *Ryder*', *Women's Studies*, 22.2 (1993), 163–79; and Marie Ponsot, 'A Reader's *Ryder*', in *Silence and Power: A Reevaulation of Djuna Barnes*, ed. Mary Lynn Broe (Carbondale and Edwardsville: Southern Illinois University Press, 1991), pp. 94–112. Even Phillip Herring's biography of Barnes, which remains the most comprehensive to date, makes the questionable decision to 'take the liberty of drawing on *Ryder* for biographical information'. See Herring, *Djuna: The Life and Works of Djuna Barnes* (New York: Penguin Books, 1996), pp. 313–4 n2.
12. Barnes's invitation is uncharacteristic of what became an increasing reticence to discuss her personal life with critics and admirers. Barnes to James B. Scott, 15 April 1971. DBP, Series 2, Box 14, Folder 57.
13. Julie Taylor, *Djuna Barnes and Affective Modernism* (Edinburgh: Edinburgh University Press, 2012), p. 74. See also Diane Warren's *Djuna Barnes' Consuming Fictions* (Aldershot: Ashgate, 2008) and Creasy's 'Of Matter and Manner'.
14. Daniela Caselli, *Improper Modernism: Djuna Barnes's Bewildering Corpus* (London and New York: Routledge, 2016), p. 199; Tyrus Miller, *Late Modernism: Politics, Fiction, and the Arts Between the World Wars* (Berkeley and London: University of California Press, 1999), pp. 129–30.
15. Louis F. Kannenstine, *The Art of Djuna Barnes: Duality and Damnation* (New York: New York University Press, 1977), p. 44.
16. Lydia Steptoe, 'Against Nature', *Vanity Fair*, XVIII (August 1922), 60, 88 (p. 60).

17. Ibid. p. 60.
18. Virginia Woolf, *The Pargiters: The Novel-Essay Portions of The Years*, ed. Mitchell A. Leaska (London: Hogarth Press, 1978), p. xliii.
19. Steptoe, 'Against Nature', p. 60.
20. Mortimer-Sandilands and Erickson, 'Introduction: A Genealogy of Queer Ecologies', p. 8. The emergence of sexology in the nineteenth century was pivotal to this process. See Anna Katharina Schaffner, *Modernism and Perversion: Sexual Deviance in Sexology and Literature, 1850-1930* (Basingstoke: Palgrave Macmillan, 2012).
21. Steptoe, 'Against Nature', p. 88.
22. See, for instance, Erin G. Carlston, *Thinking Fascism: Sapphic Modernism and Fascist Modernity* (Stanford: Stanford University Press, 1998).
23. Steptoe, 'Against Nature', p. 60.
24. Ibid. p. 88. Rachel Murray has described how the early decades of the twentieth century witnessed a growth in popular studies of insects. Murray, *The Modernist Exoskeleton: Insects, War, Literary Form* (Edinburgh: Edinburgh University Press, 2020), p. 7.
25. Mortimer-Sandilands and Erickson, 'Introduction: A Genealogy of Queer Ecologies', pp. 3–4.
26. Djuna Barnes to Emily Coleman, 7 August 1938. Emily Holmes Coleman Papers, Special Collections, University of Delaware Library (hereafter EHCP), Box 4, Folder 37.
27. Djuna Barnes to Emily Coleman, 13 August 1939. EHCP, Box 5, Folder 45.
28. Caselli, *Improper Modernism*, p. 197.
29. On Thoreau and Wald see Phillip Herring, *Djuna*, p. 34. Speculation around the origins of his name is my own.
30. For instance, Thoreau's mother continued to cook meals for him. See Dana Phillips, '"Slimy Beastly Life": Thoreau on Food and Farming', *Interdisciplinary Studies in Literature and Environment*, 19.3 (2012), 532–47.
31. Andrew Kalaidjian, 'The Black Sheep: Djuna Barnes's Dark Pastoral', in *Creatural Fictions: Human-Animal Relationships in Twentieth- and Twenty-First-Century Literature*, ed. David Herman (Basingstoke: Palgrave Macmillan, 2016), pp. 65–87 (pp. 71–2).
32. Susan Edmunds, *Grotesque Relations: Modernist Domestic Fiction and the U.S. Welfare State* (Oxford: Oxford University Press, 2008), p. 51.
33. Alex Goody, *Modernist Articulations: A Cultural Study of Djuna Barnes, Mina Loy and Gertrude Stein* (Basingstoke: Palgrave Macmillan, 2007), p. 166.
34. The *OED* gives the earliest definition of mundane as 'belonging to the earthly world, as contrasted with heaven'. 'Mundane', *OED Online* <www.oed.com/view/Entry/123748> (last accessed 16 April 2020).
35. See, for example, Wald Barnes to Djuna Barnes, 14 January 1897. DBP, Series 1, Box 6, Folder 1.
36. Jacques Derrida, *The Beast & the Sovereign, Volume I*, trans. Geoffrey Bennington (Chicago: University of Chicago Press, 2009), pp. 55–6.
37. Rosi Braidotti, *The Posthuman* (Cambridge: Polity, 2013), p. 26.

38. Jacques Derrida, *The Animal That Therefore I Am*, trans. David Wills, ed. Marie-Louise Mallet (New York: Fordham University Press, 2008), p. 16.
39. Oliver, *Animal Lessons*, p. 143.
40. Ibid. p. 131.
41. Derrida, *Beast & Sovereign*, p. 17. As outlined in Chapter 3, the beast is not synonymous with the animal in Derrida's late seminars. Nonetheless, the transgressive animal figures that Wendell frequently invokes in *Ryder* to outline his sexual identity precisely embody the beastly qualities Derrida discusses.
42. Edmunds, *Grotesque Relations*, p. 61.
43. Derrida, *Beast & Sovereign*, p. 178.
44. Rachel Potter also reads this passage through Derrida's seminars on sovereignty. Potter, '*Nightwood*'s Humans', in *Shattered Objects: Djuna Barnes's Modernism*, ed. Elizabeth Pender and Cathryn Setz (University Park: Penn State University Press, 2019), pp. 61–74.
45. Derrida, *Beast & Sovereign*, p. 283.
46. Bonnie Kime Scott, *Refiguring Modernism Volume 2: Postmodern Feminist Readings of Woolf, West and Barnes* (Bloomington: Indiana University Press, 1995), p. 73.
47. Carol J. Adams, *The Sexual Politics of Meat: A Feminist-Vegetarian Critical Theory* (New York: Continuum, 2010), p. 58; p. 25.
48. Andrew Field, *Djuna: The Life and Times of Djuna Barnes* (New York: G. P. Putnam's Sons, 1983), p. 193.
49. Adams, *Sexual Politics of Meat*, p. 13.
50. The 1917 ending to the story is more straightforward: once Amietiev has killed the rabbit, Addie becomes 'afraid of him' and is willing to submit herself to his affection.
51. Jacques Derrida, 'Eating Well, or the Calculation of the Subject', in *Points: Interviews, 1974–1994*, ed. Elizabeth Weber (Stanford: Stanford University Press, 1995), pp. 255–87 (p. 278).
52. Ibid. pp. 280–1.
53. Ibid. p. 282.
54. Henry David Thoreau, *Walden and Civil Disobedience* (New York and London: Penguin Books, 1986), pp. 261–5.
55. A parallel might be made with the satirical portrayal of the poet George Russell in *Ulysses*, who is seen coming 'from the vegetarian [restaurant]' with a 'listening woman at his side' (*U* 8.534). I have written elsewhere on the sexual politics of meat in Joyce. See Adkins, 'The Eyes of That Cow: Eating Animals and Theorizing Vegetarianism in James Joyce's *Ulysses*', *Humanities*, 6.3 (2017) <www.mdpi.com/2076-0787/6/3/46> (last accessed 22 February 2021).
56. Derrida, 'Eating Well', p. 282. Although Derrida makes clear that vegetarianism does not provide a position of moral absolution, critics have pointed out that he overlooks the possibility of a self-reflexive vegetarianism that might provide the basis for an effective mode of politics and ethics. See David Wood, 'Comment Ne Pas Manger – Deconstruction and Humanism', in *Animal Others: On Ethics, Ontology, and Animal Life*, ed. H. Peter Steeves (Albany: State University of New York Press, 1999), pp. 15–35.

57. Miller, *Late Modernism*, pp. 133–4.
58. Caselli, *Improper Modernism*, p. 203.
59. Wald Barnes, like Wendell, believed in the importance of genealogy in dogs and humans alike. Writing to Djuna in 1913, Wald explained how she was unlike the typical suffragette since she was in the 'whippet class' of women. Wald Barnes to Djuna Barnes, 12 September 1913. DBP, Series 1, Box 6, Folder 2.
60. Caselli, *Improper Modernism*, p. 208.
61. Morton, 'Queer Ecology', p. 275.
62. Ibid. p. 278.
63. Oliver, *Animal Lessons*, p. 150.
64. Ibid. p. 139.

5

THE SYMPATHETIC CLIMATE OF VIRGINIA WOOLF'S *ORLANDO*

> The age was the Elizabethan; their morals were not ours; nor their poets; nor their climate; nor their vegetables even. Everything was different. The weather itself, the heat and cold of summer and winter, was, we may believe, of another temper altogether.
>
> Virginia Woolf, *Orlando* (1928)

In 1920, Virginia Woolf reviewed a biography entitled *Mary Russell Mitford and her Surroundings* for the *Athenaeum*. Criticising the book's author, Constance Hill, for being preoccupied with facts over impressions and failing to bring her subject to life, Woolf laments the lack of attention given to the physical environment:

> The weather has varied almost as much in the course of generations as mankind. The snow of those days was more formally shaped and a good deal softer than the snow of ours, just as an eighteenth-century cow was no more like our cows than she was like the florid and fiery cows of Elizabethan pastures. Sufficient attention has scarcely been paid to this aspect of literature, which, it cannot be denied, has its importance. (*E3* 219)

Five years later when Woolf decided to include the review in *The Common Reader* (1925) she further developed this line of argument. Below the statement about the importance of weather and animals, Woolf added that '[o]ur brilliant young men might do worse, when in search of a subject, than devote a year or two to cows in literature, snow in literature' (*E4* 192). As in the original review, Woolf's addition mixes self-effacing facetiousness with a more genuine sentiment around the importance of situating the human in the more-than-human world. The sincerity of Woolf's assertion is lent weight by the degree to which weather had preoccupied her from a young age. In her earliest journals observations about the weather were an almost daily feature. In 1899, at the age of 17, for instance, she reflects on her interest in the 'thermometer rivalry' of the Victorian age, the ever-burgeoning number of amateurs and professional scientists recording meteorological data, explaining 'if I lived in the country, I should become a weather prophet or something of the kind'.[1] It was an interest that did not diminish with time. As Paula Maggio has shown, observations about weather encompass the breadth of Woolf's oeuvre.[2] From the 'fine yellow fog' that cloaks London in the opening pages of *The Voyage Out* (1915) to the sudden downpour that disrupts the pageant towards the end of *Between the Acts* (1941), Woolf's writing is highly attuned to the atmospheric events that shape the moments from which life is composed (*VO* 7; *BTA* 162).

Woolf's reflections on the amateur recording of meteorological information speaks not only to an interest in weather but, rather more accurately, climate. As Adeline Johns-Putra writes, climate is 'not just weather, but weather observed, measured and recorded – a composite of meteorological events as they are correlated, compared, and contrasted over time and space'.[3] The concept of climate implies an imperative to observe and compare, to mark variations and differences between temporally and spatially separate moments. In *Orlando: A Biography*, published in 1928, three years after Woolf revised her Mitford review, she picks up the task that the 'brilliant young men' were still neglecting, documenting the vicissitudes of the English climate as they play out across the 400 years of Orlando's life. As the epigraph to this chapter suggests, with its attention to changes in 'the English climate' (*O* 31), the biography of Orlando is also an account of changes in the environment. From the Little Ice Age, reimagined as a 'carnival of the utmost brilliancy' on the frozen Thames, to the 'irregular moving darkness' that covers the sky during the industrial nineteenth century, and the arid 'sky . . . made of metal' that accompanies the modernist era of flight and automation, Woolf's novel is, on one level, premised on showing how one cannot 'pretend that the climate was the same' over the course of centuries (*O* 32; 206; 270; 211). Yet, Woolf is interested not only in documenting changes in climate but theorising them too. Writing to Vita Sackville-West, her former lover and the inspiration for the character of Orlando, exactly one year after the book's publication, Woolf wryly suggested that she might employ Henry James's former secretary, Theodora Bosanquet, to respond to the correspondence she was receiving about the novel. Bosanquet might use a few stock responses, Woolf writes, including that in *Orlando* 'the climate changes in sympathy with the age' (*VWL4* 100). It is a sentiment which, on the surface, reiterates her earlier interest in the organic relationship between weather systems and literary history, or the idea that there might be some intrinsic relationship between eighteenth-century snow and eighteenth-century poetic representations of snow. Yet what Woolf might mean by attributing sympathy to the climate requires some attention.

The *OED* gives the primary definition of sympathy as 'a (real or supposed) affinity between certain things, by virtue of which they are similarly or correspondingly affected by the same influence', with the prefix 'sym' coming from the Greek to mean 'together' or 'alike'.[4] To understand the climate as acting in sympathy with the age, in this sense of the word, would mean to see weather systems and human activities in terms of correlation or correspondence, each shaping the other. That Woolf might have meant this is not an anachronistic proposition. By the twentieth century, enquiries into the degree to which climate determined cultural and national development and the degree to which humans, in return, could influence climate were well established. As Jan Golinski has shown, the notion of climatic determinism, or the idea that climate shaped and influenced the development of national characteristics, was an intellectual mainstay of European modernity from the seventeenth century onwards, with scientific knowledge of climate increasingly marshalled to explain the supposed superiority of cultural characteristics in the temperate global north.[5] In the same period, the question of whether human activities had influenced shifts in climate was also being explored. Debates around whether deforestation could produce changes in climate intensified during the nineteenth century, not least since it posed questions around how best to manage and exploit natural resources both in the West and its colonies.[6] Charles Lyell's 1830 *Principles of Geology*, a foundational work in establishing its field, looked to provide an answer as to whether humans could affect 'alteration of climate', concluding that while anthropogenic atmospheric changes did follow deforestation, global climate systems operated at too great a scale to be profoundly influenced by humankind.[7] Woolf's curiosity about weather and her attention to it in her writing suggests she would have been interested in the science and politics behind climate. A 1928 reprint of Arthur Holmes's *The Age of the Earth: An Introduction to Geological Ideas* (first published in 1913) is listed as present in the Woolfs' library and, as critics have shown, Woolf was aware of scientific developments taking place around her.[8] Even, Woolf's use of the word 'age' in her letter to Sackville-West teases at the influence of nineteenth-century geology, where ages, along with eons, eras, periods and epochs, had become the official demarcation of planetary time through efforts by Lyell and others to formalise geological discourse.

By the early twentieth century, however, Lyell's conclusions and his authoritative stature had come under strong scrutiny, not least by figures such as Holmes. Woolf's interest in the sympathetic relationship between stages in human development and climactic variation is, I am going to argue in this chapter, part of a generational willingness to rethink received ideas about climate. For Woolf, however, the mock-biographical form offers a way to explore sympathy beyond the merely structural relation between weather patterns and human activity, enabling her to also explore the affective charge implied in sympathy or what the OED defines as an understanding of sympathy to mean the 'quality or state of being affected by the condition of another [. . .] the fact or capacity of entering into or sharing the feelings of another or others'.[9] In her aforementioned 1920 review of the Mitford biography, Woolf describes how the difficulty of writing a good biography lies in the fact that 'the deposit of certainty is all spun over by a myriad changing shades'. Yet, Woolf goes on, if successfully captured on the page, it is precisely this ephemerality that 'stir[s] vibrations of sympathy' in the reader (E3 220–1). It is a description that positions sympathy as a bodily state that attunes the reader to the world around her; a process that is not wholly located within consciousness or cognition, but, rather, the product of molecular processes. This impersonal idea of sympathy implies an affective state not wholly identical with consciousness, but which, rather, produces subjectivity. As Kirsty Martin has shown, modernist innovations enabled new literary modes of presenting sympathy not as a discrete emotional category but a 'complex form of sensory entanglement', with Martin showing how Woolf in particular draws attention to the 'physical matter of the brain and body' in which sympathy emerges from a concatenation of 'flesh' and 'energy'.[10] Martin's work opens up new ways of reading modernism through a material understanding of sympathy that revises how we see human relations, yet for Woolf this form of sympathy goes beyond purely human concerns. In her commemorative essay on Thomas Hardy, originally published in the same year as *Orlando*, Woolf describes 'Nature as a force [. . .] that can sympathise or mock or remain the indifferent spectator of human fortunes' (E5 562–3) and in *Orlando*, we find similar moments of sympathy that present human affects in dialogue with large-scale forces of nature. As this chapter will argue, Woolf's novel shows how, as Dipesh Chakrabarty frames it, the 'wall of separation between natural and human histories that was erected in early modernity and reinforced in the nineteenth century' is no longer viable.[11]

While agreeing with Gillian Beer's description of the climate in *Orlando* as 'hyperbolical', this chapter departs from critical assessments that read the changing climate in the novel as wholly ironic or arbitrary.[12] Instead, I will suggest that while it is important to consider the satirical tone of the novel, we should take Woolf's humour seriously. Certainly, as Alexandra Harris argues, Woolf is interested in how 'as cultural preoccupations change, we find [cultural] affinities with different kinds of weather', but as this chapter will suggest, that is only half of the story.[13] *Orlando* is instead, as Jesse Oak Taylor has argued, a novel that entwines 'historical and climatic change' and 'a formative example of what has come to be called climate fiction (or "cli-fi"), novels that seek to dramatize the effects of climate change'.[14] Joining other critics, such as Ruben Borg, Helena Feder, Derek Ryan and Bonnie Kime Scott, who see Woolf as deconstructing the binary between culture and nature in *Orlando*, this chapter looks to further demonstrate the importance of examining Woolf's interest in the nonhuman.[15] Unlike Taylor's analysis of *Orlando*, however, I argue that climate is central not only to the historical narrative of *Orlando*, but its presentation of sex, gender and sexuality also. While Woolf presents the reader with broad sweeps of climatic history, she is also interested in how the macro intersects with the micro, remaining alert to questions of sex, sexuality and agency at the level of embodied life. For Woolf, this chapter will show, climate is not mere weather, but the material from which we are constituted and in which our sexed identities are entangled. Beginning by exploring how Woolf contrasts a pastoral understanding of seasonality with a notion of climate that disrupts harmony and stability, this chapter goes on to look at the extensive description of the Victorian climate that bridges the fourth and fifth chapter of the novel. Looking in detail at how Woolf presents this crucial moment in the history of the Anthropocene, I suggest that it not only restages a moment of historical climate change but also the nineteenth century's heightened attention towards climate itself. Finally, by suggesting that Woolf's idea of climate is of a 'nature' who plays 'queer tricks' (O 72), this chapter concludes by outlining how the novel's climatic ontology is central to *Orlando*'s recasting of sex. Drawing out the ways in which Woolf presents a sympathetic relation between climates and bodies, I suggest that *Orlando* broadens what is at stake when we think about climate change in the Anthropocene.

Seasonality, Poetry and Climate Change

The question of what it means to write about the environment is a sustained concern in *Orlando* and, over the course of the novel, a certain pastoral idea of seasonality is presented as a counterpoint to the notion of climate. Not only is Orlando almost immediately introduced to the reader as a poet whose subject is 'nature', but the problems that attend anyone who wishes to write about the natural world also come to the foreground:

> He was describing, as all young poets are for ever describing, nature, and in order to match the shade of green precisely he looked (and here he showed more audacity than most) at the thing itself, which happened to be a laurel bush growing beneath the window. After that, of course, he could write no more. Green in nature is one thing, green in literature another. Nature and letters seem to have a natural antipathy; bring them together and they tear each other to pieces. The shade of green Orlando now saw spoilt his rhyme and split his metre. (O 16)

It is a passage that establishes one of the subplots sustained through the centuries that follow: the writing, rejection, rewriting, publication and reception of Orlando's pastoral poem, 'The Oak Tree'. Orlando, as Jane de Gay has convincingly argued, embodies a 'Romantic desire to represent nature in an unmediated fashion' against Elizabethan literary conventions of 'artifice and rhetoric'.[16] In his desire to transcend the 'natural antipathy' between 'Nature and letters' the adolescent Orlando is, in a sense, ahead of his time. In contrast, at the turn of the twentieth century, it will be the poem's anachronistic stature, the absence of the 'modern spirit' from it, that will ensure its popular reception and accolades as a poem whose perceived 'regard to truth, to nature, to the dictates of the human heart' are celebrated (O 256). Nick Greene, the critic who disparages Orlando in the Elizabethan period, in the modern age admiringly compares 'The Oak Tree' to James Thomson's eighteenth-century early Romantic poem *The Seasons* (1726–30) (O 256). It is a comparison which not only foregrounds the celebration of the natural world that provided the original impetus to Orlando's poem – the attempt to capture the 'sights [that] exalted him – the birds and the trees [. . .] the evening sky, the homing rooks' (O 15) – but also suggests the poem's use of seasonality for its formal framework. As Tess Somervell writes, the four seasons are historically 'one of the most prevalent means by which literary texts [. . .] represent climate', offering a structuring device that can either implicitly or explicitly express a view of the natural world as harmonious, ordered and predictable.[17] In all of these respects, and as critics have long recognised, 'The Oak Tree' functions as a parody of Sackville-West's book-length poetic paean to the Kentish weald, *The Land* (1926), which, structured around the turning of the seasons, runs from winter to autumn and won the Hawthornden Prize in 1927, bringing it to wide public attention.[18]

Yet, it is also important to note that in the literary context of the 1920s Woolf's satire would have been understood to have had a broader aim. Woolf was writing at a point when nostalgic pastoralism had come to dominate English poetry. A. E. Housman's *A Shropshire Lad* (1896), for instance, had become hugely popular during the First World War and continued to grow in popularity during the 1920s, selling tens of thousands of copies in that decade alone. As Jeffrey Mathes McCarthy has argued, it was not high modernist poems such as *The Waste Land* that found a reading public in the years after the war but pastoral poetry by Housman and others such as Edward Thomas, poets whose works appealed to a cultural desire for the restoration of an imagined antebellum rural life. In contrast to Eliot's poetics of alienation, the poetry of Housman found a wide readership through its willingness to, in McCarthy's terms, place 'English readers in nature and [give] nature an essential Englishness with its village greens and cherry trees'.[19] Woolf was herself alert to the differences between the poetry of Housman and Eliot, albeit in more evaluative terms. In her 1926 diary, she describes the poetry of Housman as 'defunct' compared to attempts by Eliot and others to 'animate' poetry (*D3* 65).[20] By comparison, her 1925 essay 'The Pastons and Chaucer' offers a more ambivalent evaluation of pastoral poetry. While the 'nature worship' of Wordsworth and Tennyson is 'morbid' in its 'shrinking from human contact' their faults are diminished by the fact that both 'were great poets'. In contrast, Woolf suggests, 'modern poet[s]' of 'smaller gift' who limit their poetic subjects to 'the garden or the meadow' rely on an overly simplistic aesthetic dichotomy in which 'the country is the sanctuary of moral excellence in contrast with the town which is the sink of vice' (*E4* 27). The fact that Woolf had not read Sackville-West's *The Land* at the time she wrote this assessment of pastoral poetry (Sackville-West sent her the manuscript later in 1925) suggests the degree to which we should understand 'The Oak Tree' as having a much wider satirical aim than has been previously suggested. Orlando's poem, which will run into multiple 'editions' and win the kind of popular 'praise and fame' (*O* 297) that difficult modernist poems could not dream of achieving, is an indictment not of an individual poet, but what Woolf perceives to be an increasingly conservative and limited poetic tradition. If earlier pastoral poetry that celebrated the seasons selectively idealised certain aspects of the changing year to evoke ideals of order and harmony, Woolf suggests that the sudden poetic imperative to idealise a vanishing English pastoralism is more superficial than ever.

Moreover, in the same way that I showed in my previous chapter that Djuna Barnes was alert to how romantic constructions of nature often naturalise heteronormative configurations of gender and sexuality, Woolf presents pastoral ideals of seasonality as establishing patriarchal notions of sexual identity. As the narrator wryly explains in the first chapter, 'what the poets said in rhyme, the young translated into practice', hence if 'Girls were roses, and their seasons were as short as the flowers" then 'Plucked they must be before nightfall' (*O* 26), leading Orlando to do 'but as nature bade him' to a girl whose name is unrecorded, appearing in the text only as 'his flower' (*O* 26). This naturalisation of sexual possession through pastoral tropes, in which anonymous women are 'plucked' with Woolf, perhaps, inviting the reader to hear a near-sounding 'fucked', is presented as a correlative to Orlando's youthful 'confusion of the passions and emotions' experienced in the parkland of his great house (*O* 15). Indeed, Orlando's poetic identification with 'a place crowned by a single oak tree' within that parkland, from atop of which he is offered the prospect of all that 'was theirs' including not only buildings but the 'heath [. . .] and the forest; the pheasant and the deer, the fox, the badger and the butterfly', implies not ecological holism as suggested by some critics, but phallic mastery (*O* 17–18).[21] Nature worship, in this sense, naturalises Orlando's sense of proprietorship over his estate and the young women he comes into contact with. It also establishes the novel's sustained questioning of appeals to nature in relation to sexual identity. Orlando's transformation will later be met with a public reaction in which it is held that 'a change of sex is against nature' (O 128), a turn of phrase that foreshadows contemporary transphobic discourse.[22] I return to this question of Orlando's transformation as being against nature later in the chapter, when I examine how it relates to Woolf's material presentation of sex, gender and sexuality.

Although Orlando and the poem change over the centuries, with the female Orlando being disinherited from the estate over which the oak tree provided a phallic prospect, the novel does not indicate that her attachment to a pastoral ideal of the seasons undergoes similar transformation. As Orlando reflects in the Victorian age, 'through all these changes she had remained [. . .] fundamentally the same. She had the same brooding meditative temper, the same love of animals and nature, the same passion for the country and the seasons' (O 216). The novel's conclusion sees Orlando return to the oak tree, still 'in the prime of life', and in a romantic gesture, attempt to bury her poem at its roots in an act of 'return[ing] to the land [. . .] what the land has given to me', a deed undermined by the resistance of the tree's roots (O 296) and in which we can read Woolf's ironic attempt to 'return' or refuse *The Land*. As such, while the reader remains alert to the ways in which Orlando has undergone fundamental change, not least in sex, Orlando's self-identification as a nature poet undergoes qualification rather than transformation. While critics such as de Gay and Christine Froula have argued that the novel implicitly endorses 'The Oak Tree' as an affirmation of female creativity, the novel rather more suggests that Orlando's poem is a reflection of a poetic tradition that resists change and innovation.[23] As Dana Phillips has argued, 'ecological stability' only 'seem[s] stable to us because of our limited ability to appreciate the vast amounts of time involved in geological and climatic change, which can have and often does have cataclysmic effects'.[24] Seasonality, the predictable repetition of certain processes happening at certain points in the year, presents itself to us as the basic unit of life only because of the parochialism of human perspective. Seasons, then, are both real (in the sense that they are produced by the tilt in the Earth's axis) and a cultural construct, insofar as the motifs, associations and values of harmony and predictability attached to them are as the result of a human need to make sense of their necessarily limited perspective of planetary change.[25]

It is precisely this parochialism which Woolf's novel departs from. Although Orlando does not witness different geological epochs, her 400-year life enables her to witness first-hand climatic transitions that would remain beyond the purview of a typical human life and which disrupt the notion of seasonal stability. The young Orlando watches from the banks of the Thames as the Great Thaw apocalyptically transforms the 'whole gay city' on the frozen river into 'a race of turbulent yellow waters', effectively signalling the end of early modern

England (*O* 57). Later, Orlando will watch as a dark 'turbulent welter of cloud' suffocates London at the dawn of the nineteenth century, bringing a dampness that will again alter 'the constitution of England' in all senses of the word (*O* 206–8). As the twentieth century arrives, the sky is shown to have 'changed' again; 'no longer so thick, so watery, so prismatic' as previously, the 'dryness of the atmosphere' 'stiffen[s]' the muscles of Orlando's face, signalling the mechanised technological age (*O* 270–1). These moments of climate change in the text, some based on actual historical accounts that Woolf encountered in her reading, such as Thomas Dekker's description of the extreme winter of 1607–8, present exaggerated and fantastical figures of climate change.[26] While Orlando's lifespan is drawn out, Woolf playfully compresses gradual changes in climate into singular instances to have Orlando witness the kind of climatic cataclysms that Phillips describes as being beyond human perception. Where 'The Oak Tree', in the tradition of pastoral poetry, takes a seemingly harmonious model of seasonal cyclicality for its structure, *Orlando* figures climate in terms of hyperbolic, irreversible and singular transformations. Presenting climate in terms of tipping points and thresholds, Woolf foreshadows the neocastrophist model of geological history that has come to ascendency with the concept of the Anthropocene which, as Jeremy Davies explains, departs from 'the belief that the planet took on its current shape only through gradual and continuous operations of familiar processes' and which instead understands planetary change in terms of singular events that can rapidly alter geophysical systems.[27] Rather than drawing on realism to represent the history of the English climate, Woolf figures climate change through stark moments of 'suddenness and severity' (*O* 31) akin to a contemporary understanding of geology 'as a drama without any preestablished outcomes'.[28] As opposed to Orlando's attempt in 'The Oak Tree' to find a language that can get as close to nature as possible, *Orlando* draws on an ironically fantastic mode in order to point to the disruption, contingency and alterity of a climate that undoes any attempt to reduce the environment to a set of aesthetic ideals. In this respect *Orlando* poses a radical challenge for the Anthropocene. In contrast to the kind of writing that, like 'The Oak Tree', laments the demise of a stable seasonality threatened by the onset of climate change, *Orlando* instead affirms a planetary history that was constituted by catastrophic change all along.

Yet, while the Great Thaw, the first stark moment of climate change in the novel, arrives with the '[h]uge noises as of the tearing and rending of oak trees' (*O* 57), Orlando remains committed to his/her own oak tree, emblematic of a conservative attachment to a pastoral aesthetic of nature. Indeed, if *Orlando* is the first cli-fi novel as Taylor suggests, Orlando is also the first climate change denier. When faced with the new Victorian climate, Orlando decides to 'mew herself in her house at Blackfriars and pretend that the climate was the same', only reluctantly admitting that the 'times were changed' (*O* 210–11). At stake in this satire of pastoralism is not merely Woolf's personal feeling towards Sackville-West's literary abilities, but deeper misgiving about the parochialism of writing about nature and the pastoral mode that had risen to such prominence in the early twentieth century. The novel's hyperbolical transitions between climates upsets the idea of a holistic or harmonious nature and departs from a notion of unchanging, ahistorical seasons serving as a backdrop to human history. Claire Colebrook suggests the necessity of not seeing 'climate change as an event befalling a stable nature' but rather seeing the idea of a stable nature itself as 'a product of the European imaginary that cannot understand a world that has rhythms and transitions of a complexity greater than the human sense of seasonal change'.[29] If, as Colebrook suggests, nature is a European fiction, it is a fiction that Orlando is heavily invested in. For the young Orlando, who measures his life in terms of 'season[s]', the pastoral notion of a stable nature is pivotal to the stability of his male aristocratic identity, believing a 'mixture of brown earth and blue blood' runs through his veins (O 27). Where Orlando stakes his identity on an idealised notion of seasonality, an identity which is uprooted over the course of the novel, Woolf foregrounds not only the contingent materiality of the climate, but, as this next section explores, human identity and agency itself.

The Materiality of the Victorian Climate

The lengthy description of the 'change [which] seemed to have come over the climate of England' at the start of the nineteenth century, bridging the fourth and fifth chapters, presents the novel's most sustained description of climate change. It is worth quoting this transition at length:

> Orlando then for the first time noticed a small cloud gathered behind the dome of St Paul's. As the strokes sounded, the cloud increased, and she saw it darken and spread with extraordinary speed. At the same time a light breeze rose and by the time the sixth stroke of midnight had struck the whole of the eastern sky was covered with an irregular moving darkness, though the sky to the west and north stayed clear as ever. Then the cloud spread north. Height upon height above the city was engulfed by it. [. . .] As the ninth, tenth, and eleventh strokes struck, a huge blackness sprawled over the whole of London. With the twelfth stroke of midnight, the darkness was complete. A turbulent welter of cloud covered the city. All was darkness; all was doubt; all was confusion. The Eighteenth century was over; the Nineteenth century had begun.

> The great cloud which hung, not only over London, but over the whole of the British Isles on the first day of the nineteenth century stayed, or rather, did not stay, for it was buffeted about constantly by blustering gales, long enough to have extraordinary consequences upon those who

lived beneath its shadow. [. . .] Rain fell frequently, but only in fitful gusts, which were no sooner over than they began again. The sun shone, of course, but it was so girt about with clouds and the air was so saturated with water, that its beams were discoloured and purples, oranges, and reds of a dull sort took the place of the more positive landscapes of the eighteenth century. (O 205–7)

These passages perhaps most clearly reflect Woolf's intention that the climate should change in sympathy with the age. Arriving at the stroke of midnight, the new climate emerges as an overdetermined site of darkness, doubt and confusion that will characterise the Victorian age in contrast to the crisp airiness of the mannered and rational eighteenth century. In the paragraphs that follow, Woolf further develops the way in which changes in climate influence the material developments of the nineteenth century. The new climate brings with it a 'silent, imperceptible, ubiquitous' (O 207) damp that influences architecture and domestic spaces, with houses 'that had been of bare stone [now] smothered in greenery' and rooms so 'muffled' with furniture that 'nothing was left bare' (O 208). The climate also shapes clothing, fashion and diet: the sudden popularity of muffins, coffee and beards are all attributed to the new conditions (O 207–9). It eventually influences literary style itself, since damp 'gets into the inkpot as it gets into the woodwork' and, thus, 'sentences swelled, adjectives multiplied, lyrics became epics and little trifles that had been essays a column long were now encyclopaedias in ten or twenty volumes' (O 209). Importantly, changes in climate have unequal implications for gender. As the narrator explains, 'the change did not stop at outward things. The damp struck within. Men felt the chill in their hearts; the damp in their minds' and the 'sexes drew further and further apart' (O 209). The result is a deepening of patriarchy, as the 'life of the average woman' becomes a 'succession of childbirths' (O 209).

Woolf's ironic portrayal of the Victorian climate not only alludes to the obvious fact that the period really did see significant change in climate, or what can now be seen as the Victorian acceleration of the Anthropocene, but also to the century's heightened attention to the phenomena of climate itself. The early nineteenth century saw the emergence of a recognisably modern understanding of climate with the French scientist Joseph Fourier's study of solar radiation. Looking to answer the question of why heat from the sun does not continuously warm the planet, Fourier discovered that the surface of the planet emits infrared radiation which carries heat away. When looking for an answer to why the Earth was not therefore very cold, he found that some of this dissipated heat is retained by the planet's atmosphere.[30] Fourier's subsequent experiments with heat trapped in boxes covered by panes of glass led to the discovery of the 'Greenhouse effect' (a term not used until the 1930s) and in 1859 inspired the British scientist John Tyndall to investigate exactly which atmospheric gases trapped heat most effectively. Going against the common-sense notion that gases were transparent, Tyndall conducted experiments testing the transparency of various gases, including the coal gas piped into his laboratory's gas lamps. He made a striking discovery: coal gas was opaque to infrared radiation and, thereby, trapped heat. As the physicist Spencer B. Weart puts it, 'the Industrial Revolution, intruding into Tyndall's laboratory in the form of a gas jet, declared its significance for the planet's heat balance'.[31] Although Tyndall did not foresee the possibility of global warming as later scientists would, his discovery made clear the mechanisms through which human actions decisively influenced climatic conditions.[32]

Tyndall's interest in atmospheric gases was mirrored in the period's growing cultural and political discourse around climate. Over the course of the nineteenth century London had become the largest city in the history of the planet and the problem of air pollution was plainly visible. As Taylor details, by the 1880s events had reached crisis point: Parliament had commissioned multiple reports, chaired numerous debates and proposed various pieces of legislation to tackle what was being referred to as the 'smoke nuisance'.[33] In the same moment, cultural critics such as John Ruskin were turning their attention to the darkened skies and decrying moral as well as environmental degradation. Ruskin's essay 'The Storm Cloud of the Nineteenth Century' (1884), now often read as an outlier of social criticism on climate change, links a new 'cloud phenomena' in the skies to an incipient 'moral gloom' in society.[34] Woolf was reading and thinking about Ruskin while writing *Orlando*, reviewing his autobiography *Praeterita* in December 1927 for *T. P.'s Weekly* and, as several critics have suggested, the description in *Orlando* of a 'great cloud' rising over England and the introduction of an atmosphere that 'chill[s]' the heart of men appears to have Ruskin's essay in mind.[35] Yet, in situating Woolf's response to Ruskin as either a straightforward satire of or severance with Victorian discourse around the climate, critics have tended to overlook how Woolf's attention to aesthetics and materiality playfully develops a potentially radical understanding of climate found not only in Ruskin's essay, but in other nineteenth-century works of climatological discourse by figures such as Tyndall.

Woolf had a personal connection to Tyndall through her father, Leslie Stephen, whom he knew through the Alpine Club, and it is entirely possible that Woolf could have met the Victorian scientist at Hyde Park Gate while she was a child (he died in 1893 when Woolf was 11). Clarissa in *Mrs Dalloway* (1925) describes 'Huxley and Tyndall' as her favourite childhood reading (*MD* 66) and Woolf herself inherited two volumes of Tyndall's works from her father, suggesting that they may have been books she was fond of when given free rein in his library while growing up. Critics have also pointed to places in Woolf's oeuvre where she appears to have some knowledge of Tyndall's advances in physics. Beer, for instance, has suggested that in *Between the Acts* Mrs Swithin's sense of how the blue of the sky 'escaped registration' suggests Tyndall's discovery of light travelling in waves (*BTA* 17).[36] More recently, Justine Pizzo has highlighted how Woolf's notion of 'ethereality' appears to have been influenced by Tyndall's theories of the 'atmospheric transmission of light, heat and sound'.[37] Indeed, Pizzo suggests Woolf's often-quoted description in 'Modern Fiction' (1925) of the mind receiving a 'myriad impressions [. . .] engraved with the sharpness of steel' (*E3* 160) is a reformulation of Tyndall's material definition of consciousness in his 1874 Belfast Address to the British Association for the Advancement of Science.[38] If, as Pizzo suggests, Woolf understood not only the science behind Tyndall's discoveries but its ontological implications, *Orlando* further explores these questions in its presentation of the Victorian climate. The description of 'air [. . .] so saturated with water, that its beams were discoloured [. . .] purples, oranges, and reds of a dull sort', leaving the sky a 'bruised and sullen canopy' (*O* 207) suggests, for instance, Tyndall's research into how atmospheric gases influence how we see colour and experience the world around us.

Woolf owned a copy of Tyndall's 1860 book *The Glaciers of the Alps*, a work that is organised into two sections, the first giving an account of his travels in the Alps, replete with lavish descriptions of sunsets, and the second serving as 'an attempt [. . .] to refer the observed phenomena to their physical causes'.[39] Conceived as a popular science book, it explained in lay terms the radiation through which the planet is heated by the sun, in which the 'atmosphere acts the part of a ratchet-wheel in mechanics' as it lets heat in but not out. It also details his experiments on the opacity of gas that would pave the way for the later field of climatology. Perhaps, most suggestively in terms of an influence on Woolf is Tyndall's 'prismatic analysis' of how moisture influences light and heat, a section of the book intended to provide a physical explanation for his earlier account of 'atmospheric regions [. . .] saturated with moisture' in the Alps, where clouds 'faded from a blood-red through orange and daffodil into an exquisite green'.[40] Here, *Orlando*'s description of light as 'the effect of the sun on the water-logged air' (*O* 212) and of 'sunbeams' 'marbling the clouds with strange prismatic colours' (*O* 211) suggests that Woolf's aesthetic for *Orlando*'s Victorian climate owes a debt, either directly or indirectly, to Tyndall's discovery that the colour of the sky depends on imperceptible atmospheric conditions. Just as for Tyndall the explanation for grand sunsets resides in molecular water particles, Woolf employs a sliding scale, turning from the vast, prismatic skies 'saturated with water' to a microscopic focus on the 'silent, imperceptible' damp that enjoys an agential ability to 'stealthily' infiltrate and influence objects (*O* 207). The molecular presents a locus of meaning for the macro, and vice versa, as the damp becomes a figure of a material economy that collapses any binary distinction between earth and air, solidity and fluidity, inner and outer. Moreover, as with the 'Time Passes' section of Woolf's previous novel, *To the Lighthouse* (1927), which begins with a description of air that is said to have 'crept round corners and ventured indoors' as the Ramsay family sleep, establishing the damp conditions that will slowly transform the house from a human space to a nonhuman one (*TTL* 103), the climate in *Orlando* puts anthropocentric distinctions under pressure. The damp becomes a figure not only of invisibility but also impersonality as what appear to be personal attributes – bodily hair, taste, reproductive practices – are resituated within an inhuman continuum in which human agency is no longer autonomous.

Certainly, Tyndall is not the only influence on this opening passage. The hazy light of the Victorian age seems also to have in mind nineteenth-century English watercolour painting, or what Woolf later described in her biography of Roger Fry as the way the 'English climate' with its 'light [. . .] full of vapour' informed a national aesthetic within the visual arts.[41] As the skies appear to literally take the form of a Turner watercolour, there is also perhaps a deeper buried allusion to Oscar Wilde's argument in 'The Decay of Lying' (1889) that art does not reflect nature, but rather that nature reflects art in the sense that aesthetic norms condition how we see the world around us. Yet, in contrast to Wilde, Woolf resolutely refuses to establish a dividing line between nature and culture. Rather it is the reciprocal, or sympathetic, relationship between humans and nonhuman entities and processes that comes to the fore. For Woolf, the very categories that would look to definitively separate the human from the nonhuman come undone as the damp seeps into the 'constitution of England' (*O* 208) in such a way that the human and the nonhuman cannot be disentangled. Indeed, the damp in the Victorian inkpot presents itself as a near direct refutation of Wilde's idea that culture precedes nature, or even that the two can be safely separated, as Wilde's own writing is implicitly situated within the body of rich and verdant, if overblown, Victorian prose produced by the new climate.

Here, again, we find points of confluence with Tyndall, whose Belfast Address received considerable notoriety for insisting on the priority of science over religion in explaining the world and in which he outlined a material understanding of all life, with the search for origins necessitating retracing the point at which 'life [. . .] developed out of matter'.[42] Tyndall's material ontology, as Jeff Wallace has argued, insists that matter is not an empty capacity waiting to be animated by life but, instead, constitutes life itself.[43] Indeed, we might agree with Pizzo here that Woolf's spatial metaphor in 'Modern Fiction' of life as 'a semi-transparent envelope surrounding us from the beginning of consciousness to the end' (*E4* 160) shares with Tyndall an ontological insistence on mind and matter as indivisibly co-involved, in which, as Tyndall states, 'molecular processes and the phenomena of consciousness' cannot be safely separated.[44] *Orlando*'s opening description of the Victorian climate further develops the social implications of situating the human within a broader material ontology. The second paragraph of the chapter, which begins by marking the fact that although 'England was altered' no one could be certain of 'the exact day or hour of the change' (O 208), concludes with a lengthy sentence:

> Coffee supplanted the after-dinner port, and, as coffee led to a drawing-room in which to drink it, and a drawing-room to glass cases, and glass cases to artificial flowers, and artificial flowers to mantelpieces, and mantelpieces to pianofortes, and pianofortes to drawing-room ballads, and drawing-room ballads (skipping a stage or two) to innumerable little dogs, mats, and china ornaments, the home – which had become extremely important – was completely altered. (O 208)

As Elsa Högberg and Amy Bromley have observed, *Orlando* is a novel in which Woolf is highly attuned to the syntactic unit of the sentence and its aesthetic potential, and, here, grammar is central to conveying Woolf's presentation of materiality.[45] Consisting of eleven clauses and sub-clauses, and proceeding via a structure of anadiplosis, in which the repetition of nouns connected by the same conjunction gives rise to a sense of accretive change, by the time the reader has arrived at the apparently straightforward concluding assertion (albeit, even here, split in two by a final subclause) that the 'home' was 'completely altered', the origin of that alteration is far from clear. Akin to Tyndall and other Victorian scientists' increasing scepticism towards metaphysical searches for first causes, although the reader might retrace the sentence in search of who is responsible for having altered the home no singular agentive noun will be found. The entire paragraph refuses to name the agent responsible, despite there being plenty of verbs that insist on agency. The result is a sense of diffuseness, as the described changes in bodies, objects, buildings and social customs resist being traced solely back to the damp, and instead agency appears to arise from the way in which the damp has become hybridised with other entities and processes that have, in turn, become hybridised with others. Here, Woolf's prose not only looks back to Victorian science, but also ahead to recent new materialist philosophies, foreshadowing Rosi Braidotti's description of life as composed of 'symbiotic and material system[s] of codependence' and reflecting what Ryan describes as Woolf's 'illuminating of materiality as [. . .] the possibility of being'.[46] For Braidotti, who has written on *Orlando* in terms of a 'geology and a meteorology of forces' that gather around but extend beyond human subjects, life is best understood in terms of impersonal moments of 'affinity and sympathy' between human and nonhuman subjects.[47] In *Orlando* we see these imperceptible forces at work, as the damp becomes a figure for that which not only transgresses the binary between inner and outer, but which speaks to the very undecidability of such distinctions in themselves. Not 'stop[ping] at outward things' (O 209), the damp arrives as a transformative materialism without presence; its agency located not in itself but, like Orlando, a readiness to be transformed into something which it is not.

As opposed to seeing the chapter in terms of a material distribution of agency, critics have instead tended to read this section of *Orlando* as a satire of climatic determinism.[48] This mechanistic way of explaining cultural difference was, as I mentioned above, pervasive from the early modern period onward and Woolf's portrayal of '[l]ove, birth, and death' (*O* 209) being influenced by the weather, it has been suggested, is a sardonic presentation of such mechanistic accounts. Yet, if this is the intended aim of Woolf's description, it is notable that nowhere in the opening pages of the chapter is the word 'determine' or its synonyms used. Instead, the verbs used, such as 'changed', 'appeared', 'invented', 'supplanted' and 'altered', suggest conditionality and transformation, rather than fixity or finality. Cultural practices, such as writing, and social categories, such as gender, are shown to emerge not from some mechanistic idea of climate, but an understanding of it in which agency is dispersed and diffuse, hybridising culture and nature akin to Donna Haraway's idea of 'natureculture' in which neither term can claim priority.[49] Moreover, in contrast to climatic determinism, Woolf was herself alert to the way in which a material ontology need not erode important political or social distinctions. In her 1926 essay on the Victorian artist Thomas James Cobden-Sanderson entitled 'The Cosmos', Woolf recounts Cobden-Sanderson's discussions with Tyndall in which the former espouses a vision of the universe as an 'extraordinary ring of harmony within harmony that encircles us' and sees 'human destiny [as] the ultimate coalescence of the human intellect [. . .] with its other self, the Universe' (*E4* 370–1). Although there are parallels here with the material ontology in *Orlando*, Woolf is critical of the depoliticising Romantic thrust to Cobden-Sanderson's philosophy. His sentiment of feeling 'more related to the hills and the streams [. . .] than to men and women', Woolf writes, produced a world view in which the 'ideal got the upper hand' and the political realities of events such as 'the Boer War' or 'the Coronation' of Edward VII could have no place (*E4* 372). In contrast, Woolf is keen to stress the points of continuity between materiality and social or sexual difference. This is expressed, at least in part, through *Orlando*'s use of irony: the description of the 'essential' change of diet and household furnishings for the country gentleman, in contrast to the imposed changes in reproductive expectations for young wives, implicitly foregrounds how material adaptations and changes are always influenced in advance of time by class, gender and sex (*O* 208). This, too, is the case in the description of how changes in reproductive practices bring 'the British Empire [. . .] into existence', with an expanding population providing the bodies to be sent to manage Britain's colonies (*O* 209). Indeed, while beyond the parameters of this chapter, analysis of *Orlando*'s critique of colonialist resource extractivism would draw out the environmental dimensions to what has been described as the novel's challenging of 'prevailing assumptions about national belonging'.[50]

Woolf's sharpened satirical intent was even clearer in her initial draft of the novel, where in her description of the Great Thaw at the end of the Little Ice Age, she detailed how amidst the chaos and mass drowning '[n]obody of very high birth seemed to be included [...] which seemed to show that the upper sort had received warning and made for safety'.[51] In the same way that political commentators have emphasised the fact that climate change is not a great leveller, since 'there will be lifeboats for the rich and privileged',[52] Woolf is cognisant of the way in which, although nature and culture cannot be disentangled, it is nonetheless also the case that environmental conditions have the ability to consolidate and deepen class, gender and sexual inequalities within human society. Woolf not only avoids the depoliticising thrust of environmental determinism, then, but engages with the difficult question of how to talk about sociopolitical matters without pretending that humans are autonomous agents working against the backdrop of an inert nature. If, for Braidotti, all identity markers, including gender, class and race, must be recognised as 'historically contingent mechanism[s] of capture of the multiple potentialities of the body', Woolf draws out the historicity to such a claim as she traces this transformative materiality through transpositions that always exceed human life, showing them at work across 400 years of English history.[53] As opposed to eliding politics, especially sexual politics, such an approach heightens them, as the climate brings into crisis the two questions at the centre of the novel: 'What's an "age", indeed? What are "we"?' (O 188).

Nature's Queer Tricks

While Woolf's description of the Victorian climate eschews the language of determinism for conditionality and contingency, it is nonetheless instructive to explore where Woolf does explicitly engage with questions of determinism. Revealingly, the only place in the novel where the word 'determine' is used to mean 'to decide', 'limit' or 'pronounce, declare, state' occurs immediately after Orlando's transformation.[54] Here, the narrator takes 'pause' to 'make certain statements' that might explain Orlando's sex:

> Many people, [...] holding that such a change of sex is against nature, have been at great pains to prove (1) that Orlando had always been a woman, (2) that Orlando is at this moment a man. Let biologists and psychologists determine. It is enough for us to state the simple fact; Orlando was a man till the age of thirty; when he became a woman and has remained so ever since. (O 128–9)

Invoking a rhetoric of determinism only to disavow it, the passage suggests that biological or psychological accounts which look to determine Orlando's sex actively impose categorisation in advance of time, paralleling what Judith Butler argues is the way in which sex (one's anatomical identity) cannot absolutely precede gender (cultural definitions). Woolf, like Butler, is suggesting a more co-constitutive understanding of materiality and identity.[55] Importantly, however, the structure of the sentence also suggests that these determinations arise in response to the fear that Orlando's transformation is 'against nature'. Determinism becomes a way of attempting to naturalise Orlando's change of sex and to reconcile her transformation within a heteronormative idea of nature (ironically, exemplified in Orlando's juvenile poetry). Like Barnes's denaturalising of genealogy in *Ryder*, Woolf's narratorial aside reveals the linguistic mechanisms through which claims to nature actively regulate and determine categories of sex and sexuality. Choosing to dismiss biologists and psychologists, the narrator instead goes on to merely 'state the simple fact' of Orlando's change from 'man' to 'woman', albeit with the earlier provided caveat that gendered pronouns such as 'her' and 'his' are there only for the sake of grammatical 'convention' rather than revealing an ontological foundation (O 128). Refusing the cultural politics of biological essence, *Orlando* joins the dots between accusations of unnaturalness aimed at those with queer bodies and a form of 'nature worship' that carries with it a proscription of a binary model of gender and sexuality.

Earlier in the novel we find a queering of nature that appears to look ahead to Orlando's transformation, when the narrator describes nonhuman agency in the following terms:

> Nature, who has played so many queer tricks upon us, making us so unequally of clay and diamonds, of rainbow and granite, and stuffed them into a case, often of the most incongruous, for the poet has a butcher's face and the butcher a poet's; nature who delights in muddle and mystery, so that even now (the first of November 1927) we know not why we go upstairs, or why we come down again [. . .] nature, who has so much to answer for beside the perhaps unwieldly length of this sentence, has further complicated her task and added to our confusion by providing not only a perfect rag-bag of odds and ends within us [. . .] but has contrived that the whole assortment shall be lightly stitched together by a single thread. (O 72–3)

Another example of the novel's self-reflexive attention to the unit of the sentence, the passage foregrounds Woolf's interest not in abandoning nature as a term or concept but subverting it in service of a queer materiality. Here an apparently denaturalised and playful nature is responsible for the observable queerness that we find in human life, where appearances confound identities and causality (in actions even as quotidian as going upstairs) is not determined but subject to 'muddle'. Moreover, given Suzanne Raitt and Ian Blyth have recently shown how the word 'queer' had become a 'coded reference to dissident sexualities' by the 1920s, we should be alert to how Woolf's queer nature was quite possibly intended to suggest a mischievous unweaving of rigid sexual categories.[56] The queerness of this ironically framed nature is further suggested in the extended metaphor of life as a materiality 'lightly stitched' together into a 'rag bag of odds and ends' from a 'single thread'. It is a description which, on the one hand, looks back to the first sentence of the novel where the narrator asserts that there can 'be no doubt of his sex, though the fashion of the time did something to disguise it' (O 13). On the other, it foreshadows the moment later in the text when, after Orlando's transformation, the suggestion is raised that clothes merely stand as an outward expression of the 'vacillation from one sex to the other' within each 'human being' (O 173), contributing to a rhetorical circularity in which it is suggested that, as Christy Burns argues, 'what is essential [. . .] is to be without essence'.[57]

If elsewhere in the novel clothes are held up as symbols of cultural identity (gender) that stand in opposition to one's biological identity (sex), Woolf's queering of nature undermines such a binary by personifying nature as an artificer. As nature's queer tricks bring into crisis whether meaning is located on the surface (in someone's face or clothes) or below (their personality or concealed body), the question of what is fundamentally natural remains unclear. In this light, Orlando's self-fashioning of identity after her transformation is no different to the 'perfect rag-bag of odds and ends' from which everyone is comprised, and appears as natural (or unnatural) as nature's habit of 'stuff[ing]' people into the wrong 'case'. This queer nature, then, is central to Woolf's presentation of Orlando, enabling her to escape a binary of biological essence versus cultural difference as, instead, Orlando's transformation becomes part of a more-than-human materiality that is self-fashioning, and in which meaning and matter co-produce one another. As opposed to the pastoral idea of nature which is aligned in the novel with heterosexual structures of desire, this queered nature stands in sympathy with the climatic qualities of immanence and transformation within which Woolf couches the narrative. Or, restated slightly differently, the broader climatic processes which Woolf shows to have clear ontological implications are always already queer: they transform bodies and undo static and heteronormative categories of identity. Woolf's queer nature, as such, presents itself not in terms of essence but hybridity with Orlando's identity necessarily entangled within a continuum of 'incessant' changes that produces the 'strangest alliances' (O 295). Indeed, Woolf has alluded to this from the very start of the novel. Orlando, slicing at the Moor's skull, is in an attic 'so vast that there seemed trapped in it the wind itself, blowing this way, blowing that way, winter and summer'; a room where 'bars of darkness' compete with 'yellow pools [. . .] made by the sun falling through the stained glass'. When Orlando 'put[s] his hand on the window-sill to push the window open', he watches as it is 'instantly coloured red, blue, and yellow like a butterfly's wing' (*O* 14). Presented in terms of alien gusts of wind, bars of darkness and prismatic sunbeams, as the external climate shapes the interior human world, Orlando witnesses his body undergo a change in front of his eyes, momentarily taking on an affinity with another species. The subsequent 400 years continue in this vein, presenting a sequence of transformations shaped by and through the changing materiality of the climate. Although Orlando's change of sex might present itself as perhaps the most striking change, and certainly has the largest influence on his/her identity, it is, the novel shows us, one only instance within an ongoing climate of transformation. *Orlando*, in this light, becomes a novel not of a single transformation but singular transformations.

Later, when Orlando decides she must 'take a husband' since 'the indomitable nature of the spirit of the age [. . .] batters down anyone who tries to make stand against it', the narrator appears to again playfully combine nature and culture, continuing the emphasis on entangling the human and nonhuman that the novel has established as central to its material ontology (*O* 221–2). It is perhaps unsurprising then that Orlando's first marriage is not to a male human, but rather the nature that the novel has already signalled to the reader as queer. In rebellion against the Victorian era's dictum of compulsory marriage, Orlando vows herself to the 'cold embraces' of the earth and becomes 'nature's bride' (*O* 225–6). Pressing 'her head luxuriously' on the 'spongy pillow' of the turf, she pronounces herself the 'mate' of nature as a moment of erotic sympathy passes between Orlando and the earth itself. Comparable to what Kelly Sultzbach has described as the 'erotic encounter[s] with nature' we find in *To the Lighthouse*, Orlando's earthy matrimony is followed by a climatic vision as she turns from the earth to the sky and becomes aware of the 'marvellous golden foam into which the clouds had churned themselves', transporting her back to Turkey as, similar to the opening of the novel, the air effects transformations both material and immaterial (*O* 225–6).[58] It is a moment that speaks clearly to what Colebrook describes as Woolf's presentation of life in terms of intensity, where 'light, life, colour, sensation [and] the flux of time' put pressure on the humanist idea of the autonomous subject and reveal the priority of 'sexual desire' as that which produces a material ontology of 'becom[ing] in relation'.[59] Moreover, while Orlando's betrothal to nature appears only short-lived, since it is immediately followed by the arrival of the 'towering dark' Shelmerdine (*O* 228), nature's queer tricks continue. When Orlando shortens Shelmerdine's name to the more ambiguous Shel, Woolf invites us to hear a homonym for the kind of shell that encases or conceals a surprising interiority, which, as we have already been told, is one of nature's queer tricks, and when Orlando gives voice to her 'suspicion' that '[y]ou're a woman, Shel!' (*O* 230), the reader has already guessed as much from the androgynous shell which seems to encase an uncertain interior. The 'quickness of the [. . .] sympathy' (*O* 235) that emerges between the two presents itself not in terms of heteronormative categories of desire but is instead continuous with the broader processes of impersonal sympathy and material contingency that run throughout the novel.

This undoing of Victorian conventions around marriage is confirmed a short while later as the two prepare to wed. With the 'organ booming and the lightning playing and the rain pouring', Orlando and Shel's real marriage takes place not inside the chapel but immediately outside in the rain. Here their pre-matrimonial vows are likened to 'wild hawks together circling among the belfries' (*O* 239), joining them not only to each other but the queer nature Orlando has already given herself to. Although critics have sometimes struggled to reconcile Orlando's marriage with the feminist agency elsewhere presented in the novel, reading the marriage as a transformative event recasts this question of agency, presenting the moment as a further catalyst to transformation rather than a terminus.[60] Offering a riposte to the storm cloud which opens the Victorian century with its dim prospects for the lives of married women, the storm which closes the Victorian chapter resituates marriage in terms of a potentially queer space of climatic (not to mention climactic) transformation in which, like their vows which soar 'higher and higher, further and further, faster and faster' (*O* 239), Orlando and Shel become entangled with more-than-human processes that take them beyond their individual selves. Climate, then, is not incidental to the designs and ambitions of *Orlando*, its queering of desire and bodies, but is central to Woolf's reimagining of life. Alert to the dangers that come with essentialism – whether the climatic determinism that would look to align a national essence with geographic location or the kind of gender essentialism that the novel so clearly rejects – Woolf fulfils her ambition of becoming a 'weather prophet' by reimagining the ontological relationship between humans and nonhumans, climate and history. Defiantly queer in its undoing not only of rigid categories of sex, gender and sexuality but also of nature and culture, the sympathy that emerges between the climate and the ages in *Orlando* points towards the potential for rethinking life in the Anthropocene, attending to the climate in which we are all entangled without flattening the social, political and historical differences that matter.

Notes

1. Virginia Woolf, *A Passionate Apprentice: The Early Journals 1897–1909*, ed. Mitchell A. Leaska (London: The Hogarth Press, 1990), p. 137.
2. Paula Maggio, *Reading the Skies in Virginia Woolf: Woolf on Weather in Her Essays, Diaries and Three of Her Novels* (London: Cecil Woolf Publishers, 2009).
3. Adeline Johns-Putra, 'Introduction', in *Climate and Literature*, ed. Adeline Johns-Putra (Cambridge: Cambridge University Press, 2019), pp. 1–12 (p. 1).
4. 'Sympathy', *OED Online* <www.oed.com/view/Entry/196271> (last accessed 6 May 2020).

5. Jan Golinski, 'Weather and Climate in the Age of Enlightenment', in *Climate and Literature*, pp. 111–27 (pp. 119–20).
6. Spencer R. Weart, *The Discovery of Global Warming*, revised and expanded edition (Cambridge, MA: Harvard University Press, 2008), p. 13; Christophe Bonneuil and Jean-Baptiste Fressoz, *The Shock of the Anthropocene*, trans. David Fernbach (New York: Verso, 2016), pp. 178–9.
7. Charles Lyell, *Principles of Geology* (London: Murray, 1853), p. 697; pp. 714–17.
8. See Christina Alt, *Virginia Woolf and the Study of Nature* (Cambridge: Cambridge University Press, 2010); Holly Henry, *Virginia Woolf and the Discourse of Science* (Cambridge: Cambridge University Press, 2003); and Michael Whitworth, 'Scientific and Medical Contexts' in *Virginia Woolf* (Oxford: Oxford University Press, 2005), pp. 168–91. For a catalogue of Woolf's library see <http://ntserver1.wsulibs.wsu.edu/masc/onlinebooks/woolflibrary/woolflibraryonline.htm> (last accessed 28 September 2021).
9. 'Sympathy', *OED Online*.
10. Kirsty Martin, *Modernism and the Rhythms of Sympathy: Vernon Lee, Virginia Woolf, and D. H. Lawrence* (Oxford: Oxford University Press, 2013), p. 8; p. 99.
11. Dipesh Chakrabarty, 'Postcolonial Studies and the Challenge of Climate Change', *New Literary History*, 43.1 (2012), 1–18 (p. 10).
12. Gillian Beer, *Virginia Woolf: The Common Ground* (Ann Arbor: University of Michigan Press, 1996), p. 58.
13. Alexandra Harris, *Weatherland: Writers and Artists Under English Skies* (London: Thames & Hudson, 2015), pp. 16–17.
14. Jesse Oak Taylor, *The Sky of Our Manufacture: The London Fog in British Fiction from Dickens to Woolf* (Charlottesville: University of Virginia Press, 2016), p. 201; p. 207.
15. Ruben Borg, *Fantasies of Self-Mourning: Modernism, the Posthuman and the Finite* (Amsterdam: Brill Rodopi, 2019), pp. 109–39; Helena Feder, *Ecocriticism and the Idea of Culture: Biology and the Bildungsroman* (Farnham: Ashgate Publishing, 2014), pp. 75–96; Derek Ryan, *Virginia Woolf and the Materiality of Theory: Sex, Animal, Life* (Edinburgh: Edinburgh University Press, 2013), pp. 101–30; Derek Ryan, '*Orlando*'s Queer Animals', in *A Companion to Virginia Woolf*, ed. Jessica Berman (Oxford: Wiley-Blackwell, 2016), pp. 109–20; and Bonnie Kime Scott, *In the Hollow of the Wave: Virginia Woolf and Modernist Uses of Nature* (Charlottesville: University of Virginia Press, 2012), pp. 142–4.
16. Jane de Gay, 'Rhythms of Revision and Revisiting: Unpicking the Past in *Orlando*', in *Sentencing 'Orlando': Virginia Woolf and the Morphology of the Modernist Sentence*, ed. Elsa Högberg and Amy Bromley (Edinburgh: Edinburgh University Press, 2018), pp. 56–67 (p. 63).
17. Tess Somervell, 'The Seasons', in *Climate and Literature*, pp. 45–59 (p. 45).
18. When the reader finally gets to read a short section from Orlando's poem towards the end of the novel, they are presented with four lines taken directly from Sackville-West's poem. For a comparative reading of *Orlando* and *The Land*, see Susan Bazargan, 'The Uses of the Land: Vita Sackville West's Pastoral Writing and Virginia Woolf's *Orlando*', *Woolf Studies Annual*, 5 (1999), 25–55. See also my analysis of

The Land and *To the Lighthouse* in 'Bloomsbury and Nature', in *The Handbook to the Bloomsbury Group*, ed. Derek Ryan and Stephen Ross (London: Bloomsbury, 2018), pp. 225–38.
19. Jeffrey Mathes McCarthy, *Green Modernism: Nature and the English Novel, 1900 to 1930* (Basingstoke and New York: Palgrave Macmillan, 2015), pp. 21–2.
20. In a 1936 letter to Julian Bell, Woolf was more forthright in her verdict on Housman: 'I don't altogether [like him]; why, I cant say. Always too laden with a peculiar scent for my taste. May, death, lads, Shropshire' (*VWL6* 33).
21. Scott reads this scene as offering a holistic web image. Bonnie Kime Scott, *In the Hollow of the Wave*, p. 214.
22. For discussion of how *Orlando* relates to contemporary trans theory see Jessica Berman, 'Is the Trans in Transnational the Trans in Transgender?', *Modernism/ Modernity*, 24.2 (2017), 217–44; and Chris Coffman, 'Woolf's *Orlando* and the Resonances of Trans Studies', *Genders*, 51 (2010) <https://www.colorado.edu/gendersarchive1998-2013/2010/02/01/woolfs-orlando-and-resonances-trans-studies> (last accessed 6 May 2020).
23. De Gay, 'Rhythms of Revision and Revisiting', pp. 60–2; Christine Froula, *Virginia Woolf and the Bloomsbury Avant-Garde: War, Civilization, Modernity* (New York: Columbia University Press, 2005), pp. 180–9.
24. Dana Phillips, *The Truth of Ecology: Nature, Culture, and Literature in America* (Oxford: Oxford University Press, 2003), p. 71.
25. Somervell, 'The Seasons', pp. 45–6.
26. For Woolf's reading in the history of the Great Frost see Julia Briggs, *Virginia Woolf: An Inner Life* (London: Allen Lane, 2005), pp. 194–5; and Alice Fox, *Virginia Woolf and the Literature of the English Renaissance* (Oxford: Oxford University Press, 1990), pp. 159–62.
27. Jeremy Davies, *The Birth of the Anthropocene* (Oakland: University of California Press, 2016), pp. 9–10. Neocatastrophism is distinct from the catastrophism of the seventeenth and eighteenth centuries which looked to explain planetary change through events such as floods and was displaced by the geological discoveries of the nineteenth century, an intellectual history Woolf would have likely been aware of.
28. Davies, *Birth of the Anthropocene*, p. 26. Angeliki Spiropoulou has described how 'destruction and singularity instead of evolutionary or repetitive flow [. . .] marks the course of history and the succession of ages in *Orlando*'. See *Virginia Woolf, Modernity and History: Constellations with Walter Benjamin* (Basingstoke: Palgrave Macmillan, 2010), p. 89.
29. Claire Colebrook, 'We Have Always Been Post-Anthropocene: The Anthropocene Counterfactual', in *Anthropocene Feminism*, ed. Richard Grusin (Minneapolis: University of Minnesota Press, 2017), pp. 1–20 (p. 13).
30. Weart, *The Discovery of Global Warming*, pp. 2–3.
31. Ibid. p. 3.
32. Tyndall's work inspired the Swiss scientist Svante August Arrhenius whose research, as Christina Alt outlines, led him to conclude that 'anthropogenic CO2 emissions can cause climatic change'. Arrhenius, however, concerned about the onset of global cooling welcomed the prospect of anthropogenic climatic warming. Christina Alt,

'"Restore to Us the Necessary BLIZZARDS": Early Twentieth-Century Visions of Climatic Change', *Modernist Cultures*, 16.1 (2021), 37–61 (p. 47–8).
33. Taylor, *Sky of Our Manufacture*, p. 2.
34. John Ruskin, *Selected Writings*, ed. Dinah Birch (Oxford: Oxford University Press, 2004), p. 267; p. 277. For ecocritical analysis of the importance of Ruskin's essay see Jesse Oak Taylor, 'Storm-Clouds on the Horizon: John Ruskin and the Emergence of Anthropogenic Climate Change', *19: Interdisciplinary Studies in the Long Nineteenth Century* 26 (2018) <www.19.bbk.ac.uk/article/id/1718/> (last accessed 5 May 2020).
35. See Beer, *Virginia Woolf*, pp. 98–9; and Caroline Webb, '"All Was Dark; All Was Doubt; All Was Confusion": Nature, Culture, and *Orlando*'s Ruskinian Storm-Cloud', in *Virginia Woolf Out Of Bounds: Selected Papers from the Tenth Annual Conference on Virginia Woolf*, ed. Jessica Berman and Jane Goldman (New York: Pace University Press, 2001), pp. 243–48.
36. Beer, *Virginia Woolf*, pp. 107–8. Ann Banfield also speculates that the presentation of waves in Woolf's fiction suggests the influence of Tyndall. Banfield, *The Phantom Table: Woolf, Fry, Russell and the Epistemology of Modernism* (Cambridge: Cambridge University Press, 2000), pp. 124–5.
37. Justine Pizzo, 'Ethereal Women: Climate and Gender from Realism to the Modernist Novel', in *Climate and Literature*, pp. 179–95 (pp. 182–3).
38. Ibid. pp. 186–7.
39. John Tyndall, *The Glaciers of the Alps: Being a Narrative of the Excursions and Ascents, an Account of the Origin and Phenomena of Glaciers and an Exposition of the Physical Principles to Which They Are Related* (London: John Murray, 1860), p. v.
40. Ibid. p. 243; p. 253, p. 184.
41. Virginia Woolf, *Roger Fry: A Biography* (New York: Harcourt, Brace and Company, 1940), p. 164.
42. John Tyndall, *Address Delivered Before the British Association Assembled at Belfast* (London: Longmans, Green and Co., 1874), pp. 54–5.
43. Jeff Wallace, *D. H. Lawrence, Science and the Posthuman* (New York: Palgrave Macmillan, 2005), p. 69.
44. Pizzo, 'Ethereal Women', p. 186; Tyndall, *Belfast Address*, p. 33. I read Woolf's attack on the 'materialism' of Edwardian fiction in 'Modern Fiction' not to be a dismissal of materiality so much as a polemic on fiction that ignores the ontological liveliness, or spirit, of matter.
45. Elsa Högberg and Amy Bromley, 'Introduction: Sentencing *Orlando*', in *Sentencing 'Orlando': Virginia Woolf and the Morphology of the Modernist Sentence*, pp. 1–12 (pp. 1–2).
46. Rosi Braidotti, 'Anthropos Redux: A Defence of Monism in the Anthropocene Epoch', *Frame*, 29.2 (2016), 29–48 (p. 34); Ryan, *Virginia Woolf*, p. 3.
47. Rosi Braidotti, *Transpositions: On Nomadic Ethics* (Cambridge: Polity Press, 2006), pp. 190–1.
48. See Taylor, *Sky of our Manufacture*, p. 209; and Spiropoulou, *Virginia Woolf*, p. 87.
49. Haraway uses this term throughout her recent work but see *When Species Meet* in particular.

50. Berman, 'Is the Trans in Transnational the Trans in Transgender?', p. 218.
51. Virginia Woolf, *Orlando: The Holograph Draft*, ed. Stuart N. Clarke (London: S. N. Clarke, 1993), p. 46.
52. Andreas Malm and Alf Hornborg, 'The Geology of Mankind? A Critique of the Anthropocene Narrative', *The Anthropocene Review*, 1.1 (2014), 62–9 (p. 66).
53. Rosi Braidotti, *The Posthuman* (Cambridge: Polity, 2013), p. 98.
54. 'Determine', *OED Online* <www.oed.com/view/Entry/51244> (last accessed 6 May 2020).
55. Judith Butler, *Bodies That Matter: On the Discursive Limits of 'Sex'* (London and New York: Routledge, 2011), pp. 69–71. For a broader discussion of *Orlando* and Butler, see Christy L. Burns, 'Re-Dressing Feminist Identities: Tensions between Essential and Constructed Selves in Virginia Woolf's *Orlando*', *Twentieth-Century Literature*, 40.3 (1994), 342–64.
56. Suzanne Raitt and Ian Blyth, 'Explanatory Notes', in Virginia Woolf, *Orlando: A Biography*, ed. Suzanne Raitt and Ian Blyth (Cambridge: Cambridge University Press, 2018), p. 371. Jane Goldman has shown that the earliest use of queer in its contemporary sense can be traced back to a 1915 diary entry by Arnold Bennett, where he describes attending a party comprised of 'art students, painters and queer people' that included Vanessa Bell as well as others in Woolf's circle. See Jane Goldman, 'Queer Bloomsbury (Review)', *Woolf Studies Annual*, 23 (2017), 161–71.
57. Burns, 'Re-Dressing Feminist Identities', p. t350.
58. Kelly Sultzbach, *Ecocriticism in the Modernist Imagination: Forster, Woolf, and Auden* (Cambridge: Cambridge University Press, 2016), p. 127.
59. Claire Colebrook, 'Woolf and "Theory"', in *Virginia Woolf in Context*, ed. Bryony Randall and Jane Goldman (Cambridge: Cambridge University Press, 2012), pp. 65–78 (p. 67; p. 71).
60. See, for instance, Leslie Kathleen Hankins, '*Orlando*: "A Precipice Marked V" Between "A Miracle of Discretion" and "Lovemaking Unbelievable: Indiscretions Incredible"', in *Virginia Woolf: Lesbian Readings*, ed. Eileen Barrett and Patricia Morgane Cramer (New York: New York University Press, 1997), pp. 181–202.

6

THE DISTURBING FUTURE OF VIRGINIA WOOLF'S LATE WRITING

> Grief is a path to understanding entangled shared living and dying; human beings must grieve *with*, because we are in and of this fabric of undoing.
>
> Donna Haraway, *Staying with the Trouble*

> It was an awkward moment. How to make an end?
>
> Virginia Woolf, *Between the Acts*

The future incessantly disturbs the present in Woolf's late writings, reflecting a historical moment marked by war, social upheaval and the possibility of human extinction. In her final, unfinished novel, *Between the Acts* (1941), set on the eve of the Second World War, one of the characters reflects on the question of why the present is not itself 'enough', concluding that it is '[t]he future disturbing our present' that makes life feel so precarious (*BTA* 60). In contrast, in a letter that Woolf sent to Ethel Smyth in March 1941, three days after finishing the last typescript of *Between the Acts*, it is the lack of any future at all that disturbs the present.[1] Recounting a conversation with Leonard about the war in which she remarked that 'we have no future', Leonard is said to have retorted that the lack of a future is precisely 'what gives him hope' and that 'the necessity of some catastrophe pricks him up' (*VWL5* 475). Leonard's paradoxical hopefulness in the face of 'no future', a future whose negativity seems to disturb the present in a strangely productive way, perhaps clearing the ground for alternative forms of society, shares some resemblance with Lee Edelman's influential argument in *No Future: Queer Theory and the Death Drive* (2004). For Edelman, the negation of any apparent future also offers a new way of thinking about life in the present. Critical of what he sees as a politically conservative and sexually heteronormative logic of 'reproductive futurism', in which both political and sexual orientation are structured by a desire for current social conditions to be interminably extended into the future, Edelman suggests that a more radical thought inheres in a queer negativity which rejects all investment in the future. For Edelman, the 'ideological limit on political discourse' imposed by reproductive futurism can be resisted through the rejection of 'every realization of futurity'. That is, by embracing, rather than feeling revulsion towards, the idea of a futureless future it becomes possible to think outside of the dominant social structures.[2] Interestingly, in his monograph Edelman turns not to Leonard Woolf (whose sentiments can be linked to the increasingly anti-utopian stance that he had adopted in the 1930s)[3] but rather to Virginia, taking his epigraph from her 1941 diary: 'Yes, I was thinking: we live without a future. That's what's queer, with our noses pressed to a closed door' (*D5* 355). Although Edelman does not return to Woolf in his subsequent analysis of futurity, her position at the head of his study situates her as a kind of anti-oracular oracle, whose resistance towards a vision of the future is precisely what enables her to foreshadow contemporary questions around what it means to come to an end.

This chapter traces figures of extinction and futurity in Woolf's late writing, examining how her work both thematises and is structured by a relation to the idea of a future in which 'we' (variously understood) are not present. Looking both at the final texts she wrote and the texts which can be considered late by virtue of their being published posthumously, it examines how Woolf was deeply preoccupied with the ontological and ethical implications of extinction. I suggest that, like Edelman, Woolf suspends normative thinking around questions of posterity and, instead, engages with an aesthetics of extinction that reimagines communal relations. Yet, while the human-centred politics of Edelman's present without a future have been critiqued as environmentally irresponsible,[4] this chapter suggests that Woolf offers a broader, non-anthropocentric understanding of futurity. It argues that in Woolf's writing we find a way of thinking about extinction in which the human is no longer the barometer of existence and in which as certain worlds vanish other forms of life have the potential to emerge. In engaging with Woolf's late writing and questions of endings, this chapter also reaches the end of the narrative of modernist literary history that I have traced in this book.[5] If, as I have aimed to demonstrate in the previous chapters, Joyce, Barnes and Woolf developed modes of writing about the nonhuman world that could build upon, interrogate and critique earlier writing about nature and modernity's exploitation of the natural world, this chapter suggests that the late 1930s and early 1940s necessitated yet another reassessment of the human and its relationship to the wider material world. I also look to suggest parallels and points of intersection between Woolf's late writing and the way in which the Anthropocene arrives as a crisis for futurity. Indeed, the Anthropocene as a concept is wholly structured by a relation to the future. A geological epoch yet to fully arrive, its epistemological and political implications are based on 'stratigraphic records' that 'might appear in the future'.[6] As with the future that so profoundly disturbs characters in *Between the Acts*, the Anthropocene's threat of massive species extinction, sea-level rise, catastrophic climate change and potential societal collapse unsettle the ontological and ethical sureties of the present, drawing into the foreground the inevitability of human extinction at *some point* in the future.

For Roy Scranton, the 'imminent collapse of the agricultural, shipping, and energy networks upon which the global economy depends' necessitates an urgent re-evaluation of the philosophical notions of the good and the true.[7] Following Montaigne's famous adage that 'to philosophize is to learn to die', Scranton suggests that the future promised by the Anthropocene impels nothing less than a need to 'to learn to die not as individuals, but as a civilization'. Not a wholly macabre enterprise, but a challenge to make 'meaningful decisions in the shadow of our inevitable end', Scranton suggests that civilisational death might, paradoxically, be a way of imagining new communal ways of being better adapted to our planet.[8] In this, Scranton joins Claire Colebrook for whom the Anthropocene necessitates an ethics of extinction. As Colebrook argues, 'there was a time, and there will be a time, without humans' and, as such, we need to 'think beyond the world as it is *for us*, and yet remain mindful that the imagining of the inhuman world always proceeds from a positive human failure'.[9] Moreover, just as Edelman finds in Woolf a queering of futurity that looks ahead to his own moment, Colebrook also identifies in Woolf an aesthetics of extinction that speaks to the present, seeing her writing as containing an 'intuition of that which might be perceived after the destruction of "man"'.[10] Woolf's interest in capturing experiences and intensities that exceed human life, Colebrook suggests, shatters anthropocentrically framed ways of thinking about endings. It is this capacity to imagine life *after* life that, I suggest, means her writing is always ahead of itself, able to speak to the future that it is describing. We can find examples of this proleptic agency in the recurring tableaux of a world without humans in *Between the Acts*, where empty rooms momentarily present the reader with scenes of extinction. While it is the description of the empty barn, devoid of humans but replete with creaturely life, that is frequently highlighted in ecocritical readings of the novel, we find a perhaps more apt figure for the Anthropocene in the earlier description of the 'empty' library.[11] Here the 'light but variable breeze, foretold by the weather expert, flap[s] the yellow curtain, tossing light, then shadow' on books that 'if no human being ever came, never, never, never, would be mouldy' (*BTA* 12–13). It is a momentary image of a dehumanised space in which an archive of human thought is contextualised in relation to broader material processes and haunted by the possibility of its material erasure under the influence of such forces. Curiously foreshadowing the bombing of Leonard and Virginia's personal library in Tavistock Square in October 1940, it is a scene that articulates an anxiety around the possible extinction not only of the human species but of human thought. Woolf's mouldering library stages the moment that human systems of inscription, intended to carry human value forward into posterity, collapse into a material substrate and become part of a broader inhuman system of marks and signs. As in the Anthropocene, whose imaginary is structured by a future in which human life is 'readable' not through books or repositories of knowledge but the material 'scars' that constitute the stratigraphic 'text of the earth', Woolf's extinction scenes stage what is at stake in reading and writing the end of the human.[12]

This chapter, then, aims to show how Woolf's writing is not only in dialogue with its own historical moment of possible extinction but speaks to current ideas and debates around extinction within Anthropocene studies. Beginning by tracing Woolf's engagement with the transition from the present to the future in her diaries, letters, memoirs and essays, I suggest that we can see a working through of ideas and insights around extinction narratives. Proceeding to look in detail at how these are further explored in *Between the Acts*, the chapter argues that Woolf's final novel aims to challenge dominant ways of thinking about endings and conclusions. Although it has the distinction of perhaps being the most ecocritically discussed of Woolf's novels (and, perhaps, of all modernist novels), less attention has been paid to the way in which the non-anthropocentric aesthetics of *Between the Acts* are structured through a relation to extinction.[13] Brenda Silver's conclusion that Woolf's late writing is characterised by an 'inability to see a transition from present to future' and Christine Froula's counterargument that Woolf never 'ceased to believe in civilization's future' are representative of a critical tendency to read Woolf's late writing as either pessimistic or optimistic.[14] This chapter looks to depart from the necessity of reading Woolf along such a division, suggesting instead Woolf's preoccupations around possible futures and futurity instead open onto the radical and potentially dangerous question of whether human life as we know it should continue into the future at all.

WRITING THE END OF THE WORLD

The concept of extinction was understood in various ways during the early twentieth century. An evolutionary understanding of species extinction was well developed; Georges Curvier had established the concept at the close of the eighteenth century in his work on elephant fossils and Darwin's *The Origin of Species* (one of the books Woolf rescued from her bombed London home) ends with an extended passage that considers the 'extinction of less-improved forms'.[15] Yet, extinction was not tied solely to questions of gradual species adaptation. The Victorian period had left a legacy of concerns around energy depletion, environmental limits and anxieties that civilisation could consume itself.[16] In the interwar years of the twentieth century, fears of civilisation annihilating itself further intensified, manifesting themselves in what Paul K. Saint-Amour has described as a 'collective syndrome' in which 'a future-conditional war or attack' structured everyday reality.[17] It is unsurprising then that we find a certain apocalyptic tone running through much modernist literature. Instances include Bloom's earlier discussed musings on 'the annihilation of the world and consequent extermination of the human species' (*U* 17.464–5) in *Ulysses*, images of cities overgrown or dying in Eliot's *The Waste Land* (1922) and his later play, *The Rock* (1934), and Gerald Birkin's misanthropic desire for an extinction event in which 'humanity disappear[s] as quick as possible' in D. H. Lawrence's *Women in Love* (1920).[18] It is important, however, to distinguish between a much older notion of apocalypse, understood in religious terms as the end of history or the unveiling of a new world, and the more secular understanding of extinction that arises from the discoveries of fossils of bygone species and fears about humanity's capacity to wipe itself out through resource depletion or warfare. Indeed, where Eliot's work might seem to blend a religious and secular vision of end times (the personified wind in *The Rock* speaks of the traces of a disappeared 'godless people' in the urban ruins),[19] Woolf's writing is less interested in theological questions, than material and ontological ones. While Woolf uses the word 'extinction' (in its various forms) throughout the breadth of her oeuvre, the only use of the word 'apocalypse' to be found in her writing is a direct quotation in a *TLS* review of Arnold Bennett's *Books and Persons* (1917) and, as she wrote to Stephen Spender, her less than warm feelings towards Eliot's apocalyptic vision in *The Rock* were influenced by her 'anti-religious bias' (*L5* 315).

Questions of extinction took on new and urgent dimensions in the last part of her life, however. Writing in her diary in late January 1940, Woolf describes herself as 'cling[ing]' to a 'tiny philosophy: to hug the present moment (in which the fire is going out)' (*D5* 262). The extinguishing of light and heat sustaining the present can be read in a literal sense (Britain was experiencing an unusually severe winter), but it also invites itself to be read metaphorically in the broader context of the war, with the possibility of her world being extinguished provoking the necessity for a philosophy of the present. As Benjamin Hagen suggests, we can understand Woolf's notion of philosophy here as being premised not on metaphysical abstraction but rather lived experience: a 'creative ontology' that 'focus[es] on the here and now' while 'not taking for granted [. . .] the possibility of a future for her and others'.[20] Notably, Hagen suggests that Woolf found a philosophical predecessor for this in Montaigne, for whom, as has already been noted, to philosophise is to learn to die.[21] Woolf's diary is instructive for tracing this tiny philosophy in practice, where the present is incessantly reassessed in the face of a threatened future. As early as 1936, with the 'chaos' and 'slaughter' of the Spanish Civil War giving the impression that 'war surround[s] our island' (*D5* 32), Woolf is reflecting on the relationship between 'the future' and 'what I'm to write', and records feeling buoyed by Leonard's observation that she tends to 'work from death – or non being – to life!' (*D5* 35). A reversal of the trajectory from life to death, Leonard's insight makes Woolf feel that a 'weight [has been] rolled off' her (*D5* 35), enabling her to begin work on *Three Guineas* (1938), whose working title of *The Next War* and opening question of how to 'prevent war' are both predicated on the logic of a movement from a disturbing future back to the present (*TG* 89). By 1940, however, this tiny philosophy had developed in response to the realities of a war that had now arrived and in which, as Woolf writes to Smyth, London was already 'like a dead city' and in which invasion 'seems imminent' (*VWL5* 433). This more intimate proximity to destruction is registered in texts such as 'Thoughts on Peace in an Air Raid' (1940), which opens with the experience of 'lying in the dark and listening to the zoom of a hornet which may at any moment sting you to death', situating the present within an unfolding moment of extinction rather than as an imagined future event (*E6* 242). Moreover, for Woolf, there is more than just material destruction at stake in the bombing raids. In the 'drone of the planes' in which 'all thinking stop[s]' (*E6* 244) the war threatens to extinguish not only individual lives but collective thought itself. Like the mouldering library in *Between the Acts*, it is not only the end of certain forms of organic life that extinction threatens but forms of thought and knowledge that would otherwise inhere into the future.

Thomas S. Davis, borrowing a term from an Elizabeth Bowen short story, has described the socio-cultural moment of Woolf's late writing as the 'extinct scene', a moment of looming material and intellectual dereliction that threatened the fabric of everyday life and compelled a socially engaged 'outward turn' in modernist writing.[22] Saint-Amour makes a similar argument in his description of Woolf's interest in developing new literary forms capable of 'being and thinking and feeling in common' in response to the war.[23] For Woolf, however, the question of the future also provoked questions around the legacy of her work and other writers of her generation. We see this expressed indirectly in essays such as 'The Humane Art' (1940), where she argues that Horace Walpole's letters were written not for his contemporaries but 'for posterity' (*E6* 225) (a word which is repeated five times in the first paragraph alone) and which concludes with the enigmatic remark that 'whatever ruin may befall the map of Europe in years to come, there will still be people, it is consoling to reflect, to hang absorbed over the map of one human face' (*E6* 228). In a January 1940 diary entry, we find a more explicit engagement with possible futures. Posing the question of whom of the Bloomsbury group 'will interest posterity most', Woolf decides that John Maynard Keynes is the most probable and adds that if she had 'any regard for the future I would use this hour to record what he [had] said' a few nights previously while discussing the 'legacy' they were leaving behind them (*D5* 255). This question of posterity re-emerges the following January, when Woolf hears that 'Joyce is dead' and remembers reading the early serialised episodes of *Ulysses* in 1918 as a potential publisher. It was, Woolf reflects, 'a scene that should figure I suppose in the history of literature' (*D5* 352–3).[24] The description of 'tufts of smoke [. . .] from burning houses' and the 'desolate ruins' of central London that immediately follow these reflections situates Joyce's death and a modernist literary history she has already begun to memorialise within a broader context of 'completeness ravished and destroyed' (*D5* 353). Extinction, understood as a mass-death event in which certain forms of life are permanently ended, is shown here to bear a relation to individual death. Indeed, in the same way that Woolf appears to read Joyce's demise within a broader historical moment, her own death two months later invites itself to be read in similar terms. As both Mark Hussey and Val Gough have argued, the bleak outlook of the late 1930s shaped an intellectual culture in which taking one's life was being discussed as an act that was not only personal but ethical and political.[25] While it is important not to overlook Woolf's mental health in her decision to take her life, her diary description of a 'matter of fact' conversation with Leonard about 'suicide if Hitler lands' suggests an approach to individual death that is framed within a social context of mass extinction and an understanding of suicide as ethical as much as it is personal (*D5* 284–5).

Perhaps surprisingly, we also find in Woolf's late writing an interest in certain forms of extinction as potentially productive. This is articulated through a distinction that emerges between the end of *the* world and the end of *a* world in 'The Leaning Tower' (1940), an essay based on a paper read to the Workers Educational Authority in Brighton in April 1940. Beginning by theorising the influence of peacetime conditions on literature, Woolf discusses the current generation of 'tower conscious' male poets, whose critical self-awareness of their privileged positions in society has led them to advocate for the tearing down of social and political hierarchies (*E6* 268). These writers, who include W. H. Auden, Cecil Day Lewis and Louis MacNeice, Woolf argues, 'took over from [Yeats and Eliot] a technique which, after many years of experiment, those poets used skilfully, and [have] used it clumsily and often inappropriately' in the service of a 'didactic' political 'oratory' (*E6* 271–2). As in her diary entries, Woolf's polemic addresses modernism's afterlife. Yet her argument is not only aesthetical and political, but ontological. Woolf acknowledges that these writers face an 'appallingly difficult task' since, she argues, refashioning lines from Matthew Arnold, they are 'dweller[s] in two worlds, one dying, the other struggling to be born' (*E6* 272–3).²⁶ This figure of a dying world that represents the old order and a nascent world of new social relations, becomes an extended metaphor for the rest of the essay, as Woolf describes the 'deep gulf to be bridged' between the two and warns that it is within this gulf that 'literature may crash and come to grief' (*E6* 276). Insisting that there are 'still two worlds, two separate worlds', Woolf's language not only delineates between an understanding of the word 'world' as the totality of all material reality (*the* world) and a certain mode of existence (*a* world), it also again invokes a future that has not yet arrived, but which is already marking the present. Turning from the 'tower conscious' writers, who are too quick to disavow the social privilege that has enabled their success, Woolf instead suggests the 'next generation' of writers will come from a variety of backgrounds and will include 'outsiders' who have been historically excluded (*E6* 274; 277). To 'bridge the gulf between the two worlds' this next generation of writers will need to develop a mode of writing that can both 'preserve and create', Woolf insists; an act that involves 'read[ing] . . . critically' and 'trespass[ing] freely and fearlessly' (*E6* 277–8). Here then, despite Woolf's ambivalence towards the next generation of poets, we find a more dynamic and potentially positive relation to the future, as the material of the dead world becomes matter to be reshaped. Offering an extinction narrative of sorts, Woolf's essay foreshadows Leonard's later optimism in the face of no future, where the end of one world makes possible other and different future worlds.

ANONYMITY, IMPERSONALITY AND EXTINCTION

The instruction to 'preserve and create' which closes 'The Leaning Tower' might be read as a relatively conservative gesture; a tempered approach to social change that emphasises preservation as much as it endorses creation. Indeed, the tension between resisting extinction and embracing it can be seen as a working through of her 'tiny philosophy' of the 'present moment' as it comes under increasing pressure. Yet, Woolf's insistence on the language of worlds – future worlds, towerless worlds, dying worlds – suggests a pluralistic understanding of life in which the end of one's own world (however construed) does not amount to the end of *the* world. If this is only suggested in 'The Leaning Tower', such an idea finds clearer expression in other texts Woolf was writing at the same time, where we find an attention to the materiality that subtends human modes of thought and perception, and which promises to be there long after we have gone. Woolf's unfinished history of English literature set to be entitled *Reading at Random* or *Turning the Page* (the later title) presents itself as precisely one such attempt to preserve and create at a point when Woolf feared 'the future of language is almost extinct now', a phrase whose uncertain tense again points towards a future disturbing the present.²⁷ Woolf, however, is not interested in ensconcing literature within a humanist narrative in which by virtue of cultural ingenuity human exceptionalism might be shored against the threat of extinction. Instead, Woolf begins with a thought of extinction by attempting to imagine a world before ours, pre-empting what Colebrook frames as an ethical and ontological imperative to 'think beyond the world as it is for us'.[28] 'Anon', intended as the book's first chapter, begins by sketching out a prehistory that precedes literature, but which also provides its condition of possibility. Citing the historian George Macaulay Trevelyan's book *History of England* (1926), Woolf describes a 'moist and mossy' Britain in which the 'untamed forest was king' where, the essay speculates, the song of 'innumerable birds' in the 'matted boughs' gave rise to a 'desire to sing [among] huntsmen', providing the origins for what would become verbal art (*E6* 583). Woolf would draw upon the same passage from Trevelyan in a section of *Between the Acts* that she composed while writing 'Anon'. In the final section of the novel, as 'darkness' cloaks the village setting, Mrs Swithin reads Trevelyan's description of England as a 'swamp' where '[t]hick forests covered the land' (*BTA* 157).[29] In what is teased as the coming extinction of civilisation in *Between the Acts*, Trevelyan's prehistory is refashioned into what might be described as posthistory, or rather more accurately posthuman history, since nonhuman life, the text suggests, will keep on going.

Woolf's citations of Trevelyan are important here and not only since his text enables her to situate human life within broader forms of existence. It also presents an example of Woolf reading what can now be seen as a proto-Anthropocene narrative of extinction. Trevelyan concludes his history with a remark that would become amplified in the environmental historiographies that followed later in the century. While in 'the earlier scene, man's impotence to contend with nature made his life brutish and brief. To-day his very command over nature, so admirably and marvellously won, has become his greatest peril.'[30] Yet, where Trevelyan appears to be mourning the future demise of the human subject, situating the human as the species whose technological exceptionalism is also the cause of its own destruction, in 'Anon', the figure of the anonymous singer is resolutely not an autonomous human subject manipulating the nonhuman world to its own ends. Instead, it is continuous with the materiality that it expresses. Woolf asserts that '[t]he voice that broke the silence of the forest was the voice of Anon', later describing Anon as 'sometimes man; sometimes woman [. . .] [living] a roaming life crossing the fields, mounting the hills, lying under the hawthorn to listen to the nightingale' (*E6* 581–2). 'Anon', here, is a figure that resists taking on a recognisable human shape. It is defined by an 'impersonality' which, unlike Eliot's famous formulation, is not the expression of an individual talent since Anon cannot 'stamp his own name'. Rather it is an impersonality that expresses a broader 'generality' and extends beyond the human world since Anon stands as both the human speaker and the world that speaker is expressing (*E6* 597–8). The chapter goes on to chart the development of 'Anon' up until the development of the printing press, itself a kind of extinction event insofar as it would both 'kill' and 'preserve' the possibility of anonymous works in a new form (*E6* 583). Yet, for Woolf, this quality of anonymity, in which literature is understood to derive from a more-than-human materiality that exceeds individual human subjectivity, is not lost to a prehistoric past. Instead, 'the anonymous world' is that which lies 'beneath our consciousness' and is emphatically something 'to which we can still return' (*E6* 584). Indeed, we see Woolf reflecting on precisely this aspect of her own writing in a section of her unfinished memoir, 'A Sketch of the Past', that she was writing while planning 'Anon' and revising *Between the Acts*. Remembering her childhood holidays in St Ives, Woolf writes:

> The lemon-coloured leaves on the elm tree; the apples in the orchard; the murmur and rustle of the leaves makes me pause here, and think how many other than human forces are always at work on us. While I write this the light glows; an apple becomes a vivid green; I respond all through me; but how? (*MB* 146)

Here writing is recast as a 'response' that is subjective, but which does not wholly coincide with the human subject. These 'other than human forces', comparable with both the description in 'Anon' of the 'anonymous world' that exceeds our consciousness and *Orlando*'s damp in the inkpot discussed in Chapter 5, situate writing as an act that is profoundly impersonal. While for Eliot, impersonality is achieved through an aesthetic practice that eschews subjectivity through a 'continual extinction of personality', for Woolf it involves acknowledging one's self as a 'porous vessel' and 'yield[ing]' to a world that exceeds us (*MB* 146–7).[31] It means, Woolf explains, listening to 'a third voice' that never seems to coincide with our own (*MB* 146), as writing becomes an encounter with the world that exists without us.

Woolf's attention to the material anonymity that subtends the human and which always exceeds our own world presents itself as sympathetic to what Colebrook describes as the 'stratigraphic' imaginary. For Colebrook, stratigraphy, that is the analysis of geological layers (strata), allows 'humans [. . .] to discern a broader and inhuman history beyond their ken'.[32] More importantly, the ability to 'think stratigraphically' enables a mode of 'deterritorialization' in which it becomes possible not only to consider other scales of existence, but to glimpse how this fact of 'superimposition or co-existence' is fundamental to understanding life in terms of a 'plane of immanence, with all the temporalities, chronologies, histories and events of life existing at once'. Time and space are no longer opposed, as the stratigraphic imaginary enables a mode of perception in which it is possible to imagine multiple temporalities at once, the slow unfolding of geological processes and the fast-paced temporality of Western modernity offering two obvious examples. The result, Colebrook argues, is a deeper ontological understanding of how *our* world is not *the* world.[33] Woolf's posthumously published essay 'Flying over London', written in 1928 but not published until 1950, explores precisely this question of stratigraphy as it relates both to the ability to think beyond the human and the implications therein for understanding extinction. Describing the view from an aeroplane above London, the essay offers a defamiliarised topography of 'the River Thames [. . .] as the Romans saw it, as palaeolithic man saw it, at dawn from a hill shaggy with wood, with the rhinoceros digging his horn into the roots of the rhododendrons' (*E6* 446). Momentarily challenging what Woolf describes as the 'inveterately anthropocentric' tendency of the human mind to assimilate the 'nameless [and] unowned' into the familiar and recognisable, this superimposition of perspectives produces a stratigraphic vista from which 'England [is] earth merely, merely the world' (*E6* 445–6). Using a vocabulary that foreshadows that used by contemporary theorists of the Anthropocene, Woolf recasts both time and space in stratigraphic terms and, in Colebrook's words, suggests the possibility for 'other worlds and other forms of existence [. . .] existing in the present' to be imagined.[34]

For Deleuze and Guattari, from whom Colebrook takes her stratigraphic concept of deterritorialisation, the 'plane of consistency' beneath the everyday appearance of the world is resolutely not an ontological foundation. Instead, the plane exists as 'relations of speed and slowness' which produces a 'consolidation of [. . .] aggregates'.[35] Or, slightly simplified, everyday human reality is the product of a certain experience of speed, intensity and affect. It is a concept which undercuts the notion of either the permeance or transcendence of certain forms of life (such as 'the human') and which 'stands opposed to all [. . .] finality'.[36] For Woolf, a stratigraphic perspective also opens on to questions of finality. Flying higher, Woolf reflects on how:

> It was the idea of death that now suggested itself; not being received and welcomed; not immortality, but extinction. [. . .] [For] where there are gulls only, life is not. Life ends; life is dowsed in that cloud as lamps are dowsed with a wet sponge. That extinction has become now desirable. For it was odd in this voyage to note how blindly the tide of the soul and its desires rolled this way and that, carrying consciousness like a feather on the top, marking the direction, not controlling it. (*E6* 446–7)

Here extinction is recast in terms of affect and desire, as it is stripped of its familiar associations and comes to describe an experience in which conscious life becomes subject to intensities that exceed the conventional limits of human existence. Bringing the human into intimate proximity with a flighty animal life, experienced as a consciousness that is carried along by material flows and forces that it can mark but not control, Woolf's description of seeing 'merely the world' speaks to the defamiliarising thrust of Deleuze and Guattari's antifoundationalist stratigraphy. It also firmly links an experience of extinction with Woolf's insistence on impersonality that we find in 'A Sketch of the Past' and 'Anon'. Extinction becomes a reminder that, as Rosi Braidotti describes, just as life is both personal and impersonal, there is also a 'personal and impersonal death'. Death no longer serves as the horizon of life, but as the 'opening up of new intensities' beyond individual life, presenting itself as a nodal point within a 'synthesis of flows, energies and becomings'.[37] Yet, for Woolf, such intensities are bearable only for a certain amount of time. Eventually there is a wish to 'give up this arduous game' of flirting with extinction and to return to the solid earth of everyday life (*E6* 449). Moreover, the essay's twist ending – that due to a machine fault Woolf 'had not flown' and has imagined the whole experience from the safety of the airfield (*E6* 450) – offers a conclusion that brings the essay down to earth too, suggesting that flighty visions of extinction will always necessarily be grounded in the limits of the human imagination.

Narratives of Extinction in *Between the Acts*

There is evidence that Woolf returned to the unpublished 'Flying over London' when writing 'the airy world of Poyntz Hall [*sic*]', the fictional country house in *Between the Acts* (*D5* 141).[38] The novel's opening description of the rural surroundings as seen from an aeroplane parallels the stratigraphic vision of her essay, presenting the land in terms of material 'scars made by the Britons; by the Romans; by the Elizabethan manor house; and by the plough, when they ploughed the hill to grow the wheat in the Napoleonic wars' (*BTA* 3). Similarly, the 'rhododendrons' that provide food for the 'rhinoceros' in 'Flying Over London' (*E6* 446) are echoed in Mrs Swithin's fascination with the prehistoric 'rhododendron forests' populated with 'the mammoth, and the mastodon' that stood where Piccadilly is now (*BTA* 6–7). Gillian Beer has described Woolf's final novel as identifying 'prehistory' in terms of 'pre-narrative', understood as that which 'will not buckle to plot'; a 'story [of] extinction' that has happened before and could happen again.[39] Indeed, the very title of *Between the Acts* insists on foregrounding the temporal relation between the present and the future as well as the past, and fears of extinction are an explicit concern throughout the text. The aerial perspective that opens the novel frames a discussion of the planned installation of a village 'cesspool', firmly positioning the first scene within a broader narrative of rise and decline, in which civilisation and modernity are diminished through their relation to the longue durée of geological time (*BTA* 3). The novel's ending makes this point much more forcibly, as the end of the day also marks a greater finality:

> The window was all sky without colour. The house had lost its shelter. It was night before roads were made, or houses. It was the night that dwellers in caves had watched from some high place among rocks.
> Then the curtain rose. They spoke. (*BTA* 157–8)

The characters, too, reflect on decline and extinction. For William Dodge, visitor to Pointz Hall from London, the 'doom of sudden death' is 'hanging' in the air (*BTA* 83), a metaphor that takes material form a short while later when '[t]welve aeroplanes in perfect formation' fly overhead (*BTA* 138). It is within this same militarised context that Isa considers if she would 'mind not again to see may tree or nut tree? Not again to hear on the trembling spray the thrush sing, or to see [. . .] the yellow woodpecker' (*BTA* 76). Similarly, the romantic poetry that she spends the day secretly composing dreams of a 'dark antre of the unvisited earth' that will emerge from the ashes of the future (*BTA* 37).

Yet, as Woolf also shows us, it is not extinction in a general or abstract sense that is a source of anxiety for the inhabitants and visitors of Pointz Hall but as Isa's possessive pronoun suggests when she complains of 'the future disturbing *our* present' (*BTA* 60, emphasis added), it is rather a certain question of posterity that is at stake. As the narrator explains, referring to a guidebook to the area, what was true in '1833 was true in 1939. No house had been built; no town had sprung up [. . .] the very flat, field-parcelled land had changed only in this – the tractor had to some extent superseded the plough' (*BTA* 38). A pastoral vision of an unchanged England, the 'fine view of the surrounding country' (*BTA* 38) enjoyed by the Oliver family from the garden of Pointz Hall is framed in terms that, in contemporary terminology, would be described as relating to the sustainability of the environment for future generations. Here the novel has clear ties to the rural preservation movement, which, as Hussey has shown, looked to decry and stall what it saw at the despoliation of the English countryside by the rise in the building of new roads and houses.[40] Bound up with the rise in a conservative pastoralism that I discussed in relation to *Orlando* in Chapter 5 and buttressed by class prejudices, the movement's banner of 'Save Our Countryside' spearheaded campaigns that looked to highlight what was perceived as the encroachment of the city into the country, evident in the growing problem of litter from day trippers and the visual blight of advertising hoardings. As Hussey shows, Woolf's letters and diaries often present her as echoing such concerns, most notably in her fervent dislike of the red brick bungalows springing up in the Sussex countryside.[41] Yet, where Hussey points out confluences between the rural preservation movement and *Between the Acts* – such as the remark made by a pageant audience member that she would make 'leaving litter' 'penal' (*BTA* 88) – the novel also interrogates the grounds upon which claims for sustainability are made.[42]

Adeline Johns-Putra has argued that discourse around sustainability is invariably structured through appeals to 'future generations', an idea which we can see reflected in the anxieties voiced by the elderly Mrs Swithin and Bart Oliver that the landscape remain unchanged for the Oliver children. Moreover, Johns-Putra suggests, in this respect, the logic of sustainability has clear parallels with Edelman's notion of 'reproductive futurism'.[43] Both pivot around the idea of present material relations remaining fixed and unchanged, with the abstract notion of 'future generations' providing a rhetoric that hopes to shore the present against a disturbing future (Johns-Putra, for instance, points to the way in which much climate justice discourse is centred on the world 'our children' will 'inherit').[44] For both Edelman and Johns-Putra, it is the figure of the child that comes to take on importance within discussions of futurity and which requires critical scrutiny. Edelman argues that 'the image of the Child' regulates and enforces reproductive futurism. Cultural representations of children 'embody [. . .] the telos of the social order and come to be seen as [those] for whom that order is held in perpetual trust'.[45] These images of 'the Child', not to be confused with the lived experience of real historical children, mark 'an erotically charged investment in the rigid sameness of identity that is central to compulsory narratives of reproductive futurism'.[46] The image of the Child metonymically underpins a future in which heterosexuality is timeless and ahistorical, structuring not only the present but also the future, and in which, as Johns-Putra has shown, there is more at stake than reproductive practices but the broader question of how we relate to, interact with and conceptualise the world around us.

In *Between the Acts* we find a similar awareness of the ways in which children come to be associated with heteronormative ideas of posterity and are made to dispel a more radical thought of extinction. Although little remarked upon, Woolf's presentation of children in her final novel contrasts sharply with her earlier works. Unlike Edelman who, despite insisting that the image of the Child needs to be distinguished from real children, does not discuss the implications of his theory for them, Woolf's oeuvre displays a sustained interest in the lives of children, with works such as *To the Lighthouse* and *The Waves* developing innovative narrative perspectives to explore the way in which children see and think about the world. In contrast, except for one key scene discussed below, *Between the Acts* is noticeable for the fact that the reader only ever encounters children through and in relation to the projections, anxieties and preoccupations of adults. This is established early in the novel, where the one direct description of a child character's interior life is displaced by an adult projection in such a way that draws attention to the contrast between the two. Introduced initially through the impersonal title of 'the little boy', Isa's son George is described as 'grouting in the grass' before the narrative appears to, paradoxically, both enter his perspective and remain detached from it:

> The flower blazed between the angles of the roots. Membrane after membrane was torn. It blazed a soft yellow, a lambent light under a film of velvet; it filled the caverns behind the eyes with light. All that inner darkness became a hall, leaf smelling, earth smelling of yellow light. And the tree was beyond the flower; the grass, the flower and the tree were entire. (*BTA* 8)

Recalling Woolf's childhood memory of 'looking at the flower bed by the front door' and it becoming 'suddenly plain that the flower itself was a part of the earth' in 'A Sketch of the Past' (*MB* 80), the uncertain proximity between the child and the earth presents the antithesis to the aesthetic pleasure that the adults take in viewing the landscape from the distance of the garden. Where Bart observes the surrounding 'fields, heaths and woods' as a 'picture' to be 'framed' (*BTA* 10), for George the distinction between self and non-self, the human and the earth, is still fluid. The 'inner' 'hall' of the child, subtended by the outer world's materiality of light, smell and tactility, stands as a figure of uncertain relations that contrast with Pointz Hall, which, according to Bart, was built 'to escape from nature' (*BTA* 6). It is unsurprising then, that it is Bart who desires to tear George away from this vision, surprising him from behind a tree and then swelling with anger when the boy is revealed to be 'a cry-baby' (*BTA* 10). Later Bart thinks of this moment as an act that 'destroyed the little boy's world' (*BTA* 145) and its function in the text is not only to puncture the ecological perspective that has just been described, but to act as the first instance of a recurring narrative motif, in which children become receptacles for adult projections. We find a further instance a short while later, when Mrs Swithin is seen to 'salute the children' and 'beat up against [the] immensities' of the sky (*BTA* 17). Against this militaristic gesture, the sky embodies not merely the threat of rain for the outdoor pageant but a more disturbing reminder of the cosmological inconsequence of human life. As Mrs Swithin has been reflecting immediately prior to saluting the children, beyond the clouds is:

> blue, pure blue, black blue; blue that had never filtered down; that escaped registration. It never fell as sun, shadow, or rain upon the world, but disregarded the little coloured ball of earth entirely. (*BTA* 17)[47]

For Mrs Swithin, who, of all the adult characters, most frequently contemplates questions of life before and after humans, and whose interest in the natural world leads her to see existence in terms that are not resolutely anthropocentric, the figure of the Child nonetheless occupies a site of futurity that resists the thought of extinction.

It is through Isa, however, that the image of the Child is both most strongly expressed and resisted. In an early scene, Isa is alone in her bedroom, remembering the 'silent [and] romantic gentleman farmer' neighbour who had visited Pointz Hall the previous evening. The 'presence of his body in the room last night', Isa recalls, produced a 'tingling, tangling, vibrating' within 'a certain spot in her' (*BTA* 10–11). This implicitly orgasmic sensation, which the text suggests is being felt again in the present moment, is held in tension with competing thoughts of fidelity towards Giles, who Isa feels a duty towards not as her husband but, importantly, as '[t]he father of my children' (*BTA* 10). This phrase, which becomes a refrain, repeated by Isa a further three times (*BTA* 35; 149; 155) is, the narrator tells us, a 'cliché conveniently provided by fiction' (*BTA* 10) to suppress extramarital desires. Seeing George 'lagging behind' his nurses from her bedroom window (*BTA* 10) at the same time as she experiences sexual sensations provoked by the memory of the gentleman farmer, Isa's son becomes a figure of posterity and duty weighed against self-pleasure. There is a parallel here with 'The Leaning Tower', where the figure of the male child is similarly presented as an overdetermined site of posterity. Woolf quotes from a mother who has written a letter to the *New Statesman & Nation* explaining that although she is in favour of 'free national education' over private schooling she is unsure where she will send her own child to be educated, since she wants 'the best of both worlds for my son'. It is a sentiment Woolf sees as articulating a desire for 'the new world and the old world to unite' (*E6* 276).[48] The Child, but more particularly the son, becomes a figure not only of patriarchal lineage, establishing a historical line that consolidates the present, but is projected into the future. The image of the Child, as Edelman argues, 'shield[s] [. . .] against the persistent threat of apocalypse'.[49] It is not inconceivable that Woolf had extinction in mind when writing the scene with Isa in the bedroom. The 'tingling, tangling, vibrating' bodily sensation – which the image of the Child is meant to suppress – leads Isa to think of 'the infinitely quick vibrations of the aeroplane propeller that she had seen once at dawn at Croydon' (*BTA* 11). Again, suggesting that Woolf returned to 'Flying over London' when writing *Between the Acts*, the description that follows refashions imagery from the essay. The earlier description of a seductive impersonality, in which 'consciousness [is] like a feather' as 'the soul and its desires rolled this way and that', and 'extinction [becomes] now desirable' (*E6* 446–7) finds a correlative in Isa's reflections on 'flying, rushing through the ambient, incandescent, summer', impelling her to speak aloud an improvised poem that describes 'a feather, a blue feather [. . .] flying mounting through the air [. . .] there to lose what binds us here' (*BTA* 11). Just as Woolf's essay recasts extinction in terms of impersonality and intensity, Isa experiences a flight of the mind and senses in which the future is momentarily suspended. Yet, just as Woolf's essay insists on coming back to earth, Isa too is brought back to the present with a rough jolt, deciding that the 'words [just spoken] weren't worth writing' in her notebook 'in case Giles suspected' (*BTA* 11).

If the Oliver family embody the libidinal investments that sustain reproductive futurism, the character of William Dodge serves to disturb the filial order already rendered precarious by the threat of a futureless future. A visitor to the Oliver household whose homosexuality is identified yet unspoken by the other characters, he presents what Stephen Barber describes as Woolf's sensitivity to the way in which queerness was (and remains) subject to 'social codifications [and] regulatory labelling'. Yet, as Barber also outlines, Dodge not only resists the 'epistemic configuration' within which he has been interpellated but establishes 'conspiratorial relationships' with the women of the Oliver family.[50] What Barber does not highlight, however, is the way in which these conspiratorial relationships explicitly challenge the authority of the Child. As Mrs Swithin shows Dodge around Pointz Hall, for instance, she not only 'guesse[s] his trouble' (*BTA* 52) but in a certain sense identifies with it. Catching him looking at her in a bedroom mirror, where 'their eyes smiled' (*BTA* 52), she takes him to the nursery. A room laden with the symbolism of how the young are perceived as the 'cradle of our race', it insists on the absence rather than the presence of the children and the futurity they promise:

> The room was like a ship deserted by its crew. The children had been playing – there was a spotted horse in the middle of the carpet. The nurse had been sewing – there was a piece of linen on the table. The baby had been in the cot. The cot was empty. (*BTA* 52)

Sensing that she has shown him the abandoned room so that he can confess, as he indeed wishes to, that 'I [am] married; but my child's not my child' (*BTA* 54), Dodge's unspoken words not only articulate his homosexuality, but speak to what Edelman describes as the capacity for a 'queer negativity' to destabilise categories of identity and reproduction associated with children. As Erica Delsandro has shown in a reading which also draws on Edelman's concept of queer negativity, Dodge not only resists, qua Edelman, 'every substantiation of identity' projected onto him but challenges the 'determinate identities' that shore up 'sexual, national and historical' identities.[51] More specifically, we can see how Dodge's queerness, articulated in the space of the deserted nursery, comes to 'names the side of those not "fighting for the children", the side outside the consensus by which all politics confirms the absolute value of reproductive futurism' and which, in Pointz Hall, names the posterity of the Oliver name and a metonymic idea of Englishness.[52] As in Chapter 3, where I discussed Edelman's concept of queer negativity in relation to Robin in *Nightwood*, Dodge not only dodges the identities projected onto him but figures as a character whose queerness disturbs social organisation.[53] Mrs Swithin, who has adult children, but is seen in terms of childlessness by other characters (Bart wonders how 'she [had] ever borne children' (*BTA* 85)) momentarily enters into a queer affiliation with Dodge, smiling at him with 'a ravishing girl's smile' as he desires to 'kneel before her [and] kiss her hand' (*BTA* 53). It is a moment of queer rapport, as they identify each other as outsiders within the suffocating reproductive futurism that structures the social relations around them.

Later, when Isa finds herself alone in the greenhouse with Dodge, we find another moment of affiliation against an oppressive future. Reflecting how, on account of his homosexuality, she has 'nothing to fear, nothing to hope', Isa feels that they can talk with one another 'as if they had known each other all their lives' because, as she explains to him, 'we've never met before, and never shall again' (*BTA* 83). For Dodge this lucidity is precisely enabled because of the 'sudden death hanging over us [. . .] There's no retreating and advancing [. . .] for us as for them' (*BTA* 83). Here, as in Leonard's remarks about being perked up by the thought of the end of the world, the disruption to the future that seems to be promised is strangely productive. Conventional relations between the past, present and future are suspended and suddenly open. Significantly, Dodge's remarks lead into the following description: 'The future shadowed their present, like the sun coming through the many-veined transparent vine leaf; a criss-cross of lines making no pattern' (*BTA* 83). Although the text gives us little clue as to whether this description should be read as focalised through either Dodge or Isa or as an omniscient narratorial observation, the imagery of foliage and light implicitly parallels George's earlier observation as he sat in the grass. Whereas elsewhere the image of the Child is a figure for resisting extinction, here a childlike perspective produces a moment of impersonality in which the relationship between the present and the future is no longer required to fit a predetermined pattern. While appearing on the surface to contradict Woolf's often quoted 'philosophy' in 'A Sketch of the Past' of a 'pattern hid behind the cotton wool' of daily life (*MB* 81), we might here instead read Woolf's 'philosophy' back through the novel that she was writing at the same time. The 'criss-cross' of the sun through leaves, as in the 'swallows darting' through the trees who 'make a pattern' (*BTA* 47) and the opening aerial description of the landscape's 'scars' (*BTA* 3), suggests a relationship between form and materiality in which meaning and identity are necessarily immanent and in which patterns emerge and dissipate, rather than remain in a fixed relation. Woolf's philosophy of a pattern hidden beneath daily life might be understood to be not only subterranean in the sense of waiting to be revealed, but as taking shape through its emergence. As the encounter between Dodge and Isa shows, in which a pattern that resists interpretation becomes a simile for the relationship between the future and the present, it is a philosophy from which a radically different and potentially queer understanding of futurity might emerge, no longer beholden to the heteronormativity that structures the present.

Extinction Ethics

Woolf is not only concerned with queering futurity in *Between the Acts*; the text also explores how the question of extinction offers new ethical modes of being. For Colebrook, the question of extinction is always implicitly an ethical opportunity. As she explains, when 'faced with extinction the human species might, finally, be presented with a genuine ethics' insofar as it might return ethics to its roots in the notion of 'what it owes to place (ethos) and to those beyond its own organic life (the future)'.[54] A self-reflexive (or even nihilistic) correlative to what Trevelyan was arguing in 1926 about human ingenuity hastening its demise, such an ethics would need to ask the question of whether human life should be sustained at all, since it is precisely because 'the human species [. . .] has remained committed absolutely to its own survival as uniquely human and blessed with a duty to live' that it now faces a mass extinction event of its own making.[55] For Colebrook, an ethics of extinction involves revising how we imagine community, or what she describes as a 'justification of who "we" are' and a willingness 'to question the "we" who would subtend and be saved by the question of ethics and politics'.[56] While Woolf cannot be considered a nihilist, not least since, as I have shown above, her thoughts on extinction tended to swing between resistance towards and desire for creative destruction, she was similarly preoccupied with reconsidering what constituted a 'we' during the composition of *Between the Acts*. Her intentions are captured in an early reference to the novel in her diary:

> 'I' rejected: 'We' substituted: to whom at the end there shall be an invocation? 'We' . . . composed of many different things . . . we all life, all art, all waifs & strays – a rambling capricious but somehow unified whole – the present state of my mind? (*D5* 135)

While it is unclear whether Woolf means 'the end' to refer to the end of the novel or the greater finality facing Europe, the 'we' that emerges in *Between the Acts* explicitly articulates a collective response to impending destruction and can most clearly be seen in the village pageant organised by Miss La Trobe. As Jed Esty has shown, the rise of the pageant as a 'village rite' in the late nineteenth and early twentieth centuries was premised on its ability to 'produce a pastoral, apolitical, and doughtily cohesive version of national identity'.[57] Yet, while Esty reads Woolf's pageant as invested in refiguring national identity against the backdrop of European fascism, we also find in La Trobe's play a hesitancy and uncertainty around the 'we' of that community. Certainly, La Trobe's pageant is a performance of English history and is invested in recovering the past for the present moment, but it is also, as Delsandro has shown, a queering of the 'identities that compose' that history.[58] Moreover, it is not only the past that guides La Trobe's attempt to forge a new community. It is also given shape by a future that has not yet arrived, but which is already putting the 'we' of the present under pressure.

Like Dodge, La Trobe is a childless character whose queerness separates her not only from the Oliver family but the heteronormative familial unit. A 'swarthy, sturdy and thick set' woman with 'a passion for getting things up', La Trobe is, the narrator tells us, not seen as 'altogether a lady' by her fellow villagers (*BTA* 42–3). Like Dodge, La Trobe is self-conscious both of her difference and how it is perceived. As she paces the lawn before the pageant begins, she pauses and imagines '[t]he butterflies circling; the lighting changing; the children leaping; the mothers laughing' before muttering 'I don't get it' and resuming her pacing (*BTA* 46). Woolf would have likely been aware that La Trobe's queer resistance to motherhood had political implications. As Sam See outlines, 'Hitler's campaign against non-reproductive women attempted to institutionalize reproductivity as the only natural state of being.'[59] In the face of an impending war, La Trobe's future, like Dodge's, is threatened precisely because the horizon is dominated by a heteronormative image of the Child. It is all the more striking, then, that the pageant she has written opens with the figure of the child, as 'a small girl, like a rosebud in pink' advances to the stage and introduces herself in verse: 'England am I [. . .] A child new born [. . .] sprung from the sea whose billows blown by mighty storm cut off from France and Germany this isle' (*BTA* 56–7). From this highly gendered, anthropomorphic and patriotic figuring of Britannia, however, the pageant proceeds to undermine the essentialised 'we' that it seemingly establishes in its opening movements. The arrival of Queen Elizabeth a few scenes later, for instance, sees the boundary between the human characters within the play and the broader environment in which it is being performed become uncertain. A line stating that 'Shakespeare sang' for the queen is followed by the report that a 'cow mooed' and a 'bird twittered' that, although in parentheses, implicitly become an ironic component of the performance (*BTA* 61).[60] The more-than-human elements of the pageant become increasingly amplified as subsequent nonhuman participants heighten the pathos of the performance. The 'yearning bellow' of a cow who 'had lost her calf' offers an aural accompaniment to the tragedy of Valentine and Flavinda, while the 'swallows' darting through the comic Victorian 'Picnic Party' add to the scene's joviality (*BTA* 101; 118). Later, when rain pours down on the audience, trickling down La Trobe's cheeks 'as if they were her own tears' in a comic reversal of pathetic fallacy, she reflects on how 'Nature once more had taken her part' (*BTA* 129–30). As Louise Westling has argued, the pageant 'posits nonhuman forces and beings as crucial players in the human drama' as '[s]wallows, butterflies, trees, cows, clouds and rain interweave with human activities' and the result, as Rasheed Tazudeen similarly argues, is 'a shared affective space' that bridges human and nonhuman life.[61]

This sense of what Froula describes as the pageant's 'purposiveness without purpose', in which the performance's porousness is its condition of expression, is at its clearest in the 'present time' section of the pageant, as the audience are themselves drawn into the performance.[62] Described in the programme as 'The present. Ourselves', it is met with resistance from certain sections of the audience before it has even begun. The homophobic and, it is implied, fascistic Giles, for instance, declares that he 'hope[s] to God that's the end' (*BTA* 127). As Johns-Putra has argued, the desire for narrative resolution speaks not only to a wish for 'stability and continuity' but can also be linked to 'a desire for reproductive continuity' in which 'happy endings' shore up the 'prevalent heteronormative [. . .] logic of progress, procreation and posterity'. According to this logic, which Johns-Putra develops from Frank Kermode's *The Sense of an Ending* (1967), the conventionally linear structure of narrative establishes a reassuring relation between the past, the present and the future. The ending, necessarily written into the beginning, is always safely foreclosed ahead of time.[63] Indeed, in the figure of Giles, who cannot stand Mrs Swithin's habit of leaving 'books open' and her predilection for coming to 'no conclusion' (*BTA* 44), closure is explicitly linked to an authoritative and potentially violently enforced heteronormativity. In contrast, La Trobe is less interested in closure than what she calls 'present-time reality' (*BTA* 129). Unravelling the linear temporality that the pageant has established she resists the sense of an ending that audience members such as Giles so desire. Reversing the pageant's opening scene, where England is figured as a 'weak and small' child, what first appear to be 'children' but are revealed to be 'Imps–elves–demons' take to the stage with an assortment of discarded items, including 'tin cans', 'bedroom candlesticks' and a mother's 'cracked' 'mirror' (*BTA* 131–2). Using these 'bright' fragments of discarded domestic objects to 'reflect' the audience back upon themselves, the demon children reverse the 'distorting and upsetting' gaze of the adults (*BTA* 131–2), with the 'anonymous' voice of the megaphone instructing the audience not to 'presume there's innocency in childhood' (*BTA* 134). While elsewhere in the novel the image of the Child, projected onto children by adults, undergirds the construction of a reproductive futurism, here, at precisely the point at which the audience expects an ending, it is the return of this gaze back onto the adults that underscores La Trobe's rejection of closure, forcing them to see themselves as 'scraps, orts and fragments' (*BTA* 135) rather than as a unified whole. Accompanied by a switch from traditional forms of music, structured by melody and resolution, to a jazz which 'snapped; broke; jagged', and which the audience hear as a 'cacophony' and 'chaos' in which 'nothing ended' (*BTA* 131), the final act unravels the closure and unity that the pageant previously seemed to promise.

A moment of dissolution rather than resolution, the pageant's finale removes any lingering sense of a separation between the pageant, its audience and the external nonhuman world. The 'very cows joi[n] in', 'walloping' and 'tail lashing' with the 'leap[ing], jerk[ing]' children, as the 'barriers which should divide Man the Master from the Brute' are dissolved and 'the reticence of nature [is] undone' (*BTA* 132). It is from this more-than-human assemblage of adult and child body parts, objects, animals, and nature, or what Tazudeen describes as the pageant's presentation of 'raw materials' prior to taking on the form of subjects, that La Trobe and the audience are made to undergo the double 'indignity' of not only seeing themselves through the fragmented reflection of the demon children but not knowing whether 'the play's over' (*BTA* 133–4).⁶⁴ Akin to shapes and forms that emerge without predetermined 'patterns', the pageant becomes a space of immanence and impersonal potentiality, in which the relation between the present and the future remains undetermined. Reverend Streatfield's 'awkward' attempt to 'make an end' after the performance has concluded, an act of containment that suggests the pageant is still leaking into the future, includes an 'interpretation' in which he suggests the play's message is that 'we should unite' (*BTA* 138–9). Yet it is precisely a question of who constitutes that 'we' which the play has brought into question. If for Colebrook, a genuine ethics relies on devising a community whose 'lines [are] drawn without any preceding or ideal community', the denouement to La Trobe's pageant performs a similar function, as it both dissembles and broadens the 'we' of the audience.⁶⁵ Despite a strong collective desire for unity in the face of a coming war, the play instead insists on the uncomfortable truth that there is something to be gained from breaking up and thereby remaking the traditional bonds of relations which have sustained English life thus far.

For Woolf, the threat of extinction and questions around the end of the world that were so prevalent in the late 1930s informed a mode of writing invested in re-examining how we imagine the future and the 'we' that is constituted within such a statement. Writing as the world in which she had lived her adult life was coming to an end, and in which it could not be taken for granted that life itself would continue as it previously had, her late writing reimagines an impersonal ontology in which the human is resituated within a broader materiality that both antedates it and which will be there long after it has vanished. The human is no longer the only thing that imbues life with value. While La Trobe's pageant finishes by unsettling the present, the setting of her next play is to be firmly located in a future that departs from all preconceptions of human life continuing as it is. Organised around the motifs of 'shelter; voices; oblivion', this sequel will take place on 'high ground at midnight' with 'two scarcely perceptible figures' whose words sink into and rise up from the 'fertile' 'mud', linking language and stratigraphy and paralleling the opening aerial perspective (*BTA* 152). La Trobe's final vision, then, is of a depersonalised space in which oblivion becomes a condition for potentiality and new forms of relationality. It also foreshadows the novel's final scene between Giles and Isa, in which it is described how:

> before they slept, they must fight; after they had fought, they would embrace. From that embrace another life might be born. But first they must fight, as the dog fox fights with the vixen, in the heart of darkness, in the fields of night. (*BTA* 157)

Once more returning to the language of futurity through procreation the future is, however, this time recast not in terms of the Child but the birth of 'another life', a phrase that invites itself to be read in terms of either continuity or difference. Employing the language of uncertainty and equivocation that Giles has explicitly rejected but which Isa has increasingly been drawn towards, it situates the present in relation to a future that cannot be determined in advance and in which the end of our world is not the end of the world. A site of potentiality that necessarily encompasses all possible outcomes, it embodies what Derrida memorably describes as how, properly understood, the future can only be 'anticipated in the form of an absolute danger [. . .] [as] that which breaks absolutely with constituted normality'.[66] As Isa lets 'her sewing drop' and stands against the backdrop of a 'sky without colour' in a house that has 'lost its shelter' (*BTA* 157), Woolf's incomplete novel, like La Trobe's unfinished pageant, eschews closure and opts instead for a moment of extinction that is dangerously open to whatever might come next.

Notes

1. Although this was Woolf's last typescript it was not intended to be the final version of the novel. Mark Hussey's textual history of the novel in the Cambridge edition makes clear why *Between the Acts* should be considered an unfinished novel. Mark Hussey (ed.), 'Introduction', in Virginia Woolf, *Between the Acts* (Cambridge: Cambridge University Press, 2011), pp. xxxiv–lxxiii (p. xxxix).
2. Edelman, however, goes further than Leonard insofar as any form of hope is seen as an 'insistence of . . . affirmation' that subjects the present to pressures of reproductive futurism. Lee Edelman, *No Future: Queer Theory and the Death Drive* (Durham, NC: Duke University Press, 2004), pp. 2–4.
3. For a discussion of Virginia and Leonard's critical responses to utopianism see Caroline Pollentier, 'Between Aesthetic and Political Theory: Virginia Woolf's Utopian Pacifism', in *Virginia Woolf, Europe and Peace: Volume 2, Aesthetics and Theory*, ed. Peter Adkins and Derek Ryan (Clemson, SC: Clemson University Press, 2020), pp. 203–18.
4. Nicole Seymour has criticised Edelman for overlooking how 'corporate and governmental disregard for the future' is precisely what enables exploitation, including environmental exploitation. Nicole Seymour, *Strange Natures: Futurity, Empathy, and the Queer Ecological Imagination* (Urbana: University of Illinois Press, 2013), pp. 7–8.
5. Although, with the ascendency of the new modernist studies, the temporal and spatial parameters of what constitutes modernism have been expanded, the sense that the Second World War marks the end of at least one dominant branch within modernist literary history continues to shape how modernism is widely understood and taught. Indeed, as Paul K. Saint-Amour writes, in expanding the field beyond its 'old 1890–1940 period boundaries' and opening on to a trans-historical global context, there is a danger of an 'expansionism' that 'might encroach on adjacent fields, or at least compel them to accept the terms of the expanding field's recognition'. Moreover, as I show in my coda, suggesting that a historically situated form of modernism ends in the 1940s does not mean that we cannot trace its aesthetic

presence in later periods. Paul K. Saint-Amour, 'Weak Theory, Weak Modernism', *Modernism/Modernity*, 25.3 (2018), 437–59 (p. 441).
6. Stanley C. Finney and Lucy E. Edwards, 'The "Anthropocene" Epoch: Scientific Decision or Political Statement?', *GSA Today*, 26.3–4 (2016), 4–10 (p. 7).
7. Roy Scranton, *Learning to Die in the Anthropocene* (San Francisco: City Lights Books, 2015), pp. 19–20.
8. Ibid. pp. 19–21.
9. Claire Colebrook, *Death of the Posthuman: Essays on Extinction, Vol.1* (Ann Arbor, MI: Open Humanities Press, 2014), pp. 32–3, emphasis in original.
10. Claire Colebrook, 'Woolf and "Theory"', in *Virginia Woolf in Context*, ed. Bryony Randall and Jane Goldman (Cambridge: Cambridge University Press, 2012), pp. 65–78 (p. 77).
11. Shelley Saguaro has read the barn scene in terms of 'interconnectedness', while Louise Westling has framed it in terms of 'nonhuman community'. Shelley Saguaro, '"Something That Would Stand for the Conception": The Inseminating World in the Last Writings of Virginia Woolf', *Green Letters*, 17.2 (2013), 109–20 (p. 11); Louise Westling, 'Virginia Woolf and the Flesh of the World', *New Literary History*, 30.4 (1999), 855–75 (p. 867).
12. Colebrook, *The Death of the Posthuman*, p. 24.
13. Carol Cantrell's 1998 essay 'Woolf, Modernism and Place' was the first article to take an explicitly ecocritical approach to modernist aesthetics and championed *Between the Acts* as 'woven of multiple layers of life'. Carol H. Cantrell, '"The Locus of Compossibility": Virginia Woolf, Modernism, and Place', *Interdisciplinary Studies in Literature and Environment*, 5.2 (1998), 25–40 (p. 34). For more recent ecocritical readings see Renée Dickinson, 'Writing the Land: *Between the Acts* as Ecocritical Text', *Virginia Woolf Miscellany*, 81 (2012), 16–18; Sam See, 'The Comedy of Nature: Darwinian Feminism in Virginia Woolf's *Between the Acts*', *Modernism / Modernity*, 17.3 (2010), 639–67; Rasheed Tazudeen, '"Discordant Syllabling": The Language of the Living World in Virginia Woolf's *Between the Acts*', *Studies in the Novel*, 47.4 (2015), 491–513; and Vicki Tromanhauser, 'Animal Life and Human Sacrifice in Virginia Woolf's *Between the Acts*', *Woolf Studies Annual*, 15 (2009), 67–90.
14. Brenda Silver, '"Anon" and "The Reader": Virginia Woolf's Last Essays', *Twentieth-Century Literature*, 25.3–4 (1979), 356–441; Christine Froula, *Virginia Woolf and the Bloomsbury Avant-Garde: War, Civilization, Modernity* (New York: Columbia University Press, 2005). For an overview of approaches that divide along these lines to *Between the Acts* see Froula, *Virginia Woolf*, p. 403 n5.
15. Charles Darwin, *The Origin of Species by Means of Natural Selection or the Preservation of Favoured Races in The Struggle for Life*, ed. J. W. Burrow (London: Penguin Books, 1985), p. 459. For an extended study of Darwin's influence on Woolf see Saskia McCracken, '(R)Evolutionary Animal Tropes in the Works of Charles Darwin and Virginia Woolf' (unpublished Doctoral Thesis, University of Glasgow, 2021).
16. On Victorian questions of unsustainability see Allen MacDuffie, *Victorian Literature, Energy and the Ecological Imagination* (Cambridge: Cambridge University Press, 2014), pp. 1–22; and Wendy Parkins, 'Introduction: Sustainability and the

Victorian Anthropocene', in *Victorian Sustainability in Literature and Culture*, ed. Wendy Parkins (Abingdon: Routledge, 2018), pp. 1–13.
17. Paul K. Saint-Amour, *Tense Future: Modernism, Total War, Encyclopedic Form* (Oxford: Oxford University Press, 2015), p. 7.
18. Also see Lawrence's posthumously published *Apocalypse* (1931), a book-length commentary on the Book of Revelation. D. H. Lawrence, *Women in Love*, ed. David Farmer, Lindeth Vasey and John Worthen (London: Penguin Books, 2000), p. 59.
19. T. S. Eliot, *Collected Poems 1909–1962* (New York: Harcourt, Brace & World, Inc., 1963), p. 156.
20. Benjamin Hagen, 'Bloomsbury and Philosophy', in *The Handbook to the Bloomsbury Group*, ed. Stephen Ross and Derek Ryan (London: Bloomsbury, 2018), pp. 135–50 (p. 146).
21. Ibid. p. 146. Judith Allen's *Virginia Woolf and the Politics of Language* (Edinburgh: Edinburgh University Press, 2010) discusses Montaigne's influence on Woolf at length.
22. Thomas S. Davis, *The Extinct Scene: Late Modernism and Everyday Life* (New York: Columbia University Press, 2016), pp. 1–2.
23. Saint-Amour, *Tense Future*, p. 94.
24. The Hogarth Press turned down the opportunity to publish *Ulysses* in 1918. Woolf here recounts how she read the novel at Monks House 'one summer [. . .] with spasms of wonder, of discovery, & then again with long lapses of intense boredom' (*D5* 353).
25. Hussey, 'Introduction', p. xliv; Val Gough, '"A Responsible Person Like Her": Woolf's Suicide Culture', in *Virginia Woolf: Turning the Centuries: Selected Papers from the Ninth Annual Conference on Virginia Woolf*, ed. Ann Ardis and Bonnie Kime Scott (New York: Pace University Press, 2000), pp. 183–91 (p. 186).
26. See Arnold's 'Stanzas from the Grand Chartreuse' (1869) where he describes 'Wandering between two worlds, one dead | The other powerless to be born'. Stuart N. Clarke notes this allusion in his endnotes to Woolf's essay. Arnold, *Poems* (New York: Macmillan and Co., 1880), p. 338.
27. The quoted sentence appears in an early draft of the book. Quoted in Silver, '"Anon" and "The Reader"', p. 416. My dating of Woolf's manuscripts throughout this chapter is taken from Silver.
28. Colebrook, *Death of the Posthuman*, p. 33.
29. Although Woolf uses a near-direct quotation from Trevelyan in *Between the Acts* he is not named and the book that Swithin reads from is instead called *Outline of History*. This has led critics such as Tromanhauser to see it as an amalgamation of Trevelyan's work and H. G. Wells's *The Outline of History* (1920), which Woolf also likely read. Like Trevelyan's book, Wells juxtaposes human history with inhuman scales of time, highlighting a prehistory which, as Christina Alt has argued, shows how 'changes in climate and environment' bring about massive change in life forms. Tromanhauser, 'Animal Life and Human Sacrifice', p. 69; Alt, *Virginia Woolf and the Study of Nature* (Cambridge: Cambridge University Press, 2010), p. 136.
30. Quoted in See, 'The Comedy of Nature', p. 657.
31. T. S. Eliot, *Selected Prose*, ed. Frank Kermode (New York: Harcourt Brace Jovanovich Farrar, Straus and Giroux, 1975), p. 40.

32. Claire Colebrook, '"A Grandiose Time of Coexistence": Stratigraphy of the Anthropocene', *Deleuze Studies*, 10.4 (2016), 440–54 (p. 442).
33. Ibid. pp. 450–1.
34. Ibid. p. 452.
35. Gilles Deleuze and Félix Guattari, *A Thousand Plateaus: Capitalism and Schizophrenia*, trans. Brian Massumi (London: Bloomsbury, 2014), pp. 589–90.
36. Ibid. p. 589.
37. Rosi Braidotti, *Transpositions: On Nomadic Ethics* (Cambridge: Polity Press, 2006), p. 235; p. 248.
38. *Pointz Hall* was the working title of the novel until February 1941.
39. Gillian Beer, *Virginia Woolf: The Common Ground* (Ann Arbor: University of Michigan Press, 1996), p. 9.
40. Mark Hussey, *'I'd Make It Penal': The Rural Preservation Movement in Virginia Woolf's 'Between the Acts'* (London: Cecil Woolf Publishers, 2011), p. 9.
41. Ibid. pp. 10–11. See also Clara Jones, 'Virginia Woolf and "The Villa Jones" (1931)', *Woolf Studies Annual*, 22 (2016), 75–96.
42. Tellingly, this remark arises from within a montage of reported speech that implicitly links it to fears of 'refugees' and European 'Jews' arriving in the countryside (*BTA* 88), suggesting Woolf could be self-reflexive of the politics underpinning anxieties around rural preservation.
43. Adeline Johns-Putra, 'The Unsustainable Aesthetics of Sustainability: The Sense of an Ending in Jeanette Winterson's *The Stone Gods*', in *Literature and Sustainability: Concept, Text and Culture*, ed. Adeline Johns-Putra, John Parham, and Louise Squire (Manchester: Manchester University Press, 2017), pp. 177–94 (pp. 181–2).
44. Adeline Johns-Putra, '"My Job Is to Take Care of You": Climate Change, Humanity, and Cormac McCarthy's *The Road*', *Modern Fiction Studies*, 62.3 (2016), 519–40 (p. 534).
45. Edelman, *No Future*, pp. 10–11.
46. Ibid. p. 21.
47. This is the passage highlighted in Chapter 5 as suggesting Woolf's familiarity with John Tyndall's theory of how light travels as waves. See Beer, *Virginia Woolf*, pp. 112–24.
48. Also see Saint-Amour's argument that Woolf's 'Thoughts on Peace' contains a 'critique of reproductive futurism'. Saint-Amour, *Tense Future*, pp. 128–9.
49. Edelman, *No Future*, p. 18.
50. Stephen Barber, 'Lip-Reading: Woolf's Secret Encounters', in *Novel Gazing: Queer Readings in Fiction*, ed. Eve Kosofsky Sedgwick (Durham, NC: Duke University Press, 1997), pp. 401–34 (pp. 402–3).
51. Erica Delsandro, '"Myself It Was Impossible": Queering History in *Between the Acts*', *Woolf Studies Annual*, 13 (2007), 87–109 (p. 96).
52. Edelman, *No Future*, p. 3.
53. Ibid. p. 17.
54. Claire Colebrook, *Sex After Life: Essays on Extinction, Vol. 2* (Ann Arbor, MI: Open Humanities Press, 2014), p. 137.
55. Ibid. p. 138.

56. Ibid. p. 137; p. 148.
57. Jed Esty, *A Shrinking Island: Modernism and National Culture in England* (Princeton: Princeton University Press, 2003), p. 55.
58. Delsandro, '"Myself It Was Impossible"', p. 107.
59. See, 'The Comedy of Nature', p. 646.
60. Hussey's choice in the 2011 Cambridge edition of the novel not to italicise the dialogue from the pageant – the italics being an editorial decision made by Leonard Woolf in the first edition of the novel, followed in all subsequent editions despite not being present in Woolf's final draft – further emphasises the continuity between the performance and the world which frames it.
61. Westling, 'Virginia Woolf', p. 865; Tazudeen, p. 505. See also Derek Ryan's argument that the pageant enacts a 'deterritorialisation of humanity where the human makes an animal connection'. Ryan, '"The Reality of Becoming": Deleuze, Woolf and the Territory of Cows', *Deleuze Studies*, 7.4 (2013), 537–61 (p. 549).
62. Froula, *Virginia Woolf*, p. 302.
63. Johns-Putra, 'Unsustainable Aesthetics', p. 181.
64. Tazudeen, '"Discordant Syllabling"', p. 506.
65. Colebrook, *The Death of the Posthuman*, pp. 44–5.
66. Jacques Derrida, *Of Grammatology*, trans. Gayatri Chakravorty Spivak (Baltimore: Johns Hopkins University Press, 1997), p. 5.

FALLOUT: MODERNISM IN THE NUCLEAR ANTHROPOCENE

> Only within the moment of time represented by the present century has one species – man – acquired significant power to alter the nature of his world.
>
> Rachel Carson, *Silent Spring*

> Nuclear as the song of the siren marked silent sprung, no rhythm of which to speak, just algorithms of decay.
>
> Drew Milne and John Kinsella, 'Nuclear Theory Degree Zero'

The threat of extinction that Woolf was writing in response to in her late works serves as a conclusive (if not final) moment in the Modernist Anthropocene that I have outlined in this book. As discussed in Chapter 6, both Woolf and Joyce died in 1941, with their deaths shaped and perhaps hastened by a world war that must have seemed even more far reaching, both geographically and technologically, than the one through which they had previously lived. The events of the Second World War also marked an important turning point in Barnes's life. In 1939 Barnes, suffering from alcoholism and living in Paris as war broke out, was given an ultimatum by her benefactor Peggy Guggenheim to either return to the US or have her finances cut off. Placed on a train to Bordeaux by Guggenheim and Helena Joyce (James Joyce's daughter-in-law), Barnes set sail to New York on 12 October 1939. She would not see Europe again. By April 1941, when she heard of Woolf's death, writing to Emily Coleman asking, 'What is this about

Virginia Wolf [*sic*] killing herself?', Barnes was living in 5 Patchin Place in Greenwich Village, where she would remain until her death in 1982.¹ The sense that a certain world had come to an end was apparent. A few months later, in June 1941, Barnes would recount to Coleman having bumped into Eugene Jolas in a library in New York: 'He says Joyce's son and boy [Giorgio and Stephen Joyce] are starving [. . .] Nora, poor lost creature, is so stunned (also starving more or less) that she can hardly speak, not even to her son.'²

The pre-nuclear world was also coming to an end. At 5.30 a.m. on 16 July 1945, as the Second World War continued to be fought in Asia, the United States military detonated the Trinity A-Bomb at their test site in Alamogordo, New Mexico. The event marked a turning point not only in the war but in geological history, with human-made radioactive material released into the atmosphere for the first time. Following the bombing of Hiroshima and Nagasaki, and the end of Second World War, the Soviet Union, the United Kingdom and France would all join the United States in developing and testing nuclear weaponry. Between 1945 and the 1996 Comprehensive Nuclear-Test-Ban Treaty, more than 2,000 nuclear bombs were detonated, leaving a chemostratigraphic inscription that will remain detectable long into the deep future.[3] For members of the Anthropocene Working Group (AWG), the first explosion in New Mexico stands of such importance as a boundary event that they have argued that it should formally mark the beginning of the Anthropocene as a geological epoch.[4] While the AWG's conclusion is reached through an approach necessarily guided by scientific methods of empirical observation, measurement and calculation, this book has shown that many of its fundamental insights and ideas run much deeper and longer than a mid-twentieth-century dating implies. Indeed, in ascribing too neat a division it becomes easy to overlook not only the causes of the Anthropocene, but earlier insights that still retain critical purchase today. What I want to suggest in this final section is that, instead of seeing a dividing line between a pre- and post-Anthropocene epoch, we might see the nuclear detonation in the New Mexico desert as ushering in the Nuclear Anthropocene, which, like the Modernist Anthropocene, should be understood both in terms of its historical significance and the cultural practices that responded to it. As this coda will suggest, in tracing the material fallout from that first nuclear detonation, we can also trace the aesthetic fallout from a modernism whose world also seemed to have ended.

If, as I have suggested, the Modernist Anthropocene is characterised by entanglement, then the Nuclear Anthropocene might be aptly described as captured by the trope of suffusion. As Drew Milne and John Kinsella write in their essay, 'Nuclear Theory Degree Zero', in the nuclear age we are 'caught in a symbiotic intertwining in which "nature" can no longer be imagined as a backdrop, but has become a dark ecology prefigured by the nuclear, and *suffused* with it'.[5] Suffusion might be understood as the dark side of entanglement, sharing an insistence on a loss of autonomy and co-becoming, but to an overwhelming and destructive degree. To be suffused is to encounter the 'too-much-ness' that Rosi Braidotti describes as always marking the limits of becoming, the point of saturation at which the subject can take no more.[6] This is entanglement accelerated in the direction of moribund mutations. We might think, for instance, of the case of James Yeatts, a participant in the US Army's Desert Rock nuclear test exercises in 1952 who described how his company was exposed to a flash 'so bright we could see the bones in our hands'. Suffused with radiation, his teeth would later fall from his mouth and his son would be born with profound deformities.[7] Indeed, the word 'suffuse' offers phonic traces that resonate with the nuclear project, suggesting processes of fusion and fission necessary in the production of nuclear weapons, as well as the fusing of desert sand at the test sites, turning into radioactive glass named 'trinitite' after the first test.[8] Such suffusion is not restricted to localised events, either spatially or temporally. Every plant, animal and human born in the aftermath of nuclear tests carries the trace of those explosions in their bodies in the form of higher than naturally occurring amounts of the radioactive isotope carbon-14.

There can be no doubt that had they lived to witness the birth of the Nuclear Anthropocene, Joyce and Woolf would have understood the significance of events in New Mexico in July 1945. As critics have shown, both writers were aware of developments in quantum mechanics in the first half of the twentieth century and its revelation that 'the atom is not an indivisible particle [and] that subatomic particles can be transformed into energy and vice versa'.[9] As Andrzej Duszenko writes, in *Finnegans Wake* there are 'numerous references' to quantum mechanics and, on one level, the novel can be seen as a response to the 'new vision of the universe' that was coming into view.[10] Indeed, Joyce reimagines the moment in 1917 that the atom was first split by Ernest Rutherford:

> *The abnilisation of the etym by the grisning of the grosning of the grinder of the grunder of the first lord of Hurtreford expolodotonates through Parsuralia with an ivanmorinthorrorumble fragoromboassity amidwhiches general uttermosts confusion are perceivable moletons skaping with muliculus which coventry plumpkins fairlygosmotherthemeslves in the Landaunelegants of Pinkadindy.* (FW 353, emphasis in original)

Rutherford, recast as the sinister Hurtreford, grins as he grinds atoms and sets off an explosive detonation, with the violent 'confusion' of 'perceivable moletons skaping with muliculus' serving as an apparent moment of nuclear fission as molecules scrape against each other (thus fusing in the text Rutherford's 1917 'chipping' of the atom with the first successful splitting of a nucleus in a particle accelerator by John Cockroft and Ernest Walton, overseen by Rutherford, in 1932). It is a moment that demonstrates modernism's half-life: short of seeing nuclear warfare, Joyce intuits the implications of nuclear fission for the planet, encoding (intentionally or otherwise) the threat of atomic destruction into his text. As Duszenko suggests, the atomic grinder 'conjures a parallel image of solid bodies being pulverized' and in the impact of the explosion through the subsequent words – captured in the reverberating phonics of the '*ivanmorinthorrorumble fragoromboassity*' – we find shockwaves spreading outwards from ground zero, contaminating all that they come into contact with.[11] While Joyce's late work seems to forecast the sub-atomic implications of the Nuclear Anthropocene, Woolf's *Between the Acts* offers a similar moment of textual prolepsis, albeit at a macroscopic scale, in Mrs Swithin's cosmological vision of the planet as a 'little coloured ball of earth' suspended in the colourlessness of space (*BTA* 17). An image of the Earth as if viewed from a position outside of it, the moment foreshadows a planetary aesthetic that would become ubiquitous after the 1968 *Earthrise* photographs of the Earth as seen from the Moon (figure 7.1). Mrs Swithin's imagining of the Earth as a little ball captures the sense of post-nuclear planetary vulnerability that accompanies such an image – one that confuses the categories of the macro and the micro as the planet and all life on it is imagined in diminutive terms. Indeed, Woolf's language is here surprisingly close to that of the first lunar astronauts, with William Anders (who took the *Earthrise*

Figure 7.1 *Earthrise* (1968) by William Anders. Public Domain.

photographs) recounting how from the Moon, Earth looked like a 'Christmas-tree ball, which we should handle with care'.[12]

Modernism's ability to proleptically speak to life in the Nuclear Anthropocene also inspired the choice of artwork for the cover of this book. Georgia O'Keeffe's *Light Coming on the Plains No. II* (figure 7.2), painted in Texas in 1917 (the same year that Rutherford conducted his experiment on the atom) presents a powerful white light rising from the horizon and spreading into the dark blue of the desert night sky, the watery hues presenting a 'seamless fusion of color washes'.[13] The second in a series of three paintings that O'Keeffe produced over the course of a summer in which she would stay up all night for the arrival of dawn, the artworks were produced by a spontaneous layering of deep ultramarine pigment on newsprint paper, 'allowing the fluidity of the medium to form the final design'.[14] As Judith Zilczer describes, the paintings were a response to her surroundings, wavering 'between evocative naturalism and pure abstraction'.[15] O'Keeffe was also responding to theories of modern art she had read from figures such as Wassily Kandinsky, Arthur Jerome Eddy and Clive Bell (Woolf's brother-in-law and fellow Bloomsbury Group member), taking ideas that were emerging in Europe and reworking them to evoke the 'sensation of

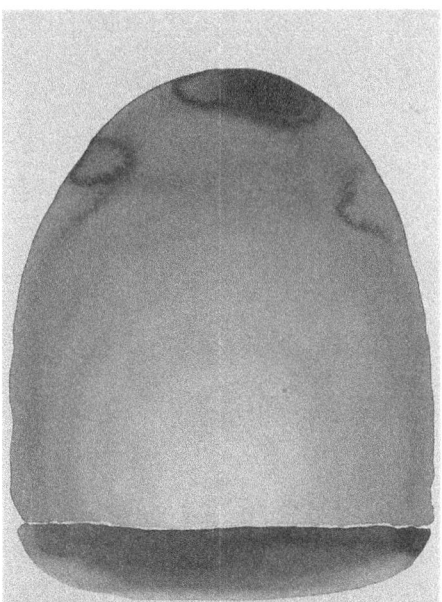

Figure 7.2 *Light Coming on the Plains No. II* (1917) (detail) by Georgia O'Keeffe. Amon Carter Museum of American Art, Fort Worth, Texas, 1966.32, © Amon Carter Museum of American Art.

201

diurnal time' felt in the American desert.[16] The result can be seen as fusing post-impressionism's emphasis on form, medium and abstraction with the expansiveness of the American west, its sparseness also looking ahead to the minimalist works that would follow the modernist epoch. Yet, when I look at the painting, I see not only a sun rising over Texas in 1917 but also that first dawn detonation of a nuclear weapon in the desert of New Mexico in 1945. A white-hot centre radiates outwards, blanching the dark blue sky around it, its core an energy source of force simultaneously centrifugal and centripetal. The painting embodies suffusion at a material level, a visual rendering of the *OED*'s definition of 'suffuse' to mean to 'overspread as with a fluid, a colour, a gleam of light'.[17] Such an interpretation is lent further weight by the comparisons that have been made between O'Keeffe's series of paintings and later visually similar works of postmodernist art that drew on an aesthetics of abstraction and minimalism to respond to the Nuclear Anthropocene, such as Adolph Gottlieb's *Blast, I* (1957) (figure 7.3).[18] Gottlieb's painting, part of his *Burst* series of responses to postwar planetary existence, shows a deep red circle hovering above a mass of black brushstrokes angled in different directions and suggesting jagged movement outwards. Cutting away all of the lingering naturalism of O'Keeffe's painting

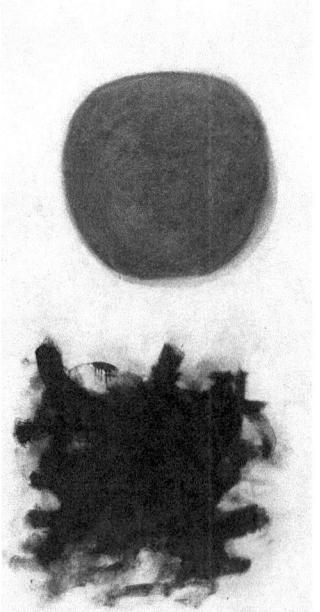

Figure 7.3 *Blast, I* (1957) by Adolph Gottlieb
Digital image, The Museum of Modern Art, New York/Scala, Florence, © Adolph and Esther Gottlieb Foundation/VAGA at ARS, NY and DACS, London 2021.

for a stark and threatening post-nuclear visual idiom, it is a work that suggests both continuity with and departure from the earlier modernist paintings that came before. Here, then, we might again understand modernism's influence in terms of fallout, the works emitting a half-life that seep into the future as the catalyst for new mutations that still carry the traces of the past age.

Like Barnes, O'Keeffe would outlive many of her modernist contemporaries, living until 1986 and seeing the Nuclear Anthropocene unfold around her. Indeed, she would be witness to its birth first-hand. On 16 July 1945, when the first nuclear bomb lit up the dawn sky, O'Keeffe was living at Ghost Ranch, north of the test site in the New Mexico desert. In the lead-up to the first test, the fifty-acre dude ranch had also hosted a number of the scientists involved in the Manhattan Project responsible for developing the bomb, including J. Robert Oppenheimer, Edward Teller and Richard Feynman.[19] There can be little doubt that O'Keeffe, who had moved to Ghost Ranch in 1940 and would become deeply associated with New Mexico, understood the significance of the moment, despite the fact that, for me, it is her pre-nuclear paintings of the American south-west that most clearly seem to respond to the new era. Barnes was well aware of O'Keeffe's work. In 1917, the same year that the *Light Coming on the Plains* series was produced, Barnes published a pen portrait of Alfred Stieglitz (O'Keeffe's future husband) and his 291 gallery, where O'Keeffe's work had been exhibited the previous year. In the article, O'Keeffe is listed among the 'revolutionary' artists to whom Barnes looks to draw her readers' attention.[20] Barnes also parallels O'Keeffe in not only outliving many of her contemporaries but remaining active well into the second half of the twentieth century. A range of recent studies have challenged what Scott Herring has called the once 'pervasive and gerontophobic image of Barnes as an aging recluse who had laid down her pen', instead seeing her, in Cathryn Setz's terms, as a *late* late modernist.[21] Although after returning to the US in 1939, Barnes's published output was largely restricted to five short poems, the verse-drama *The Antiphon*, republication of earlier work and the posthumous *Creatures in an Alphabet* poetry collection, she remained enormously busy as a writer, composing and endlessly revising poems that she hoped would eventually find a readership. Archived along with her correspondence and personal library, there are least 2,400 unpublished draft poems in the Djuna Barnes Papers at the University of Maryland.[22]

Particularly striking in the context of this coda is the fact that of the five poems Barnes published in her final decades, two of them directly address the Nuclear Anthropocene.[23] Published in 1958 in a Festschrift on the occasion of T. S. Eliot's seventieth birthday, the ominously titled 'Fall-out Over Heaven' opens with the lines:

> The atom, broken in the shell,
> Licks up Eden's reach, and Hell.

> To Adam back his rib is thrown,
> A mole of woman quakes, undone. (*CP* 133)

Framed by epigraphs from *The Waste Land* ('I'll show you fear in a handful of dust') and the Book of Isaiah ('And dust shall be the serpent's meat'), the landscape of the poem is one of environmental, spiritual and bodily despoliation. The fallout of the atom bomb both seems to reverse time and any attendant notion of historical progress, while also undoing the bodily integrity of both men and women. Womankind is diminished to a mole, a noun that suggests not only material blemish and beastly animality, but which since 1902 has been a unit of scientific measurement for mass, insinuating a reduction of life to a brute, unformed matter. Setz argues that the poem's title might also suggest a falling out between Barnes and Eliot 'over heaven' and could be read as a polemic against an 'unfeasible piety in the face of the atrocities of World War II'.[24] This interpretation is furthered by the syntactical ambiguity of the opening couplets, where not only does the splitting of the atom 'lick up Eden' but 'Hell' too, and the closing lines, in which 'Lucifer roars up from earth. | Down falls Christ into his death . . .' (*CP* 133). Narratives of redemption and punishment are not merely reversed but rendered unrecognisable, scrambled into couplets that resist the closure of clear exegesis.

For Milne and Kinsella, the nuclear epoch is embodied by 'the negation of future proof tense constructions' and 'decaying syntax'; an era in which language and literature is understood in terms of half-lives that go on, never whole in themselves, always on the verge of breaking down.[25] Poetry, in this sense, 'is a textual Geiger counter registering the spread of toxicity and contamination'.[26] Such a description fits Barnes's response to the Nuclear Anthropocene, where we find her engaging with a poetics that, through fragmentation and ambiguity, emits an unstable half-life. In 1969, eleven years after 'Fall-out over Heaven', Barnes would return to a similar theme in 'Quarry', a nine-line lyric published in the *New Yorker*. The poem opens:

> While I unwind duration from the tongue-tied tree,
> Send carbon fourteen down for time's address.
> [. . .]
> I come, I come that path and there look in
> And see the capsized eye of sleep and wrath
> And hear the beaters' 'Gone to Earth!' (*CP* 136)

Here, the poem literally takes on the function of a Geiger counter, as the temporal markers offered in tree-rings, with which one can 'unwind duration', are made to compete with the more precise analysis of 'time's address' offered by radiocarbon dating technology using carbon-14. Barnes's unpublished notebooks show that she took down many notes from popular scientific radio broadcasts in her final decades, and it is easy to imagine that, in addition to knowing about radiocarbon dating, she would have known that the higher than natural carbon-14 levels present in the cells of all humans (and, indeed, all trees too) were the material-semiotic signs of life in the Nuclear Anthropocene. Phillip Herring and Osías Stutman in their commentary on Barnes's *Collected Poems* suggest that we might read the lyric as being about 'winding down our personal spool of fate until we reach death's door'.[27] Yet, it is not clear that the poem's 'I' is the quarry being pursued. Instead, the 'I' that unwinds duration, calls for carbon-14 and comes down the path appears to hold a deathly power over the quarry who appears immobilised with 'capsized eye of sleep and wrath'. Akin to the 'I' of Oppenheimer's remark that on seeing the first Trinity test site detonation he was reminded of the lines from the *Bhagavad Gita*, 'Now I am become Death, the destroyer of worlds' (first broadcast in a television documentary four years before the poem's publication), we might understand the 'I' of 'Quarry' as a similarly destructive nuclear agent. In such a reading, the 'Quarry' of the poem's title presents itself not only as an allusion to the pursued subject of the poem, who has '"Gone to Earth"' like a fox hounded by the hunt, but to the mining of the radioactive materials which will pursue the hunted subject through the poem. Understood as such, we might read in the 'unwind[ing]' of the 'tongue-tied tree' an image of its rotting from the outside in, silently falling apart in a landscape of radioactive desolation. The poem, in this light, becomes less about the existential nature of old age and more the contingent realities of the nuclear present.

Barnes's activities in the final decades of her life present a writer who, far from turning inwards and away from the world, was alive to emergent ideas and theories of the nonhuman in the Nuclear Anthropocene. We find jottings on cybernetics, entropy and quantum mechanics in her notebooks, drafts of poems where 'electric quanta' rip matter apart in the creation of new forms of life and correspondence that speaks in the language of an emergent popular environmentalism.[28] Writing to Natalie Clifford Barney, in the summer of 1963, Barnes complains of the 'death-dealing smog' that has led to an air-conditioning unit being fitted in her small apartment. In the face of 'air fouled by auto gasses, D.D.T. spraying, refuse burning, [and] manufacturing fumes' Barnes's only respite, she explains, is in 'reading my stout Montaigne'.[29] In Barnes's awareness not only of pollution in general but the threats presented by the mass spraying of the pesticide DDT we find an echo of Rachel Carson's *Silent Spring*, which a year previously had been serialised in the *New Yorker* (one of the few publications that Barnes continued to have a working relationship with during this time). Carson's book had drawn the public's attention to the dangerous effects of chemical pesticides such as DDT to plant, animal and human populations, insisting on the urgency of recognising the catastrophic ecological implications of new chemical technologies. For Carson human-made chemicals were of a threat equal to nuclear radiation, describing the present as a moment of 'universal contamination' in which 'chemicals are the sinister and little-recognized partners of radiation in changing the very nature of the world'.[30] The suggestive influence of Carson on Barnes can be found in titles of poems such as 'Phantom Spring' and 'Ancient Spring' that she drafted over and over from the 1960s onwards and in the amplified themes of decay and decline in her poetry, an awareness that, as she put it to Barney, 'the end of the world coincides with our end'.[31] Thelma Wood, too, would register a similar sentiment of personal and planetary decline when, writing to Barnes in 1969 (a year before her death), she described how 'spring is here but as Rachel Carson said it is silent, the people have taken everything'.[32]

Although throughout this book I have been careful to avoid making the claim that Joyce, Woolf or Barnes held proto-environmentalist views, it is clear that Barnes was inspired by the emergence of a more visible and mainstream environmentalism in the post-war decades. Scientists such as Carson were inspiring her to respond to increasingly visible evidence of ecological degradation. In one undated poem with two titles, one typewritten, 'The Girls of [illegible]' and, one above in felt-tip pen, 'A Life of Lewd Plenty', the words 'Rachel Carson's *Silent Spring*' are handwritten in the bottom right-hand corner.[33] The short poem, which gives a portrait of an impotent elderly man named Corvé, includes the lines:

> 'A lazy, costly helpless man, and still
> A most humanly man'
> :the green-fly's got him;
> There's no swarming in him, his heart's an hive,
> That's banished all its bees; the green-fly's [above: gnat's] got him,
> Disintegration's all his progress[34]

As in 'Quarry', death is the keynote here. Bees, greenflies and gnats swarm around this 'most humanly man' as, having used his chest for a hive, they leave him to a future in which he must endure 'disintegration' from the inside out. Perhaps inspired by Carson's opening to *Silent Spring*, which describes a spring in which 'no bees droned among the blossoms, so there was no pollination and there would be no fruit', the poem presents a figure of 'man' and insect at odds with one another, unable to live in harmony, as both the disintegrating human body and the hive 'banished' of its bees stand as figures of infertility.[35] An image of permeability and contamination, it is a striking poetic expression of suffusion as the dark side of entanglement. In its imagining of entomological revenge on humankind, the poem accords with the stark warning in Carson's book that:

> The 'control of nature' is a phrase conceived in arrogance, born of the Neanderthal age of biology and philosophy, when it was supposed that nature exists for the convenience of man. The concepts and practices of applied entomology for the most part date from that Stone Age of science. It is our alarming misfortune that so primitive a science has armed itself with the most modern and terrible weapons, and that in turning them against the insects it has also turned them against the earth.[36]

As Milne and Kinsella write, poetry 'lets us know our vulnerability to the nuclear, and our own culpability in attempting to humanise or aestheticise it to appease guilts and doubts'.[37] Barnes's poem turns on precisely this fact of vulnerability. The hubristic human who has deluded himself that he is a transcendent subject with sovereignty over the planet and all the beasts that inhabit it, discovers that what he thought was 'progress' was, instead, extinction. Yet, it is not only poetry that can express such ideas. Barnes's late work, in turning to poetry to respond to the Nuclear Anthropocene, suggests points of continuity with the modernist fiction that I have examined in this book. Her poem is, among other things, a further instance of the beastly writing that stretches the entirety of her oeuvre. Moreover, in the ease with which Barnes was able to turn her attention to themes inspired by popular environmentalism, her late works suggest the degree to which the innovations developed in the modernist works of fiction analysed in this study had the potential to be developed to environmental ends. The degree to which later environmentalist literature explicitly or implicitly adapted modernist techniques and innovations is an area of enquiry that warrants further investigation and could extend the points of contiguity between the Modernist Anthropocene and Nuclear Anthropocene that I have begun to outline in this concluding chapter.

Research for this book began in 2015, the year when the average surface temperature of the planet crossed the threshold of one degree Celsius above pre-industrial averages, making it the warmest in 11,000 years. As I write this conclusion in early 2021, England is in a state of lockdown because of a viral pandemic that has brought back into the headlines the connection between environmental issues and public health that was at the heart of Carson's book, so disturbingly captured in Barnes's poem. For Dipesh Chakrabarty, the emergence of the Anthropocene implies not merely a new context for our thinking but necessitates the emergence of a '"new" humanities' whose 'primary purpose' will be 'to develop points of view that seek to place the current constellation of environmental crises in the larger context of the deeper history of natural reproductive life on this planet'.[38] I hope that this book has contributed to that project by showing how the point we have arrived at was not inevitable and that the future is similarly yet to be determined.

Understanding the historical conditions that Joyce, Woolf and Barnes were responding to and the literary strategies that they developed presents itself as an important task in reassessing the ecology of modernism. In showing how revising the human and the nonhuman were central to a range of modernist works of fiction, I have looked to demonstrate the usefulness of the Anthropocene concept for modernist studies, showing how a different historical optic and scale of reference might help us revise established literary histories and create new critical constellations. Reading modernist literature not only offers a history of the Anthropocene but also a way of making sense of it in the present. The attempt to re-write and re-present nonhuman life that we find in the modernist fiction that I have examined presents us with ways of writing, reading and thinking that remain provocative, challenging and productive in the twenty-first century. In Joyce's opposition to the pastoral foundations of the Revival's proto-environmental politics and his posthuman rendering of Molly as a Gaian Earth Mother, in Barnes's beastly subversion of human exceptionalism and her insistence on the centrality of sexual difference to the way we approach the nonhuman, and in Woolf's presentation of a climatic ontology and her openness to extinction, we find modernist texts already at work theorising the challenges of our present moment. It is clear to me that Anthropocene studies stands to benefit from the insights of these modernist writers, as much as modernist studies stands to benefit from these new critical approaches. In the introduction to this book, I quoted Christophe Bonneuil and Jean-Baptiste Fressoz's assertion of the need to recover 'the conceptual grammars' through which we have historically understood the planet and our relation to it.^{39} Yet, in modernism's attempt to create startlingly new literary grammars, through innovative linguistic, aesthetic and conceptual frameworks of meaning, we can find the materials for not only historicising the Anthropocene but for theorising its implications and helping to create the futures that have not yet arrived.

Notes

1. Djuna Barnes to Emily Coleman, 19 April 1941. Djuna Barnes Papers, Special Collections, University of Maryland Libraries (hereafter DBP), Series 2, Box 3, Folder 17.
2. Djuna Barnes to Emily Coleman, 6 June 1941. DBP, Series 2, Box 7, Folder 4.
3. Colin N. Waters et al., 'Artificial Radionuclide Fallout Signals', in *The Anthropocene as a Geological Time Unit*, ed. Jan Zalasiewicz et al. (Cambridge: Cambridge University Press, 2019), pp. 192–9 (p. 192).
4. In 2019, the AWG voted overwhelmingly in favour of a mid-twentieth-century start date for the Anthropocene. Jan Zalasiewicz et al., 'When Did the Anthropocene Begin? A Mid-Twentieth Century Boundary Level Is Stratigraphically Optimal', *Quaternary International*, 383 (2015), 196–203 (pp. 200–1).
5. Drew Milne and John Kinsella, 'Nuclear Theory Degree Zero, with Two Cheers for Derrida', *Angelaki*, 22.3 (2017), 1–16 (p. 1), emphasis added.

6. Rosi Braidotti, *Transpositions: On Nomadic Ethics* (Cambridge: Polity Press, 2006), p. 214.
7. Quoted in Jeremy Davies, *The Birth of the Anthropocene* (Oakland: University of California Press, 2016), p. 209.
8. Waters et al., 'Artificial Radionuclide Fallout Signals', p. 194.
9. Andrzej Duszenko, 'Abnihilization of the Etym: Joyce, Rutherford, and Particle Physics', *Irish University Review*, 46.2 (2016), 275–86 (p. 275). For more on Joyce and the new physics see Katherine Ebury, *Modernism and Cosmology: Absurd Lights* (Basingstoke: Palgrave Macmillan, 2014). For Woolf, see Chapter 5 of Derek Ryan, *Virginia Woolf and the Materiality of Theory: Sex, Animal, Life* (Edinburgh: Edinburgh University Press, 2013).
10. Duszenko, 'Abnihilization of the Etym', p. 276.
11. Ibid. p. 282.
12. Quoted in Timothy Clark, *Ecocriticism on the Edge: The Anthropocene as a Threshold Concept* (London: Bloomsbury, 2015), p. 34.
13. Judith Zilczer, '"Light Coming on the Plains:" Georgia O'Keeffe's Sunrise Series', *Artibus et Historiae*, 20.40 (1999), 191–208 (p. 193).
14. Quotation taken from the curatorial description that accompanies the painting in the Amon Carter Museum of American Art in Fort Worth, Texas. Digital reproductions of all three paintings can be seen on the museum's website.
15. Zilczer, '"Light Coming on the Plains:"', p. 191.
16. Ibid. p. 196.
17. 'Suffuse', *OED Online* <www.oed.com/view/Entry/193611> (last accessed 15 February 2021).
18. Zilczer points to aspects that suggest influence and aesthetic continuity between O'Keeffe and Gottlieb. Zilczer, '"Light Coming on the Plains:"', p. 204.
19. Christopher Reynolds, 'Witness to Creation – and Destruction', *Los Angeles Times*, 9 November 2004 <https://www.latimes.com/archives/la-xpm-2004-nov-09-os-wildwest9-story.html> (last accessed 15 February 2021).
20. Djuna Barnes, *Interviews*, ed. Alyce Barry (Washington DC: Sun & Moon Press, 1985), p. 216.
21. Scott Herring, 'Djuna Barnes and the Geriatric Avant-Garde', *PMLA*, 130.1 (2015), 69–91 (p. 70); Cathryn Setz, '"Tree of Heaven": Djuna Barnes's Late Metaphysical Verse', in *Shattered Objects: Djuna Barnes's Modernism*, ed. Elizabeth Pender and Cathryn Setz (University Park: Penn State University Press, 2019), pp. 130–46 (p. 144).
22. 2,400 is the figure that Scott Herring gives in his assessment of the archive. Herring, 'Djuna Barnes', p. 71.
23. A similar analysis could be made of the way in which *The Antiphon* is a response to the Nuclear Anthropocene. Eliot, who oversaw its publication at Faber and Faber, wrote to Barnes, describing how 'some sort of explosion of nuclear fission seems to take place [in the play] in which language disintegrates into some sort of primitive constituents of violent energy'. Barnes responded by warning him of 'rather more than less' nuclear explosions to come. Quoted in Peter Nicholls, 'Afterword', in *Shattered Objects: Djuna Barnes's Modernism*, pp. 207–12 (p. 210).

24. Setz, '"Tree of Heaven"', p. 135.
25. Milne and Kinsella, 'Nuclear Theory Degree Zero', p. 15.
26. Ibid. p. 2.
27. Phillip Herring and Osías Stutman, 'Commentary', in Djuna Barnes, *Collected Poems with Notes Towards the Memoirs*, ed. Phillip Herring and Osías Stutman (Madison: University of Wisconsin Press, 2005), p.137.
28. A comprehensive account of Barnes's late writing and the large volume of unpublished material in her archive remains to be published, as does an edition of her late poetry that manages to capture the ceaseless process of revision and amendment that shaped her late work. Herring and Stutman's 2005 edition of Barnes's *Collected Poems* succeeded in making a selection of Barnes's unpublished late poems available to a wider audience for the first time but necessarily made editorial decisions about which draft of a poem constituted a final version. With the rise of digital editions, it might now be possible to capture the way in which Barnes's late poems exist in multiple, rather than singular, states of completion. For the poem see the sheet headed 'When gravitational decay tears us apart', DBP, Series 3, Box 7, Folder 13.
29. Djuna Barnes to Natalie Clifford Barney, 16 May 1963. DBP, Series 2, Box 1, Folder 45.
30. Rachel Carson, *Silent Spring* (London and New York: Penguin Books, 2000), p. 23.
31. Djuna Barnes to Natalie Clifford Barney, 20 October 1963. DBP, Series 2, Box 1, Folder 45.
32. Thelma Wood to Djuna Barnes, 14 April 1969. DBP, Series 2, Box 16, Folder 49.
33. Like many of Barnes's drafts, parts of this poem were recycled within different poems. For a poem that uses lines from this poem see 'There Should Be Gardens' in her *Collected Poems*.
34. Djuna Barnes, 'A Life of Lewd Plenty', Typescript, c. 1962–3. DBP, Series 3, Box 8, Folder 5.
35. Carson, *Silent Spring*, p. 22.
36. Ibid. p. 257. For an account of how the science of entomology influenced the development of modernism see Rachel Murray, *The Modernist Exoskeleton: Insects, War, Literary Form* (Edinburgh: Edinburgh University Press, 2020).
37. Milne and Kinsella, 'Nuclear Theory Degree Zero', p. 2.
38. Dipesh Chakrabarty, 'Humanities in the Anthropocene: The Crisis of an Enduring Kantian Fable', *New Literary History*, 47.2–3 (2016), 377–97 (p. 394).
39. Christophe Bonneuil and Jean-Baptiste Fressoz, *The Shock of the Anthropocene*, trans. David Fernbach (New York: Verso, 2016), p. 172.

BIBLIOGRAPHY

ARCHIVE SOURCES

Connecticut, New Haven, Beinecke Rare Book and Manuscript Library:
 James Joyce Collection
Delaware, Newark, University of Delaware Library:
 Emily Holmes Coleman Papers (EHCP)
Maryland, College Park, University of Maryland Libraries:
Djuna Barnes Papers (DBP)

OTHER SOURCES

Adams, Carol J., *The Sexual Politics of Meat: A Feminist-Vegetarian Critical Theory* (New York: Continuum, 2010).
Adkins, Peter, 'Bloomsbury and Nature', in *The Handbook to the Bloomsbury Group*, ed. Derek Ryan and Stephen Ross (London: Bloomsbury, 2018), pp. 225–38.
———, 'The Eyes of That Cow: Eating Animals and Theorizing Vegetarianism in James Joyce's *Ulysses*', *Humanities*, 6.3 (2017) <www.mdpi.com/2076-0787/6/3/46> (last accessed 22 February 2021).
———, '"There All the Time without You": Joyce, Modernism, and the Anthropocene', in *Eco-Modernism: Ecology, Environment and Nature in Literary Modernism*, ed. Jeremy Diaper (Clemson, SC: Clemson University Press, forthcoming).

———, 'Transatlantic Dialogues in Sustainability: Edward Carpenter, Henry David Thoreau and the Literature of Simplification', in *Victorian Sustainability in Literature and Culture*, ed. Wendy Parkins (London and New York: Routledge, 2018), pp. 51–68.

Agamben, Giorgio, *The Open: Man and Animal*, trans. Kevin Attell (Stanford: Stanford University Press, 2004).

Allen, Judith, *Virginia Woolf and the Politics of Language* (Edinburgh: Edinburgh University Press, 2010).

Alt, Christina, '"Restore to Us the Necessary BLIZZARDS": Early Twentieth-Century Visions of Climatic Change', *Modernist Cultures*, 16.1 (2021), 37–61.

———, *Virginia Woolf and the Study of Nature* (Cambridge: Cambridge University Press, 2010).

Aristotle, *The Complete Works of Aristotle*, ed. Jonathan Barnes, rev. edn (Oxford: Oxford University Press, 1995).

Arnold, Matthew, *Poems* (New York: MacMillan and Co., 1880).

Ayers, David, 'De Anima: Or, *Ulysses* and the Theological Turn in Modernist Studies', *Humanities*, 6.3 (2017) <www.mdpi.com/2076-0787/6/3/57> (last accessed 25 February 2021).

Azzarello, Robert, *Queer Environmentality: Ecology, Evolution and Sexuality in American Literature* (Farnham: Ashgate, 2012).

Bakhtin, Mikhail, *Rabelais and His World*, trans. Hélène Iswolsky (Bloomington: Indiana University Press, 1984).

Banfield, Ann, *The Phantom Table: Woolf, Fry, Russell and the Epistemology of Modernism* (Cambridge: Cambridge University Press, 2000).

Barber, Stephen, 'Lip-Reading: Woolf's Secret Encounters', in *Novel Gazing: Queer Readings in Fiction*, ed. Eve Kosofsky Sedgwick (Durham, NC: Duke University Press, 1997), pp. 401–34.

Barnes, Djuna, *The Antiphon* (Los Angeles: Green Integer, 2000).

———, *Collected Poems with Notes Towards the Memoirs*, ed. Phillip Herring and Osías Stutman (Madison: The University of Wisconsin Press, 2005).

———, *The Collected Stories of Djuna Barnes*, ed. Phillip Herring (Los Angeles: Sun & Moon Press, 1996).

———, 'The Girl and the Gorilla', *New York World Magazine*, 18 October 1914, p. 9.

———, *Interviews*, ed. Alyce Barry (Washington DC: Sun & Moon Press, 1985).

———, *Ladies Almanack* (New York: New York University Press, 1992).

———, *New York*, ed. Alyce Barry (Los Angeles: Sun & Moon Press, 1989).

———, *Nightwood* (London: Faber and Faber, 2007).

———, *Ryder* (London: Dalkey Archive Press, 2010).

Barrows, Adam, 'Joyce's Panarchy: Time, Ecological Resilience, and *Finnegans Wake*', *James Joyce Quarterly*, 51.2–3 (2014), 333–52.

Bazargan, Susan, 'The Uses of the Land: Vita Sackville West's Pastoral Writing and Virginia Woolf's *Orlando*', *Woolf Studies Annual*, 5 (1999), 25–55.

Beer, Gillian, *Virginia Woolf: The Common Ground* (Ann Arbor: University of Michigan Press, 1996).

Bergson, Henri, *Creative Evolution*, trans. Arthur Mitchell (New York: Random House, 1944).

Berman, Jessica, 'Is the Trans in Transnational the Trans in Transgender?', *Modernism/Modernity*, 24.2 (2017), 217–44.

Black, Elizabeth, *The Nature of Modernism: Ecocritical Approaches to the Poetry of Edward Thomas, T. S. Eliot, Edith Sitwell and Charlotte Mew* (Abingdon: Routledge, 2018).

Blake, Elizabeth, 'Obscene Hungers: Eating and Enjoying *Nightwood* and *Ulysses*', *The Comparatist*, 39.1 (2015), 153–70.

Bonneuil, Christophe, and Jean-Baptiste Fressoz, *The Shock of the Anthropocene*, trans. David Fernbach (New York: Verso, 2016).

Borg, Ruben, *Fantasies of Self-Mourning: Modernism, the Posthuman and the Finite* (Amsterdam: Brill Rodopi, 2019).

———, 'Figures of the Earth: Non-Human Phenomenology in Joyce', *Humanities*, 6.3 (2017) <www.mdpi.com/2076-0787/6/3/71> (last accessed 22 February 2021).

Bowler, Peter J., *The Norton History of the Environmental Sciences* (New York: W. W. Norton, 1993).

Braidotti, Rosi, 'Anthropos Redux: A Defence of Monism in the Anthropocene Epoch', *Frame*, 29.2 (2016), 29–48.

———, 'Critical Posthuman Knowledges', *The South Atlantic Quarterly*, 116.1 (2017), 83–96.

———, 'Four Theses on Posthuman Feminism', in *Anthropocene Feminism*, ed. Richard Grusin (Minneapolis: University of Minnesota Press, 2017), pp. 21–48.

———, *The Posthuman* (Cambridge: Polity Press, 2013).

———, *Posthuman Knowledge* (Cambridge: Polity Press, 2019).

———, *Transpositions: On Nomadic Ethics* (Cambridge: Polity Press, 2006).

Brannigan, John, *Archipelagic Modernism: Literature in the Irish and British Isles, 1890–1970* (Edinburgh: Edinburgh University Press, 2015).

Brazeau, Robert, and Derek Gladwin (eds), *Eco-Joyce: The Environmental Imagination of James Joyce* (Cork: Cork University Press, 2014).

Briggs, Julia, *Virginia Woolf: An Inner Life* (London: Allen Lane, 2005).

Broglio, Ron, *Surface Encounters: Thinking with Animals and Art* (Minneapolis: University of Minnesota Press, 2011).

Brown, Richard (ed.), *Joyce, 'Penelope' and the Body* (Amsterdam: Rodopi, 2006).
Budgen, Frank, *James Joyce and the Making of 'Ulysses' and Other Writings* (Oxford: Oxford University Press, 1972).
Burke, Carolyn, '"Accidental Aloofness": Barnes, Loy, and Modernism', in *Silence and Power: A Reevaulation of Djuna Barnes*, ed. Mary Lynn Broe (Carbondale and Edwardsville: Southern Illinois University Press, 1991), pp. 67–79.
Burke, Kenneth, *Language as Symbolic Action: Essays on Life, Literature and Method* (Berkeley: University of California Press, 1966).
Burns, Christy L., 'Re-Dressing Feminist Identities: Tensions between Essential and Constructed Selves in Virginia Woolf's *Orlando*', *Twentieth-Century Literature*, 40.3 (1994), 342–64.
Butler, Judith, *Bodies That Matter: On the Discursive Limits of 'Sex'* (London and New York: Routledge, 2011).
Cantrell, Carol H., '"The Locus of Compossibility": Virginia Woolf, Modernism, and Place', *Interdisciplinary Studies in Literature and Environment*, 5.2 (1998), 25–40.
Carlston, Erin G., *Thinking Fascism: Sapphic Modernism and Fascist Modernity* (Stanford: Stanford University Press, 1998).
Carson, Rachel, *Silent Spring* (London and New York: Penguin Books, 2000).
Caselli, Daniela, '"If Some Strong Woman": Djuna Barnes's Great Capacity for All Things Uncertain', in *Shattered Objects: Djuna Barnes's Modernism*, ed. Elizabeth Pender and Cathryn Setz (University Park: Penn State University Press, 2019), pp. 147–62.
———, *Improper Modernism: Djuna Barnes's Bewildering Corpus* (London and New York: Routledge, 2016).
Castle, Gregory, '"I Am Almosting It": History, Nature, and the Will to Power in "Proteus"', *James Joyce Quarterly*, 29.2 (1992), 281–96.
———, 'Introduction: Matter in Motion in the Modernist Novel', in *A History of the Modernist Novel*, ed. Gregory Castle (Cambridge: Cambridge University Press, 2015), pp. 1–36.
———, 'Irish Revivalism: Critical Trends and New Directions', *Literature Compass*, 8.5 (2011), 291–303.
———, *Modernism and the Celtic Revival* (Cambridge: Cambridge University Press, 2001).
Chakrabarty, Dipesh, 'The Anthropocene and the Convergence of Histories', in *The Anthropocene and the Global Environmental Crisis: Rethinking Modernity in a New Epoch*, ed. Clive Hamilton (Abingdon: Routledge, 2015), pp. 44–56.
———, 'The Climate of History: Four Theses', *Critical Inquiry*, 35.2 (2009), 197–222.
———, 'Humanities in the Anthropocene: The Crisis of an Enduring Kantian Fable', *New Literary History*, 47.2–3 (2016), 377–97.

——, 'Postcolonial Studies and the Challenge of Climate Change', *New Literary History*, 43.1 (2012), 1–18.
Cheng, Vincent J., *Joyce, race, and empire* (Cambridge: Cambridge University Press, 1995).
Cixous, Hélène, 'The Laugh of the Medusa', trans. Keith Cohen and Paula Cohen, *Signs*, 1.4 (1976), 875–93.
Clark, Adele, and Donna Haraway (eds), *Making Kin Not Population: Reconceiving Generations* (Chicago: Prickly Paradigm Press, 2018).
Clark, Timothy, *Ecocriticism on the Edge: The Anthropocene as a Threshold Concept* (London: Bloomsbury, 2015).
Coffman, Chris, 'Woolf's *Orlando* and the Resonances of Trans Studies', *Genders*, 51 (2010) <https://www.colorado.edu/gendersarchive1998-2013/2010/02/01/woolfs-orlando-and-resonances-trans-studies> (last accessed 6 May 2020).
Colebrook, Claire, '"A Grandiose Time of Coexistence": Stratigraphy of the Anthropocene', *Deleuze Studies*, 10.4 (2016), 440–54.
——, *Death of the Posthuman: Essays on Extinction, Vol.1* (Ann Arbor, MI: Open Humanities Press, 2014).
——, 'The Future in the Anthropocene: Extinction and the Imagination', in *Climate and Literature*, ed. Adeline Johns-Putra (Cambridge: Cambridge University Press, 2019), pp. 263–80.
——, *Sex After Life: Essays on Extinction, Vol.2* (Ann Arbor, MI: Open Humanities Press, 2014).
——, 'We Have Always Been Post-Anthropocene: The Anthropocene Counterfactual', in *Anthropocene Feminism*, ed. Richard Grusin (Minneapolis: University of Minnesota Press, 2017), pp. 1–20.
——, 'Woolf and "Theory"', in *Virginia Woolf in Context*, ed. Bryony Randall and Jane Goldman (Cambridge: Cambridge University Press, 2012), pp. 65–78.
Colebrook, Claire, Peter Adkins and Wendy Parkins, 'Victorian Studies in the Anthropocene: An Interview with Claire Colebrook', *19: Interdisciplinary Studies in the Long Nineteenth Century*, 26 (2018) <https://doi.org/10.16995/ntn.819> (last accessed 21 February 2021).
Creasy, C. F. S., 'Of Matter and Manner: Djuna Barnes's *Ryder* and Censorship as Style', *Modern Philology*, 117.3 (2020), 370–92.
Crossland, Rachel, *Modernist Physics: Waves, Particles, and Relativities in the Writings of Virginia Woolf and D. H. Lawrence* (Oxford: Oxford University Press, 2018).
Crowley, Ronan, 'Things Actually Said: On Some Versions of Joyce's and Yeats' First Meeting', *Joyce Studies in Italy*, 17 (2015), 31–54.
Crutzen, Paul, 'Geology of Mankind', *Nature*, 415 (2002), 23.
Crutzen, Paul, and Eugene Stoermer, 'The "Anthropocene"', *IGBP Newsletter*, 41 (2000), 17–18.

Dalton, Anne B., 'Escaping from Eden: Djuna Barnes' Revision of Psychoanalytic Theory and Her Treatment Of Father-Daughter Incest in *Ryder*', *Women's Studies*, 22.2 (1993), 163–79.
Darwin, Charles, *The Origin of Species by Means of Natural Selection or the Preservation of Favoured Races in The Struggle for Life*, ed. J. W. Burrow (London: Penguin Books, 1985).
Davies, Jeremy, *The Birth of the Anthropocene* (Oakland: University of California Press, 2016).
Davis, Thomas S., *The Extinct Scene: Late Modernism and Everyday Life* (New York: Columbia University Press, 2016).
De Man, Paul, *The Rhetoric of Romanticism* (New York: Columbia University Press, 1984).
Deleuze, Gilles, and Félix Guattari, *A Thousand Plateaus: Capitalism and Schizophrenia*, trans. Brian Massumi (London: Bloomsbury, 2014).
Delsandro, Erica, '"Myself It Was Impossible": Queering History in *Between the Acts*', *Woolf Studies Annual*, 13 (2007), 87–109.
Derrida, Jacques, *The Animal That Therefore I Am*, trans. David Wills, ed. Marie-Louise Mallet (New York: Fordham University Press, 2008).
———, *The Beast & the Sovereign, Volume I*, trans. Geoffrey Bennington (Chicago: University of Chicago Press, 2009).
———, 'Eating Well, or the Calculation of the Subject', in *Points: Interviews, 1974–1994*, ed. Elizabeth Weber (Stanford: Stanford University Press, 1995), pp. 255–87.
———, *Of Grammatology*, trans. Gayatri Chakravorty Spivak (Baltimore: Johns Hopkins University Press, 1997).
Diaper, Jeremy, *T. S. Eliot and Organicism* (Clemson, SC: Clemson University Press, 2018).
Dickinson, Renée, 'Writing the Land: *Between the Acts* as Ecocritical Text', *Virginia Woolf Miscellany*, 81 (2012), 16–18.
Douglass, Paul, 'Bergson, Vitalism, and Modernist Literature', in *Understanding Bergson, Understanding Modernism*, ed. Paul Ardoin, S. E. Gontarski, and Laci Mattison (London: Bloomsbury, 2013), pp. 107–27.
Doyle, Patrick, *Civilising Rural Ireland: The Co-Operative Movement, Development and the Nation-State, 1889–1939* (Manchester: Manchester University Press, 2019).
Duffy, Enda, *The Speed Handbook: Velocity, Pleasure, Modernism* (Durham, NC: Duke University Press, 2009).
Dukes, Hunter, '*Ulysses* and the Signature of Things', *Humanities*, 6.3 (2017) <www.mdpi.com/2076-0787/6/3/52> (last accessed 23 February 2021).
Duszenko, Andrzej, 'Abnihilization of the Etym: Joyce, Rutherford, and Particle Physics', *Irish University Review*, 46.2 (2016), 275–86.

Ebury, Katherine, 'Becoming-Animal in the Epiphanies: Joyce Between Fiction and Non-Fiction', in *Joyce's Non-Fiction Writings: Outside His Jurisfiction*, ed. Katherine Ebury and James Alexander Fraser (Cham: Palgrave Macmillan, 2018), pp. 175–94.

———, *Modernism and Cosmology: Absurd Lights* (Basingstoke: Palgrave Macmillan, 2014).

Edelman, Lee, *No Future: Queer Theory and the Death Drive* (Durham, NC: Duke University Press, 2004).

Edmunds, Susan, *Grotesque Relations: Modernist Domestic Fiction and the U.S. Welfare State* (Oxford: Oxford University Press, 2008).

Edwards, Erin E., *The Modernist Corpse: Posthumanism and the Posthumous* (Minneapolis: University of Minnesota Press, 2018).

Eglinton, John, *Anglo-Irish Essays* (Dublin: The Talbot Press, 1917).

Eliot, T. S., *Collected Poems 1909–1962* (New York: Harcourt, Brace & World, Inc., 1963).

———, *Selected Prose*, ed. Frank Kermode (New York: Harcourt Brace Jovanovich Farrar, Straus and Giroux, 1975).

Ellmann, Maud, '"Penelope" Without the Body', in *Joyce, 'Penelope' and the Body*, ed. Richard Brown (Amsterdam: Rodopi, 2006), pp. 97–108.

———, '*Ulysses*: The Epic of the Human Body', in *A Companion to James Joyce*, ed. Richard Brown (Oxford: Wiley-Blackwell, 2011), pp. 54–70.

Ellmann, Richard, *James Joyce*, rev. edn (Oxford: Oxford University Press, 1983).

———, *Ulysses on the Liffey* (Oxford: Oxford University Press, 1982).

Esty, Jed, *A Shrinking Island: Modernism and National Culture in England* (Princeton: Princeton University Press, 2003).

Fairhall, James, 'The Bog of Allen, the Tiber River, and the Pontine Marshes: An Ecocritical Reading of "The Dead"', *James Joyce Quarterly*, 51.4 (2014), 567–600.

———, 'Ecocriticism, Joyce, and the Politics of Trees in the "Cyclops" Episode of *Ulysses*', *Irish Studies Review*, 20.4 (2012), 367–87.

Faltejskova, Monika, *Djuna Barnes, T. S. Eliot and the Gender Dynamics of Modernism: Tracing 'Nightwood'* (New York and Abingdon: Routledge, 2010).

Feder, Helena, *Ecocriticism and the Idea of Culture: Biology and the Bildungsroman* (Farnham: Ashgate Publishing, 2014).

Field, Andrew, *Djuna: The Life and Times of Djuna Barnes* (New York: G. P. Putnam's Sons, 1983)

Finney, Stanley C., and Lucy E. Edwards, 'The "Anthropocene" Epoch: Scientific Decision or Political Statement?', *GSA Today*, 26.3–4 (2016), 4–10.

Fordham, Finn, '*Finnegans Wake*: Novel and Anti-Novel', in *A Companion to James Joyce*, ed. Richard Brown (Oxford: Wiley-Blackwell, 2011), pp. 71–89.

———, *Lots of Fun at 'Finnegans Wake': Unravelling Universals* (Oxford: Oxford University Press, 2007).
Forster, E. M., *Howards End*, ed. Oliver Stallybrass (London: Penguin Books, 1989).
Foster, R. F., *Modern Ireland 1600–1972* (London: Penguin Books, 1988).
Fox, Alice, *Virginia Woolf and the Literature of the English Renaissance* (Oxford: Oxford University Press, 1990).
Frank, Joseph, *The Widening Gyre: Crisis and Mastery in Modern Literature* (Bloomington: Indiana University Press, 1963).
Friedman, Susan Stanford, 'Definitional Excursions: The Meanings of Modern/Modernity/Modernism', *Modernism/Modernity*, 8.3 (2001), 493–513.
Froula, Christine, *Virginia Woolf and the Bloomsbury Avant-Garde: War, Civilization, Modernity* (New York: Columbia University Press, 2005).
De Gay, Jane, 'Rhythms of Revision and Revisiting: Unpicking the Past in *Orlando*', in *Sentencing 'Orlando': Virginia Woolf and the Morphology of the Modernist Sentence*, ed. Elsa Högberg and Amy Bromley (Edinburgh: Edinburgh University Press, 2018), pp. 56–67.
Ghosh, Amitav, *The Great Derangement: Climate Change and the Unthinkable* (Chicago: University of Chicago Press, 2017).
Giffney, Noreen, and Myra Hird (eds), *Queering the Non/Human* (Aldershot: Ashgate, 2008).
Gifford, Don, and Robert J. Seidman, *'Ulysses' Annotated: Notes for James Joyce's 'Ulysses'* (Berkeley and Los Angeles: University of California Press, 1986).
Gilbert, Stuart, *James Joyce's 'Ulysses': A Study* (London: Penguin Books, 1963).
Gillies, Mary Ann, *Henri Bergson and British Modernism* (Montreal: McGill Queen's University Press, 1996).
Goldman, Jane, *Modernism, 1910–1945: Image to Apocalypse* (Basingstoke: Palgrave Macmillan, 2004).
———, 'Queer Bloomsbury (Review)', *Woolf Studies Annual*, 23 (2017), 161–71.
Golinski, Jan, 'Weather and Climate in the Age of Enlightenment', in *Climate and Literature*, ed. Adeline Johns-Putra (Cambridge: Cambridge University Press, 2019), pp. 111–27.
Goody, Alex, 'Djuna Barnes on the Page', in *Shattered Objects: Djuna Barnes's Modernism*, ed. Elizabeth Pender and Cathryn Setz (University Park: Penn State University Press, 2019), pp. 26–45.
———, *Modernist Articulations: A Cultural Study of Djuna Barnes, Mina Loy and Gertrude Stein* (Basingstoke: Palgrave Macmillan, 2007).
Gough, Val, '"A Responsible Person Like Her": Woolf's Suicide Culture', in *Virginia Woolf: Turning the Centuries: Selected Papers from the Ninth*

Annual Conference on Virginia Woolf, ed. Ann Ardis and Bonnie Kime Scott (New York: Pace University Press, 2000), pp. 183–91.

Gould, Peter C., *Early Green Politics: Back to Nature, Back to the Land, and Socialism in Britain, 1880–1900* (Brighton: The Harvester Press, 1988).

Greene, Graham, 'Fiction Chronicle', *Tablet*, 14 November 1936, pp. 678–9.

Griffiths, Matthew, *The New Poetics of Climate Change: Modernist Aesthetics for a Warming World* (London: Bloomsbury, 2017).

Grosz, Elizabeth, *Becoming Undone: Darwinian Reflections on Life, Politics, and Art* (Durham, NC: Duke University Press, 2011).

Guattari, Félix, *The Three Ecologies*, trans. Ian Pindar and Paul Sutton (New Brunswick, NJ: The Athlone Press, 2000).

Hagen, Benjamin, 'Bloomsbury and Philosophy', in *The Handbook to the Bloomsbury Group*, ed. Stephen Ross and Derek Ryan (London: Bloomsbury, 2018), pp. 135–50.

Hankins, Leslie Kathleen, '*Orlando*: "A Precipice Marked V" Between "A Miracle of Discretion" and "Lovemaking Unbelievable: Indiscretions Incredible"', in *Virginia Woolf: Lesbian Readings*, ed. Eileen Barrett and Patricia Morgane Cramer (New York: New York University Press, 1997), pp. 181–202.

Haraway, Donna, *The Companion Species Manifesto: Dogs, People, and Significant Otherness* (Chicago: Prickly Paradigm Press, 2003).

———, 'Situated Knowledges: The Science Question in Feminism and the Privilege of Partial Perspective', *Feminist Studies*, 14.3 (1988), 575–99.

———, *Staying with the Trouble: Making Kin in the Chthulucene* (Durham, NC: Duke University Press, 2016).

———, *When Species Meet* (Minneapolis: University of Minnesota Press, 2007).

Harris, Alexandra, *Weatherland: Writers and Artists Under English Skies* (London: Thames & Hudson, 2015).

Heise, Ursula K., *Sense of Place and Sense of Planet: The Environmental Imagination of the Global* (Oxford: Oxford University Press, 2008).

Henke, Suzette A., and Elaine Unkeless, 'Introduction', in *Women in Joyce*, ed. Suzette A. Henke and Elaine Unkeless (Brighton: The Harvester Press, 1982), pp. xi–xxii.

Henry, Holly, *Virginia Woolf and the Discourse of Science* (Cambridge: Cambridge University Press, 2003).

Herman, David, 'Introduction: Literature Beyond the Human', in *Creatural Fictions: Human-Animal Relationships in Twentieth- and Twenty-First-Century Literature*, ed. David Herman (Basingstoke: Palgrave Macmillan, 2016), pp. 1–18.

Herring, Phillip, *Djuna: The Life and Works of Djuna Barnes* (New York and London: Penguin Books, 1996).

Herring, Scott, 'Djuna Barnes and the Geriatric Avant-Garde', *PMLA*, 130.1 (2015), 69–91.
Hesiod, *Theogony and Works and Days*, trans. Catherine Schlegel and Henry Weinfeld (Ann Arbor: University of Michigan Press, 2010).
Hewitt, Seán, 'Yeats's Re-Enchanted Nature', *International Yeats Studies*, 2.2 (2018), 1–19.
Hirsch, Edward, 'The Imaginary Irish Peasant', *PMLA*, 106.5 (1991), 1116–33.
Högberg, Elsa, and Amy Bromley, 'Introduction: Sentencing *Orlando*', in *Sentencing 'Orlando': Virginia Woolf and the Morphology of the Modernist Sentence*, ed. Elsa Högberg and Amy Bromley (Edinburgh: Edinburgh University Press, 2018), pp. 1–12.
Hovanec, Caroline, *Animal Subjects: Literature, Zoology and British Modernism* (Cambridge: Cambridge University Press, 2018).
Howell, Ted, 'An Imperialist Inherits the Earth: *Howards End* in the Anthropocene', *Modern Language Quarterly*, 77.4 (2016), 547–72.
Human Animal Research Network Editorial Collective (ed.), *Animals in the Anthropocene: Critical perspectives on non-human futures* (Sydney: Sydney University Press, 2015).
Hussey, Mark, *'I'd Make It Penal': The Rural Preservation Movement in Virginia Woolf's 'Between the Acts'* (London: Cecil Woolf Publishers, 2011).
———, 'Introduction', in Virginia Woolf, *Between the Acts* (Cambridge: Cambridge University Press, 2011), pp. xxxiv–lxxiii.
Hutton, Clare, 'Joyce and the Institutions of Revivalism', *Irish University Review*, 33.1 (2003), 117–32.
Johns-Putra, Adeline, 'Introduction', in *Climate and Literature*, ed. Adeline Johns-Putra (Cambridge: Cambridge University Press, 2019), pp. 1–12.
———, '"My Job Is to Take Care of You": Climate Change, Humanity, and Cormac McCarthy's *The Road*', *Modern Fiction Studies*, 62.3 (2016), 519–40.
———, 'The Unsustainable Aesthetics of Sustainability: The Sense of an Ending in Jeanette Winterson's *The Stone Gods*', in *Literature and Sustainability: Concept, Text and Culture*, ed. Adeline Johns-Putra, John Parham and Louise Squire (Manchester: Manchester University Press, 2017), pp. 177–94.
Jolas, Eugene, 'Glossary', *transition*, 16–17 (1929), 326–8.
Jones, Clara, 'Virginia Woolf and "The Villa Jones" (1931)', *Woolf Studies Annual*, 22 (2016), 75–96.
Joyces, James, *Finnegans Wake*, ed. Robbert-Jans Henkes, Erik Bindervoet and Finn Fordham (Oxford: Oxford University Press, 2012).
———, 'From Work in Progress', *Transatlantic Review*, 1.4 (1924), 215–23.
———, *Joyce's 'Ulysses' Notesheets in the British Museum*, ed. Phillip Herring (Charlottesville: University Press of Virginia, 1972).

—, *Letters Of James Joyce*, ed. Stuart Gilbert (London: Faber and Faber, 1957).
—, *The Letters of James Joyce Volume II*, ed. Richard Ellmann (London: Faber, 1966).
—, *The Letters of James Joyce Volume III*, ed. Richard Ellmann (London: Faber, 1966).
—, *Occasional, Critical and Political Writing*, ed. Kevin Barry (Oxford: Oxford University Press, 2008).
—, *Poems and Exiles*, ed. J. C. C. Mays (London: Penguin Books, 1992).
—, *A Portrait of the Artist as a Young Man*, ed. Jeri Johnson (Oxford: Oxford University Press, 2000).
—, 'The Sisters', *The Irish Homestead*, 13 August 1904, pp. 676–7.
—, *Stephen Hero*, ed. Theodore Spencer, rev. edn (St Albans: Granada Publishing, 1982).
—, *Ulysses: A Critical and Synoptic Edition*, ed. Hans Walter Gabler, Wolfhard Steppe and Claus Melchior (New York: Garland Publishing, 1984).
—, *Ulysses: The Corrected Text*, ed. Hans Walter Gabler with Wolfhard Steppe and Claus Melchior (London: Penguin Books, 1986).
Kaivola, Karen, 'The "Beast Turning Human": Constructions of the "Primitive" in *Nightwood*', *Review of Contemporary Fiction*, 13.3 (1993), 172–85.
Kalaidjian, Andrew, *Exhausted Ecologies: Modernism and Environmental Recovery* (Cambridge: Cambridge University Press, 2020).
—, 'The Black Sheep: Djuna Barnes's Dark Pastoral', in *Creatural Fictions: Human-Animal Relationships in Twentieth- and Twenty-First-Century Literature*, ed. David Herman (Basingstoke: Palgrave Macmillan, 2016), pp. 65–87.
Kannenstine, Louis F., *The Art of Djuna Barnes: Duality and Damnation* (New York: New York University Press, 1977).
Kenner, Hugh, *Ulysses* (London: George Allen & Unwin, 1980).
Kershner, Brendan, 'Joyce Beyond the Pale', in *Eco-Joyce: The Environmental Imagination of James Joyce*, ed. Robert Brazeau and Derek Gladwin (Cork: Cork University Press, 2014), pp. 123–35.
Kiberd, Declan, *Inventing Ireland: The Literature of a Modern Nation* (London: Jonathan Cape, 1995).
Kipling, Rudyard, *Selected Poems* (London: Penguin Books, 2001).
Klaus, H. Gustav, and John Rignall, 'Introduction: The Red and The Green', in *Ecology and the Literature of the British Left: The Red and The Green*, ed. Valentine Cunningham, H. Gustav Klaus, and John Rignall (Farnham: Ashgate, 2012), pp. 1–17.
Kupinse, William J., 'Private Property, Public Interest: Bloom's Ecological Fantasy in "Ithaca"', *James Joyce Quarterly*, 52.3–4 (2015), 593–621.

Lacivita, Alison, *The Ecology of 'Finnegans Wake'* (Gainesville: University Press of Florida, 2015).

———, 'Wild Dublin: Nature Versus Culture in Irish Literature', *Green Letters*, 17.1 (2013), 27–41.

Lai, Yi-Peng, 'The Tree Wedding and the (Eco)Politics of Irish Forestry in "Cyclops": History, Language and the Viconian Politics of the Forest', in *Eco-Joyce: The Environmental Imagination of James Joyce*, ed. Robert Brazeau and Derek Gladwin (Cork: Cork University Press, 2014), pp. 91–110.

Larbaud, Valery, 'The *Ulysses* of James Joyce', *The Criterion*, 1.1 (1922), 94–103.

Latour, Bruno, *Facing Gaia: Eight Lectures on the New Climatic Regime*, trans. Catherine Porter (Cambridge: Polity, 2017).

———, *Politics Of Nature: How to Bring the Sciences into Democracy*, trans. Catherine Porter (Cambridge, MA: Harvard University Press, 2004).

———, *We Have Never Been Modern*, trans. Catherine Porter (Cambridge, MA: Harvard University Press, 1993).

Lawrence, D. H., *The Rainbow*, ed. Mark Kinkead-Weekes (London: Penguin Books, 1995).

———, *Women in Love*, ed. David Farmer, Lindeth Vasey and John Worthen (London: Penguin Books, 2000).

Lawrence, Karen, *The Odyssey of Style in 'Ulysses'* (Princeton: Princeton University Press, 1981).

Le Roy, Edouard, 'The Origins of Humanity and the Evolution of the Mind', in *The Biosphere and Noosphere Reader*, ed. Paul R. Samson and David Pitt (London and New York: Routledge, 1999), pp. 60–70.

Levin, Harry, *James Joyce: A Critical Introduction* (London: Faber and Faber, 1971).

Levine, Nancy J., '"Bringing Milkshake to Bulldogs": The Early Journalism of Djuna Barnes', in *Silence and Power: A Reevaulation of Djuna Barnes*, ed. Mary Lynn Broe (Carbondale and Edwardsville: Southern Illinois University Press, 1991), pp. 27–37.

Lewis, Simon L., and Mark A. Maslin, 'Defining the Anthropocene', *Nature*, 519.7542 (2015), 171–80.

Lewis, Sophie, 'Cthulhu Plays No Role For Me', *View Point Mag*, 2017 <https://viewpointmag.com/2017/05/08/cthulhu-plays-no-role-for-me/> (last accessed 12 May 2020).

Lorimer, Jamie, 'The Anthropo-Scene: A Guide for the Perplexed', *Social Studies of Science*, 47.1 (2017), 117–42.

Lovejoy, Laura, 'The Bestial Feminine in *Finnegans Wake*', *Humanities*, 6.3 (2017) <https://www.mdpi.com/2076-0787/6/3/58> (last accessed 25 February 2021).

Lovelock, James, *Gaia: A New Look at Life on Earth*, rev. edn (Oxford: Oxford University Press, 2000).

———, *The Revenge of Gaia: Why the Earth Is Fighting Back – and How We Can Still Save Humanity* (London: Penguin Books, 2007).

Lyell, Charles, *Principles of Geology* (London: Murray, 1853).

McCarthy, Jeffrey Mathes, *Green Modernism: Nature and the English Novel, 1900 to 1930* (Basingstoke and New York: Palgrave Macmillan, 2015).

McCormick, Kathleen, 'Reproducing Molly Bloom: A Revisionist History of "Penelope", 1922–1970', in *Molly Blooms: A Polylogue on 'Penelope' and Cultural Studies*, ed. Richard Pearce (Madison: University of Wisconsin Press, 1994), pp. 17–39.

McCourt, John, 'Introduction: Joyce, Yeats, and the Revival', *Joyce Studies in Italy*, 17 (2015), 7–70.

McCracken, Saskia, '(R)Evolutionary Animal Tropes in the Works of Charles Darwin and Virginia Woolf' (unpublished Doctoral Thesis, University of Glasgow, 2021).

MacDuffie, Allen, *Victorian Literature, Energy and the Ecological Imagination* (Cambridge: Cambridge University Press, 2014).

Maggio, Paula, *Reading the Skies in Virginia Woolf: Woolf on Weather in Her Essays, Diaries and Three of Her Novels* (London: Cecil Woolf Publishers, 2009).

Mak, Cliff, 'Joyce's Indifferent Animals: Boredom and the Subversion of Fables in *Finnegans Wake*', *Modernist Cultures*, 11.2 (2016), 179–205.

Malm, Andreas, *Fossil Capital: The Rise of Steam Power and the Roots of Global Warming* (London: Verso, 2016).

Malm, Andreas, and Alf Hornborg, 'The Geology of Mankind? A Critique of the Anthropocene Narrative', *The Anthropocene Review*, 1.1 (2014), 62–9.

Marcus, Jane, 'Laughing at Leviticus: *Nightwood* as Woman's Circus Epic', in *Silence and Power: A Reevaulation of Djuna Barnes*, ed. Mary Lynn Broe (Carbondale and Edwardsville: Southern Illinois University Press, 1991), pp. 221–50.

Margulis, Lynn, *The Symbiotic Planet: A New Look at Evolution* (London: Phoenix, 1999).

Martin, Kirsty, *Modernism and the Rhythms of Sympathy: Vernon Lee, Virginia Woolf, and D. H. Lawrence* (Oxford: Oxford University Press, 2013).

Mathews, P. J., *Revival: The Abbey Theatre, Sinn Féin, The Gaelic League and the Co-Operative Movement* (Notre Dame, IN: University of Notre Dame Press, 2003).

Menely, Tobias, *The Animal Claim: Sensibility and the Creaturely Voice* (Chicago and London: University of Chicago Press, 2015).

Miller, Tyrus, *Late Modernism: Politics, Fiction, and the Arts Between the World Wars* (Berkeley and London: University of California Press, 1999).

Milne, Drew, and John Kinsella, 'Nuclear Theory Degree Zero, with Two Cheers for Derrida', *Angelaki*, 22.3 (2017), 1–16.

Monaco, Beatrice, *Machinic Modernism: The Deleuzian Literary Machines of Woolf, Lawrence and Joyce* (Basingstoke: Palgrave Macmillan, 2008).

Mortimer-Sandilands, Catriona, and Bruce Erickson, 'Introduction: A Genealogy of Queer Ecologies', in *Queer Ecologies: Sex, Nature, Politics, Desire*, ed. Catriona Mortimer-Sandilands and Bruce Erickson (Bloomington and Indianapolis: Indiana University Press, 2010), pp. 1–51.

Morton, Timothy, *The Ecological Thought* (Cambridge, MA: Harvard University Press, 2010).

——, *Ecology Without Nature: Rethinking Environmental Aesthetics* (Cambridge, MA: Harvard University Press, 2007).

——, 'Queer Ecology', *PMLA*, 125.2 (2010), 273–82.

Murray, Rachel, *The Modernist Exoskeleton: Insects, War, Literary Form* (Edinburgh: Edinburgh University Press, 2020).

Nagai, Kaori, '"'Tis Optophone Which Ontophanes": Race, The Modern and Irish Revivalism', in *Modernism and Race*, ed. Len Platt (Cambridge: Cambridge University Press, 2011), pp. 58–76.

Nicholls, Peter, 'Afterword', in *Shattered Objects: Djuna Barnes's Modernism*, ed. Elizabeth Pender and Cathryn Setz (University Park: Penn State University Press, 2019), pp. 207–12.

Nolan, Emer, *James Joyce and Nationalism* (New York: Routledge, 1995).

——, 'Modernism and the Irish Revival', in *The Cambridge Companion to Modern Irish Culture*, ed. Joe Cleary and Claire Connolly (Cambridge: Cambridge University Press, 2005), pp. 157–72.

Norris, Margot, 'The Animals of James Joyce's *Finnegans Wake*', *Modern Fiction Studies*, 60.3 (2014), 527–43.

——, *Beasts of the Modern Imagination: Darwin, Nietzsche, Kafka, Ernst and Lawrence* (Baltimore and London: Johns Hopkins University Press, 1985).

——, *The Decentered Universe of 'Finnegans Wake': A Structuralist Analysis* (Baltimore: Johns Hopkins University Press, 1977).

——, *Virgin and Veteran Readings of 'Ulysses'* (New York: Palgrave Macmillan, 2011).

O'Connor, Ulick, *The Joyce We Knew: Memoirs of Joyce* (Dingle: Brandon Books, 2004).

O'Dea, Dathalinn, 'Joyce the Regionalist: *The Irish Homestead*, *Dubliners* and Modernism's Regional Affect', *Modern Fiction Studies*, 63.3 (2017), 475–501.

Oliver, Kelly, *Animal Lessons: How They Teach Us to Be Human* (New York: Columbia University Press, 2009).

O'Neal, Hank, *'Life Is Painful, Nasty and Short . . . in My Case It Has Only Been Painful and Nasty': An Informal Memoir* (New York: Paragon House, 1990).

Onishi, Norimitsu, 'France's Far Right Wants to Be an Environmental Party, Too', *The New York Times*, 17 October 2019 <www.nytimes.com/2019/10/17/world/europe/france-far-right-environment> (last accessed 25 February 2021).

Parkins, Wendy, 'Introduction: Sustainability and the Victorian Anthropocene', in *Victorian Sustainability in Literature and Culture*, ed. Wendy Parkins (Abingdon: Routledge, 2018), pp. 1–13.

Parkins, Wendy, and Peter Adkins, 'Introduction: Victorian Ecology and the Anthropocene', *19: Interdisciplinary Studies in the Long Nineteenth Century*, 26 (2018) <https://19.bbk.ac.uk/article/id/1717/> (last accessed 25 February 2021).

Parsons, Deborah, *Theorists of the Modernist Novel: James Joyce, Dorothy Richardson, Virginia Woolf* (London: Routledge, 2007).

Pearce, Richard (ed.), *Molly Blooms: A Polylogue on 'Penelope' and Cultural Studies* (Madison: University of Wisconsin Press, 1994).

Phillips, Dana, '"Slimy Beastly Life": Thoreau on Food and Farming', *Interdisciplinary Studies in Literature and Environment*, 19.3 (2012), 532–47.

———, *The Truth of Ecology: Nature, Culture, and Literature in America* (Oxford: Oxford University Press, 2003).

Pick, Anat, *Creaturely Poetics: Animality and Vulnerability in Literature and Film* (New York: Columbia University Press, 2011).

Pizzo, Justine, 'Ethereal Women: Climate and Gender from Realism to the Modernist Novel', in *Climate and Literature*, ed. Adeline Johns-Putra (Cambridge: Cambridge University Press, 2019), pp. 179–95.

Platt, Len, *Joyce and the Anglo-Irish: A Study of Joyce and the Literary Revival* (Amsterdam: Rodopi, 1998).

Plock, Vike Martina, 'Bodies', in *The Cambridge Companion to 'Ulysses'*, ed. Sean Latham (Cambridge: Cambridge University Press, 2014), pp. 184–99.

———, *Joyce, Medicine and Modernity* (Gainesville: University Press of Florida, 2010).

Plumb, Cheryl J., 'Introduction', in Djuna Barnes, *Nightwood: The Original Version and Related Drafts*, ed. Cheryl J. Plumb (Normal, IL: Dalkey Archive Press, 1995), pp. vii–xxvi.

Pollentier, Caroline, 'Between Aesthetic and Political Theory: Virginia Woolf's Utopian Pacifism', in *Virginia Woolf, Europe and Peace: Volume 2, Aesthetics and Theory*, ed. Peter Adkins and Derek Ryan (Clemson, SC: Clemson University Press, 2020), pp. 203–18.

Ponsot, Marie, 'A Reader's *Ryder*', in *Silence and Power: A Reevaulation of Djuna Barnes*, ed. Mary Lynn Broe (Carbondale and Edwardsville: Southern Illinois University Press, 1991), pp. 94–112.

Potter, Rachel, '*Nightwood*'s Humans', in *Shattered Objects: Djuna Barnes's Modernism*, ed. Elizabeth Pender and Cathryn Setz (University Park: Penn State University Press, 2019), pp. 61–74.
Pound, Ezra, *Pound/Joyce: The Letters of Ezra Pound to James Joyce, with Pound's Essays on Joyce*, ed. Forrest Read (New York: New Directions Books, 1967).
Power, Arthur, *Conversations with Joyce* (Dublin: Lilliput Press, 1999).
Proust, Marcel, *The Past Recaptured*, trans. Frederick A. Blossom (New York: Albert & Charles Boni, 1932).
Rabaté, Jean-Michel, *Think, Pig!: Beckett at the Limit of the Human* (New York: Fordham University Press, 2016).
Raffnsøe, Sverre, *Philosophy of the Anthropocene: The Human Turn* (Basingstoke: Palgrave Macmillan, 2016).
Raitt, Suzanne, and Ian Blyth, 'Explanatory Notes', in Virginia Woolf, *Orlando: A Biography*, ed. Suzanne Raitt and Ian Blyth (Cambridge: Cambridge University Press, 2018), pp. 304–543.
Reynolds, Christopher, 'Witness to Creation – and Destruction', *Los Angeles Times*, 9 November 2004 <https://www.latimes.com/archives/la-xpm-2004-nov-09-os-wildwest9-story.html> (last accessed 15 February 2021).
Rohman, Carrie, *Stalking the Subject: Modernism and the Animal* (New York: Columbia University Press, 2009).
Ross, Stephen, 'Introduction: The Missing Link', in *Modernism and Theory: A Critical Debate*, ed. Stephen Ross (Abingdon: Routledge, 2009), pp. 1–18.
Ruddiman, William F., Erle C. Ellis, Jed O. Kaplan and Dorian Q. Fuller, 'Defining the Epoch We Live In: Is a formally designated "Anthropocene" a good idea?', *Science*, 348.6230 (2015), 38–9.
Ruskin, John, *Selected Writings*, ed. Dinah Birch (Oxford: Oxford University Press, 2004).
Ryan, Derek, 'Following Snakes and Moths: Modernist Ethics and Posthumanism', *Twentieth-Century Literature*, 61.3 (2015), 287–304.
———, 'Literature', in *The Edinburgh Companion to Animal Studies*, ed. Lynn Turner, Undine Sellbach and Ron Broglio (Edinburgh: Edinburgh University Press, 2017), pp. 321–36.
———, '*Orlando*'s Queer Animals', in *A Companion to Virginia Woolf*, ed. Jessica Berman (Oxford: Wiley-Blackwell, 2016), pp. 109–20.
———, '"The Reality of Becoming": Deleuze, Woolf and the Territory of Cows', *Deleuze Studies*, 7.4 (2013), 537–61.
———, *Virginia Woolf and the Materiality of Theory: Sex, Animal, Life* (Edinburgh: Edinburgh University Press, 2013).
Saguaro, Shelley, '"Something That Would Stand for the Conception": The Inseminating World in the Last Writings of Virginia Woolf', *Green Letters*, 17.2 (2013), 109–20.

Saint-Amour, Paul K., *Tense Future: Modernism, Total War, Encyclopedic Form* (Oxford: Oxford University Press, 2015).
———, 'Weak Theory, Weak Modernism', *Modernism/Modernity*, 25.3 (2018), 437–59.
Samson, Paul R., and David Pitt, 'Introduction: Sketching the Noosphere', in *The Biosphere and Noosphere Reader*, ed. Paul R. Samson and David Pitt (London and New York: Routledge, 1999), pp. 1–10.
Sandilands, Catriona, *The Good Natured Feminist: Ecofeminism and the Quest for Democracy* (Minneapolis: University of Minnesota Press, 1999).
Sandquist, Brigitte L., 'The Tree Wedding in "Cyclops" and the Ramifications of Cata-Logic', *James Joyce Quarterly*, 33.2 (1996), 195–209.
Sands, Danielle, 'Gaia, Gender, and Sovereignty in the Anthropocene', *PhiloSOPHIA*, 5.2 (2015), 287–307.
Santner, Eric L., *On Creaturely Life: Rilke, Benjamin, Sebald* (Chicago: University of Chicago Press, 2006).
Schaffner, Anna Katharina, *Modernism and Perversion: Sexual Deviance in Sexology and Literature, 1850–1930* (Basingstoke: Palgrave Macmillan, 2012).
Schuster, Jonathan, *The Ecology of Modernism: American Environments and Avant-Garde Poetics* (Tuscaloosa: The University of Alabama Press, 2015).
Scott, Bonnie Kime, *In the Hollow of the Wave: Virginia Woolf and Modernist Uses of Nature* (Charlottesville: University of Virginia Press, 2012).
———, *Joyce and Feminism* (Bloomington: Indiana University Press, 1984).
———, 'Joyce, Ecofeminism and the River as Woman', in *Eco-Joyce: The Environmental Imagination of James Joyce*, ed. Robert Brazeau and Derek Gladwin (Cork: Cork University Press, 2014), pp. 56–69.
———, *Refiguring Modernism Volume 2: Postmodern Feminist Readings of Woolf, West and Barnes* (Bloomington: Indiana University Press, 1995).
Scott, James B., *Djuna Barnes* (Boston: Twayne Publishers, 1976).
Scranton, Roy, *Learning to Die in the Anthropocene* (San Francisco: City Lights Books, 2015).
See, Sam, 'The Comedy of Nature: Darwinian Feminism in Virginia Woolf's *Between the Acts*', *Modernism / Modernity*, 17.3 (2010), 639–67.
Seitler, Dana, *Atavistic Tendencies: The Culture of Science in American Modernity* (Minneapolis: University of Minnesota Press, 2008).
Setz, Cathryn, *Primordial Modernism: Animals, Ideas, transition (1927–1938)* (Edinburgh: Edinburgh University Press, 2019).
———, '"Tree of Heaven": Djuna Barnes's Late Metaphysical Verse', in *Shattered Objects: Djuna Barnes's Modernism*, ed. Elizabeth Pender and Cathryn Setz (University Park: Penn State University Press, 2019), pp. 130–46.
Seymour, Nicole, *Strange Natures: Futurity, Empathy, and the Queer Ecological Imagination* (Urbana: University of Illinois Press, 2013).

Sheehan, Paul, *Modernism, Narrative and Humanism* (Cambridge: Cambridge University Press, 2002).

Sherlock, R. L., *Man as Geological Agent: An Account of His Action on Inanimate Nature* (London: H. F. & G. Witherby, 1922).

Shin, Ery, 'The Apocalypse for Barnes', *Texas Studies in Literature and Language*, 57.2 (2015), 182–209.

Silver, Brenda, '"Anon" and "The Reader": Virginia Woolf's Last Essays', *Twentieth-Century Literature*, 25.3–4 (1979), 356–441.

Somervell, Tess, 'The Seasons', in *Climate and Literature*, ed. Adeline Johns-Putra (Cambridge: Cambridge University Press, 2019), pp. 45–59.

Sourvinou-Inwood, Christiane, 'Gaia, Gē', *The Oxford Classical Dictionary*, <https://oxfordre.com/classics> (last accessed 22 September 2020).

Spiropoulou, Angeliki, *Virginia Woolf, Modernity and History: Constellations with Walter Benjamin* (Basingstoke: Palgrave Macmillan, 2010).

Spoo, Robert, *James Joyce and the Language of History: Dedalus's Nightmare* (Oxford: Oxford University Press, 1994).

Steffen, Will, Jacques Grinevald, Paul Crutzen and John McNeill, 'The Anthropocene: Conceptual and Historical Perspectives', *Philosophical Transactions of the Royal Society*, A369.1938 (2011), 842–67.

Stein, Gertrude, *Picasso* (New York: Dover Publications, 1984).

Stengers, Isabelle, *In Catastrophic Times: Resisting the Coming Barbarism*, trans. Andrew Goffey (Ann Arbor, MI: Open Humanities Press, 2015).

Steptoe, Lydia, 'Against Nature', *Vanity Fair*, XVIII (August 1922), 60, 88.

Stevenson, Sheryl, 'Writing the Grotesque Body: Djuna Barnes's Carnival Parody', in *Silence and Power: A Reevaulation of Djuna Barnes*, ed. Mary Lynn Broe (Carbondale and Edwardsville: Southern Illinois University Press, 1991), pp. 81–93.

Sultzbach, Kelly, *Ecocriticism in the Modernist Imagination: Forster, Woolf, and Auden* (Cambridge: Cambridge University Press, 2016).

Taylor, Jesse Oak, *The Sky of Our Manufacture: The London Fog in British Fiction from Dickens to Woolf* (Charlottesville: University of Virginia Press, 2016).

———, 'Storm-Clouds on the Horizon: John Ruskin and the Emergence of Anthropogenic Climate Change', *19: Interdisciplinary Studies in the Long Nineteenth Century*, 26 (2018) <www.19.bbk.ac.uk/article/id/1718/> (last accessed 5 May 2020).

Taylor, Julie, *Djuna Barnes and Affective Modernism* (Edinburgh: Edinburgh University Press, 2012).

———, 'Making Contact: Affect, Queer Historiography, and "Our Djuna"', in *Shattered Objects: Djuna Barnes's Modernism*, ed. Elizabeth Pender and Cathryn Setz (University Park: Penn State University Press, 2019), pp. 193–206.

Tazudeen, Rasheed, '"Discordant Syllabling": The Language of the Living World in Virginia Woolf's *Between the Acts*', *Studies in the Novel*, 47.4 (2015), 491–513.

Teilhard de Chardin, Pierre, 'The Phenomenon of Man', in *The Biosphere and Noosphere Reader*, ed. Paul R. Samson and David Pitt (London and New York: Routledge, 1999), pp. 70–80.

Thoreau, Henry David, *Walden and Civil Disobedience* (New York and London: Penguin Books, 1986).

Tønnessen, Morten, Kristin Armstrong Oma and Silver Rattasepp (eds), *Thinking about Animals in the Age of the Anthropocene* (Lanham, MD: Lexington Books, 2016).

Tromanhauser, Vicki, 'Animal Life and Human Sacrifice in Virginia Woolf's *Between the Acts*', *Woolf Studies Annual*, 15 (2009), 67–90.

Tyndall, John, *Address Delivered Before the British Association Assembled at Belfast* (London: Longmans, Green and Co., 1874).

——, *The Glaciers of the Alps: Being a Narrative of the Excursions and Ascents, an Account of the Origin and Phenomena of Glaciers and an Exposition of the Physical Principles to Which They Are Related* (London: John Murray, 1860).

Vernadsky, Vladimir, 'Geochemistry', in *The Biosphere and Noosphere Reader*, ed. Paul R Samson and David Pitt, trans. Paul R. Samson (London and New York: Routledge, 1999), pp. 26–8.

Wallace, Jeff, *D. H. Lawrence, Science and the Posthuman* (New York: Palgrave Macmillan, 2005).

——, 'Modern', in *The Cambridge Companion to Literature and the Posthuman*, ed. Bruce Clarke and Manuela Rossini (Cambridge: Cambridge University Press, 2017), pp. 41–53.

Walsh, Erin, 'Word and World: The Ecology of the Pun in *Finnegans Wake*', in *Eco-Joyce: The Environmental Imagination of James Joyce*, ed. Robert Brazeau and Derek Gladwin (Cork: Cork University Press, 2014), pp. 70–90.

Warren, Diane, *Djuna Barnes' Consuming Fictions* (Aldershot: Ashgate, 2008).

Waters, Colin N., Irka Hajdas, Catherine Jeandel and Jan Zalasiewicz, 'Artificial Radionuclide Fallout Signals', in *The Anthropocene as a Geological Time Unit*, ed. Jan Zalasiewicz, Colin N. Waters, Mark Williams and Colin Summerhayes (Cambridge: Cambridge University Press, 2019), pp. 192–9.

Waters, Colin N., Jan Zalasiewicz, Colin Summerhayes, Anthony D Barnosky, Clément Poirier, Agnieszka Gałuszka et al., 'The Anthropocene is Functionally and Stratigraphically Distinct from the Holocene', *Science*, 351.6269 (2016) <https://doi.org/10.1126/science.aad2622> (last accessed 21 September 2021).

Weart, Spencer R., *The Discovery of Global Warming*, revised and expanded edition (Cambridge, MA: Harvard University Press, 2008).

Webb, Caroline, '"All Was Dark; All Was Doubt; All Was Confusion": Nature, Culture, and *Orlando*'s Ruskinian Storm-Cloud', in *Virginia Woolf Out Of Bounds: Selected Papers from the Tenth Annual Conference on Virginia Woolf*, ed. Jessica Berman and Jane Goldman (New York: Pace University Press, 2001), pp. 243–8.

Westling, Louise, 'Virginia Woolf and the Flesh of the World', *New Literary History*, 30.4 (1999), 855–75.

White, T. H., *The Book of Beasts: Being a Translation from a Latin Bestiary of the Twelfth Century* (London: Jonathan Cape, 1956).

Whitworth, Michael, *Einstein's Wake: Relativity, Metaphor, and Modernist Literature* (Oxford: Oxford University Press, 2004).

———, *Virginia Woolf* (Oxford: Oxford University Press, 2005).

Whitworth, Michael, and Anna Snaith, 'Introduction: Approaches to Space and Place in Woolf', in *Locating Woolf: The Politics of Space and Place*, ed. Michael Whitworth and Anna Snaith (Basingstoke: Palgrave Macmillan, 2007), pp. 1–31.

Williams, Raymond, *Keywords: A Vocabulary of Culture and Society* (Abingdon: Routledge, 2011).

Winning, Joanne, 'Djuna Barnes, Thelma Wood and the Making of the Lesbian Modernist Grotesque', in *Shattered Objects: Djuna Barnes's Modernism*, ed. Elizabeth Pender and Cathryn Setz (University Park: Penn State University Press, 2019), pp. 26–45.

Winter, James H., *Secure From Rash Assault: Sustaining the Victorian Environment* (Berkeley and Los Angeles: University of California Press, 1999).

Wolfe, Cary, *What Is Posthumanism?* (Minneapolis: University of Minnesota Press, 2010).

Wood, David, 'Comment Ne Pas Manger – Deconstruction and Humanism', in *Animal Others: On Ethics, Ontology and Animal Life*, ed. H. Peter Steeves (Albany: State University of New York Press, 1999), pp. 15–35.

Woolf, Virginia, *Between the Acts*, ed. Mark Hussey (Cambridge: Cambridge University Press, 2011).

———, *The Diary of Virginia Woolf*, ed. Anne Olivier Bell, 5 vols (London: Penguin Books, 1979–85).

———, *The Essays of Virginia Woolf*, ed. Andrew McNeillie (vols 1–4) and Stuart N. Clarke (vols 5–6), 6 vols (London: Hogarth Press, 1986–2011).

———, *The Letters of Virginia Woolf*, ed. Nigel Nicolson and Joanne Trautmann, 6 vols (London: The Hogarth Press, 1975–80).

———, *Moments of Being*, ed. Jeanne Schulkind (London: Grafton Books, 1989).

———, *Mrs Dalloway*, ed. David Bradshaw (Oxford: Oxford University Press, 2009).

———, *Orlando: A Biography*, ed. Suzanne Raitt and Ian Blyth (Cambridge: Cambridge University Press, 2018).
———, *Orlando: The Holograph Draft*, ed. Stuart N. Clarke (London: S. N. Clarke, 1993).
———, *The Pargiters: The Novel-Essay Portions of The Years*, ed. Mitchell A. Leaska (London: Hogarth Press, 1978).
———, *A Passionate Apprentice: The Early Journals 1897–1909*, ed. Mitchell A. Leaska (London: The Hogarth Press, 1990).
———, *Roger Fry: A Biography* (New York: Harcourt, Brace & Company, 1940).
———, *A Room of One's Own and Three Guineas*, ed. Anna Snaith (Oxford: Oxford University Press, 2015).
———, *The Voyage Out*, ed. Lorna Sage (Oxford: Oxford University Press, 2009).
Yeats, W. B., *Autobiographies* (London: Macmillan, 1955).
———, *Collected Poems* (London: Macmillan, 1982).
———, *The Cutting of an Agate* (New York: Macmillan, 1912).
———, *Writings on Irish Folklore, Legend and Myth*, ed. Robert Welch (London: Penguin Books, 1993).
Zalasiewicz, Jan, Colin N. Waters, Mark Williams, Anthony D. Barnosky, Alejandro Cearreta, Paul Crutzen et al., 'When Did the Anthropocene Begin? A Mid-Twentieth Century Boundary Level Is Stratigraphically Optimal', *Quaternary International*, 383 (2015), 196–203.
Zilczer, Judith, '"Light Coming on the Plains:" Georgia O'Keeffe's Sunrise Series', *Artibus et Historiae*, 20.40 (1999), 191–208.

INDEX

Abbey Theatre, 38
Adams, Carol J., 133–6
A. E. *see* Russell, George
Alt, Christina, 167–8n, 194n
Anders, William, 200–1
Anglocene, 10
animal studies, 14–15, 22, 90–1, 96–7
Anthropocene studies, 2–3, 19–20, 23, 34, 173, 208
Anthropocene Working Group, 6,198, 208n
anthropomorphism, 22, 103–11, 116n, 127–8
Anthropos, 21–2, 31, 89–91
apocalypse, 92, 97–8, 174
Aristotle, 31, 45, 59n47, 66–7, 69–70, 85n
Arnold, Matthew, 37, 176–7, 194n
Arrhenius, Svante August, 167n
Artaud, Antonin, 34
Athenaeum, 145
atomic physics, 199–200
Auden, W. H., 176

Back to Nature movement, 20–1, 35–7
Bakhtin, Mikhail, 93

Banfield, Ann, 168n
Barber, Stephen, 185–6
Barnes, Djuna
   'Against Nature', 18, 22, 123–4, 126, 139
   'Aller et Retour', 108
   The Antiphon, 93, 98–9, 133–4, 203, 209n
   'The Coward', 92
   Creatures in an Alphabet, 115n, 203
   'Dusie', 92–3
   'Fall-out over Heaven', 203–4
   'The Girl and the Gorilla', 105–8, 111
   Ladies Almanack, 93
   'Love and the Beast', 92
   Nightwood, 4–5, 14, 16, 22, 89–96, 98, 100–4, 106, 109–12, 114n, 116n, 116n, 116n, 118, 120, 130–2
   'Oscar', 92
   'The People and the Sea: How They Get Together', 91–2
   'Quarry', 204–6
   'The Rabbit', 134–6, 143n50

INDEX

Ryder, 22, 93–6, 98–100, 106–9, 120–2, 124–40, 141n, 141n, 143n, 162
Spillway, 134
Barnes, Wald, 106, 117n, 121, 124–5, 127, 134, 144n
Barney, Natalie Clifford, 92–3, 94, 205–6
Barrows, Adam, 81
beastliness, 4–5, 21–2, 81, 89–112, 126–7, 130–2, 136,143n, 204, 207–8
Beckett, Samuel, 34
Beer, Gillian, 148, 156–7, 181
Bell, Clive, 201
Bell, Julian, 167n
Bell, Vanessa, 169n
Benjamin, Walter, 97
Bennett, Arnold, 169n, 174
Bergson, Henri, 13–14, 18, 28n, 29n
Bhagavad Gita, 205
biosphere, 12, 28n
Black, Elizabeth, 3
Blake, Elizabeth, 116n
Blake, William, 92
Blatchford, Robert, 35–6
Bloomsbury Group, 176, 201
Blyth, Ian, 163
Boheemen-Saaf, Christine Van, 86n
Boni & Liveright, 121
Bonneuil, Christophe, 5, 10, 35–6, 208
Borg, Ruben, 65, 67, 70, 82, 149
Bosanquet, Theodora, 146–7
Bowen, Elizabeth, 175
Braidotti, Rosi, 18–19, 33–4, 70, 90, 104–5, 128, 159, 161, 181, 199
Brannigan, John, 34, 36
Broglio, Ron, 104–5, 109
Brokeback Mountain, 120
Bromley, Amy, 159
Bronx Zoo, 105–6
Brooklyn Daily Eagle, 91
Budgen, Frank, 48, 62, 66, 71, 73
Burke, Kenneth, 94–5
Burns, Christy, 163
Butler, Judith, 162

Capitalocene, 10, 27n
carnophallogocentrism, 135–8
Carpenter, Edward, 35–6, 58n
Carson, Rachel, 24, 59n, 197, 205–7

Caselli, Daniela, 92, 113n, 115n, 115n, 125, 138–9
Castle, Gregory, 17, 32–3, 37, 43, 45, 51, 60n
Castletown, Lord, 50, 53
Celtic mythology, 36–7, 48, 68–9
Chakrabarty, Dipesh, 19, 54, 148, 207
Cheng, Vincent, 38, 46, 86n
Cixous, Hélène, 74–5
Clark, Timothy, 2–3, 19–20
climate change, 1–4, 6–7, 22–3, 90, 145–65, 167n, 172, 183, 194n, 207
Cobden-Sanderson, Thomas James, 160
Cockroft, John, 199
Colebrook, Claire, 2, 9, 111, 154, 164, 172, 178–80, 187–8, 191
Coleman, Emily, 4–5, 14, 16, 18, 94, 102–3, 111, 116n, 117n, 118–9, 124–5, 140, 197–8
Conrad, Joseph, 71
Costelloe, Karin, 14
creaturely, the 22, 96–100, 103, 114n, 115n
Criterion, 63
Crutzen, Paul, 2, 5–6, 11, 14, 112n
cubism, 10, 12
Curiver, Georges, 173

Dana (Celtic goddess), 68
Dana (magazine), 48, 59n, 68
Dante Alighieri, 92
Darwin, Charles, 173–4
Davies, Jeremy, 153
Davis, Thomas S., 175
Davitt, Michael, 38
Day Lewis, Cecil, 176
d'Eaubonne, Françoise, 75
de Gay, Jane, 150, 152
De Man, Paul, 104–5, 111, 57n, 180
Dekker, Thomas, 153
Deleuze, Gilles, 19, 53–5
Delsandro, Erica, 186, 188
Derrida, Jacques, 19, 22, 30n, 52, 60n, 91, 94, 96, 100–1, 107–9, 111–12, 117n, 119, 127–8, 130–2, 135–7, 143n, 143n, 192
Descartes, Rene, 17
Dial, The, 63

233

Donne, John, 92
Douglass, Paul, 14
Dukes, Hunter, 46
Duszenko, Andrzej, 199–200

Earth Mother myths, 21, 38, 45, 48, 62–84, 208
Earth sciences, 5–6, 198
Earthrise, 200–1
Ebury, Katherine, 43, 65, 81
ecofascism, 53–4
ecofeminism, 74–80
Eddy, Arthur Jerome, 201
Edelman, Lee, 101–2, 115–16n, 170–2, 182–3, 185–6, 192n, 192n
Edmunds, Susan, 125–6, 131
Edward VII, King, 160
Eglinton, John, 20, 38, 45, 48, 51–2, 68
Eliot, T. S., 9, 14, 16, 63, 71, 77, 98, 116n, 118, 150–1, 174, 176, 178–9, 203–4, 209n
Ellmann, Maud, 68, 75
Ellmann, Richard, 74, 80
Emerson, Ralph Waldo, 125
environmentalism, 20–1, 24, 35–8, 50–2, 54, 56, 75, 81, 84, 156, 205–8
Erickson, Bruce, 119–20, 123–4
Esty, Jed, 188
evolution, 12–16, 89–90, 119–21, 129–30, 137, 139, 173–4
extinction, 1–2, 6, 23, 77, 97, 170–192, 197, 207–8

Fairhall, James, 50, 60n
Fallon, William G., 13
Feder, Helena, 149
Feynman, Richard, 203
Field, Andrew, 103, 133–4
First World War, 7, 12–13, 51, 111, 150
Fitzgerald, Eleanor, 102–3, 116n
Fordham, Finn, 81, 83
Forster, E. M., 7–8, 26n
Foster, Roy, 50
Foucault, Michel, 123
Fourier, Michel, 155
Fressoz, Jean-Baptiste, 5, 10, 35–6, 208
Freud, Sigmund, 5
Froula, Christine, 152, 173, 189

Gaelic Athletic Association, 38
Gaelic League, 38, 50
Gaia (Greek mythology), 21, 62–84, 208
Gaia (scientific hypothesis), 13, 21, 64–6, 72, 74–80, 83–4
Garner, Richard L., 105, 107
Garnett, David, 107
geology, 2–4, 5–7, 10–16, 19–20, 27n, 28n, 32, 44–5, 70, 73, 77, 82, 147, 152–3, 159, 167n, 172, 179–81, 198
Ghosh, Amitav, 27n
Gilbert, Stuart, 63, 73–5, 86n
Gillies, Mary Ann, 14
Gladstone, William, 50
Goethe, Johann Wolfgang von, 34
Goldberg, S. L., 74
Golding, William, 64
Goldman, Jane, 169n
Golinski, Jan, 147
Good Housekeeping, 9
Goody, Alex, 95, 113n, 126
Gottlieb, Adolph, 202–3
Gough, Val, 176
Graves, Robert, 68
Great Acceleration, 6–7, 26n
Greene, Graham, 93
Greenhouse effect, 155–6
Gregory, Lady, 32
Griffiths, Matthew, 3–4
Grosz, Elizabeth, 13–14
Guattari, Félix, 19, 21, 33–4, 43–4, 48–9, 53–6, 57n, 76, 180–1
Guggenheim, Peggy, 102–3, 197

Hagen, Benjamin, 174–5
Haraway, Donna, 10, 21, 31, 34, 51, 66–8, 76–7, 79, 83–4, 87n, 88n, 90, 97–8, 115n, 115n, 160, 168n, 170
Hardy, Thomas, 148
Harris, Alexandra, 148
Harte, Bret, 124
Henke, Suzette, 63, 74
Herman, David, 97
Herring, Phillip, 29n, 116n, 141n, 205, 210n
Herring, Scott, 203, 209n
Hesiod, 71, 82, 88n
Hewitt, Seán, 37

Hill, Constance, 145
Hirsch, Edward, 58n
Hogarth Press, 9, 16, 194n
Högberg, Elisa, 159
Holmes, Arthur, 147
Holocene, 5–7, 11
Homer, 63
Housman, A. E., 23, 150–1, 167n
Hulme, T. E., 14
Husserl, Edmund, 65
Hussey, Mark, 176, 182, 196n
Huxley, Julian, 15
Huxley, T. H., 15, 156
Huysmans, Joris-Karl, 123
Hyde, Douglas, 48

Ibsen, Henrik, 42
International Commission on Stratigraphy, 6
Irish Agricultural Organisation Society, 35–6, 39–41, 57n
Irish Homestead, 39–41, 58n
Irish Literary Revivalism, 20–1, 32–3, 36–43, 45–51, 56, 68–9, 208
Irish Literary Society, 36
Irish National Land League, 35–6

James, Henry, 138, 146
Johns-Putra, Adeline, 146, 182–3, 189–90
Jolas, Eugene, 108, 120, 198
Joyce, Giorgio, 198
Joyce, Helena, 197
Joyce, James
  Dubliners, 9
  Exiles, 71
  Finnegans Wake, 16, 21, 33, 54, 80–4, 88n, 108–9, 199–200
  The Letters of James Joyce 38, 62–3, 71, 74, 77, 78–9, 80
  'A Portrait of the Artist', 59n
  A Portrait of the Artist as a Young Man, 20–1, 33, 38–48, 55–6
  Stephen Hero, 20–1, 33, 40–4, 48–9, 56
  'The Study of Languages', 4
  Triestine Journalism, 36, 50–1, 56
  Ulysses see also 4, 14, 16, 19, 21, 31–6, 38–9, 44–6, 48–56, 62–3, 66–84, 93, 124, 128–9, 143n, 174, 176, 194n
  Chapters of *Ulysses* (in chronological order)
  'Telemachus', 67, 68–9
  'Proteus', 31–2, 45–6, 66–8, 80, 83
  'Calypso', 69, 73
  'Lotus Eaters', 72
  'Hades', 31, 35, 69–70
  'Aeolus', 34
  'Lestrygonians', 34, 69
  'Scylla and Charybdis', 36, 38–9, 45, 48–50, 68
  'Cyclops', 21, 49–56, 60n, 72
  'Nausicaa', 46, 69, 71
  'Oxen of the Sun', 39, 128–9
  'Eumaeus', 69
  'Ithaca', 4, 54–6, 62–4, 70–1, 73, 77–80, 87n, 124, 174
  'Penelope', 21, 62–3, 67, 71–80, 84n, 85n, 86n
  Work in Progress, 108–9
Joyce, Nora, 198
Joyce, Stanislaus, 38
Joyce, Stephen, 198

Kafka, Franz, 19, 107
Kalaidjian, Andrew, 125
Kandinsky, Wassily, 201
Kannenstine, Louis, 121
Keats, John, 59n
Kenner, Hugh, 74
Kermode, Frank, 190
Kershner, Brendan, 33
Keynes, John Maynard, 176
Kiberd, Declan, 48–9
King James Bible, 107, 126
Kinsella, John, 197–8, 204, 207
Kipling, Rudyard, 106
Klaus, H. Gustav, 38
Kupinse, William, 55, 61n

Lacivita, Alison, 33, 37–8, 54, 61n, 80–1
Lai, Yi-Peng, 50
Land War, 35
Larbaud, Valéry, 63
Latour, Bruno, 3, 8, 21, 24n, 38, 64–5, 72, 78, 82–3

Lawrence, D. H., 7–8, 19, 71, 174, 194n
Lawrence, Karen, 49
Le Roy, Edouard, 12–13
Levine, Nancy, 105
L'Imagerie Populaire, 109
Little Ice Age, 146, 152–4, 161
Little Review, 52–3, 92
Louis XIV, King, 107, 109
Lovelock, James, 13, 64–5, 72, 74–5, 84, 85n
Lyell, Charles, 147

McCarthy, Jeffrey Mathes, 3, 18, 150
McCormick, Kathleen, 74
McCourt, John, 33
MacNeice, Louis, 176
Maffi, Bruno, 94
Magee, William Kirkpatrick *see* Eglinton, John
Maggio, Paula, 146
Malm, Andreas, 27n
Marcus, Jane, 90
Margulis, Lynn, 64–6, 83–4
Marinetti, F. T., 7–8
Martin, Kirsty, 148
Marx, Karl, 35
Mathews, P. J., 39
Medb, 68
Menageries of Versailles, 107
Menely, Tobias, 97
Milesians, 68
Miller, Hugh, 44
Miller, Tyrus, 137
Milne, Drew, 197–8, 204, 207
Milton, John, 92
Mitford, Mary Russell, 145–6, 148
Montaigne, Michel de, 172, 174–5, 194n, 205
Morrell, Ottoline, 15–16
Morris, William, 35–6, 61n
Mortimer, Raymond, 8
Morton, Timothy, 18, 22, 25n, 119–20, 139
Muir, Edwin, 113n
Murray, Rachel, 142n

Nagai, Kaori, 53
Nazism, 53, 189

Neocatastrophism, 153, 167n27
Neoplatonism, 45
New Statesmen & Nation, 185
New Yorker, 204–5
New York World Magazine, 105
Nicolson, Harold, 8
Nietzsche, Friedrich, 117n
Nolan, Emer, 35, 85n
noosphere, 12–14
Norris, Margot, 14–15, 77, 82, 88n, 90, 113n7
Nouvelle Revue Française, 63
Nuclear Anthropocene, 23–4, 197–208
nuclear warfare, 6, 23–4, 198–205, 207

O'Dea, Dathalin, 58n
oil, 8–9, 27n
O'Keeffe, Georgia, 24, 201–3
Oliver, Kelly, 22, 119, 130–31, 140
O'Neal, Hank, 116n
Oppenheimer, J. Robert, 203, 205
Ovid, 109

Parmelee, Maurice, 80
Parnell, Charles Stewart, 35, 38
Parsons, Deborah, 15
pastoralism, 3–4, 7, 18, 23, 26n, 32–3, 35–9, 43, 48, 54–6, 119–21, 123–6, 132–6, 149–54, 163, 182, 188, 208
Pavlov, Aleksey, 11
Pen, Jean-Marie Le, 53
Pen, Marine Le, 53
Phillips, Dana, 152–3
Pick, Anat, 97
Pitt, David, 12–13
Pizzo, Justine, 157–8
Plantationocene, 51
Plato, 45
Platt, Len, 32–3, 49
Plock, Vike Martina, 34, 87n
Plunkett, Horace, 35
posthumanism, 18–19, 30n, 30n, 47, 63, 79–83, 178, 208
postmodernism, 6–7, 26n, 202–3
Potter, Rachel, 89
Pound, Ezra, 63, 74, 124
Power, Arthur, 17
Proust, Marcel, 19, 34, 110

queer ecology, 22, 66, 76, 84, 119–20, 123–4, 138–40, 149, 161–5

Rabaté, Jean-Michel, 80
Raffnsøe, Sverre, 89–90
Raitt, Suzanne, 163
Richardson, Dorothy, 15
Rignall, John, 38
Rohman, Carrie, 5, 14–15, 90, 92
Ross, Stephen, 30n
Ruskin, John, 35–6, 57n, 156
Russell, George, 20, 35, 36, 38, 39–41, 45, 50, 68, 143n
Rutherford, Ernest, 199, 201
Ryan, Derek, 4, 19, 149, 159,196n
Ryan, Frederick, 48, 68

Sackville-West, Vita, 8, 16, 23, 146–7, 150–4, 166n
Saint-Amour, Paul K., 174–5, 192n, 195n
Samson, Paul, 12–13
Sandilands-Mortimer, Catriona, 119–20, 123–4
Sands, Danielle, 75–6, 83
Schuster, Joshua, 3–4, 8
Scott, Bonnie Kime, 3, 68, 81, 90, 93–4, 106, 109, 113n, 133, 149, 167n
Scott, James B., 101, 114n, 121
Scranton, Roy, 172
seasonality, 132–3, 149–54
Second World War, 7, 23–4, 170–7, 187–91, 192n, 197–8, 204
See, Sam, 189
Setz, Cathryn, 16, 204
sexology, 119–20, 123–4
Seymour, Nicole, 192n
Shakespeare, William, 1, 4, 31, 189
Shaw, George Bernard, 106
Sheehan, Paul, 16–17
Shelley, Percy Bysshe, 71
Sherlock, R. L., 11–12
Shin, Ery, 115n
Silver, Brenda, 173
sixth great extinction event, 2, 6
Smyth, Ethel, 170–1
Snaith, Anna, 10
Somervell, Tess, 150

Spanish Civil War, 175
Spender, Stephen, 174
Spiropoulou, Angeliki, 167n
Spoo, Robert, 79
Stein, Gertrude, 10–12
Stengers, Isabelle, 3, 65
Stephen, Leslie, 156
Stevenson, Sheryl, 99–100
Stieglitz, Alfred, 203
Stoermer, Eugene, 26n
Stutman, Osías, 205, 210n
Suess, Eduard, 28n
Sultzbach, Kelly, 3, 26n, 164
sustainability, 55, 182–3, 193n
Swift, Jonathan, 127
Synge, J. M., 32, 42

T. P.'s Weekly, 156
Tablet, the, 93
Taylor, Jesse Oak, 148–9, 153, 156
Taylor, Julie, 108, 113n
Tazudeen, Rasheed, 189–90
Teilhard de Chardin, Pierre, 12–13, 15, 28n
Teller, Edward, 203
Tellus, 21, 63–6, 68, 70, 73–6, 79–80, 82, 84
Tennyson, Lord Alfred, 151
Thomas, Edward, 150
Thomson, James, 150
Thoreau, Henry David, 22, 36–7, 56, 124–6, 136
Tindall, William York, 74
transatlantic review, 108
transcendentalism, 22, 124–6, 136
transition, 108, 120
Trevelyan, George Macaulay, 178, 187–8, 194n
Turner, J. M. W., 158
Twain, Mark, 124
Tyndall, John, 23, 155–9, 160, 167n, 168n, 195n

Ulster Cycle, the, 68
uniformitarianism, 11, 27n
United States National Aeronautics and Space Administration, 64
Unkeless, Elaine, 63, 74

vegetarianism, 133, 135–7, 143n, 143n
Vernadsky, Vladimir, 11–13

Wallace, Jeff, 19, 28n, 47, 158
Walpole, Horace, 175
Walsh, Erin, 88n
Walton, Ernest, 199
Watt, James, 6
Weart, Stephen B., 156
Weaver, Harriet Shaw, 63, 80
Weil, Simone, 97
Wells, H. G., 194n
Weston, Jessie, 71
White, T. H., 98, 101
Whitman, Walt, 124–5
Whitworth, Michael, 10
Wilde, Oscar, 58n, 158
Williams, Raymond, 118–9
Winning, Joanne, 114n
Winter, James, 10–11
Witt, Carl, 86n
Wolfe, Cary, 18–19
Wood, Thelma, 206
Woodward, Arthur Smith, 11
Woolf, Leonard, 28n, 170–1, 173, 175–7, 187, 196n
Woolf, Virginia
   A Room of One's Own, 1–2, 16
   Between the Acts, 4, 20, 23, 146, 156–7, 170, 172–3, 175, 178–9, 181–92, 200
   The Common Reader, 22, 145–6
   'The Cosmos', 160
   The Diaries of Virginia Woolf, 8–9, 16, 151, 171, 174–6, 181, 188, 194n
   'The Docks of London', 9–10
   'Flying over London', 179–81, 185
   'Henry David Thoreau', 125
   'The Humane Art', 175
   'Kew Gardens', 5
   'The Leaning Tower', 176–7
   The Letters of Virginia Woolf, 14, 16, 146–7, 167n, 170, 175
   'Modern Fiction', 157–8, 168n
   Mrs Dalloway, 156
   Orlando: A Biography, 22–3, 145–65, 179, 182
   'The Pastons and Chaucer', 151
   'Poetry, Fiction and the Future', 15–17, 20
   Reading at Random; or Turning the Page, 177–81
   Roger Fry, 158
   'A Sketch of the Past', 179, 180–1, 184, 187
   'Thoughts on in Peace in an Air Raid', 175, 195n
   Three Guineas, 123, 175
   To the Lighthouse, 157–8, 164, 183
   The Voyage Out, 4, 146
   The Waves, 183
   The Years, 123
Wordsworth, William, 18, 151

Yeats, W. B., 20, 32–3, 36–9, 42, 47–8, 68, 92, 176
Yeatts, James, 199

Zilczer, Judith, 201, 209n
Zola, Émile, 42

EU representative:
Easy Access System Europe
Mustamäe tee 50, 10621 Tallinn, Estonia
Gpsr.requests@easproject.com